Microsoft

Windows 10
Step by Step

Second Edition

Joan Lambert

Windows 10 Step by Step, Second Edition
Published with the authorization of Microsoft Corporation by:
Pearson Education, Inc.

ISBN-13: 978-1-5093-0672-5
ISBN-10: 1-5093-0672-2

Library of Congress Control Number: 2017955971

1 17

Microsoft and the trademarks listed at http://www.microsoft.com on the "Trademarks" webpage are trademarks of the Microsoft group of companies. All other marks are property of their respective owners.

For information about buying this title in bulk quantities, or for special sales opportunities (which may include electronic versions; custom cover designs; and content particular to your business, training goals, marketing focus, or branding interests), please contact our corporate sales department at corpsales@pearsoned.com or (800) 382-3419.

For government sales inquiries, please contact governmentsales@pearsoned.com.

For questions about sales outside the U.S., please contact intlcs@pearson.com.

Editor-in-Chief
Greg Wiegand

Senior Acquisitions Editor
Laura Norman

Senior Production Editor
Tracey Croom

Editorial Production
Online Training Solutions, Inc.
(OTSI)

Compositor/Indexer
Susie Carr (OTSI)

Copy Editor
Jaime Odell (OTSI)

Proofreader
Kathy Krause (OTSI)

Technical Reviewer
Laura Acklen

Editorial Assistant
Cindy J. Teeters

Interior Designer
Joan Lambert (OTSI)

Cover Designer
Twist Creative • Seattle

Contents

Part 1: The Windows 10 environment

Give us feedback
Tell us what you think of this book and help Microsoft
improve our products for you. Thank you!
https://aka.ms/tellpress

Part 2: Apps and files

Part 3: Devices and resources

Part 4: Behind the scenes

Give us feedback
Tell us what you think of this book and help Microsoft
improve our products for you. Thank you!
https://aka.ms/tellpress

Introduction

Welcome to the wonderful world of Windows 10! This *Step by Step* book has been designed so you can read it from the beginning to learn about Windows 10 and then build your skills as you learn to perform increasingly specialized procedures. Or, if you prefer, you can jump in wherever you need ready guidance for performing tasks. The how-to steps are delivered crisply and concisely—just the facts. You'll also find informative, full-color graphics that support the instructional content.

Who this book is for

Windows 10 Step by Step, Second Edition is designed for use as a learning and reference resource by home and business users of desktop and mobile computers and devices running Windows 10 Home or Windows 10 Pro. The content of the book is designed to be useful for people who have previously used earlier versions of Windows and for people who are discovering Windows for the first time.

What this book is (and isn't) about

This book is about the Windows 10 operating system. Your computer's operating system is the interface between you and all the apps you might want to run, or that run automatically in the background to allow you to communicate with other computers around the world, and to protect you from those same computers.

In this book, we explain how you can use the operating system and the accessory apps, such as Cortana, File Explorer, Microsoft Edge, and Windows Store, to access and manage the apps and data files you use in your work and play.

Many useful apps that are part of the Windows "family" are installed by manufacturers or available from the Store. You might be familiar with common apps such as Calendar,

Camera, Groove Music, Mail, Maps, News, Photos, and Windows Media Player. This book isn't about those apps, although we do mention and interact with a few of them while demonstrating how to use features of the Windows 10 operating system.

> **SEE ALSO** For information about working with apps, see Chapter 4, "Work with apps and notifications."

The *Step by Step* approach

The book's coverage is divided into parts that represent general computer usage and management skill sets. Each part is divided into chapters that represent skill set areas, and each chapter is divided into topics that group related skills. Each topic includes expository information followed by generic procedures. At the end of the chapter, you'll find a series of practice tasks you can complete on your own by using the skills taught in the chapter. You can use the practice files that are available from this book's website to work through the practice tasks, or you can use your own files.

Features and conventions

This book has been designed to lead you step by step through all the tasks you're most likely to want to perform in Windows 10. If you start at the beginning and work your way through all the procedures, you'll have the information you need to administer all aspects of the Windows 10 operating system on a non-domain-joined computer. However, the topics are self-contained, so you can reference them independently. If you have worked with a previous version of Windows, or if you complete all the exercises and later need help remembering how to perform a procedure, the following features of this book will help you locate specific information.

- **Detailed table of contents** Search the listing of the topics, sections, and sidebars within each chapter.

- **Chapter thumb tabs and running heads** Identify the pages of each chapter by the colored thumb tabs on the book's open fore edge. Find a specific chapter by number or title by looking at the running heads at the top of even-numbered (verso) pages.

- **Topic-specific running heads** Within a chapter, quickly locate the topic you want by looking at the running heads at the top of odd-numbered (recto) pages.

- **Practice task page tabs** Easily locate the practice task sections at the end of each chapter by looking for the full-page colored stripe on the book's fore edge.

- **Glossary** Look up the meaning of a word or the definition of a concept.

- **Keyboard shortcuts** If you prefer to work from the keyboard rather than with a mouse, find all the shortcuts in one place in the appendix, "Keyboard shortcuts and touchscreen tips."

- **Detailed index** Look up specific tasks and features in the index, which has been carefully crafted with the reader in mind.

You can save time when reading this book by understanding how the *Step by Step* series provides procedural instructions and auxiliary information and identifies on-screen and physical elements that you interact with. The following table lists content formatting conventions in use in this book.

Convention	Meaning
TIP	This reader aid provides a helpful hint or shortcut to simplify a task.
IMPORTANT	This reader aid alerts you to a common problem or provides information that is necessary to successfully complete a procedure.
SEE ALSO	This reader aid directs you to more information about a topic in this book or elsewhere.
1. 2.	Numbered steps guide you through generic procedures in each topic and hands-on practice tasks at the end of each chapter.
■ ■	Bulleted lists indicate single-step procedures and sets of multiple alternative procedures.
Interface objects	In procedures and practice tasks, semibold black text indicates on-screen elements that you should select (click or tap).
User input	Bold green formatting identifies specific information that you should enter when completing procedures or practice tasks.
Ctrl+P	A plus sign between two keys indicates that you must select those keys at the same time. For example, "press Ctrl+P" directs you to hold down the Ctrl key while you press the P key.
Emphasis and *URLs*	In expository text, italic formatting identifies web addresses and words or phrases we want to emphasize.

Adapt procedures for your environment

The instructions in this book assume that you're interacting with on-screen elements on your computer by selecting or clicking them with a mouse, or on a touchpad or other hardware device. If you're using a different method—for example, if your computer has a touchscreen interface and you're tapping the screen (with your finger or a stylus)—substitute the applicable tapping action when the book directs you to select a user interface element.

> **SEE ALSO** For information about touchscreen interaction with Windows 10 devices, see the appendix "Keyboard shortcuts and touchscreen tips."

Instructions in this book refer to user interface elements that you select or tap on the screen as *buttons*, and to physical buttons that you press on a keyboard as *keys*, to conform to the standard terminology that is used in documentation for these products.

Multistep procedural instructions provide detailed instructions the first time they're presented. For example:

1. Select the **Start** button, and then select the **Settings** button to open the Settings window.

2. In the **Settings** window, select **System**.

3. On the **System** settings page, select **Power & sleep**.

4. In the **Power & sleep** settings pane, in the **Sleep** section, expand the **When plugged in...** list, and then do one of the following:

   - If you want the computer to go to sleep after a specific length of idle time, select a time from **1 minute** to **5 hours**.

   - If you don't want the computer to go to sleep when its idle, select **Never**.

On subsequent instances of instructions that require you to follow the same process, the instructions might be simplified in this format because the working location has already been established:

1. Display the **System** settings page, and then select **Power & sleep**.

2. In the **Screen** section of the pane, in the **When plugged in** list, select an idle time from **1 minute** to **5 hours** after which you want the screen to turn off, or select **Never** to leave the screen on when the computer is idle.

When the instructions tell you to enter information, you can do so by typing on a connected external keyboard, tapping an on-screen keyboard, or even speaking aloud, depending on your computer setup and your personal preferences.

Download the practice files

Although you can complete the practice tasks in this book by using your own files, for your convenience we have provided practice files for many of the tasks. You can download these practice files to your computer by going to *https://aka.ms/win10sbs2e/files* and following the instructions on the webpage.

> ⚠ **IMPORTANT** Windows 10 is not available from the book's website. You should install that operating system before working through the procedures and practice tasks in this book.

You can use the files that are supplied for the practice tasks to perform the tasks, and if there are changes, you can save the finished versions of each file. If you later want to repeat practice tasks, you can download the original practice files again.

> 🔍 **SEE ALSO** For information about working with files, see Chapter 6, "Manage folders and files."

The following table lists the practice files for this book.

Chapter	Folder	File
1: Get started using Windows 10	None	None
2: Personalize your working environment	Win10SBS\Ch02	Background01.jpg through Background08.jpg
3: Work with shortcuts and tiles	Win10SBS\Ch03	Image01.jpg through Image05.jpg
4: Work with apps and notifications	None	None

5: Explore files and folders	Win10SBS\Ch05	Files\Brochure.pptx Photos\Backgrounds\Background.jpg Photos\Backgrounds\Background03.jpg Photos\Backgrounds\Background08.jpg Photos\Lucy.jpg Photos\Lucy2.jpg Events.docx Expenses.xlsx PackingList.docx Password01.jpg through Password03.jpg Survey.docx TravelChecklist.xlsx
6: Manage folders and files	Win10SBS\Ch06	Files\Brochure.pptx Photos\Backgrounds\Background.jpg Photos\Backgrounds\Background03.jpg Photos\Backgrounds\Background08.jpg Photos\Lucy.jpg Photos\Lucy2.jpg Reports\ (folder) Events.docx Expenses.xlsx Password01.jpg through Password03.jpg Survey.docx
7: Manage peripheral devices	None	None
8: Manage network and storage resources	Win10SBS\Ch08	Folder only
9: Get assistance from Cortana	None	None
10: Safely and efficiently browse the internet	None	None
11: Manage user accounts and settings	Win10SBS\Ch11	Account01.jpg through Account05.jpg Password01.jpg through Password03.jpg
12: Manage computer settings	None	None
13: Manage power and access options	None	None
14: Work more efficiently	None	None
15: Protect your computer and data	None	None

E-book edition

If you're reading the e-book edition of this book, you can do the following:

- Search the full text
- Print
- Copy and paste

You can purchase and download the e-book from the Microsoft Press Store at *https://aka.ms/win10sbs2e/detail*.

Get support and give feedback

This topic provides information about getting help with this book and contacting us to provide feedback or report errors.

Errata and support

We've made every effort to ensure the accuracy of this book and its companion content. If you discover an error, please submit it to us at *https://aka.ms/win10sbs2e/errata*.

If you need to contact the Microsoft Press Support team, please send an email message to *mspinput@microsoft.com*.

For help with Microsoft software and hardware, go to *https://support.microsoft.com*.

We want to hear from you

At Microsoft Press, your satisfaction is our top priority, and your feedback our most valuable asset. Please tell us what you think of this book at *https://aka.ms/tellpress*.

The survey is short, and we read every one of your comments and ideas. Thanks in advance for your input!

Stay in touch

Let's keep the conversation going! We're on Twitter at *http://twitter.com/MicrosoftPress*.

Part 1

The Windows 10 environment

CHAPTER 1

CHAPTER 2

Get started using Windows 10

If you're reading this book, it's likely that you already have a Windows 10 computer or plan to acquire one, and you want to know how to get the most out of it. This chapter will help you quickly come up to speed with the basic elements of the Windows 10 user experience and environment—including that of the Windows 10 2017 Fall Creators Update.

The first public release of Windows 10, in July 2015, combined popular elements of Windows 7 and Windows 8 with new technology to create a powerful, easy-to-use operating system. Since that time, additional functionality has been added to Windows 10 through periodic public releases. Windows 10 can interact with you through commands that you enter on a keyboard, on screen, or verbally; from information and activities on your phone; and (with your permission) by gleaning information from email messages.

Windows 10 is designed to work not only on desktop and laptop computers, but also on smaller mobile devices, such as tablets and phones. The user interface is clean and simple so that it can scale gracefully across device formats. If you're new to Windows 10 but familiar with operating system concepts, many Windows 10 features will be familiar to you.

This chapter guides you through procedures related to signing in to Windows, exploring the primary user interface areas, managing content and app windows, and various methods of ending a computing session.

In this chapter

- Sign in to Windows
- Explore the desktop and taskbar
- Explore the Start menu
- Explore Windows settings
- Manage content and app windows
- End a computing session

Sign in to Windows

Between computing sessions, Windows displays one of two screens: the Lock screen and the Welcome screen.

About the Lock screen

When your Windows 10 computer first starts or has been idle for a while, it displays the Lock screen. As the name indicates, the Lock screen is a security layer between the world outside the computer and the information inside the computer. The Lock screen displays a background picture (or a slideshow of pictures), the time and date, and network connection information. It can also display information from some of the core Windows 10 apps, including Alarms & Clock, Calendar, Mail, Messaging, Phone, Skype, Store, Weather, and Xbox. The Lock screen doesn't display user account information or specific message content that you might not want to share with people who happen to walk past the computer.

Windows 10 comes with a set of attractive Lock screen images. You can choose a static background from among those, enjoy the daily Windows spotlight photos, or choose a specific picture or set of pictures that you have access to from your computer.

> **SEE ALSO** For information about specifying the image and app information that appear on the Lock screen, see "Customize the Lock screen" in Chapter 2, "Personalize your working environment."

About the Welcome screen

When you dismiss the Lock screen, the Welcome screen appears. The Welcome screen displays a list of the user accounts that are registered on the computer in its lower-left corner; provides access to the internet, accessibility, and power settings in its lower-right corner; and displays the image and password entry box or Sign In button for the most recent user in the center.

> **TIP** This book contains many images of the Windows 10 user interface elements (such as the Lock screen, Welcome screen, desktop, taskbar, Start menu, and Settings window) that you'll work with while performing tasks on a computer running Windows 10. Unless we're demonstrating an alternative view of content, the screenshots shown in this book were captured on a horizontally oriented display at a screen resolution of 1600 × 900 and a magnification of 100 percent. If your settings are different, user interface elements on your screen might not look the same as those shown in this book.

From the Welcome screen, you sign in to Windows with your user account credentials to begin or return to your computing session.

Choose a user account type

To start a Windows 10 computing session, you sign in to Windows with a user account that is registered on that computer. The user account can be linked to a *Microsoft account* that connects to all the resources associated with that account, or it can be a *local account* that exists only on one computer.

Use a Microsoft account or local account

You can choose one of two account types when signing in to Windows 10:
a Microsoft account or a local account. Here's a quick overview of the two
account types.

Microsoft accounts

Microsoft accounts are single sign-on (SSO) accounts that you can use to sign
in to any Microsoft service, to services provided by other companies that
have adopted Microsoft accounts as standard credentials, or to computers
running Windows 10, Windows 8.1, or Windows 8.

TIP Single sign-on isn't unique to Microsoft: Google, Facebook, Amazon, and many other
organizations use it. Many web services allow you to sign in by using one of the major SSO
accounts, rather than requiring you to create new accounts on their sites.

Any email account hosted on a Microsoft webmail service—designated domain
(hotmail.com, live.com, msn.com, outlook.com, passport.com, passport.net, or
any country/region-specific variant) is automatically configured as a Microsoft
account. If you don't already have a Microsoft account, you can easily create
a free email account on a Microsoft webmail domain, or enroll any valid email
address or phone number that you already have as a Microsoft account.
These options are available through the user interface when setting up your
Windows 10 user account, and at *https://signup.live.com*.

IMPORTANT If someone is already signed in to a Microsoft account in your computing
session, you must sign out of that account (but not the computing session) from your web
browser before you can create a new one, or use an InPrivate browsing session to mask
the account credentials. For information about InPrivate browsing, see Chapter 10, "Safely
and efficiently browse the internet."

Local accounts

A local account is exactly what it sounds like: a user account that exists only
on your computer. You (or someone with administrative privileges) can create
multiple local accounts on one computer, and each account can sign in to
that computer and access a combination of private and shared information.

■■ Microsoft

Create account

Microsoft account opens a world of benefits.

someone@example.com

Create password

☐ Send me promotional emails from Microsoft

Next

Use a phone number instead

Get a new email address

Local accounts are good for young children who don't yet need an email account. Local accounts might also be a good choice when you don't want to link the computer to other computers that you sign in to by using your Microsoft account. A local account doesn't require a password (but can have one), doesn't have an associated OneDrive storage folder, and might have only limited access to Windows apps and Office 365 tools.

If you create a local account but later decide that you would prefer to sign in by using a Microsoft account, you can easily connect the local account to a Microsoft account or create a new user profile on the computer for the Microsoft account.

TIP You can designate any account as a child's account to add parental controls. For more information about setting up accounts and about parental controls, see Chapter 11, "Manage user accounts and settings."

When you install Windows 10, or the first time you sign in to a new Windows 10 computer, Windows guides you through the processes of configuring your basic settings, connecting to the internet, and connecting to or setting up a computer user account.

Microsoft encourages you to use a Microsoft account rather than a local account to sign in. The advantages of signing in to Windows 10 by using a Microsoft account include the following:

- You can easily connect to other computers on your network that you sign in to by using that account, because the computers have the same sign-in credentials.

- You can synchronize settings for the computer theme, web browser, passwords, language preferences, Ease Of Access tools, printers, mouse options, File Explorer, and notifications among the computers you sign in to by using the same account.

- You can pass credentials to other Microsoft services that require you to sign in (such as Microsoft Office 365).

- You have access to 5 gigabytes (GB) of free Microsoft OneDrive online storage, or 1 terabyte (TB) with an Office 365 subscription (at the time of this writing).

The first time you sign in to a computer by using a new user account, Windows sets up the user account–specific folders and settings, and synchronizes settings with other computers that your Microsoft account is configured on, if you've chosen that option. While Windows goes through this process (which takes about two minutes), it displays a series of reassuring messages on the screen. At the end of this initial setup process, your personal Windows desktop appears.

> **SEE ALSO** For information about synchronizing system settings on multiple computers, see "Customize your sign-in options" in Chapter 11, "Manage user accounts and settings."

Depending on the processes that are configured to run when you sign in, there could be some activity, such as windows opening and closing, as various apps start. Some of these will be apps that you want to interact with—for example, you might want a communication app such as Skype or Skype for Business to start automatically. Others will be tools that support the apps that are installed on your computer. For example, installing an app such as Adobe Acrobat or Apple iTunes also installs a tool that checks the internet for updates to the app each time you start a new computing session. (This is usually for the purpose of increasing app security rather than adding new functionality.)

> **TIP** Some apps and services start automatically when any user signs in to Windows, and others run specifically when you sign in. You can review a list of apps that start automatically and remove apps from the list to conserve startup resources. For more information, see "Manage app startup" in Chapter 14, "Work more efficiently."

To dismiss the Lock screen

- Click or tap a blank area of the screen.
- Flick the screen upward by using your finger.
- Press any keyboard key.

To sign in to Windows 10

1. Dismiss the Lock screen.

   If the computer has multiple user accounts, the Welcome screen displays a link to each account in the lower-left corner.

2. If the user account picture and name in the center of the screen aren't for the account you want to sign in to, select the account in the lower-left corner of the Welcome screen.

3. Do one of the following:

   - If your account doesn't have a password, select **Sign in** below your account name.

   - If your account has a password, enter the password in the box below your account name, and then press Enter or select **Submit** (the arrow button to the right of the password box).

> **SEE ALSO** For information about signing in to Windows from within an existing Windows session, see "Explore the Start menu" later in this chapter. For information about configuring and signing in by using PINs, picture passwords, and biometric recognition, see "Customize your sign-in options" in Chapter 11, "Manage user accounts and settings."

> **TIP** If you're working on a touchscreen device and want to enter your account credentials from the On-Screen Keyboard app, tap the password box once to display the keyboard. For more information about the On-Screen Keyboard app, see "Configure Windows accessibility features" in Chapter 13, "Manage power and access options."

Sign in on a touchscreen device

Windows 10 is optimized for touchscreen interaction. You control most options in the Settings window by using a simple on/off toggle switch that's easy to select whether you're using a mouse, a stylus, or your finger. Windows 10 has two on-screen keyboards—both of which are available from the Welcome screen before you sign in.

If you're working on a touchscreen device and want to enter your account credentials on the Welcome screen by using one of the on-screen keyboards, do either of the following:

- Tap the **Password** or **PIN** box to display an on-screen keyboard that is docked to the bottom of the screen.

- Tap the **Ease of Access** button and then select **On-Screen Keyboard** to display the floating keyboard that is one of the Ease Of Access tools.

To close the keyboard, tap away from the docked keyboard or tap the Close button on the floating keyboard.

> **TIP** When you buy a new computer, you might be surprised to find your desktop cluttered with shortcuts. Computer manufacturers or resellers frequently install trial versions of apps on a computer in hopes that you will use those apps instead of others that are available to you. Most of these are benign, but often they include a well-known antivirus app that provides a short trial period for free, and then prompts you to pay for a subscription. This app can interfere with the free Windows Defender security system that is built into Windows 10. You can delete the shortcuts to tidy up the desktop, but that won't uninstall the apps. For information about cleaning up desktop shortcuts and uninstalling apps, see Chapter 3, "Work with shortcuts and tiles" and Chapter 4, "Work with apps and notifications."

Explore the desktop and taskbar

Your starting point after you sign in to Windows is the desktop. The Windows 10 desktop has a picture or color background that fills your screen; hosts icons for system tools such as the Recycle Bin; might have app shortcuts, folders, and files stored on it; and has a taskbar that provides access to the computer content and functionality.

Explore the desktop

The initial desktop background picture is configured as part of the Windows installation. If you upgrade from another version of Windows and choose to keep your personal settings, your desktop background won't change. If you purchase a computer that has Windows 10 preinstalled on it, it might feature a background specific to the computer manufacturer (for example, a Dell computer desktop might display the Dell logo).

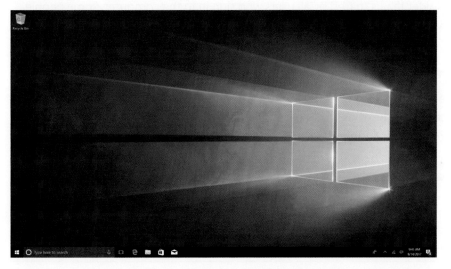

The only icon that is typically displayed by default with a clean installation is the one for the Recycle Bin, which is a temporary storage folder for deleted files. The Recycle Bin is initially located in the upper-left corner of the desktop (but can be moved by you), and might appear empty or full, depending on whether you've deleted files.

Apps that you install later might place (or offer to place) shortcuts on the desktop to provide a quick way to start them. You can place app shortcuts on the desktop yourself, too. Most computer manufacturers preinstall apps from companies they have alliances with, and place shortcuts to these apps on the desktop. The appearance of your desktop might be different from the one shown in this book, but the functionality will be the same. You might find it more convenient to pin app tiles to the Start menu (as described later in this chapter), to keep your desktop free of shortcuts and start all apps from the Start menu.

> **SEE ALSO** For information about creating shortcuts on the desktop, Start menu, and taskbar, see Chapter 3, "Work with shortcuts and tiles."

The desktop itself is really just a background for the display of items that are stored in one of two folders—the Desktop folder that is part of your user account, or the Public Desktop folder that is shared by all users who sign in to the computer. Some people like to save files or folders to their desktops for easy access.

Explore the taskbar

The bar across the bottom of the desktop is the *Windows taskbar*. The taskbar provides access to all the apps, files, settings, and information on the computer. The fixed tools are on the left and right ends of the taskbar.

> **TIP** By default, the taskbar is displayed at the bottom of your screen. You can move it to the top or one of the sides, or hide it to provide additional screen space. For more information, see "Customize the taskbar" in Chapter 3, "Work with shortcuts and tiles."

The Windows 10 taskbar looks very similar to the taskbar in earlier versions of Windows, but there are some pleasant surprises here.

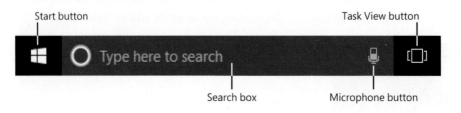

1

The Start button, search box, and Task View button are located at the left end of the taskbar. Each of these has an important function:

- Selecting the Start button displays the Start menu, the primary location from which you access apps and settings. The Start menu has new functionality in Windows 10. We discuss this at length in the next topic.

- Right-clicking the Start button displays the Quick Link menu, your fastest route to many frequently used computer management tools. The Quick Link menu options are specific to the computer; on a laptop computer, the menu also includes a link to Mobility Center.

Apps and Features

Power Options

Event Viewer

System

Device Manager

Network Connections

Disk Management

Computer Management

Windows PowerShell

Windows PowerShell (Admin)

Task Manager

Settings

File Explorer

Search

Run

Shut down or sign out   >

Desktop

> **TIP** A menu that appears when you right-click a button, file, folder, or other item is referred to as a *shortcut menu*. Most shortcut menus don't have names, but this is the *Quick Link menu*.
> On a touchscreen device, tap and hold an item to perform the right-click action. For more information about touchscreen interaction with Windows 10 devices, see the appendix "Keyboard shortcuts and touchscreen tips."

- Entering a term in the search box displays relevant apps, files, and settings stored on your computer and, when you have an active internet connection, relevant online information. Search results are grouped by type—selecting a group (such as Apps, Settings, Folders, Documents, or Store) displays all results of that type.

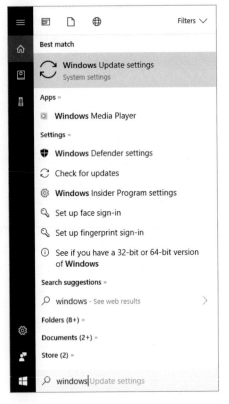

The icons to the left of the search results represent the app or system area of each result. For example, an app icon indicates the default app for that file type; a folder indicates a folder; a gear indicates a Settings page, pane, or setting; and a key indicates a security feature setting.

> **TIP** The search box is also your interaction point with Cortana, your "personal assistant" on any Windows device (also available on Android and iOS). After you initially configure Cortana, the service will alert you to upcoming appointments; help you check in for flights or track packages; provide information about local restaurants, traffic conditions, and investment performance; and much more. If you install Cortana on your smartphone, you can also receive alerts from that device on your computer. For more information, see the sidebar "Hey, Cortana!" later in this chapter.

- Selecting the Task View button displays Task View (new in Windows 10), which is a large-thumbnail view of all the open windows and running apps on your desktop.

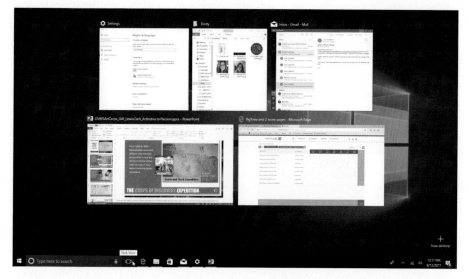

From Task View, you can easily switch among or close apps and windows. You can also create virtual desktops, which are secondary instances of the Windows desktop. When you create one or more virtual desktops, you can organize the windows of running apps, files, and folders across them.

> **SEE ALSO** For information about virtual desktops, see "Organize apps on multiple desktops" in Chapter 14, "Work more efficiently."

The center area of the taskbar, to the right of the Task View button, can display shortcut buttons and toolbars. In a default installation of Windows 10, shortcuts to the Microsoft Edge web browser, File Explorer, the Store app, and the Mail app are pinned here. You can easily move or delete these and pin additional items that you want quick access to.

Microsoft Edge button   Store button

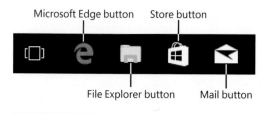

File Explorer button   Mail button

> **SEE ALSO** For information about pinning apps to the taskbar, see "Create and manage app shortcuts" in Chapter 3, "Work with shortcuts and tiles."

The right end of the taskbar is the *notification area*. The icons displayed here represent apps that run on your computer that might need to notify you of events or system status. You can choose which app icons appear in the notification area, and set them either to always display or to display an alert if something happens. You can also select or right-click notification area icons to interact with the underlying apps in various ways.

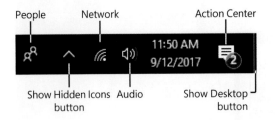

Some of the apps that you install on your computer, such as Microsoft OneDrive, Outlook, OneNote, and Teams, will display icons in the notification area. By default, the notification area contains the following items:

- The People icon links to the People bar, a feature introduced in the 2017 Fall Creators Update of Windows 10. You can quickly pin contacts from the messaging apps installed on your computer to the People bar.

- The Show Hidden Icons button displays a pane of notification icons that are for apps rather than for Windows functions. You can access app-management commands from these icons.

- The standard Windows notification icons provide access to network and sound settings, app and operating system notifications, and other tools. The specific icons depend on your computer configuration.

- The Action Center icon opens the Action Center, which provides quick access to messages, notifications, and settings. When you have unread communications from apps (such as Cortana, Microsoft Mail, or Outlook), or from Windows or other sources (such as mobile devices), the icon is white and displays a number; otherwise, it is hollow.

Notification management buttons

- The time and date displayed on the taskbar also provide access to configure the time and date settings on your computer.

- The narrow bar at the rightmost end of the taskbar is the Show Desktop button, which you can use to minimize (hide) all open windows (and thereby display the desktop).

> **TIP** You can opt to display the Windows Ink Workspace, Touch Keyboard, and Touchpad buttons in the notification area of the taskbar. For more information, see "Customize the taskbar" in Chapter 3, "Work with shortcuts and tiles."

To search for content on the computer or internet

1. Activate the taskbar search box by doing either of the following:

   - Click or tap the search box.

   - Press the Windows logo key.

    TIP We abbreviate the Windows logo key name as "Win" in keyboard shortcuts so that it's easier to read.

2. Enter the search term.

3. To refine the results, select **Apps**, **Settings**, **Folders**, **Documents**, or **Store** in the search results list to display only results in that category.

To display or hide the Task View of all active apps and desktops

- On the taskbar, to the right of the search box, select the **Task View** button.

- Press Win+Tab.

- On a touchscreen device, swipe in from the left edge of the screen.

To manage windows in Task View

- To close a file or app, point to the thumbnail, and then select the **Close** button (the X) in the upper-right corner.

- To switch to a specific window, select the window thumbnail (not the window title).

To display app-management icons and commands

1. At the left end of the notification area of the taskbar, select the **Show hidden icons** button.

2. In the icon pane, right-click the icon of the app you want to display commands for.

    TIP On a touchscreen device, tap and hold an item to perform the right-click action. For more information about touchscreen interaction with Windows 10 devices, see the appendix "Keyboard shortcuts and touchscreen tips."

To display recent, unread messages from Windows and communication apps

- Near the right end of the taskbar, select the **Action Center** icon.

To manage messages in the Action Center

- To preview message content, select the arrow to the right of the message subject.

- To remove a message from the Action Center (but not from the app that generated the message), point to the message header and then select the X that appears in its upper-right corner.

- To open a message in its app, select the message header.

> **SEE ALSO** For information about managing settings from the Action Center, see "Manage app notifications" in Chapter 4, "Work with apps and notifications."

To minimize all open windows

- To minimize the windows, select the **Show Desktop** button or press Win+D. Use the same technique to restore the minimized windows.

- To temporarily minimize the windows, point to the **Show Desktop** button. (This is called "peeking" at the desktop.)

> **TIP** The Peek function can be turned on or off in the taskbar settings. For more information, see "Customize the taskbar" in Chapter 3, "Work with shortcuts and tiles." For information about other techniques for minimizing, maximizing, and restoring windows, see "Manage content and app windows" later in this chapter.

Hey, Cortana!

Cortana is a curiously useful technology from Microsoft that is described as a "personal assistant," but is really a complex information-analysis tool that monitors your activities and communications and proactively provides you with relevant information about them. You can interact with Cortana through the taskbar search box, or if your computer or device has a microphone input you can configure Cortana for speech recognition and then activate it by saying, "Hey, Cortana."

O Type here to search

Cortana can track your incoming packages and outgoing flights; remind you of appointments, meetings, and tasks from email conversations; keep shopping and to-do lists; and provide information about pretty much any-thing—local restaurants and events, stock prices, traffic conditions, public transit options, movies and television shows, news, sports, weather, and more. You can set timers and alarms, and ask Cortana to remind you to do things at a certain time, on a certain date, or when you arrive at a specific location.

You can connect Cortana to a variety of services, including Microsoft Dynamics CRM, Knowmail, LinkedIn, Office 365, Outlook.com, Skype, and Wunderlist, to get all your notifications in one place.

The concept of having your messages and location monitored can take some getting used to, but in trade you'll get proactive reminders and relevant information that Cortana locates just for you.

To access Cortana, activate the taskbar search box, or press Win+Q. To display your personalized content, at the bottom of the Cortana pane, select **I've got more for you...** on a desktop computer or **Cortana can do much more...** on a laptop computer.

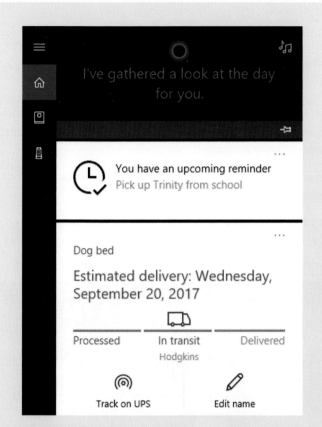

If you like using Cortana on your computer and want to have it available in other places, you can install the Cortana app on your Windows, Android, or iOS phone, and link it to your computer so that information is available to you on any of your devices. You can also purchase a Cortana speaker, through which you can make and receive Skype calls, control smart home devices, get information, and play music.

SEE ALSO For more information, see Chapter 9, "Get assistance from Cortana."

Explore the Start menu

The Windows 10 Start menu provides access to computer-management commands, your account folders, the apps installed on your computer, and any apps, folders, files, websites, or other things you want to pin to it. The Start menu has commands in three areas:

- The left side of the Start menu displays icons for Power, Settings, and Account information by default, and you can add other links to it. The Start menu is collapsed by default to display only the icons.

- The app list displays an alphabetical list of all the apps that are installed on your computer. Recently installed apps appear at the top of the menu.

- The right side of the Start menu displays groups of app tiles that the computer manufacturer pinned there for you or you choose to pin there. Some apps support "Live Tiles" that display current information such as weather, stock prices, or news.

SEE ALSO For information about Live Tiles, see Chapter 3, "Work with shortcuts and tiles."

1

You can configure the content of the Start menu however you want by adding, removing, resizing, and grouping tiles. If you prefer a cleaner look, you can opt to display a full-size Start screen instead of the partial-screen Start menu. The full-size Start screen displays either Pinned Tiles view or All Apps view, with the commands minimized on the left.

SEE ALSO For information about switching to the full-size Start screen, see "Configure the Start menu" in Chapter 2, "Personalize your working environment." For information about pinning tiles to the Start menu, see Chapter 3, "Work with shortcuts and tiles."

Selecting your user account image at the top of the Start menu icon area displays a list of options. You can access your user account settings, lock the computer, or sign out of Windows from this user account menu. (You can also do all those things from other places.) If multiple user accounts are configured on your computer, they appear at the bottom of this menu, and you can switch to those accounts without signing out of your current Windows session. For example, you might switch between accounts if your home computer has user accounts configured on it for other family members or guests, and you want to let one of those people use the computer without ending your computer session, or if you have a user account that is linked to your Microsoft account and a local user account that isn't.

Change account settings

Lock

Sign out

Rudy
Signed in

Susie

If the other user account is already signed in to Windows, this is indicated by the words "Signed in" under the user account name. Switching to an account that has an active Windows session resumes that Windows session; otherwise, switching to the account starts a new Windows session. Either way, when you switch accounts Windows displays the Welcome screen, so you can either sign in to Windows with the other user account credentials (including the account password, if it has one) or sign in to the existing Windows session.

You can choose whether to display the Most Used and Recently Added sections above the app list. Windows populates these sections automatically based on your computer usage and displays the section headings only when it also displays apps in those sections. Apps that you use more than others stay on the Most Used list until others take their place. Newly installed apps stay on the Recently Added list for about a day.

A hidden gem on the Start menu is the ability to quickly access jump lists of app-management commands, recent files, or common tasks. *Jump lists* are a marvelous time-saving feature. You can display a jump list by right-clicking an app in the app list or in the pinned tile area.

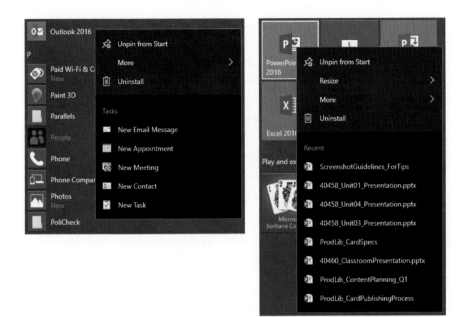

To display the Start menu (default configuration)

- Select the **Start** button.

- Press the Windows logo key.

- Press Ctrl+Esc.

To display user account controls

- On the left side of the **Start** menu, select your user account button.

To switch to another user account

1. On the left side of the **Start** menu, select your user account button, and then select the account you want to switch to.

2. On the Welcome screen, do one of the following:

   - If the account has a password, enter the password in the box below the account name, and then press Enter or select **Submit**.

   - If the account doesn't have a password, select **Sign in** below the account name.

To display recent files for a specific app

- On the **Start** menu, right-click the app name or tile.

Explore Windows settings

In versions of Windows prior to Windows 10, the various settings that controlled the behavior of the computer were available from Control Panel. Navigating through the Control Panel screens could be somewhat tricky. Control Panel still exists in Windows 10, but most of the settings have been moved from Control Panel to a much simpler interface: the Settings window. (The settings that haven't yet been moved are available through links from the Settings window. It's likely that future Windows 10 updates will result in the continued migration of Control Panel content to Settings.) This topic provides an overview of where you can find various settings that you'll work with throughout later chapters of this book.

In its default configuration, the Settings window displays iconic representations of the 13 categories of settings that are present in the Fall 2017 Creators Update of Windows 10.

TIP Four categories of settings are new since the initial release of Windows 10: Phone, Apps, Gaming, and Cortana.

The Settings window is an example of the type of changes Microsoft made in Windows 10 so that the operating system can run on devices of any size, from desktop computers to smartphones. As the window width decreases, the icons become smaller and move to a list format. Regardless of the format, each category icon and name is accompanied by a short (and by no means complete) list of settings available in that category, to give you an indication of where to find specific settings that you're looking for.

Settings	— □ ×

Find a setting 🔍

System
Display, notifications, power

Devices
Bluetooth, printers, mouse

Phone
Link your Android, iPhone

Network & Internet
Wi-Fi, airplane mode, VPN

Personalization
Background, lock screen, colors

Apps
Uninstall, defaults, optional features

Accounts
Your accounts, email, sync, work, family

One of the benefits of the Settings interface over Control Panel is that each category is only one level deep, so it's relatively easy to browse to the feature or setting you want to configure. In the standard (wider) Settings window configuration, each category page displays a list of features in the left pane; selecting any feature displays the settings for that feature in the right pane.

Active category   Features within   The Multitasking pane of
                   the category   the System settings page

Settings	— □ ✕
⚙ Home	**Multitasking**
Find a setting 🔎	**Snap**
System —	Arrange windows automatically by dragging them to the sides or corners of the screen
🖵 Display	⬤ On
🖵 Notifications & actions	When I snap a window, automatically size it to fill available space
⏻ Power & sleep	⬤ On
▭ Storage	When I snap a window, show what I can snap next to it
🖥 Tablet mode	⬤ On
▭ Multitasking	When I resize a snapped window, simultaneously resize any adjacent snapped window
🖵 Projecting to this PC	⬤ On
✕ Shared experiences	**Virtual desktops**
⟩ Remote Desktop	On the taskbar, show windows that are open on
ⓘ About	Only the desktop I'm using ⌄
	Pressing Alt+Tab shows windows that are open on
	Only the desktop I'm using ⌄

When the Settings window is narrower, selecting a category name displays only the feature list, and then selecting a feature displays that pane of settings.

It's easy to locate a specific setting from the Find A Setting search box at the top of each page of the Settings window. The following table lists the features you can configure settings for in each of the thirteen categories.

1

Settings category	Features included in the category
System	Display
	Notifications & actions
	Power & sleep
	Battery (on mobile devices)
	Storage
	Tablet mode
	Multitasking
	Projecting to this PC
	Shared experiences
	Remote Desktop
	About (Windows and system information)
Devices	Bluetooth & other devices
	Printers & scanners
	Mouse
	Touchpad (on mobile devices)
	Typing
	Pen & Windows Ink
	AutoPlay
	USB
Phone	General settings
Network & Internet	Status
	Wi-Fi
	Ethernet (on devices that have an Ethernet port)
	Dial-up
	VPN
	Airplane mode
	Mobile hotspot
	Data usage
	Proxy
Personalization	Background
	Colors
	Lock screen
	Themes
	Start
	Taskbar

Settings category	Features included in the category
Apps	Apps & features Default apps Offline maps Apps for websites Video playback
Accounts	Your info Email & app accounts Sign-in options Access work or school Family & other people Sync your settings
Time & language	Date & time Region & language Speech
Gaming	Game bar Game DVR Broadcasting Game Mode TruePlay Xbox Networking
Ease of Access	Narrator Magnifier Color & high contrast Closed captions Keyboard Mouse Other options
Cortana	Talk to Cortana Permissions & History Notifications More details

Settings category	Features included in the category
Privacy	General
	Location
	Camera
	Microphone
	Notifications
	Speech, inking, & typing
	Account info
	Contacts
	Calendar
	Call history
	Email
	Tasks
	Messaging
	Radios
	Other devices
	Feedback & diagnostics
	Background apps
	App diagnostics
	Automatic file downloads
Update & security	Windows Update
	Windows Defender
	Backup
	Troubleshoot
	Recovery
	Activation
	Find my device
	For developers
	Windows Insider Program (by subscription)

You can locate the configuration options for a specific feature by selecting the category and then the feature, or by searching from the Settings window search box or the taskbar search box.

When you configure settings in the Settings window, your changes are implemented as soon as you make them; it isn't necessary to save your changes, and it's not possible to undo your changes other than by manually reversing each change. If you ever need to identify the default settings for a feature, one way to do so is to create a new local user account, switch to that user account, and then check the settings in that account.

> **SEE ALSO** For information about creating new user accounts, see "Create and manage user accounts" in Chapter 11, "Manage user accounts and settings." For information about switching accounts, see "Explore the Start menu" earlier in this chapter.

As previously mentioned, Control Panel still exists and you can configure many of the less frequently used settings there. The standard Control Panel configuration displays category names followed by tasks you can perform in the categories.

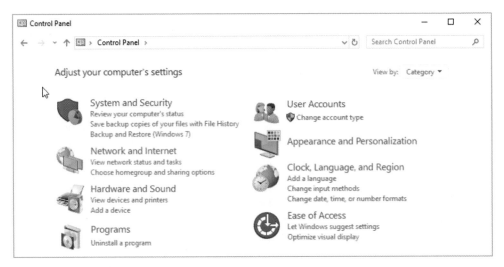

Alternatively, you can display features instead of categories by switching to Icon view, where you have the choice of displaying large or small icons. The content in both views is the same, but it can be much simpler to navigate through Control Panel in Icon view than in Category view. In either view, a search box is located in the upper-right corner of the window. Searching from this box returns results only from Control Panel.

1

View selector

| All Control Panel Items | — □ × |

← → ∨ ↑ 🖳 › Control Panel › All Control Panel Items › ∨ ↻ 🔍 Search Control Panel

Adjust your computer's settings

View by: Small icons ▾

Administrative Tools	AutoPlay	Backup and Restore (Windows 7)
BitLocker Drive Encryption	Color Management	Credential Manager
Date and Time	Default Programs	Device Manager
Devices and Printers	Ease of Access Center	File Explorer Options
File History	Flash Player (32-bit)	Fonts
HomeGroup	Indexing Options	Infrared
Intel® HD Graphics	Internet Options	Keyboard
Language	Mail (Microsoft Outlook 2016) (32-bit)	Mouse
Network and Sharing Center	Pen and Touch	Phone and Modem
Power Options	Programs and Features	Recovery
Region	RemoteApp and Desktop Connections	Security and Maintenance
Sound	Speech Recognition	Storage Spaces
Sync Center	System	Tablet PC Settings
Taskbar and Navigation	Troubleshooting	User Accounts
Windows Defender Firewall	Windows To Go	Work Folders

You can access the settings in Control Panel directly (by navigating or searching in Control Panel or from the taskbar search results list), by selecting links on the Quick Link menu, and also by selecting links in the feature settings panes. Links that lead from the Settings window to Control Panel are located in a Related Settings section adjacent to the settings pane, and are often labeled as advanced or additional settings. (For example, "Additional power settings" and "Change advanced sharing options" both link directly to Control Panel.)

We'll work with individual settings in later chapters of this book. In this first chapter, we're just making you aware of them in case you want to investigate them on your own or need to configure something before you get to the relevant topics.

To open the Settings window

- On the left side of the **Start** menu, select the **Settings** icon.

- Press Win+I.

- Near the right end of the taskbar, select the **Action Center** icon and then, in the **Quick Actions** section at the bottom of the Action Center, select **All settings**.

To display a category of settings

- In the **Settings** window, select the category you want to display.

To display settings for a specific feature

1. From the **Settings** window, display the category page.

2. On the category page, select the feature you want to configure.

To display the Quick Link menu

- Right-click the **Start** button.

- Press Win+X.

To display the Control Panel home page

- In the taskbar search box, enter **control**, and then in the search results list, select **Control Panel**.

- In the **Start** menu app list or on the **All apps** screen, select any index letter. In the alphabetic index, select **W**, expand the **Windows System** folder, and then select **Control Panel**.

Manage content and app windows

As the name of the Windows 10 operating system indicates, most of the information you view on your computer is displayed in windows—rectangular content frames. Files open in app windows, folders open in File Explorer windows, and operating system elements open in system windows. Regardless of the content they display, all windows share certain common characteristics and can be manipulated in the same ways.

In this topic, we discuss managing windows on the desktop.

Resize, minimize, and close windows

A window can either fill the entire screen or occupy only part of the screen. You can open and close a window, move a window, and change the size of a window. (These features help us to differentiate windows from other user interface elements such as panes or dialog boxes.) When an app (including File Explorer) or system element is active, its window has a corresponding taskbar button.

Windows have common features. Depending on which system or app generates the window, its controls might look slightly different, but in general, a window has a title bar at the top that has a title in the middle and window-management buttons on the right side.

The three buttons on the right end of the title bar are:

- **Minimize** Minimizing a window doesn't close the file or app in the window, but closes the window on the screen. You can reopen the window by selecting the corresponding taskbar button.

- **Maximize/Restore** When a window fills only part of the screen, maximizing it increases it to full-screen size. When a window is maximized, restoring it returns it to its previous part-screen size.

- **Close** Closing a window also closes the file or app that the window contains.

Pointing to (hovering over) the controls displays ScreenTips to help you identify them.

You can also use the title bar at the top of a window or the window frame to manage the window size.

To resize a window

- To manually change only the window height, point to the top or bottom of the window frame, and when the pointer changes to a double-headed arrow, drag the arrow up or down.

- To manually change only the window width, point to the left or right side of the window frame, and when the pointer changes to a double-headed arrow, drag the arrow left or right.

- To manually change the window size in any direction, point to a corner of the window frame, and when the pointer changes to a diagonal arrow, drag the arrow in any direction.

> **TIP** You cannot resize a maximized window by dragging its frame; you must first restore the window to a non-maximized state.

To maximize the height of a window without changing the width

- Point to the top or bottom of the window frame, and when the pointer changes to a double-headed arrow, double-click.

To maximize a window

- Double-click the window title bar.

- At the right end of the title bar, select the **Maximize** button.

- Drag the window by its title bar to the top of the screen, and then release it.

- Press Win+Up Arrow to maximize a non-snapped window.

> **SEE ALSO** For information about snapping windows, see the "Move and arrange windows" section of this topic.

To restore a maximized window

- Double-click the window title bar.

- At the right end of the title bar, select the **Restore** button.

- Drag the window by its title bar away from the top of the screen, and then release it.

- Press Win+Down Arrow to restore a non-snapped window.

1

To minimize the active window

- At the right end of the title bar, select the **Minimize** button.

- Press Win+Down Arrow to minimize a non-maximized window.

To minimize all windows other than the active window

- Press Win+Home.

- Shake (rapidly wiggle) the active window by its title bar.

To minimize all windows

- Press Win+M.

To restore minimized windows

- Press Win+Shift+M.

- Press Alt+Tab to cycle through thumbnails of windows; release the Alt key to open the window of the selected thumbnail.

- Press Win+[a number from 0 to 9] to open the first instance of the first through tenth active app on the taskbar. (The number 0 represents the app to the right of the **Task View** button on the taskbar, the number 1 represents the next app, and so on.)

To close a window

- At the right end of the title bar, select the **Close** button.

Move and arrange windows

Some people might never open more than one window at a time. But most people have at least a few windows open at the same time, and a business computer user could easily have a dozen or more windows open on a single screen, multiple monitors, or multiple desktops.

Earlier in this chapter, we looked at Task View, in which you can display a tiled view of thumbnails of all your open windows at the same time, and switch to or close individual windows. In this section, we discuss managing windows on the desktop.

You can move and arrange windows by dragging them around the screen, by using keyboard shortcuts, or by using commands on the taskbar shortcut menu.

Toolbars	>
Cortana	>
✓ Show Task View button	
✓ Show People button	
Show Windows Ink Workspace button	
Show touch keyboard button	
Show touchpad button	
Cascade windows	
Show windows stacked	
Show windows side by side	
Show the desktop	
Task Manager	
Lock the taskbar	
⚙ Taskbar settings	

Window-management commands

You can arrange open windows in traditional cascaded, stacked, and side-by-side arrangements or by snapping them to a half or quarter of the screen. Cascading and snapping windows also changes the window sizes.

Snapping a window is a technique that sizes and positions a window to occupy the left or right portion of the screen or one corner of the screen. Snapping a window to the left or right side of the screen in Windows 10 resizes it to half the screen width, unless another window is snapped to a screen edge. In that case, snapping a window to the same edge matches the existing window width, and snapping a window to the opposite edge fills the available space.

To drag a window

1. Press and hold the window title bar by using the primary mouse button, your finger, or a stylus.

2. Move the pointing device until the window is where you want it.

To move a window

- ▪ Drag the window by its title bar to the new position.

- ▪ Press Win+Left Arrow or Win+Right Arrow to cycle the active window through the left, right, and center of each screen.

To cascade all open windows

1. Right-click the taskbar.

2. On the taskbar shortcut menu, select **Cascade windows**.

To arrange all open windows in a grid

- Right-click the taskbar, and then select **Show windows stacked** or **Show windows side by side**.

To restore cascaded, stacked, or side-by-side windows

- Right-click the taskbar, and then select the relevant **Undo** command.

To snap a window to the left or right side of a screen

1. Do either of the following:

   - Drag the window until the pointer touches the left or right side of the display area (the contact point will flash briefly), and then release it.

   - Activate the window, and then press Win+Left Arrow or Win+Right Arrow to cycle the window through the left, right, and center of each screen.

   > **TIP** If you have multiple monitors (as opposed to virtual desktops), selecting the right or left arrow keyboard shortcut repeatedly acts on the window on the current monitor, then moves it to the next monitor and cycles through the positions on that screen. This is true whether the monitors are arranged horizontally or vertically.

2. Select the thumbnail of the window you want to display in the remaining space, or to close the thumbnail view without filling the other space, press Esc, select the active window, or select the taskbar.

To snap a window to a quarter screen

1. Do any of the following:

   - Drag the window until the pointer touches a corner (not a side) of the display area, and then release it.

   - Press Win+Up Arrow or Win+Down Arrow to snap a half-screen window to the upper or lower quarter.

   - Press Win+Left Arrow or Win+Right Arrow to move a quarter-screen window to another corner.

2. Select the thumbnail of the window you want to display in the remaining space, or to close the thumbnail view without filling the other space, press Esc, select the active window, or select the taskbar.

End a computing session

If you're going to stop working with your computer for any length of time, you can use one of these four options to leave the Windows session:

- **Lock the computer** This leaves your Windows computing session active, saves the state of any running apps and open files, and displays the Lock screen. Signing in to Windows resumes your computing session.

- **Sign out of Windows** This exits any running apps, ends your Windows computing session, and displays the Lock screen. Signing in to Windows starts a new computing session.

- **Put the computer to sleep** This leaves your Windows computing session active, saves the state of any running apps and open files, turns off the monitor, and puts the computer into a power-saving mode. When you wake the computer up, the monitor turns on, the Lock screen appears, and signing in to Windows resumes your computing session.

- **Shut down the computer** This signs all active users out of Windows, shuts down the computer processes in an orderly fashion, and turns off the computer.

You can access these processes from your account button and the Power button on the Start menu and full-size Start screen. The Sign Out, Sleep, and Shut Down processes are also available from the Quick Link menu.

The other available Power option is to restart the computer. When you do so, Windows shuts down the computer, and then starts it again. It is sometimes necessary to restart a computer to complete the installation of an update, when the update affects system files that are in use during the computing session. Restarting can also fix things if your computer is overtaxed with too many processes and begins to run slowly or erratically.

If apps are running when you sign out of Windows or shut down or restart the computer, Windows manages the process of exiting the apps. If files are open and have unsaved changes, Windows pauses the sign-out process and prompts you to save the files. At that point, you have the option of canceling the sign-out process and returning to your Windows session.

To lock the computer

- Display the **Start** menu. On the left side of the **Start** menu, select your user account button, and then select **Lock**.

- Press Win+L.

To sign out of Windows

1. Do either of the following:

   - Display the **Start** menu, select your user account button, and then select **Sign out**.

   - Right-click the **Start** button to display the **Quick Link** menu, select **Shut down or sign out**, and then select **Sign out**.

2. Respond if Windows asks whether to save unsaved changes to specific files or apps.

> ✓ **TIP** Watch the taskbar for flashing buttons that indicate an app that needs attention; sometimes notifications end up behind other on-screen processes. Select the button to activate the app, and then provide any necessary feedback.

To put the computer to sleep

- From within an active computing session, do either of the following:

   - On the left side of the **Start** menu, select the **Power** button, and then select **Sleep**.

   - On the **Quick Link** menu, select **Shut down or sign out**, and then select **Sleep**.

- In the lower-right corner of the Welcome screen, select the **Power** button, and then select **Sleep**.

To wake up a computer from sleep

Wake methods might vary depending on the computer. The following methods are common:

- Press and release the computer's power button.
- Press any keyboard key.
- Wiggle the mouse.

To shut down the computer

- From within an active computing session, do either of the following:

  - On the left side of the **Start** menu, select the **Power** button, and then select **Shut down**.

  - On the **Quick Link** menu, select **Shut down or sign out**, and then select **Shut down**.

- In the lower-right corner of the Welcome screen, select the **Power** button, and then select **Shut down**.

> **TIP** If your Shut Down option is labeled *Update and Shut Down*, Windows has installed an update that affects files and settings that are in use in the current computing session. When you select Update And Shut Down, Windows completes the update process before shutting down the computer.

To restart the computer

- From within an active computing session, do either of the following:

  - On the left side of the **Start** menu, select the **Power** button, and then select **Restart**.

  - On the **Quick Link** menu, select **Shut down or sign out**, and then select **Restart**.

- In the lower-right corner of the Welcome screen, select the **Power** button, and then select **Restart**.

> **TIP** If your Restart option is labeled *Update and Restart*, Windows has installed an update that affects files and settings that are in use in the current computing session. When you select Update And Restart, Windows completes the update process before restarting the computer.

Key points

- You start a computing session by signing in from the Welcome screen with a user account. The user account can be either a Microsoft account or a local computer account. If you sign in by using a Microsoft account, you can share settings across multiple computers and synchronize more easily with online services.

- After you sign in to Windows, you work from the desktop, which is a display panel for the contents of two folders—your personal Desktop folder and a Public Desktop folder available to all user accounts on the computer. The desktop displays shortcuts to system tools such as the Recycle Bin and might display shortcuts to apps, files, folders, and webpages.

- The taskbar located at the bottom of the desktop hosts the Start button, the search box (which also provides access to Cortana), the Task View button, and shortcuts to apps such as Microsoft Edge, File Explorer, the Store app, the Mail app, and any apps that are currently running. You can modify the shortcuts as you want.

- The notification area at the right end of the taskbar includes the People icon, notification icons for various apps and processes running on your computer, the date and time, and the Action Center icon.

- The Action Center provides quick access to messages and notifications that you receive, and to settings that you might want to access quickly.

- The Start menu provides links to your user account settings, the Settings window, and power options. (You can add other links.) The alphabetical app list on the Start menu provides access to all the apps installed on your computer. You can pin app tiles to the Start menu and group them for easy access.

- In Windows 10, you access most computer settings from the Settings window. Settings are organized into 13 categories of features.

- Most of the content displayed on your computer screen is within content frames called *windows*. These windows have common controls for resizing and closing the windows. You can move and resize windows on the screen and quickly snap them to a half or quarter of the screen.

- You can leave a computing session by locking the session or putting the computer to sleep. You can end the session by signing out of Windows or shutting down the computer. If your computer isn't running well or an update requires that the system files be released from use, it might be necessary to restart the computer.

Practice tasks

No practice files are necessary to complete the practice tasks in this chapter.

Sign in to Windows

Perform the following tasks:

1. Start your Windows 10 computer.

2. Dismiss the Lock screen, and then sign in to Windows 10.

Explore the desktop and taskbar

Sign in to Windows, and then perform the following tasks:

1. From the taskbar search box, search for **desktop**. Filter the search results list to display only folders, and then open the **Desktop** folder for your user account.

2. Search for **taskbar**. Filter the search results list to display only settings. Then display the settings pane in which you can specify which icons appear on the taskbar.

3. In the notification area of the taskbar, right-click the **Speakers** icon, and then select **Sounds** to open the Sound dialog box.

4. Display Task View to view all active apps and dialog boxes in your computing session. From Task View, close the **Sound** dialog box and then go to the **Settings** window.

5. Display the hidden icons in the notification area of the taskbar. Point to each icon in the window to display a ScreenTip that identifies the app. Then right-click any icon to display the available commands for that app.

6. From the notification area of the taskbar, display the Action Center.

7. If the Action Center contains messages, preview the content of a message, and then remove that message from the Action Center.

8. Minimize all open windows. (You'll use them in upcoming tasks.)

Explore the Start menu

Perform the following tasks:

1. Display the **Start** menu, and then display your user account menu.

2. From the user account menu, lock the computer. Then sign in to Windows again.

3. Display the **Start** menu. Examine the app list for apps that have jump lists, and notice the recent files and common actions for those apps.

Explore Windows settings

Perform the following tasks:

1. Open the **Settings** window.

2. Display any category of settings that interests you.

3. Within the selected category, display the settings for a specific feature.

4. Open Control Panel.

5. Leave the **Settings** window and Control Panel open for later use.

Manage content and app windows

Ensure that the Settings window and Control Panel are open, and then perform the following tasks:

1. Activate the **Settings** window. Change only the width of the window so it is approximately half the width of the screen. Then drag the window to the approximate center of the screen.

2. Use the mouse or pointer to resize the **Settings** window in the following ways:

   a. Maximize the window height without changing its width.

   b. Maximize the window to fill the screen.

   c. Snap the window to the left side of the screen, and select Control Panel to fill the right side of the screen.

3. Activate Control Panel, and then use keyboard shortcuts to resize it in the following ways:

   a. Snap the window to the upper-right quadrant of the screen.

   b. Move the window to the left side of the screen.

4. Temporarily minimize all the open windows to display the desktop.

5. Stack the open windows.

6. Minimize all the active windows, and then restore them.

7. Activate the **Settings** window, and then minimize all windows other than the active window.

8. Close the **Settings** window. Then activate and close Control Panel (and any other windows that you opened earlier).

End a computing session

Sign in to Windows, and then perform the following tasks:

1. From the user account menu at the top of the **Start** menu, lock the computer. Then sign in to Windows again.

2. From the **Power** button at the bottom of the **Start** menu, put the computer to sleep. Then sign in to Windows again.

3. From the **Start** shortcut menu, sign out of Windows to end your computing session.

4. From the Welcome screen, restart the computer.

Personalize your working environment

In Chapter 1, "Get started using Windows 10," you looked at the Windows user interface elements that you encounter in every Windows session—the Lock screen, the Welcome screen, the desktop, the taskbar, and the Start menu. (The other place you'll probably spend a lot of time is in File Explorer, which Chapter 5, "Explore files and folders," covers at length.)

Some of the Windows user interface elements might look different on your computer from those shown in this book, because the colors and images might have been set to something other than the defaults. One of the things people like to do with their Windows computers is personalize the user interface to reflect things they like and want to see rather than things that other people have decided they should see. And that's what this chapter is about!

This chapter guides you through procedures related to modifying the Start menu, setting the desktop background and system colors, selecting the Lock screen background and content, and applying and managing themes.

In this chapter

- Configure the Start menu
- Set the desktop background and system colors
- Customize the Lock screen
- Apply and manage themes

Configure the Start menu

The Start menu is your primary entry point to the apps that are installed on your computer. As mentioned in Chapter 1, "Get started using Windows 10," you have the choice of two Start menu configurations:

- A partial-screen Start menu that displays the folder list, the app list, and pinned tiles

- A full-size Start screen that displays the folder list and either pinned tiles or the app list

The partial-screen Start menu configuration is the default.

TIP The Windows 10 user interface has three distinct Start elements—the Start button, Start menu, and full-size Start screen. Windows documentation often refers to each of these simply as *Start*. For clarity, we refer to each of these elements separately in this book.

Resize the Start menu

The Start menu configuration that is best for you depends on the way you work—considerations include whether you primarily interact with Windows by selecting or tapping the screen, which method you prefer to use to start apps, whether you depend on Live Tiles for information, whether you make use of jump lists, and how large your screen is. Your initial preference might be based solely on what you're used to and comfortable with. You can easily try out both configurations to determine which is more efficient for the way that you work.

Changing the Start menu configuration is a simple one-step process. When you turn the full-screen setting on or off, the change takes place immediately. It isn't necessary to sign out of Windows or restart your computer to implement it.

You can change to the full-size Start screen or revert to the default Start menu size, and configure other Start menu settings, from the Start settings pane on the Personalization page in the Settings window.

You can adjust the height and width of the Start menu. When you make the Start menu wider or narrower, the width of the tile groups might also change.

> **SEE ALSO** For information about arranging tiles and tile groups on the Start menu, see "Manage Start menu tiles" in Chapter 3, "Work with shortcuts and tiles."

To resize the Start menu

- Drag the top border of the **Start** menu up or down to increase or decrease its height.

- Drag the right border of the **Start** menu right or left to increase or decrease its width.

To display pinned tiles that don't fit on the Start menu

1. Point to the **Start** menu to display the vertical scroll bar on the right edge.

> ✓ **TIP** The scroll bar appears only when there are more tiles than fit on the Start menu at the current size.

2. Drag the scroll box or select the scroll bar to scroll the **Start** menu content.

To switch between the default Start menu and full-size Start screen

1. Open the **Settings** window by selecting **Start** and then **Settings** or pressing Win+I.

2. Select **Personalization**, and then on the **Personalization** page, select **Start**.

3. In the **Start** settings pane, select **Use Start full screen**.

4. Select the **Start** button to test the setting.

To display commands on the full-size Start screen

- In the upper-left corner of the **Start** screen, select the **Expand** button.

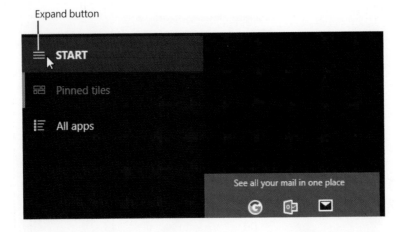

Expand button

Configure the Start menu folder list

The default Start menu has three sections: the folder list on the left, the app list in the middle, and the pinned tiles on the right. The folder list is collapsed to display only icons, but you can open it by selecting the Expand button at the top.

The folder list always displays a link to manage your user account and displays the Power button. By default, it also displays a link to the Settings window. In addition to these, you can display links to the following items:

- File Explorer
- Your Documents, Downloads, Music, Pictures, and Videos folders
- The HomeGroup and Network windows
- Your personal folder, from which you can access all your user account–specific folders and settings

The folders you select are always displayed in the same order.

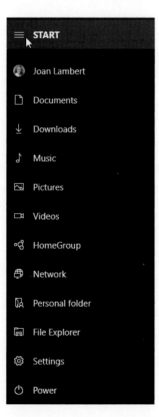

To add or remove folders on the Start menu

1. Display the **Start** pane of the **Personalization** settings page.

2. At the bottom of the pane, select **Choose which folders appear on Start** to display the list of options.

3. On the **Choose which folders appear on Start** page, turn on the folders that you want to appear on the Start menu, and turn the others off.

> ✅ **TIP** You can't turn off the user account management or Power buttons.

Configure the Start menu app list

The app list appears in the center pane of the Start menu. It displays an alphabetical list of the apps installed on your computer (some within folders). It can also display the following lists:

- **Recently added apps** This list displays apps for a short time after you install them. If no apps have been installed recently, the list disappears from the Start menu.

- **Most used apps** On a new Windows 10 installation, this list contains links to some standard Windows tools, or to apps that were selected by the computer manufacturer. As you use Windows, the apps you use most often appear in this list.

- **Recently opened items** When this setting is turned on, you can quickly access files that you've opened with apps that support the jump list feature (such as Microsoft Office apps) from the Start menu or taskbar.

If you prefer to not see the app list, you can remove the app list from the Start menu, or switch to the full-size Start screen.

To remove the app list from the Start menu

1. Display the **Start** pane of the **Personalization** settings page.

2. Turn off **Show app list in Start menu**.

3. Select the **Start** button to test the setting.

To display or hide contextual app lists on the Start menu

1. Display the **Start** pane of the **Personalization** settings page.

2. Do either of the following:

   - To turn off or on the Most Used list, select **Show most used apps**.

   - To turn off or on the Recently Added list, select **Show recently added apps**.

> **TIP** The Recently Added app list and jump lists are turned on by default. The Most Used app list is not on by default, but this can be a handy feature, so you might want to turn it on.

3. Select the **Start** button to test the setting.

To display or hide jump lists on the Start menu and taskbar

1. Display the **Start** pane of the **Personalization** settings page.

2. Select **Show recently opened items in Jump Lists on Start or the taskbar** to turn jump lists on or off.

Set the desktop background and system colors

You can use the options on the Personalization page of the Settings window to set the desktop background image or color, and the accent color that is used for various operating system elements, including the Start menu, taskbar, Action Center, and window title bars.

> **TIP** In addition to the changes described in this topic, you can apply a custom theme, which sets the background, color scheme, and other properties. For more information, see "Apply and manage themes" later in this chapter.

Set the desktop background

Your choice of desktop background usually reflects your personal taste—what you like to see when your app windows are minimized or closed. Some people prefer simple backgrounds that don't obscure their desktop icons, some prefer photos that reflect a specific theme, and some prefer personal photos of family members, pets, or favorite places.

You can set your desktop background to any of the following:

- **A picture** You can choose one of the photos that come with Windows, or a digital image of your own. The image can be any of several file types, including BMP, GIF, JPG, PNG, TIF, and the less common DIB, JFIF, JPE, JPEG, TIFF, and WDP file types.

- **A solid color** If you want to keep things simple, you can opt for a plain, colored background. You can choose from a palette of 24 colors, or select a custom color that you choose from a gradient or specify as an RGB (Red, Green, Blue), HSV (Hue, Saturation, Value), or hexadecimal value.

- **A slideshow** You can display the contents of a folder of your choice, with the background image changing as frequently as every minute or every 10 minutes, 30 minutes, hour, six hours, or day. You can display the images in the order they appear in the folder, or in a random order.

When you select a background option, a preview of the option appears at the top of the Background settings pane and Windows implements the option on the desktop. It isn't necessary to save your changes.

When displaying an image or slideshow as your desktop background, you can specify the position of the image as follows:

- **Fill** The image is centered on the screen. The image fills the screen horizontally and vertically and maintains its original aspect ratio. Parts of the image might overrun the left and right sides or the top and bottom edges (but not both).

- **Fit** The image is centered on the screen. The image fills the screen horizontally or vertically and maintains its original aspect ratio. Parts of the image might not fill the left and right sides or the top and bottom edges.

- **Stretch** The image is centered on the screen. The image fills the screen horizontally and vertically but does not maintain its original aspect ratio. No part of the image overruns the screen.

- **Tile** The image is anchored in the upper-left corner of the screen at its original size, followed by as many copies as are necessary to fill the screen. Parts of the rightmost and bottom tiles might overrun the edges of the screen.

- **Center** The image is centered on the screen at its original size.

- **Span** When you have multiple monitors connected to the computer, this option stretches the image across the monitors.

When you select a picture position that doesn't fill the screen (such as Fit or Centered), the rest of the desktop is filled with the currently selected desktop background color.

To set one desktop background image

1. Open the **Settings** window, select **Personalization**, and then on the **Personalization** settings page, select **Background**.

2. In the **Background** settings pane, select the **Background** list and then **Picture**.

3. In the **Choose your picture** area, do either of the following:

   - Select a thumbnail to select a Windows 10 image or a previously selected picture.

   - Select **Browse**. In the **Open** dialog box, browse to and select the image you want to use. Then select **Choose picture**.

4. In the **Choose a fit** list, select **Fill**, **Fit**, **Stretch**, **Tile**, **Center**, or **Span** to indicate the way you want to position the image.

5. When the preview image updates to reflect your settings, make any necessary changes to configure the desktop background the way you want it.

 IMPORTANT If you choose Fit or Centered and don't like the desktop background color behind the image, change it and then reselect the desktop background image.

Or

1. Start the Photos app.

2. Locate and select the photo that you want to display as the desktop background.

3. At the right end of the **Photos** menu bar, select **See more** (...) > **Set as** > **Set as background**.

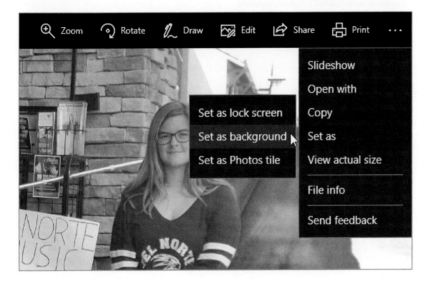

To display a series of desktop background images

1. Place the images you want to display into one folder.

2. Display the **Background** pane of the **Personalization** settings page.

3. In the **Background** list, select **Slideshow**.

4. If you want to use a folder other than the one shown in the **Choose albums for your slideshow** area (by default, this is your Pictures folder), select **Browse**. In the **Select Folder** dialog box, browse to and select the folder of images you want to use. Then select **Choose this folder**.

> 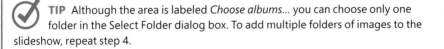 **TIP** Although the area is labeled *Choose albums...* you can choose only one folder in the Select Folder dialog box. To add multiple folders of images to the slideshow, repeat step 4.

5. If you want the background image to change more or less frequently than the default of every 30 minutes, expand the **Change picture every** list and then select **1 minute, 10 minutes, 1 hour, 6 hours,** or **1 day**.

6. If you want to display the folder contents in a random order, turn on **Shuffle**.

7. In the **Choose a fit** list, select **Fill, Fit, Stretch, Tile, Center,** or **Span** to indicate the way you want to position the images. Consider that image sizes in the slideshow might vary.

8. When the preview image updates to reflect your settings, make any necessary changes to configure the desktop background the way you want it.

To set a standard desktop background color

1. Display the **Background** pane of the **Personalization** settings page.

2. In the **Background** list, select **Solid color** to display the color grid. An outline and check mark indicate the current background color.

3. In the color grid, select the color swatch you want to use.

To set a custom desktop background color

1. In the **Background** pane of the **Personalization** settings page, in the **Background** list, select **Solid color**.

2. Below the color grid, select **Custom color** to open the Pick A Background Color pane.

3. Do one of the following, and then select **Done**:

   - Select or drag on the gradient panel to specify a color.

   - Select **More**, and then enter an RGB or hexadecimal color value.

   - Select **More**, expand the **RGB** list, and select **HSV**. Then enter an HSV color value.

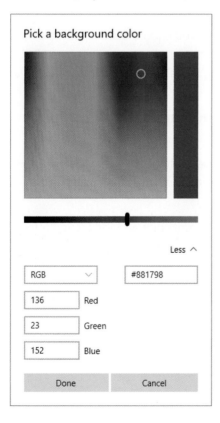

Set an accent color

The preview at the top of the Background settings pane displays an image of the desktop background, Start menu, and taskbar. The preview at the top of the Colors settings pane also displays a content window, either with or without a colored title bar, because the window title bar is one of the optional areas to which you can apply the accent color. The other optional areas are the Start menu, taskbar, and Action Center.

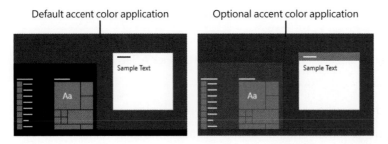

When selecting an accent color, you can choose from four configurations based on combinations of two settings:

- The tiles can be an accent color that you choose from a palette of 48 colors; a custom color that you choose from a gradient or specify as an RGB (Red, Green, Blue), HSV (Hue, Saturation, Value), or hexadecimal value; or a color that Windows chooses based on the desktop background.

- The Start menu, taskbar, and Action Center can be black or a darker shade of the accent color.

- The system window title bars can be white or the accent color. (This setting doesn't affect the color of Microsoft Office app title bars, for example, which have their own color scheme setting.)

You have two options in addition to the accent color and the areas it affects: transparency and light or dark app mode. The transparency option, which is turned on by default, makes the Start menu, taskbar, and Action Center slightly transparent so you can see the desktop and open windows behind them. This Windows Aero feature was introduced for windows frames and the taskbar in Windows Vista, was relegated to only the taskbar in Windows 8, and has returned in Windows 10. You can't control the percentage of transparency (or rather, opacity) of the user interface elements—they're either transparent or opaque—but the low transparency level does seem to be less distracting than in previous versions of Windows.

⚙ Colors

Choose your color

☐ Automatically pick an accent color from my background

Recent colors

Windows colors

+ Custom color

More options

Transparency effects

⬤ On

Show accent color on the following surfaces

☐ Start, taskbar, and action center

☐ Title bars

Choose your default app mode

◉ Light

○ Dark

To set an accent color based on the desktop background

1. Display the **Personalization** settings page, and then select **Colors**.

2. In the **Colors** settings pane, select the **Automatically pick an accent color from my background** check box.

> **TIP** If your desktop background is set to Slideshow and you have Windows pick an accent color based on the background, the accent color will change when the desktop background changes. If you like change, you'll like this combination; if you don't, you might find it distracting.

To set a standard accent color

1. Display the **Colors** pane of the **Personalization** settings page.

2. In the **Choose your color** area, clear the **Automatically pick an accent color from my background** check box. An outline and check mark indicate the current accent color if it is one from the grid.

3. In the color grid, select the color swatch you want to use. Windows implements the change and updates the preview image.

To set a custom accent color

1. Display the **Colors** pane of the **Personalization** settings page.

2. In the **Choose your color** area, clear the **Automatically pick an accent color from my background** check box.

3. Below the color grid, select **Custom color**.

4. In the **Choose a custom accent color** pane, do one of the following:

   - Select or drag on the gradient panel to specify a color.

   - Select **More**, and then enter an RGB or a hexadecimal color value.

   - Select **More**, expand the **RGB** list, and select **HSV**. Then enter an HSV color value.

To apply the accent color to the Start menu, taskbar, and Action Center

1. Display the **Colors** pane of the **Personalization** settings page.

2. In the **More options** area, below **Show accent color on the following surfaces**, select the **Start, taskbar, and action center** check box.

To apply the accent color to system window title bars

1. Display the **Colors** pane of the **Personalization** settings page.

2. In the **More options** area, below **Show accent color on the following surfaces**, select the **Title bars** check box.

To switch between transparent and opaque user interface elements

1. Display the **Colors** pane of the **Personalization** settings page.

2. In the **More options** area, do one of the following:

   - If you want the Start menu, taskbar, and Action Center to be transparent, turn on **Transparency effects**.

   - If you want the Start menu, taskbar, and Action Center to be opaque, turn off **Transparency effects**.

   Windows implements the change. This setting doesn't affect the preview image, but if your desktop background has content at the bottom of the screen, the effect might be apparent on your taskbar.

3. To check the effect of the setting, display the Start menu or Action Center.

Customize the Lock screen

When your computer comes out of sleep mode (and between computing sessions), Windows displays the Lock screen. By default, the Lock screen displays the current time, date, network connection status, and battery charge (for devices running on battery power). However, it can be configured to display much more information, including status updates from up to eight apps. It can also double as an electronic picture frame and display a slideshow of pictures stored in multiple folders on your computer and in the cloud.

The Lock screen has four primary purposes:

- To act as a screensaver to prevent people from seeing your open files and apps or using your computer when you're away from it.

- To display a single photo, or a slideshow of one or more folders of photos. (Windows 10 can display photos from multiple folders.)

- To display information from selected apps when the computer session isn't active, so you can be aware of upcoming appointments or other information without signing in.

- To deter accidental sign-in on a touch device.

Set the Lock screen background

On a clean installation of Windows 10, the Lock screen is configured to display one of the Windows 10 theme images. You can choose any photo or a slideshow of photos that are contained in one or more folders. The latter option displays more than a simple slideshow; it displays from one to five images at a time and mixes photos from the selected folders. When displaying your own images, you also have the option to display fun facts and tips about Windows and Cortana on the Lock screen. If you don't want to use your own photos, you can choose the Windows Spotlight slideshow, which features beautiful high-definition images, information about the image subjects, and Windows and Cortana information.

> **TIP** It is possible to disable the Lock screen by editing the registry or Group Policies, but these activities shouldn't be undertaken lightly and are beyond the scope of a *Step by Step* book.

To display one image on the Lock screen

1. Display the **Personalization** page of the **Settings** window, and then select **Lock screen**. The Preview area of the Lock Screen settings pane displays your current Lock screen background.

   If the current background is a single picture, the pane shows thumbnails of other recent picture backgrounds (or background options from the current theme) for quick selection. If the background is a slideshow, the pane shows the folders that contain the slideshow photos.

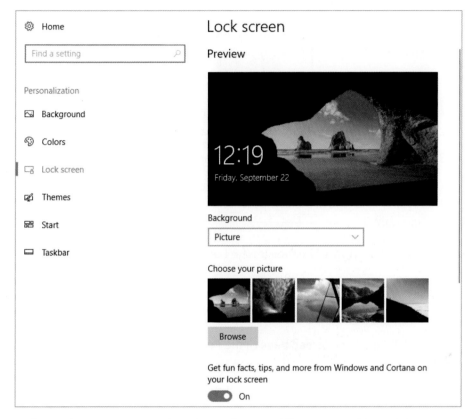

2. In the **Lock screen** pane, select the **Background** list to expand it, and then select **Picture**.

3. Select the background picture by doing either of the following:

- If the **Choose your picture** section includes a thumbnail of the picture you want to use, select the thumbnail.

- If the **Choose your picture** section doesn't show the picture you want to use, select **Browse**. In the **Open** dialog box, browse to the picture you want to use, and then select **Choose picture**.

> **TIP** The pretty pictures provided with Windows 10 are stored in C:\Windows \Web\Screen and are also provided as part of the Windows 10 theme. You can download similar artwork from *windows.microsoft.com/windows/wallpaper*.

Your selection is shown in the Preview area. If the picture you select doesn't have the same aspect ratio as the screen, Windows fills the screen with the picture, which might cut off part of what you want to see.

4. Press Win+L to lock the computer and verify that the background looks the way you want it.

Or

1. Start the Photos app.

2. Locate and select the photo that you want to display on the Lock screen.

3. At the right end of the **Photos** menu bar, select **See more (…)** > **Set as** > **Set as Lock screen**.

4. Press Win+L to lock the computer and verify that the background looks the way you want it.

To display a slideshow of images on the Lock screen

1. Identify one or more folders that contain pictures you want to display as a slideshow. If you want to use only some of the photos from each folder, create a new folder (Lock Screen Pics, for example) and copy the photos to it.

2. Display the **Lock screen** pane of the **Personalization** settings page.

3. Expand the **Background** list, and select **Slideshow**. The Choose Albums For Your Slideshow area displays your Pictures folder and any other folders that were previously selected for a slideshow.

> **TIP** The advanced slideshow settings can be configured to include Camera Roll folders from your computer and Microsoft OneDrive, without displaying those folders in the Choose Albums section, and to include pictures that don't entirely fit on the screen. It's a good idea to specifically configure those settings the way you want them.

4. Do either of the following:

- To add a folder to the slideshow, select **Add a folder**, browse to the folder you want to add, select the folder, and then select **Choose this folder**.

- To remove a folder from the slideshow album, select the folder to display its controls, and then select **Remove**.

Configure a screen saver

Screen savers are blank screens or moving images that appear on your screen after some period of inactivity. Originally, screen savers were used to prevent screens from being permanently "imprinted" with a static image that remained on the screen for too long. (This was back in the dark ages of computer history, when monitors fired a stream of electrons at the back of a CRT (cathode ray tube) or plasma screen to create little white dots that combined to display text you could read from the front side of the screen.) Modern monitors are not susceptible to this kind of damage, so screen savers are now primarily for visual entertainment.

The original screen saver was a simple app that made the screen blank after a period of inactivity. It was created by John Socha, and its code was published in the December 1983 issue of the *Softalk* magazine.

The Lock screen can display a series of images, but if you're looking for something less specific, Windows 10 still has six built-in screen saver options:

- **3D Text** Displays a rotating version of the text you specify. If you don't specify text, it displays "Windows 10."

- **Blank** Clears the screen of content.

- **Bubbles** Displays colorful round bubbles that bounce around the screen.

- **Mystify** Displays colorful repeating lines in geometric and curving patterns.

- **Photos** Displays a slideshow of the files in any folder that you specify. If you don't specify a folder, it displays the content of your Pictures folder.

- **Ribbons** Displays ribbons of color that dance across the screen.

2

When you select a screen saver, you can preview the effect, set the interval of inactivity before it will be displayed, and specify whether a password is required to stop the screen saver after it is set in motion. For some screen savers, you can set options such as size, motion pattern, and style.

To configure a screen saver, follow these steps:

1. Display the **Personalization** page of the **Settings** window, and then select **Lock screen**.

2. Near the bottom of the **Lock screen** settings pane, select **Screen saver settings** to open the Screen Saver Settings dialog box.

3. In the **Screen saver** list, select the screen saver you want to use. The dialog box displays a preview of the screen saver.

4. If the screen saver you select has options, the Settings button becomes active. To configure nondefault options, select the **Settings** button and provide the requested information.

5. If you want to preview the screen saver at full size on your screen, select the **Preview** button. The preview ends as soon as you move the mouse, tap the screen, or press a key.

6. In the **Wait** box, set the number of minutes of inactivity after which you want the screen saver to start.

7. If you want Windows to display the Lock screen when the screen saver stops, select the **On resume, display logon screen** check box.

   TIP The term "logon screen" in the Screen Saver Settings dialog box is left over from a previous version of Windows, but refers to the Windows 10 Lock screen.

8. In the **Screen Saver Settings** dialog box, select **OK**.

To configure advanced slideshow settings

1. Configure the Lock screen to display a slideshow of images.

2. In the **Lock screen** settings pane, below the **Choose albums for your slideshow** area, select the **Advanced slideshow settings** link to display the **Advanced slideshow settings** pane.

> ⚙ Advanced slideshow settings
>
> Include Camera Roll folders from this PC and OneDrive
> ⬤ Off
>
> Only use pictures that fit my screen
> ⬤ On
>
> When my PC is inactive, show lock screen instead of turning off the screen
> ⬤ On
>
> Turn off screen after slideshow has played for
> Don't turn off ⌄

> ✓ **TIP** On a mobile device, the Advanced Slideshow Settings pane includes an option to play or not play a slideshow when using battery power.

3. Configure the advanced settings the way you want them for your slideshow.

To display the Windows Spotlight Lock screen

1. Display the **Lock screen** pane of the **Personalization** settings page.

2. Expand the **Background** list, and select **Windows spotlight**. A preview of the current Spotlight background appears at the top of the Lock Screen pane.

> ✓ **TIP** On the Windows Spotlight Lock screen, you can vote for the backgrounds you like, and Windows 10 will select future backgrounds that reflect your preferences. To vote for or against a background, select *Like What You See?* and then select *I like it!* or *Not a fan.*

To display tips on the Lock screen

1. Configure the Lock screen to display a picture or slideshow.

2. On the **Lock screen** settings pane, below the **Choose your picture** or **Choose albums** section, turn on **Get fun facts, tips, and more from Windows and Cortana on your lock screen**.

> ⚠️ **IMPORTANT** The Get Fun Facts option is available only when the Lock screen is configured to display a picture or slideshow; the feature is automatically built in to Windows Spotlight.

Display app status information on the Lock screen

In addition to the background photo or photos and the time, date, network, and battery information, you can choose to display detailed status information on the Lock screen from one Store app, and quick status information from up to seven Store apps. The primary purpose of this display is to provide you with quick but basic information about something, such as the number of new emails or an upcoming meeting, without requiring you to unlock your screen.

The apps that are available to you depend on the apps that are installed on your computer. Run each app at least once to configure any required settings (for example, to specify the location you want the Weather app to monitor), so it can display updates at the bottom of the Lock screen.

To display app information on the Lock screen

1. Display the **Personalization** page of the **Settings** window, and then select **Lock screen**. The controls to set Lock screen apps are below the background settings.

2. In the **Choose an app to show detailed status** area, select the tile to display a list of apps that can display status information on the Lock screen. At the time of this writing, the eligible apps are Calendar, Mail, Messaging, Phone, Xbox, and Weather. (You can also choose None.) Other apps or games that you install might also be available.

3. In the app list, select one app to display detailed status updates on the Lock screen.

4. In the **Choose apps to show quick status** area, select any tile, and then select an app in the list. Repeat this process to select up to seven apps.

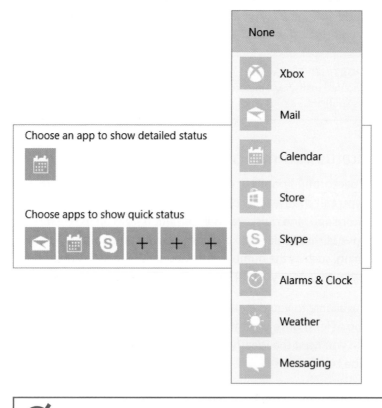

> ✓ **TIP** The order of the app icons determines the order of status updates on the Lock screen. An empty icon space displays a gap between the other status updates.

Apply and manage themes

Previously in this chapter, we worked with the desktop background and system colors. You can configure those elements individually, or you can apply an entire package of personalization elements at one time by applying a *theme*. Windows 10 has two types of themes:

- Decorative themes that provide a desktop background image or series of images, and a corresponding system accent color (or colors that change with the background image). These are the same elements covered in "Set the desktop background and system colors" earlier in this chapter. A decorative theme can also include custom notification sounds that play to notify you of Windows events (such as a low battery or a User Account Control request for Administrator approval of a change) and app events (such as an incoming instant message, a blocked pop-up window, or a completed transaction).

- High contrast themes that are designed to make system elements easier for people with visual limitations (such as color blindness) to see and use. The high contrast themes increase the color contrast of text, window borders, and images on your screen to make them more visible and easier to read and identify.

This topic is about decorative themes. For information about high contrast themes, see "Configure Windows accessibility features" in Chapter 13, "Manage power and access options."

The availability and necessity of decorative themes within Windows has changed over the last few years as digital images have become more common; it's easy to use a favorite picture of your own or that you download from the web as a desktop background, or to enjoy the Windows Spotlight imagery on your Lock screen. But if you'd like to apply a theme, they're still available and offer a wide range of motifs with impressive imagery and artwork.

Three decorative themes (Windows, Windows 10, and Flowers) are provided with Windows 10. Most of the images in this book depict the "Windows" theme desktop background.

TIP If you use your own images as a desktop background and later want to regain access to the original "Windows" or "Windows 10" theme images, you can do so by applying that theme.

2

The manufacturer of your computer might also install a theme that is specific to the brand of computer you have. If you work in a managed computer environment, your company might have a corporate theme that is installed by default with the base computer image.

In addition to these theme options, many others are available from the Store app and from the Desktop Themes page of the Microsoft Support website. The desktop backgrounds of these themes feature some breathtaking photography and creative artwork across multiple subject categories that include not only general photography (landscapes, animals, plants, people, and places) but also themes tied to specific movies or games. You could spend hours browsing through the options. The Store app is the preferred installation location for Windows 10 themes. More than 75 themes are available from the Store at the time of this writing.

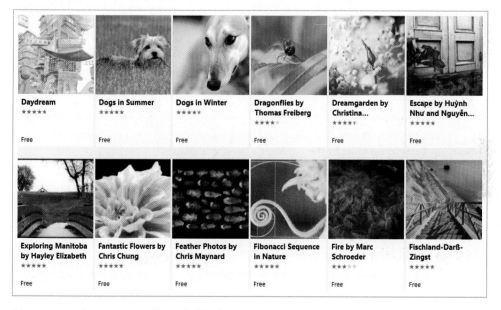

Many more themes are still available from the Microsoft Support website. They're also somewhat easier to sort through in this location, because they're divided into categories that include both content and functionality.

> **TIP** Themes that include custom sounds are easy to locate by selecting With Custom Sounds in the category list.

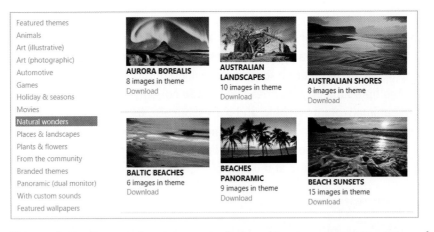

Themes in the Panoramic category are designed to span across two screens, for people who work with a second monitor that is connected to their computer system. For panoramic themes to work as intended, both screens must have the same resolution.

> **SEE ALSO** For information about screen resolution, see "Display your desktop on multiple screens" in Chapter 7, "Manage peripheral devices."

Most themes include multiple desktop background images. The number of images included with the theme appears below the theme thumbnail and name. Most themes are provided by Microsoft Corporation, but many of those in the From The Community category are contributed by photographers to showcase their work.

After you apply a theme, you can customize elements of it to suit your individual taste. For example, many themes come with multiple desktop background images, and you can choose the one that you like best, or choose a selection to display in slideshow fashion. If you use your Microsoft account credentials to sign in to multiple computers, you can choose to synchronize a custom theme among all of your accounts.

2

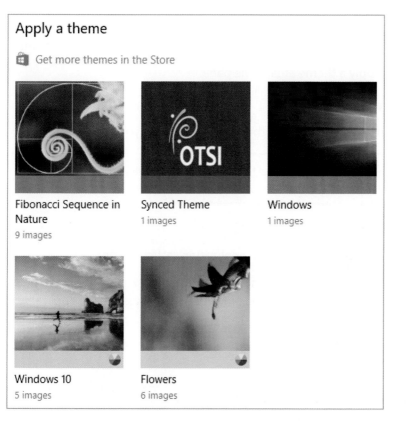

At the time of this writing, themes are ultimately managed in Control Panel, but you can also get to the theme settings through the Personalization page of the Settings window.

Any changes you make to the background, colors, sounds, or cursors after you apply a theme create a customized version of that theme, which is designated in the Themes settings pane as Unsaved Theme. For example, you can change the system color or select a single background image from among several that come with a theme. If you like the changes you make to a theme, you can save it as a custom theme, either for your own use or for distribution to other people.

> **IMPORTANT** You can have only one unsaved theme at a time; until you save it, any additional changes you make will remove that specific background/color/sound combination from your themes.

To display the installed themes

1. Display the **Personalization** page of the **Settings** window, and then select **Themes**.

2. Scroll to the **Apply a theme** area of the pane.

To apply an installed theme

- Display the installed themes, and then select the theme you want to apply.

> **TIP** You can display the updated desktop background by pointing to or selecting the Show Desktop button located at the right end of the taskbar, or by pressing Win+D.

To modify an element of the current theme

1. Display the **Themes** pane of the **Personalization** settings page.

2. In the **Current theme** area of the Themes pane, select the element you want to change: **Background**, **Sounds**, **Color**, or **Mouse cursor** to go to the applicable settings pane or dialog box.

3. Select the new element or settings you want.

To save a custom theme

1. Apply a theme and modify one or more theme elements.

2. Display the **Themes** setting pane. A customized theme is indicated by *Current theme: Custom* at the top of the pane.

3. At the bottom of the **Current theme** area, select **Save theme**.

4. In the **Save your theme** box, enter a name for the theme, and then select **Save**.

> **SEE ALSO** For information about synchronizing your theme among the computers associated with your Microsoft account, see "Customize your sign-in options" in Chapter 11, "Manage user accounts and settings."

2

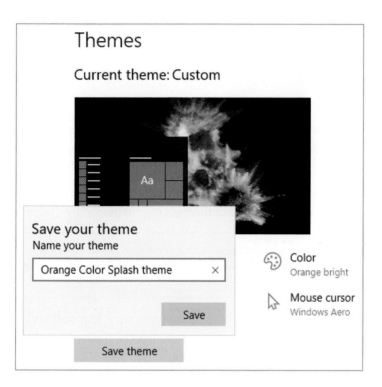

To apply a theme from the Store app

1. Do either of the following to display the Windows Themes page of the Store:

   - Select the Store icon on the taskbar. Enter **windows themes** in the search box, and then select **Windows Themes** in the filtered list.

   - Display the **Themes** settings pane of the **Personalization** settings page. Near the bottom of the pane, select **Get more themes in the Store** (not *Get more themes*).

2. Scroll the page to review the representative thumbnails of each theme.

3. Select any thumbnail to display the theme-specific page, which previews up to three images from the theme and provides additional information and the installation controls.

4. To display all images from the theme, select **Show all** adjacent to the Screenshots heading.

5. To install the theme, select **Get** at the top of the theme page. After the theme installs, select **Launch** to return to the Themes settings pane.

To apply a theme from the Windows website

1. Do either of the following to display the Desktop Themes page of the Windows website in your default browser:

   - Go to *windows.microsoft.com/windows/themes*.

   - Display the **Personalization** settings window, and then select **Themes**. Near the bottom of the Themes settings pane, under **Get more personality in Windows**, select **Get more themes** (not *Get more themes in the Store*).

2. Scroll the page to review the representative thumbnails of each theme. The number of images included with each theme is shown below the theme name.

> ✓ **TIP** The Store app is the preferred theme installation location and offers more preview options than the website. You can't preview themes on the website before installing them.

3. Select **Download** below the name of the theme you want to install, and then select **Open** in the download notification to unpack the theme file, add the theme to the Themes settings pane, and apply the theme.

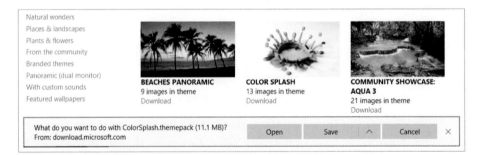

> ✓ **TIP** The installed theme elements are saved in the hidden AppData\Local\Microsoft \Windows\Themes folder in your user account folder. For information about displaying hidden files and folders, see "Change the File Explorer display options" in Chapter 5, "Explore files and folders."

To remove a theme

- In the **Apply a theme** area of the **Themes** settings pane, right-click the theme you want to remove, and then select **Delete**.

Key points

2

- The Start menu is your gateway to the apps installed on your computer. The Start menu can occupy all or part of your screen, and can display the app list and pinned tiles. You can modify the size and content of the Start menu.

- If you want to, you can display a full-size version of the Start menu called the *Start screen*. The Start screen has two views: Pinned Tiles and All Apps.

- The desktop background can display an image, a slideshow of images, or a solid color. You can choose the accent color that appears on app tiles or have Windows choose a color that complements the desktop background. You can optionally choose to apply a shade of the accent color to the Start menu, task-bar, and Action Center.

- You can set the desktop background, accent color, system sounds, and mouse cursor individually, or by installing a theme from the Store app or Windows website.

- The Lock screen serves as a screen saver and can also display current informa-tion from selected apps. You can display a built-in image, one or more images of your own, or the Windows Spotlight imagery as the Lock screen background.

- Six of the traditional screen savers, including the popular 3D Text, Bubbles, and Ribbons options, are still available if you want to configure them to display over the Lock screen.

Chapter 2

Practice tasks

Before you can complete these practice tasks, you need to copy the book's practice files to your computer. The practice files for these tasks are located in the **Win10SBS\Ch02** folder. The introduction includes a complete list of practice files.

Configure the Start menu

Open the Settings window, and then perform the following tasks:

1. Display the Start menu personalization settings.

2. Turn on the full-size Start screen (or leave it on if it already is).

3. Display the **Start** screen and note the organization of tiles and tile groups on the screen.

4. Display the app list on the Start screen, and scroll the list to note how this is different on the Start screen than on the Start menu.

5. Return to the Start menu personalization settings. Turn off the Recently Added app list, Most Used app list, and jump lists.

6. Configure the Start menu to display only these folders:

   - File Explorer

   - Settings

   - Documents

   - Downloads

   - Pictures

   - Network

7. Display the **Start** screen to observe the results of the changes.

8. Return to the Start menu personalization settings. Turn off the full-size Start screen.

9. Display the **Start** menu, and drag the corner of the screen until it is at its minimum size.

10. If a vertical scroll bar appears, scroll down to display the hidden tiles.

11. Return to the Start menu personalization settings, and implement the Start menu configuration, lists, and folders that you like best.

Set the desktop background and system colors

Open the Settings window, and then perform the following tasks:

1. Display the system accent color personalization settings.

2. Configure the settings so that Windows selects an accent color from the desktop background.

3. Apply the accent color to the Start menu, taskbar, Action Center, and title bars.

4. Turn on transparency effects.

5. Display the desktop background personalization settings.

6. Set the desktop background to a solid color of your choice. In the preview image, note any change in the accent color.

7. Set the desktop background to the **Background01** image located in the practice file folder. In the preview image, note any change in the accent color.

8. Configure the background settings to display the image in the center of the screen without resizing it.

9. Minimize all open windows to show the desktop, and observe the change. Notice that the background color you set in step 6 surrounds the image.

10. Return to the background personalization settings. Configure the background settings as follows:

    - Display a slideshow of the images in the practice file folder.

    - Display the images in a random order, with the image changing every minute.

    - Choose the fit option that will display all the images at full-screen size without affecting the image aspect ratios.

11. Minimize all open windows to show the desktop and observe the change.

12. Expand the **Start** menu. Notice that the desktop background is visible through the Start menu and taskbar.

13.   Wait for the desktop background to change. Notice that the accent color on the taskbar and other interface elements changes with the background image. Locate the source of the accent color for each new background image.

14.   Return to the **Settings** window. Configure the desktop background and accent color as you want them.

Customize the Lock screen

Display the Lock Screen settings pane, and then perform the following tasks:

1.   Configure the Lock screen to display a slideshow of the images from the practice file folder.

2.   Lock your computer and observe the slideshow. Notice that the picture layout changes from a single photo to multiple photos.

3.   Unlock your computer, and then display the advanced slideshow settings. Turn on the option to display photos from the Camera Roll folders on your computer and on OneDrive. Then lock your computer and note any changes from the previous Lock screen slideshow.

4.   Unlock your computer, and then configure the Lock screen to display any image from the practice file folder. Select the option to display Windows and Cortana tips.

5.   Lock your computer and observe the Lock screen.

6.   Unlock your computer, and then configure the Lock screen to display Windows Spotlight background images.

7.   Select one app to display detailed information on the Lock screen, and at least one app to display quick status information. If you haven't yet done so, start and configure each of the selected apps.

8.   Lock your computer and observe the Lock screen. Take note of the app information at the bottom of the screen. If you have the option to do so, indicate whether you like or dislike the current Windows Spotlight background.

9.   Unlock your computer, and then configure the Lock screen to display the information you want.

Apply and manage themes

Display the Theme settings pane, and then perform the following tasks:

1. Locate the themes that are installed on your computer.

2. Apply the built-in **Flowers** theme.

3. Open the Store app. Locate a theme that you like, and install it.

4. Go to the **Desktop Themes** webpage. Locate a theme that you like, and install it.

5. Change the system color for the installed theme. Then return to the **Themes** pane, and note that the unsaved theme reflects your changes.

6. Save the customized theme as MyCustomTheme.

7. Remove any of the new themes you installed that you don't want to keep.

Part 2

Apps and files

Work with shortcuts and tiles

In Chapters 1 and 2, you worked with the Windows user interface rather than with apps that run on Windows. There are many ways to start the apps that are installed on your computer. Chapter 4, "Work with apps and notifications," discusses some of the common preinstalled Windows 10 apps and how to install others. This chapter covers configuring the Windows environment to make apps available where you want them.

When you install an app on your computer, the app and the files that support it are copied to folders within the Windows system folder structure. You can start an app by navigating to those files and running the primary app executable file, but that's a lot of work. It's easier to start the app from the Start menu app list or from a shortcut that you create in the area that's most convenient to the way you work: the desktop, taskbar, or Start menu pinned tiles area.

This chapter guides you through procedures related to creating and managing app shortcuts, managing Start menu tiles, and configuring the taskbar.

In this chapter

- Create and manage app shortcuts
- Manage Start menu tiles
- Customize the taskbar

Create and manage app shortcuts

Installing an app adds it to the app list on the Start menu, and you can start the app by locating it in the list and selecting it. If you plan to use the app often, you can save time by creating a shortcut to the app in a more convenient location. You can create app shortcuts in these locations:

- On the Start menu, where the shortcut is a tile

- On the taskbar, where the shortcut is a button

- On the desktop, where the shortcut is indicated by an arrow on the icon

- In a folder, where the shortcut is indicated by an arrow on the item

Start menu shortcuts

All Start menu tiles are actually shortcuts to files and folders that are stored else-where. You can pin any app to the Start screen. To start an app from the Start menu shortcut, simply select the tile.

By default, pinning an app to the Start menu creates a Medium tile. Start menu tiles that link to desktop apps can be Small or Medium; Start menu tiles that link to Store apps can be Small, Medium, Wide, or Large.

> **SEE ALSO** For information about changing the size and location of tiles, see "Manage Start menu tiles" later in this chapter. For information about Store apps and desktop apps, see "Locate and start apps" in Chapter 4, "Work with apps and notifications."

3

Many Store apps are configured to display live tile content (but not all apps that are configured for it have live tile content available at this time). If a Start menu tile links to an app that is configured for live tile content, the tile shortcut menu includes the command Turn Live Tile On or Turn Live Tile Off, depending on the current setting. You can turn on live tile content for an app at any tile size, but only Medium, Wide, and Large tiles can display live content.

To create an app shortcut on the Start menu

1. Do either of the following:

   - Locate the app in the app list on the **Start** menu.

   - In File Explorer, navigate to and select the app executable file.

2. On the menu or in File Explorer, right-click the app or the selected executable file, and then select **Pin to Start**. (If the command says *Unpin from Start*, the app is already pinned to the Start menu.)

To display or hide live content on an app tile

1. Do either of the following:

   - On the **Start** menu, right-click the tile.

   - On a touchscreen device, press and hold the tile until the Unpin and Options buttons appear on the tile to indicate that it is active for editing. Then in the lower-right corner of the tile, select the **Options (...)** button.

2. Select **More**, and then **Turn Live Tile on** or **Turn Live Tile off**.

> **TIP** There might be a short delay after you turn on Live Tile content while Windows connects to the app source to fetch and then display the current content.

To remove an app shortcut from the Start menu

- In the app list, right-click the app and then select **Unpin from Start**.

- On the **Start** menu, right-click the app tile, and then select **Unpin from Start**.

- On a touchscreen device, press and hold the tile until it becomes active for editing. Then in the upper-right corner of the tile, select the **Unpin** button.

Touchscreen tile management

If you're working on a touchscreen device, you can display the equivalent of the tile shortcut menu commands by pressing and holding a tile until the Unpin and Options buttons appear.

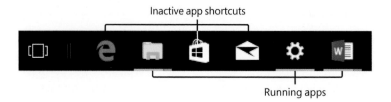

Selecting the Options (...) button displays the available tile sizes and live content options for the active tile. Tapping More displays the available app management commands for the active tile. The commands available for a tile depend on the app that it links to and the current state of the tile.

Taskbar shortcuts

Because the taskbar is always available from the desktop, it can be much faster to access apps, files, and folders from shortcuts that are on the taskbar than from the Start menu. You can pin any Store app or desktop app to the taskbar. Taskbar shortcuts look like buttons. To start an app from the taskbar shortcut, simply select the button. App shortcuts display only icons until the app is active. An underline appears below the taskbar icon for each open file.

Inactive app shortcuts

Running apps

On the taskbar, you can arrange shortcuts and active app buttons by dragging them into the order you want. You can make all the taskbar buttons smaller at the same time, but you can't change the size of individual taskbar buttons.

> 🔍 **SEE ALSO** For information about changing the size of taskbar buttons, see "Customize the taskbar" later in this chapter.

3

To create an app shortcut on the taskbar

1. Do either of the following:

   - Locate the app in the app list or pinned tiles area on the **Start** menu.

   - In File Explorer, navigate to the app's executable file.

2. Right-click the app, the app tile, or the app executable file, select **More**, and then select **Pin to taskbar**.

Or

1. On a touchscreen device, press and hold the Start menu tile until it becomes active for editing.

2. In the lower-right corner of the tile, tap the **Options** button, tap **More**, and then tap **Pin to taskbar**.

> ⚠ **IMPORTANT** Pinning an app to the taskbar replaces the command Pin To Taskbar with the command Unpin From Taskbar. You can't pin two instances of an app to the taskbar.

To create a taskbar shortcut to a currently running app

- On the taskbar, right-click the app button, and then select **Pin to taskbar**.

To create a taskbar shortcut to a file

- Open File Explorer and locate the file. Drag the file to the taskbar. When the ScreenTip *Pin file to <app>* appears, release the file to create a taskbar shortcut to the app, with the file in the Pinned section of the shortcut menu.

- With the file open, right-click the taskbar shortcut, locate the file in the **Recent** section of the shortcut menu, point to the file, and then select the **Pin to this list** button (the thumbtack) that appears.

Manage apps from the taskbar

You can start or switch to a pinned or running app by clicking its taskbar button. If you prefer to use a keyboard shortcut, you can start or switch to any of the first 10 apps in the taskbar button area by pressing Win+*n*, where *n* is a number from 0 through 9 (with 0 representing 10).

When an app is running, a thick underline appears below the app icon. A color variation on the bar indicates when multiple instances of an app are running. Pointing to (hovering over) an active taskbar button displays thumbnails of each instance of the app. You can switch to a specific app window by selecting its thumbnail. You can close an app window by pointing to its thumbnail, and then selecting the Close button (the X) that appears in the upper-right corner.

Right-clicking a taskbar button (or dragging the button up slightly above the taskbar) displays a jump list and a shortcut menu. Depending on the app, the jump list displays tasks that are related to the app or files that were recently

To move an app shortcut on the taskbar

- Drag the taskbar button left or right to its new location.

To remove an app shortcut from the taskbar

- Right-click the taskbar button, and then select **Unpin from taskbar**.

opened in that app. (In the case of a web browser such as Chrome, the jump list displays webpages opened in the browser.)

You can right-click files on the jump list to display additional commands. The taskbar button shortcut menu typically displays commands for starting or quitting the app and pinning or unpinning the app.

You can manually pin items to a jump list by dragging files or folders of the appropriate type to the taskbar button. For example, you can drop a Word document on the Word icon, or drop a folder on the File Explorer icon, to pin the document or folder to the relevant jump list.

Desktop shortcuts

Traditionally, many desktop app installation processes create app shortcuts on the desktop. There is no interface to "pin" an app to the desktop, but you can easily create a desktop shortcut to any app. You can also create shortcuts to webpages, files, and folders, or save files and folders directly on the desktop. Items on the desktop are represented by icons, usually of the app that opens them.

A shortcut is differentiated from an item that is stored directly on the desktop by an arrow in the lower-left corner of the icon.

By default, desktop icons are created at a Medium size and aligned to a grid that helps to maintain a bit of order. You can change the icon size to Small or Large. Unlike the Start menu icons, which are individually sizable, this change affects all icons on the desktop.

Large icons	View	>
● Medium icons	Sort by	>
Small icons	Refresh	
Auto arrange icons	Paste	
✓ Align icons to grid	Paste shortcut	
	Undo Move	Ctrl+Z
✓ Show desktop icons	Graphics Properties...	
	Graphics Options	>
	New	>
	Display settings	
	Personalize	

If you want to organize (or disorganize) icons without using the grid, you can turn off grid alignment, and then drag items to whatever desktop position you want.

Some people like to organize their active files, folders, and apps on the desktop so they have everything they need in one place. You can organize content on the desktop manually, in whatever order you want, or you can have Windows manage the order for you.

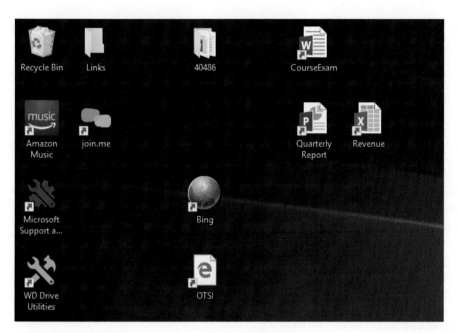

3

When you turn on the Auto Arrange Icons feature, Windows moves all desktop icons so they line up from the upper-left corner of the screen in the order (from top to bottom and then left to right) that you specify on the Sort By submenu.

The desktop content is actually stored in a folder—or rather, in two folders. In addition to system icons (such as the Recycle Bin), your desktop displays content from two locations:

- Content that is specific to your user account and displayed on only *your* desktop is stored in the C:\Users\[user account name]\Desktop folder.

- Content that is displayed for all users of the computer is stored in the C:\Users \Public\Public Desktop folder.

If you want your desktop to appear totally clean, you can hide the desktop icons without affecting the content of the Desktop folders.

You can open either folder in File Explorer to display a different view of the shortcuts, folders, and files on the desktop.

To create an app shortcut on the desktop

> **TIP** The first procedure option works only for desktop apps; the second procedure option works for any app.

1. Display the desktop and minimize any open windows.

2. Open the **Start** menu. Right-click the app in the app list, or the app tile, select **More**, and then select **Open file location** to open the *Start Menu\Programs* folder. This folder contains shortcuts to all the installed apps that are available from these locations.

> **IMPORTANT** Some built-in apps, such as Calculator, don't have Open File Location links, so you have to use the alternative method to create desktop shortcuts for them.

3. Do either of the following to create the desktop shortcut:

   • Right-click and drag the shortcut from the *Start Menu\Programs* folder to the desktop, and then select **Copy here** on the menu that appears after you release the shortcut.

   • Select the shortcut in the *Start Menu\Programs* folder, right-click the selected shortcut, select **Send to**, and then select **Desktop (create shortcut)**. Use this method to avoid accidentally removing the shortcut from the Start menu.

Or

1. Right-click an empty area of the desktop, select **New**, and then select **Shortcut**.

2. In the **Create Shortcut** dialog box, enter or browse to the location of the app executable file. Then select **Next**.

3. Enter a name for the shortcut, and select **Finish**.

 TIP Use the same steps to create app shortcuts in File Explorer that you do to create app shortcuts on the desktop.

To arrange desktop icons

-   Drag icons to any location on the desktop to snap them to the nearest grid location.

-   If you want to force icons into the grid positions from top to bottom and left to right, right-click the desktop, select **View**, and then select **Auto arrange icons**.

-   If you want to permit less-precise arrangements, right-click the desktop, select **View**, and then turn off **Auto arrange icons** and **Align icons to grid**.

-   If you want Windows to set the order for you, right-click the desktop, select **Sort by**, and then select the order you want: **Name**, **Size**, **Item type**, or **Date modified**.

To set the size of desktop icons

-   Right-click the desktop, select **View**, and then select **Large icons**, **Medium icons**, or **Small icons**.

To hide or display desktop icons

-   Right-click the desktop, select **View**, and then select **Show desktop icons**.

To remove an app shortcut from the desktop

-   Right-click the shortcut, and then select **Delete**.

> ⚠️ **IMPORTANT** An arrow in the lower-left corner of the icon indicates that the icon represents a shortcut to a file or folder rather than an actual file or folder. Deleting a shortcut does not delete the file or folder the shortcut links to. Deleting a file or folder icon that doesn't have a shortcut arrow deletes the file or folder. If you do this accidently, you can retrieve the file or folder from the Recycle Bin.

Configure desktop system icons

The default desktop displays the Recycle Bin. You can configure the display of this and four other system icons—Computer, Control Panel, Network, and your user account folder—in the Desktop Icon Settings window. If you want to get creative, you can personalize the system folders by assigning nonstandard icons to them.

To access the desktop icon settings, open the Settings window, select Personalization, and then Themes. Then in the Related Settings area of the Themes pane, select Desktop Icon Settings.

Manage Start menu tiles

The right pane of the Start menu displays content in the form of *tiles*. Each tile is actually a shortcut to something else—usually an app, but tiles can also link to other things, such as folders in File Explorer or individual songs in your Groove Music library. You can pin many kinds of tiles to the Windows 10 Start menu, including shortcuts to apps, files, folders, web links, contact cards, songs, movies, and pictures—almost anything you want to get to quickly.

3

Wide tile   Medium tile   Large tile   Small tile

Tiles are square or rectangular and can be set to four different sizes: Small, Medium, Large, and Wide. All tiles support the Small and Medium sizes. App tiles also support the Large and Wide sizes, which are most appropriate for Live tiles that display information (other than the app name and/or icon). (Of course, you can also use them if you just want a big target.) When you pin an item to the Start menu, the new app tile defaults to the Medium size and usually appears at the bottom of the Start menu.

Tiles for some Store apps that provide access to frequently updated information (such as news, weather, traffic, stock market data, messages, social media network updates, and calendar events) can display and update content directly on the Start menu. These are called *live tiles*. Some apps even permit you to pin multiple live tiles that display different data to the Start menu. Only Medium, Wide, and Large tiles display live content; the larger the tile, the more information it supports.

The content displayed on a live tile can come from an online source, such as a news service, or from a local source, such your Pictures folder. Live content is not available for Small tiles, and if the on-screen movement bothers you, you can turn off the live content for any tile. When live content is off, the tile displays the app icon and name.

Tiles always align on the Start menu in a grid format. When you place tiles next to each other, they form a group. Each group has a title bar area in which you can assign a name to the tile group. You can create additional groups of tiles by dropping them a bit further away from an existing group. After you create a group, you can easily move tiles into or out of the group, or move the entire group of tiles to a different location on the Start menu.

Tile group   Title bar handle   Tile folder

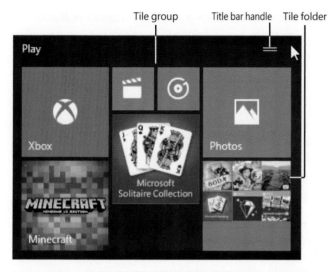

3

To provide another layer of organization for pinned tiles, the Windows 10 2017 Fall Creators Update introduced tile folders, into which you can insert multiple tiles; the first nine are visible on a Medium tile (4 on a Small tile, 18 on a Wide tile, 36 on a Large tile). Opening a tile folder expands it below the tile group that it's in, pushing other tile groups out of the way.

Close Folder button

An open tile folder

You can organize tiles on the Start menu in whatever grouping is most logical and convenient to you—by type, by purpose, by project, alphabetically—there is no magic formula that will satisfy everyone. Fortunately, the Start menu content is easy to customize.

Computer manufacturers place tiles on the Start menu to help you find apps and tools that you might want to use (for example, a link to the support department for the computer manufacturer, or to a free app that comes with the computer). You can remove the tiles you don't use. Removing tiles does not uninstall apps, delete folders, or otherwise affect the item that the tile links to. You can still start apps from the app list or locate folders in File Explorer.

> **SEE ALSO** For information about files and folders, see Chapter 6, "Manage folders and files."

> **IMPORTANT** The procedures in this topic pertain to the mechanics of the Start menu rather than its content. For information about managing the content of the Start menu, see "Configure the Start menu" in Chapter 2, "Personalize your working environment."

To move a pinned tile

- Select and hold the tile you want to move, and then drag it to its new location.

  > **TIP** The screen becomes shaded to indicate change when you move the tile, but until then there is no specific indicator that you're editing the screen.

- Do the following:

  a. On a touchscreen device, tap and hold the tile to activate the Start menu elements for editing. The screen changes to a shaded color and the tile group title boxes are visible.

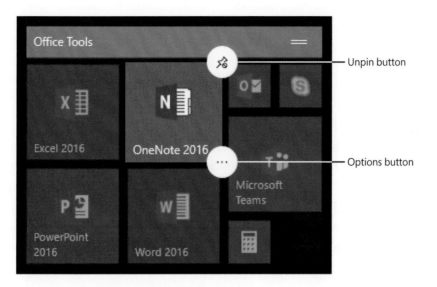

Unpin button

Options button

3

b. Drag the tile to its new location.

c. Move any additional tiles, and then tap an empty area of the **Start** menu to return it to its normal state.

To resize a pinned tile

1. Do one of the following:

   • Right-click the tile, and then select **Resize**.

   • Tap and hold the tile, tap the **Options** button that appears in its lower-right corner, and then tap **Resize**.

2. Select the tile size you want (**Small**, **Medium**, **Large**, or **Wide**).

 TIP Moving or resizing a tile might change the layout of the surrounding tiles.

To add a tile to an existing tile group

■ Drag the tile to slightly overlap with an existing tile in the group you want to add it to, and then release it.

To create and name a tile group

1. Drag a tile to an open space above, below, or to the side of an existing group.

2. When a shaded bar (a blank tile group title bar) appears, release the tile to create the tile group.

3. Do either of the following:

   • Point to the area above the tile. When **Name group** appears, select it to activate it for editing, and then enter the title you want to assign to the tile group.

   • If you create a tile group by tapping and dragging a tile on a touchscreen device, the tile group title bar is active for editing when you release the tile. Tap **Name group**, and then enter the title you want to assign to the tile group.

To rename a tile group

1. Point to the tile group title, and then select the title bar or the handle that appears at its right end to activate the title bar for editing.

2. Edit the existing title, or select the **X** at the right end of the title box to delete the existing content, and then enter the new title.

3. Press Enter, or select or tap away from the title box to return the Start menu to its normal state.

To move a tile group

1. Select and hold the tile group title bar, and then drag the group to its new location. As you drag, the group tiles collapse into the group title bar, and other groups move to make space for the group you're dragging.

2. When the group is in the location you want it, release the title bar.

To create and work with tile folders

- To create a tile folder, drag a tile onto another tile.

- To add a tile to an existing tile folder, drag the tile onto the folder.

- To add an app tile to a tile folder, drag the app from the app list to the folder.

- To open or close a tile folder, select it.

- To remove a tile from a tile folder, open the folder and then drag the tile from the folder to the pinned tiles area of the Start menu.

Customize the taskbar

In Chapter 1, "Get started using Windows 10," you reviewed the functionality available from the taskbar. This topic discusses the changes you can make to the taskbar to customize it so that you can work more efficiently.

Change taskbar appearance

As previously mentioned, you can move the taskbar from its default location at the bottom of the screen to any other edge of the screen. You might find it easier to access the taskbar when it's on the side or top of the screen than when it's at the bottom of the screen. If you're working on a small screen, you might also like to have the additional vertical space that you gain by moving the taskbar to the left or right side of the screen. Wherever you position the taskbar, the Start menu expands from the Start button.

Search button

When you move the taskbar to the left or right side of the screen, it changes in the following ways:

- The width changes to accommodate the time and date, which are at the bottom of the vertical taskbar.

- The Start button is at the top of the vertical taskbar, and the Show Desktop button is at the bottom. The Start menu expands from the Start button location.

- The search box changes to a search button. Selecting the search button expands the usual search pane.

- Buttons, icons, and taskbar toolbars rotate to a horizontal orientation.

Regardless of the taskbar location, you can change the height (when horizontal) or width (when vertical) to accommodate more buttons and toolbars. Other ways to fit more onto the taskbar include the following:

- Switch to "small taskbar buttons." This change affects not only the size of the buttons, it also changes the search box to a search button, which provides significantly more space for buttons and toolbars.

- If you don't use Task View, or use a keyboard shortcut to access it, you can remove the Task View button from the taskbar. Similarly, if you don't use the People bar, you can remove the People button.

TIP If you frequently use the Windows Ink Workspace, the touch keyboard, or the touchpad—for example, on a Windows 10 tablet—you can add these buttons to the notification area of the taskbar for easy access.

By default, you can move and resize the taskbar freely, but if you prefer you can lock the taskbar so that you don't accidentally drag the taskbar or its border. You can make changes to the taskbar only when it's unlocked.

You manage some taskbar features from the taskbar shortcut menu and others from the Taskbar pane of the Personalization settings page.

To display the taskbar shortcut menu

- Right-click an empty area of the taskbar.

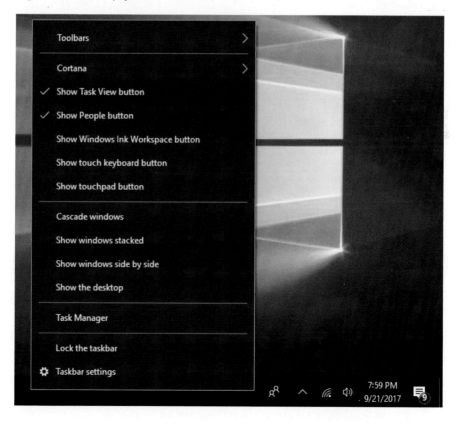

To display the Taskbar pane of the Personalization settings window

- Open the **Settings** window, select **Personalization**, and then select **Taskbar**.

- Right-click an empty area of the taskbar, and then select **Taskbar settings**.

To prevent or allow changes to the taskbar

- Display the taskbar shortcut menu, and then select **Lock the taskbar**. (A check mark indicates that the option is active.)

- Display the **Taskbar** pane of the **Personalization** settings page, and then turn on **Lock the taskbar** to prevent changes, or turn it off to allow changes.

To move the taskbar

- Drag the taskbar to any edge of the screen.

 TIP The movement of the taskbar across the screen might not be apparent; instead, it might appear to jump from location to location.

- Display the **Taskbar** pane of the **Personalization** settings page. Select the **Taskbar location on screen** list to expand it, and then select **Left**, **Right**, or **Top** (or select **Bottom** to return the taskbar to its default location).

To change the taskbar height

1. Point to the inside edge (nearest to the center of the screen) of the taskbar.

2. When the pointer changes to a double-headed arrow, drag the inside edge of the taskbar to change its height (or width, when vertical) to the size you want it. The height or width can be up to 50 percent of the screen height or width.

To display small taskbar buttons

- In the **Taskbar** pane of the **Personalization** settings page, turn on **Use small taskbar buttons**.

To hide standard taskbar buttons

- On the taskbar shortcut menu, select **Show Task View button** or **Show People button** to remove the check mark from the item and hide the button.

To display optional buttons in the notification area

- On the taskbar shortcut menu, select **Show Windows Ink Workspace button**, **Show touch keyboard button**, or **Show touchpad button**.

Change taskbar behavior

You can make a few other changes to the way that the taskbar functions, from the Taskbar pane of the Personalization settings page.

By default, each app (or each instance of an app) that you open displays a button on the taskbar. Active app buttons are differentiated from app shortcuts by a colored bar below the button. By default, multiple buttons for the same app stack on top of each other so that each app has only one button, and pointing to the button displays thumbnails of each instance of the app. If you prefer, you can display individual buttons for each instance of an app, or display individual buttons until your taskbar is full and then combine them.

If you prefer to not have the taskbar taking up space on your screen, you can hide it (on any edge of the screen) so that it appears only when you point to it. This could be convenient if you have a small screen or are simply distracted by the busyness of the taskbar.

If you find that you accidentally invoke the Peek function when your mouse pointer wanders into the corner of the screen above the Show Desktop button, you can turn off that function. Turning off Peek doesn't affect the Show Desktop function.

To hide the taskbar when it isn't active

1. Display the **Taskbar** pane of the **Personalization** settings page.

2. Do either or both of the following:

   - Turn on **Automatically hide the taskbar in desktop mode.**

   - Turn on **Automatically hide the taskbar in tablet mode.**

To change the display of multiple app taskbar buttons

- In the **Taskbar** pane of the **Personalization** settings page, select the **Combine taskbar buttons** list to expand it, and then select one of these options:

  - **Always, hide labels** (the default)

  - **When taskbar is full**

  - **Never**

To turn the Peek function off or on

- In the **Taskbar** pane of the **Personalization** settings page, turn off **Use Peek to preview the desktop...** to disable the feature, or turn it on to re-enable it.

- At far-right end of the taskbar, right-click the **Show desktop** button, and then select **Peek at desktop**. A check mark next to the option indicates it's turned on.

> **TIP** When the toolbar is unlocked, two vertical lines appear to the left of each taskbar toolbar. You can change the width of a toolbar on the taskbar by dragging this handle. Depending on the space allocated and the toolbar configuration, toolbars might display names or icons on the taskbar or on a menu. If all the toolbar links don't fit on the taskbar, a chevron button is available at its right end. Selecting the button displays a menu of hidden links.

Display and manage toolbars on the taskbar

Windows provides three "toolbars" that you can display on the taskbar to provide easy access to information that you'd otherwise have to open a separate app to get to. Toolbars can display names and icons on the taskbar or on a menu. The three built-in toolbars are:

3

- **Address** The Address toolbar displays a browser address bar directly on the taskbar and retains a list of recent entries. You can display websites, perform web searches, and start apps from this toolbar.

- **Links** The Links toolbar displays information from the same source as your Internet Explorer Favorites bar. You can add and remove links (to websites, files, folders, and apps) on either bar to share those changes with the Favorites bar and Links toolbar on all computers that you sign in to by using your Microsoft account.

> ⚠ **IMPORTANT** At the time of this writing, the Links toolbar is connected to Internet Explorer and not to Microsoft Edge. We expect that in a future release of Windows, the Links menu will display favorites from the Microsoft Edge browser, or a shared list of favorites from both Internet Explorer and Microsoft Edge.

- **Desktop** The Desktop toolbar provides quick access to the storage locations that are available in the File Explorer Navigation pane and on your desktop.

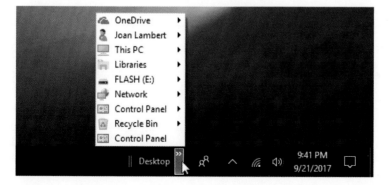

When you add a toolbar to the taskbar, the toolbar name appears at the left end of the toolbar, next to the toolbar handle. You can remove the name from the taskbar to save space.

In addition to displaying the built-in toolbars, you can create custom toolbars. A custom toolbar points to a folder, which can contain shortcuts to files, apps, and other folders. You can use this technique to quickly access files for a specific project, client, or process.

To display or hide a built-in toolbar on the taskbar

- On the taskbar shortcut menu, select **Toolbars**, and then select the toolbar you want to display or hide. A check mark indicates that a toolbar is on the taskbar.

To display a custom toolbar on the taskbar

1. Put the files and shortcuts you want to display on the custom toolbar into a folder.

     TIP Because the folder name will appear on the taskbar as the toolbar name, it's a good idea to give the folder a short name rather than a long name.

2. On the taskbar shortcut menu, select **Toolbars**, and then select **New toolbar**.

3. In the **New Toolbar – Choose a folder** window, browse to and select the folder you worked with in step 1. Then select the **Select Folder** button.

To work from the Address toolbar

- To display a website in your default browser, enter a URL in the address bar and then press Enter or select the Go button (the arrow).

- To conduct a web search by using the default browser search engine, enter a search term in the address bar.

- To start an installed app, enter the app executable name (for example, *calc* to start the Calculator, *excel* to start Microsoft Excel, or *cmd* to display the command prompt window.

- To reopen a recent website or app or refresh a recent search, select the arrow at the right end of the address bar, and then select the entry you want.

To change the width of a taskbar toolbar

- Drag the toolbar handle (the double line to the left of the toolbar) to change the taskbar space allocated to it.

To hide or display the name of a taskbar toolbar

- Right-click the toolbar, and then on the extended taskbar shortcut menu, select **Show title**.

To hide or display item names on a built-in or custom taskbar toolbar

- Right-click the toolbar, and then on the extended taskbar shortcut menu, select **Show Text**.

To remove a toolbar from the taskbar

- On the taskbar shortcut menu, point to **Toolbars**, and then select the toolbar you want to remove).

- Right-click the toolbar, and then on the extended taskbar shortcut menu, select **Close toolbar**.

> **TIP** Removing a custom toolbar from the taskbar removes that folder from the taskbar and from the Toolbars list. The folder remains in File Explorer, and you can redisplay it as a toolbar if you want to.

Key points

- You can create app shortcuts as tiles pinned to the Start menu, buttons pinned to the taskbar, or icons pinned to the desktop.

- You can organize pinned tiles on the Start menu in named tile groups and in tile folders.

- You can dock the taskbar on any edge of the screen, change the height of the taskbar and the size of the taskbar icons, and add and remove standard taskbar buttons to suit your needs. You can also change the way the taskbar shows multiple taskbar buttons from the same app.

Practice tasks

Before you can complete these practice tasks, you need to copy the book's practice files to your computer. The practice files for these tasks are located in the **Win10SBS\Ch03** folder. The introduction includes a complete list of practice files.

Create and manage app shortcuts

Perform the following tasks:

1. In the app list, identify two apps that are not yet pinned to the Start menu or to the taskbar.

2. Pin the first app to the **Start** menu, and then locate its Start menu tile. Right-click the tile, and then examine the shortcut menu to determine whether the app supports live tile content. Then start the first app from the **Start** menu.

3. Pin the second app to the taskbar, and then locate its taskbar button. Right-click the taskbar button to examine the shortcut menu options for the app. Then start the app from the taskbar.

4. On the taskbar, locate the button of the first app. Move the button to the right end of the taskbar button area. Then pin the running app to the taskbar.

5. From the app list, open the **Start Menu\Programs** folder. From the folder, create a desktop shortcut to any app.

6. Experiment with arranging and ordering the icons on your desktop.

7. Open the **Desktop** folder associated with your user account, and locate the shortcut you created in step 5. Start the app from the **Desktop** folder.

8. Exit all the running apps, and delete any of the shortcuts you created in this exercise that you think you won't use in the future.

Manage Start menu tiles

Perform the following tasks:

1. Display the **Start** menu, and observe the configuration of the existing tiles.

2. Move a Start menu tile from an existing tile group and use it to create a new tile group. Set the tile size to the largest size it supports.

3. Move another tile into the new group, and set its size to **Small**.

4. Name the new tile group **Practice Tiles**.

5. Move the **Practice Tiles** group to the upper-left corner of the **Start** menu.

6. Rename the **Practice Tiles** group as **Favorite Apps**.

7. Arrange and resize the tiles on your Start menu to suit the way you work.

Customize the taskbar

Perform the following tasks:

1. Check whether the taskbar is locked. If it is locked, unlock it.

2. Move the taskbar to the left edge of the screen.

3. Configure the taskbar to display small buttons and to hide it when it isn't active.

4. When the taskbar is hidden, point to the edge of the screen to display it. Then stretch it to twice its current width.

5. Hide the **Task View** button.

6. Move the taskbar to the top of the window.

7. Display the **Desktop** toolbar on the taskbar.

8. Hide the title and text of the Desktop toolbar.

9. Resize the Desktop toolbar so that three icons appear on the taskbar and the rest are available on a menu at the right end of the toolbar.

10. Configure the taskbar to display large buttons, and to never combine taskbar buttons.

11. Create a custom toolbar that links to the **Ch03** practice file folder. From the toolbar, open the **Image01** file in your default photo app.

12. From the **Ch03** toolbar, open the **Image03** file. Verify that a new taskbar button appears for the photo app as you open each image.

13. Close the **Desktop** toolbar, and remove the custom **Ch03** toolbar from the taskbar.

14. Configure the taskbar content the way you want it, and then lock the taskbar.

Work with apps and notifications

4

The Windows 10 operating system provides the interface through which you communicate with your computer. When you do or create something on your computer, you're using software applications, or *apps*, that runs on Windows to accomplish that task.

There are many types of apps, and you can get them from many sources. Wherever you get your apps, after you install them on your Windows 10 computer, you can run them and manage access to them in the same ways.

Many apps communicate status, new activity, and other information to you in the form of *notifications*. These might pop up in the corner of your screen—to notify you of a message that has arrived or an update that is available. When these pop-up windows appear (they are sometimes called *pop-ups* or *toast* because they pop up like a piece of toast from a toaster), you can select them to open or dismiss them. In Windows 10, recent notifications are available from the Action Center that opens from the notification area of the taskbar.

This chapter guides you through procedures related to locating and starting installed apps, exploring built-in apps and accessories, installing apps from the Windows Store, and managing app notifications.

In this chapter

- Locate and start apps
- Explore built-in apps
- Install Store apps
- Manage app notifications

Locate and start apps

At the time of this writing, software programs that install components on a computer or mobile device that runs Windows are divided into two groups: desktop apps and Store apps. Store apps are those that you install on your Windows 10 device from the Windows Store, which is called simply Store. (Somewhat confusingly, Store itself is an app.) In general, Store apps have a smaller installation footprint than desktop apps, and aren't as powerful as desktop apps.

When you purchase a new computer, it's likely that the computer will have a variety of apps installed on it by the computer manufacturer. These apps generally fall into the following categories:

- Apps provided by Microsoft with the Windows operating system. These are installed with Windows 10 regardless of whether you upgrade to this version of the operating system or have a clean installation.

- Apps that are specific to the management of the hardware elements of your computer, such as a touchpad or network adapter. These are usually related to hardware support and firmware update functions.

- Free full or trial versions of apps. Software companies often allow computer manufacturers to provide full or limited-use versions of apps with their computers as a way to add value to the package. You're usually required to register your information with the software company to use the app, and they can then offer you updates and upgrades over time. This is a win-win for the hardware and software manufacturers, and sometimes for you.

You can start an app by selecting it in the app list on the Start menu, or by selecting a Start menu, desktop, or taskbar shortcut to the app.

> **SEE ALSO** For more information about app shortcuts, see "Create and manage app shortcuts" in Chapter 3, "Work with shortcuts and tiles."

The app list provides access to most of the apps and tools that are installed on your computer. These include apps that are installed as part of Windows 10, by the computer manufacturer, and by you. The app list is integrated into the Start menu.

It is also an alternative view on the full-size Start screen.

Pinned Tiles button   All Apps button

The app list on the Start menu provides an alphabetical listing of apps, separated by index letters. You can scroll through the menu manually or select any index letter to display a menu from which you can go directly to recently added apps (represented by a clock); apps with names that begin with a symbol (represented by an ampersand), a number, or a specific letter; or apps with names that begin with characters that aren't in the alphabetical index (represented by a globe). When an index letter has no menu entries, the letter is dimmed. This is a nice improvement over the All Programs menu that was available in earlier versions of Windows.

Most apps in the app list are in order by app name, but some are in folders and therefore don't appear on the menu where you might expect them to.

> **TIP** As software development models and installation footprints have changed, so has terminology. At one time, there were only software applications, which were called *programs*. With the development of small-footprint mobile technology came apps. Over time, different types of apps were referred to as desktop apps, Windows apps, modern apps, gadgets, and other terms. In this book, unless there's a specific reason to differentiate among app types, we simply refer to programs in both categories as *apps*.

This is one reason why it's almost always faster to locate an app by entering the first few letters of its name in the search box, and selecting it from the search results list.

> ⚠️ **IMPORTANT** Many apps and services start automatically when Windows starts. This can be very helpful, but it can also add unnecessary overhead to your computer's startup tasks, and slow down the process. You can identify and disable apps that start automatically. For more information, see "Manage app startup" in Chapter 14, "Work more efficiently."

To display the app list

- Open the **Start** menu.
- Open the full-size **Start** screen and then select the **All apps** button.

> ✓ **TIP** You can navigate through the Start menu by pressing the arrow keys.

To scroll the app list to apps beginning with a specific letter

1. In the app list, select any index letter to display the alphanumeric index.
2. In the index, select any letter or symbol to jump to those entries on the menu.

> ✓ **TIP** The clock symbol represents recently installed apps. The ampersand represents numbers and symbols. The globe symbol represents international apps (with names that begin with characters that aren't in the alphabetical index).

To start an app

- In the app list, select the app name.

- On the **Start** screen, select the app tile.

- On the taskbar, select the app button.

- Enter the app name in the taskbar search box. In the search results, select the app name, or select the **Apps** heading and then select the app name in the filtered results pane.

To start a second instance of a running app

- On the taskbar, right-click the button and then select the app name.

> **TIP** On a touchscreen device, select and release instead of right-clicking. For more information about touchscreen interaction, see the appendix "Keyboard shortcuts and touchscreen tips."

> **TIP** If you experience problems with a desktop app, it might be necessary to run the app with elevated permissions so you can resolve the issue. To do so, right-click the app, select More, and then select Run As Administrator. The Run As Administrator command is available only for desktop apps. It is not available for Store apps.

Explore built-in apps

Windows 10 includes many fun and functional apps—for example, the Alarms & Clock app, which includes a world time map, timer, and stopwatch. Some of these apps are part of Windows and others are powered by MSN or Bing. It is not the purpose of this book to teach you how to use those apps. We do preview some of the more useful apps and work with them in the practice tasks, but you should explore them further on your own.

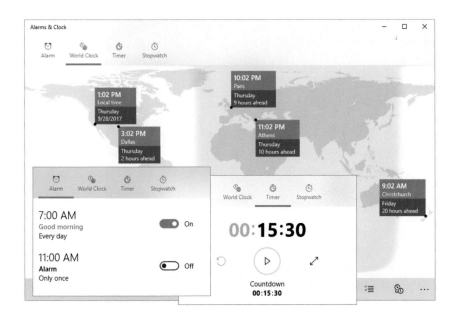

Productivity and information management apps

The many and varied Microsoft apps that you can use on a day-to-day basis to get things done have been brought together under the Windows umbrella. Although they have simple names and are free, they're quite fully featured and updated on a regular basis. These apps include Alarms & Clock, Calculator, Calendar, Camera, Cortana, Food & Drink, Groove Music, Health & Fitness, Mail, and Maps.

Other apps that fall loosely into the productivity category but have more specialized purposes include Scan and Voice Recorder.

The apps draw information from many sources and are designed to be useful both on your desktop and on the go. Many of them coordinate across the devices that you sign in to by using your Microsoft account.

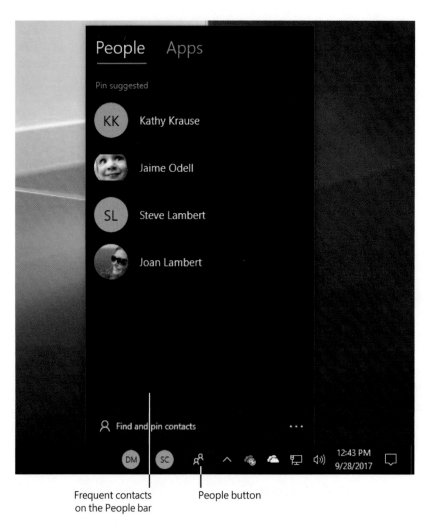

Frequent contacts
on the People bar

People button

The People bar was introduced as a default part of the Windows 10 experience in the Fall 2017 Creators Update. From the People bar, you can pin frequent contacts to the taskbar. You can easily perform the following tasks after pinning a contact:

- Start an email message, instant message, call, or video call from the contact's taskbar button, so you don't have to go through an app to initiate a conversation.

- Share a file by dragging it to the contact's taskbar button (and then selecting the app you want to use for sharing, if multiple apps support sharing that type of file).

- Display contact information in the People app and collate information from multiple apps, including Mail, People, Outlook, and Skype.

- Display a list of recent communications with the contact.

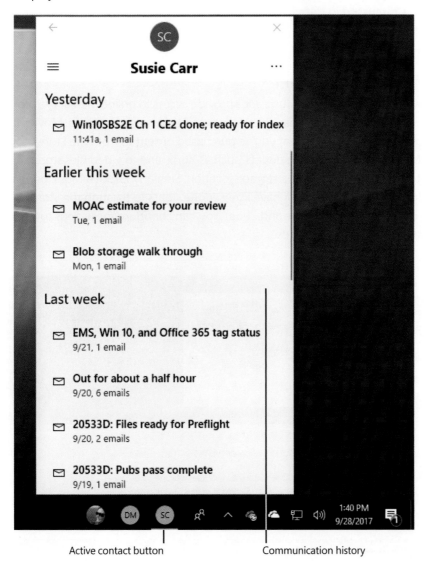

Active contact button   Communication history

Web browsers

Microsoft Edge and Internet Explorer are both installed with Windows 10. Microsoft Edge, which is new in Windows 10, is now the preferred browser. This browser is discussed in detail in Chapter 10, "Safely and efficiently browse the internet."

Media management apps

The Movies & TV and Groove Music apps provide access to online media. The branding of the site behind these apps has changed several times over the years. Movies & TV provides access to video content you've purchased or rented from the Store or from one of Microsoft's earlier video outlets, such as Xbox, and to video files stored on your computer or on a local or online storage location. Similarly, Groove Music provides access to music that you own or have licensed the rights to through the Store or one of its predecessors (Xbox Music and Zune). You can configure these apps to link to multiple media storage locations.

Windows 10 also includes Windows Media Player, which has been around for quite a long time now. You can use this app to play and manage media files, and to manage the transfer of media to discs. It doesn't interact directly with the Store, but it's a dependable media manager.

If your computer or device has a built-in camera, you can take pictures by using the Camera app.

The Photos app is a convenient and easy-to-use app in which you can efficiently manage and enhance pictures. The app tracks pictures stored in multiple locations (including your Microsoft OneDrive storage) and automatically catalogs photos by date. You can organize photos in albums, and edit and enhance them in various ways, and share them through apps that provide that functionality. The Photos app also provides a shortcut to setting a photo as your desktop background or Lock screen image.

Live information apps

The information apps are frequently featured on Start screen tiles in new or updated installations of Windows. They all have Live Tile functionality, although they might not show anything specific or pertinent until you configure them. When their Live Tiles are turned on (as they are by default), these apps can provide interesting and timely updates about things that are happening in the world around you, courtesy of Bing or MSN. The apps include Money, News, Sports, and Weather.

> **TIP** Having the latest headlines constantly available can be quite distracting. If you don't want to see the headlines, but still want to have easy access to the information, you can turn off the Live Tile content for individual apps.

The information apps provide general information but also allow you to identify information that is specific to you and pin that information to the Start screen. For example, you can track a specific stock in Money, pin a specific person's contact information in People, select a representative picture in Photos, or select a specific location in Weather.

Accessories

Along with the shiny new Store apps, Windows 10 comes with several useful desktop apps that have been around for a long time and perform a lot of useful functions. (For that reason, they're frequently referred to as *tools* or *utilities*.) These apps (and others) are available from the Windows Accessories folder in the app list on the Start menu:

- **Math Input Panel** You can use Math Input Panel, which was originally designed for tablet PC users, to convert simple and complex mathematic equations from touchscreen input to text.

- **Notepad** You can use this simple text editor to edit unformatted documents or HTML files.

- **Paint 3D** You can use this exciting new graphics app (which replaces the traditional Paint app) to create and edit three-dimensional images.

- **Quick Assist** You can use this app to share control of your computer with another person, or take control of another person's computer (with his or her explicit approval) for the purpose of providing technical support.

- **Snipping Tool** You can use this tool to capture an image of a screen area and then annotate it with handwritten notes, save it as a .gif, .jpg, .mht, or .png file, and send it by email.

- **Windows Fax and Scan** You can use this desktop app to send and receive faxes through an analog phone line and a modem, or through a fax server. If a scanner is connected to your computer, you can also use Windows Fax And Scan to scan text documents and graphics to your computer as digital files that you can then send as faxes or email message attachments. The Scan app that also comes with Windows 10 is a more modern Store app that does the same thing.

- **WordPad** You can use this word-processing app to work with documents that include rich text formatting and character and paragraph styles.

> **TIP** The Sticky Notes app that was available as a Windows accessory in earlier releases of Windows is now available to install from the Store. You can use this app to attach electronic notes to your computer desktop in the same way you'd stick the paper version of a sticky note to your physical desktop.

Other tried and true accessories include Character Map, Remote Desktop Connection, Steps Recorder, and XPS Viewer. New accessories include 3D Builder and Print 3D, which support Paint 3D.

> ✅ **TIP** Like the Portable Document Format (PDF), the XML Paper Specification (XPS) format allows a file to be saved in such a way that it can be viewed but not changed without the use of special software. Windows 10 comes with the XPS Viewer, in which you can view XPS files, and with the software that is required to create XPS files from any app you can print from. Simply open the file in its originating app, display the Print dialog box, specify the Microsoft XPS Document Writer as the printer, and select Print. When prompted, save the file with the name and in the location you want.

4

Tools for geeks

Experienced computer users who want to be able to run apps and manage their computers in traditional ways might find the following tools useful:

- **Windows PowerShell** With a text-based interface similar to that of Command Prompt, Windows PowerShell provides command-line tools that can be used to automate administrative tasks. Windows 10 also includes PowerShell ISE (Integrated Scripting Environment), which substantially extends the Windows PowerShell user interface.

- **Command Prompt** The Windows 10 Command Prompt (cmd.exe) is the latest in a progression of command-line interpreters in the tradition of MS-DOS and command.com. You can use it to run many DOS and Windows command-line tools. Windows 10 has enhanced the user interface in a number of ways, including the ability to use standard keyboard shortcuts to copy and paste text.

Install Store apps

Windows 10 works across multiple form factors (desktop, laptop, tablet, and phone), which has two notable effects. First, the simplified Windows user interface adapts gracefully to different screen sizes; and second, developers can more easily create (and support) apps that provide the same user experience on multiple devices. As the relentless rush to become constantly connected, more mobile, and less tied to desktop computers continues, these changes benefit both the software companies and the software users.

You can install software on a Windows 10 computer from multiple locations. In the past, the most common installation source was a CD or DVD, but software distribution has rapidly moved toward an online installation model. You can purchase or subscribe to software and install it on your computer or device immediately.

Thousands of apps (and games, music, movies, and television programs) that are specifically designed and optimized for use on Windows 10 are available from the Store, many for free. You can also purchase and install apps from websites or use the old-fashioned method and install them from CDs or DVDs.

Shop in the Store

The Store was first introduced in Windows 8. It has been substantially updated in Windows 10 and changes frequently. This chapter includes some images for guidance, but it's quite possible that by the time you read this book, the Store interface will be different from what's depicted in this book. This section gives an overview of the Store and describes Store functionality that we think is likely to stay in place over time.

You access the Store by starting the Store app, which is installed by default and can't be uninstalled (though it can be unpinned from your Start menu if you don't want it there).

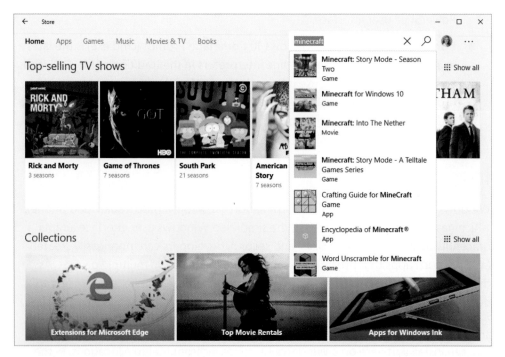

From the home page of the Store, you can search for specific apps, search by category, or browse through collections of apps such as the most popular free or paid apps or games, new music or movies, top-selling television shows, or various collections of apps that are related by a common feature (such as music, zombies, or productivity).

If you know the app, or the type of app, that you're looking for, the simplest method of finding it is to enter the name or descriptive information into the search box located at the top of the Store window. Generally, the more text you enter into the search box, the more you limit the search results.

> **TIP** At the time of this writing, the Store search engine doesn't support Boolean search restrictions such as AND, OR, or wildcards.

Regardless of your choice of navigation method, the Store presents consistent information, including app tile, name, rating, and price for each app.

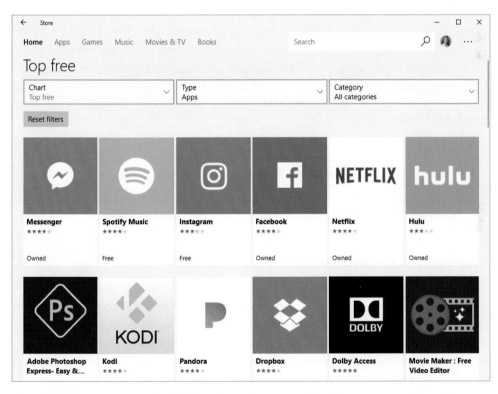

Most Windows apps are classified as Free. Some app developers accept donations. Some apps are free only for a trial period, or require that you purchase an upgrade or accompanying service to unlock the really useful functionality. Because there are variations of "free," it's a good idea to read the details before you actually install an app. You can select any app tile for more information.

Some of the useful details provided for apps in the Store include these:

- Screenshots of the app user interface

- Ratings and reviews that can be filtered by device type

- Feature lists

- The publisher's name, website, support site, and privacy policy

- Hardware and storage space requirements

- Category and age rating

- Supported processors and languages

- The access permissions the app requires, which might include permission to use your location, access your internet connection, access your local network, act as a server, read data from other apps, use your device's camera, record audio, and more

To start the Store app

- On the taskbar, select the **Store** icon.

- On the **Start** menu, select the **Store** tile.

- On the **Start** menu, in the app list, select any index letter, and then select **S**. In the list of apps that have names beginning with *S*, select **Store**.

Manage your Store account and settings

The Store is linked to your Microsoft account, so you can access your purchased apps on any device that you sign in to by using that account. Information about business that you've transacted when signed in to a site or service with that account is stored with your account information. Transactions include those for free and paid apps, services, and subscriptions through entities such as the Store app, the online Microsoft Store, Xbox Live, Groove Music, Bing Rewards, Office 365, and OneDrive.

You can manage your Store settings from within the Store app, and you can also link from the Store account menu directly to specific areas of your online Microsoft account information.

> ⚠️ **IMPORTANT** To use the Store, you must be signed in with a Microsoft account, or your local user account must be associated with a Microsoft account.

The Store settings you can configure at the time of this writing are whether to:

- Automatically update apps.
- Activate Live Tiles.
- Run limited-license games and apps offline.
- Require a password for app purchases.

The Settings window in the Store is similar to the pages of the Settings window in Windows 10. A toggle button controls each of the settings.

> ✓ **TIP** When you narrow the Store app window, a menu button appears in the upper-left corner. Selecting the menu button displays all the menu items that usually appear on the Store menu bar and all the items that usually appear on the Store account menu.

Selecting any link other than Downloads And Updates, Settings, My Library, or Send Feedback on the Store account menu starts or opens your default browser and displays information from your Microsoft account. You must sign in to your account (if you haven't already) and reconfirm your credentials when accessing pages that contain financial information. The following table describes the actions you can take from these pages that are relevant to Store purchases.

Menu item (page)	Description
Redeem a code	Enter a gift card number or promotional code to add credit to your Microsoft account. If your Microsoft account has a credit balance, Store purchases use the credit first and then charge only the difference to your selected payment option.
View account	Review recent purchases and your devices. Browse from here to any other account information.

Menu item (page)	Description
Payment options	Add, edit, and remove payment options that are linked to your account. Valid forms of payment include credit cards (Visa, MasterCard, American Express, and Discover), debit cards, direct bank account debit, PayPal accounts, physical and digital gift cards, and Microsoft account credit that is added from a Bitcoin digital wallet. You can remove only payment options that aren't associated with an active subscription. (If you want to remove a payment option that's assigned to a subscription, you must first assign a different form of payment to the subscription.)
Purchased	Display the date, description, form of payment, and amount for transactions that are associated with your Microsoft account.

> **SEE ALSO** For more information about Microsoft accounts, see the sidebar "Use a Microsoft account or local account" in Chapter 1, "Get started using Windows 10."

You can go directly to a specific page of your account information from the Store account menu, or navigate among the pages within the browser window. When you install an app or game from the Store on any Windows 10 device, you own that app and can install it on up to 10 devices. If you want to install the same app on another device, you can locate the app in your list of apps and install it from there.

To access your Microsoft account settings from the Store

- On the Store menu bar, select the **See more** button (**...**), and then do any of the following:

  - To display the home page of your Microsoft account, select **View account**.

  - To display the Payment Options page, select **Payment options**.

  - To display the Purchase History page, select **Purchased**.

  - To display the gift card/promotional code–entry interface, select **Redeem a code**.

> **TIP** All these links display a page of the Microsoft account management website, and you can move to any other page of the website from there.

Install, reinstall, and uninstall apps

Most apps are free. When you purchase an app that isn't free and doesn't include a free trial, you select a payment method in the Payment & Billing section of your Microsoft account. Most require only a one-time payment, but some are managed on a subscription basis, and until you cancel the subscription, the payment option that you select is charged each month.

The Store tracks all the apps, games, music, movies, and television episodes that you purchase. From your library, you can display information about the items you've purchased, and you can install, reinstall, and share those items.

4

The My Library page displays recent purchases that you made when signed in with your Microsoft account, on any device, in order from most recent to least recent. Selecting the Show All link adjacent to any category heading displays all the items of that type that are installed on any device that is associated with your Microsoft account. Depending on your installation history, the entries on your My Library page might be divided into sections that are titled "Works on this device" and "Doesn't work on this device." For example, when you're in the Store on your Windows 10 computer, Windows phone apps that were developed for versions of Windows Mobile earlier than Windows 10 appear in the "Doesn't work" list because they won't run on your Windows 10 computer.

You can start (launch) an app or game from your library if it's already installed on your computer. Apps and games that work on your Windows 10 computer and aren't already installed on it have an Install icon on the right side.

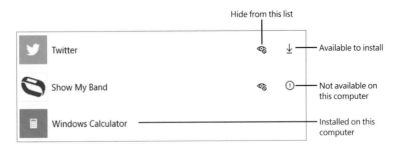

Hide from this list

Twitter — Available to install

Show My Band — Not available on this computer

Windows Calculator — Installed on this computer

When you select the icon, the Store app checks your current installations to make sure that you haven't exceeded the 10-device limit. It then assigns one of your 10 device licenses to the app, downloads the app, and installs it. During that process, the app appears on the Downloads And Updates page, which is an interim staging location for apps and updates that are pending installation on your computer.

To install an app or game for the first time

1. In the Store, search for or browse to the app or game you want to install.

2. Select the app or game thumbnail to display its information page.

3. On the information page, below the description, select the button labeled either **Free** or with the price of the app or game.

4. If you selected an app or game that requires a purchase, enter your Microsoft account password when prompted to do so. Then select a payment option and approve the purchase to install the app and add it to the app list.

Apps or updates ready to install

By default, Store apps automatically download and install updates. If you would prefer to approve updates, you can turn off the automatic update option and manage the updates from this page. When an app or update is ready for installation, the installation icon appears on the Store menu bar, next to your user account icon.

To display your purchased and installed apps and games

1. On the Store menu bar, select the **See more** button (...), and then select **My Library**.

2. By default, the My Library pane displays recently installed apps and games. To display *all* apps or games, do either of the following:

   - Select the **Show All** link to the right of the **Apps** heading to display the Your Apps pane.

   - Select the **Show All** link to the right of the **Games** heading to display the Your Games pane.

To install a purchased app or game on a different computer

1. On the computer where you want to install the app or game, start the Store app.

2. On the Store menu bar, select the **See more** button (...), and then select **My Library**.

3. If the app or game you want to install doesn't appear in this pane, display the **Your Apps** or **Your Games** pane.

4. Locate the app or game, and select the **Install** icon on the right side of its entry.

> **IMPORTANT** If there is no Install icon, then the app is already installed on or incompatible with the current device.

You can monitor the installation process from the Downloads And Updates pane.

To manage downloads and updates

1. On the Store menu bar, select the **See more** button (...), and then select **Downloads and updates**.

2. In the **Queue** area of the **Downloads and Updates** pane, do any of the following:

   - Select the **Get updates** button to search for any available updates that haven't yet been registered on your computer.

   - Select an available update to download and install it.

   - Select the **Pause** or **Restart** button near the right end of an in-process update to pause or restart the process.

   - Select the **Close** button at the right end of an in-process update to remove the update from the queue.

To turn off automatic app updates

1. Start the Store app.

2. On the menu bar, select the **See more** button (...), and then **Settings** to display the Settings pane for the Store app.

3. In the **Settings** pane, turn off **Update apps automatically** to immediately implement the change.

To uninstall a Store app

1. Open the Start menu, and locate the app in the app list.

2. Right-click the app, and then select **Uninstall**.

> ⚠ **IMPORTANT** Some apps (such as Calculator, Calendar, and Camera) can't be uninstalled, and the Uninstall option doesn't appear on the shortcut menu.

Manage app notifications

A notification is a short message that is generated when an event happens in an installed app. Not all apps generate notifications; the app developer determines whether notifications will be issued and for which events.

When an event issues a notification, it might play a sound and briefly display a banner in the lower-right corner of your screen. You can point to the notification banner to keep it visible, select the banner to display pertinent information (if available) in the app that generated it, or select the Close button that appears in its upper-right corner to dismiss it. The notification is also stored in the Action Center.

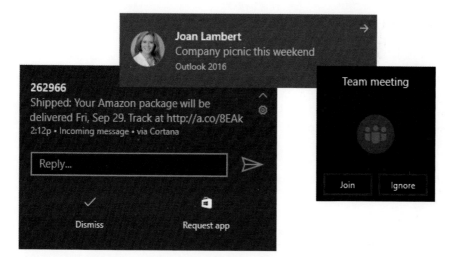

You might or might not notice notifications when they appear, but the Action Center icon on the taskbar changes to indicate that you have unread notifications, and the number of unread notifications appears in a circle in the lower-right corner of the icon. You can open the Action Center to display and process the notifications.

> 🔍 **SEE ALSO** For more information about the Action Center, see "Explore the desktop and taskbar" in Chapter 1, "Get started using Windows 10."

You manage these three aspects of notifications in the Notifications & Actions pane of the Settings window:

- The general behavior of notifications

- Which apps generate notifications

- The specific types of notifications each app generates

You manage the general behavior of notifications in the Notifications section of the Notifications & Actions pane. In this section, you can turn on or off the display of Windows system notifications and of app notifications; the display of notifications, alarms, reminders, and incoming calls on the Lock screen; and whether Windows automatically hides notifications when you're sharing your screen in an online presentation.

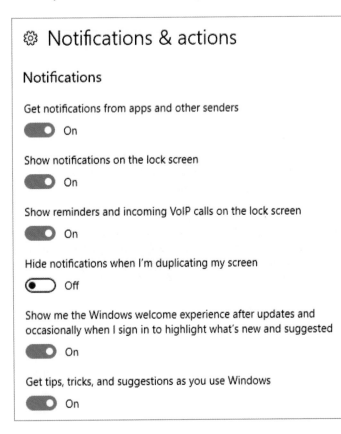

After the notification settings, there is a list of all the apps installed on the computer that are configured to generate notifications. You can turn notifications on or off for individual apps.

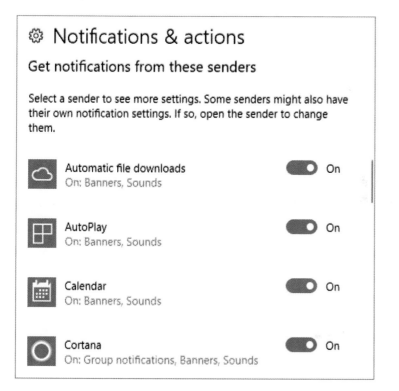

You can turn notifications on or off for each individual app. Selecting an app name takes you to a page of notification settings specific to the app.

> **TIP** If you leave Notifications turned on and turn off banners and sounds, the app generates notifications and delivers them to the Action Center for you to review at your leisure. You can also add a few apps to the Lock screen, and they will show very basic notifications. For more information about this, see "Customize the Lock screen" in Chapter 2, "Personalize your working environment."

⚙ **Cortana**

Notifications

🔘 On

Show notification banners

🔘 On

Keep notifications private on the lock screen

🔘 Off

Show notifications in action center

🔘 On

Play a sound when a notification arrives

🔘 On

Number of notifications visible in action center

3	⌄

Priority of notifications in action center

⦿ Top

Show at the top of action center

You can temporarily disable all banners and sounds by using the Quiet Hours feature. When Quiet Hours is turned on, the Action Center icon includes a crescent moon to indicate that notifications are not active.

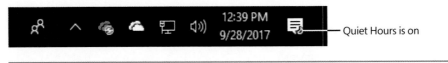
Quiet Hours is on

⚠ **IMPORTANT** When the Quiet Hours feature first debuted, you could configure it to turn on and off automatically at specific times so you wouldn't be disturbed by notifications from a Windows 10 computer or device while sleeping. At the time of this writing, the Quiet Hours options have been reduced to On and Off, so it's basically just a quick way to turn off notifications.

Notifications are still available in the Action Center when Quiet Hours is turned on. The Action Center icon changes to a filled white icon when notifications are available.

To open the Action Center

- In the notification area of the taskbar, select the **Action Center** icon.

- Press Win+A.

To limit system notifications

1. In the **Settings** window, select **System**, and then select **Notifications & actions**.

2. In the **Notifications** area of the **Notifications & actions** pane, turn off **Show me the Windows welcome experience...** and **Get tips, tricks, and suggestions as you use Windows**.

To turn off all notifications for an app

1. Display the **Notifications & actions** settings pane.

2. In the **Get notifications from these senders** list, locate the app, and then select the toggle button to turn it off.

To turn off banners or audio notifications for an app

1. Display the **Notifications & actions** settings pane.

2. In the **Get notifications from these senders** list, select the app that you want to configure notifications for.

3. In the pane that is specific to the app, do either of the following:

   - To turn off notification banners, turn off **Show notification banners**.

   - To turn off audio notifications, turn off **Play a sound when a notification arrives**.

4. If the app supports Group Notifications (synchronized notifications across devices), this section appears separately near the bottom of the pane. You can turn on or off each device in the list.

5. In the upper-left corner of the pane, select the **Back** arrow to return to the app list and check the settings.

Notification details

To temporarily turn off banner and audio notifications

- In the notification area of the taskbar, right-click the **Action Center** icon, and then select **Turn on quiet hours**.

- Open the Action Center, expand the **Quick actions** section if necessary, and then select the **Quiet Hours** button.

Key points

- Installing a Store app or desktop app on your Windows 10 computer makes it available in the app list on the Start menu. You can start the app from the app list or from a shortcut on the Start menu, taskbar, or desktop.

- Several common productivity and information management apps and tools are installed with Windows 10. You can install additional apps from the Store, from online sources, or from external installation media.

- The installation routines for some apps configure them to start automatically when you sign in to Windows. A list of these apps is available for review and management from the Startup tab of Task Manager. You can review the memory resource impact of each app and choose whether to permit it to start automatically.

- Many apps display notifications when specific events occur. You can review a list of these apps and choose whether to permit the apps to display audio, banner, and group notifications. To temporarily turn off all notifications, turn on the Quiet Hours feature.

Practice tasks

No practice files are necessary to complete the practice tasks in this chapter.

Locate and start apps

Perform the following tasks:

1. Open the **Start** menu or **Start** screen and display the app list.

2. Manually scroll the list to display apps that begin with the letter **G**. Along the way, notice the apps that are installed on your computer.

3. Display the alphabetic index of the app list. From the index, jump to the apps that begin with the letter **M**.

4. From the app list, start the **Maps** app.

5. In the taskbar search box, enter *weather*. Locate and start the **Weather** app.

6. Leave both apps running for the next task.

Explore built-in apps

Start the Maps and Weather apps, and then perform the following tasks:

1. Switch to the Maps app.

2. Enter your address in the search box. If the app locates an address match, select the address to display it on the map.

3. On the button bar in the right pane, select the **Map views** button to display the available views of the location.

Map Views button

4. Display each of the available views of the map. Experiment with zooming in and out in each view, and note the details that are available in each view.

5. Switch to the **Weather** app. In the search box, enter the name of the nearest large city to you. Experiment to find out what types of information are available in this app.

6. In the app list, scroll or jump to the **W** section. Open and browse the contents of the folders in that section to familiarize yourself with the apps, accessories, and tools that are available.

7. Exit all the running apps.

Install Store apps

Perform the following tasks:

1. Start the Store app.

2. Locate a free app that interests you, and install it. Then locate another free app that you don't want to keep and install that, too.

3. Display your library of recent apps and games, and then display the list of apps associated with your account.

4. In the **Your Apps** pane, look for an app that has an Install icon. If you find one, install the app on your computer.

5. From the Store, display your Microsoft account information. Locate your list of purchases and identify the apps you installed in steps 2 and 4.

6. If you've had a Microsoft account for a while, identify the first year for which your account has a record of transactions.

7. In the app list, locate the apps that you installed in step 2. (Hint: If you display the Recently Added section on the Start menu, it will be easy to find the new apps.)

8. Uninstall one or both of the apps.

Manage app notifications

Perform the following tasks:

1. Open the **Action Center** and examine any current notifications.

2. In the **Settings** window, on the **System** settings page, display the **Notifications & actions** pane. Review your current notification settings.

3. Review the list of apps installed on your computer that can generate notifications.

4. Display the notification options for the Calendar app. Turn off audio notifications for Calendar. Then return to the list of apps and note the change.

5. Review and modify the notification settings to meet your needs.

6. Turn on the **Quiet Hours** feature and note that the Action Center icon changes. Then turn off **Quiet Hours**.

Explore files and folders

You view all the drives, folders, and files that are stored on your computer and on storage drives it is connected to through a network or over the internet, in File Explorer. File Explorer can display the contents of a folder, a library of folders, or a virtual collection of items (such as the Quick Access list).

To simplify the way that you work with files, Windows presents files in File Explorer as though the files are organized in a hierarchical storage system of folders and subfolders (folders within folders). In reality, files are stored on the computer's hard drive and in other locations (such as Microsoft OneDrive) wherever they fit, and the storage structure that File Explorer displays is only a series of pointers to the files. This provides you with easy access to files while still maintaining an organizational system.

You can organize files in folders and create virtual libraries of folders so that you can access files in multiple ways. If you forget where you stored a file, you can use the simple yet powerful search features of Windows 10 to quickly locate files and other information on your computer based on the file name, content, or type.

This chapter guides you through procedures related to getting to know File Explorer, changing the File Explorer display options, and searching for files.

In this chapter

- Understand files, folders, and libraries
- Get to know File Explorer
- Change the File Explorer display options
- Find specific files

Understand files, folders, and libraries

There are many different types of files, but they all fall into these two basic categories:

- **Files used or created by apps** These include executable files (such as the Microsoft Office app files) and dynamic-link libraries (DLLs) (files used by apps to provide functionality). Some of these files might be hidden (not shown in a standard folder window view) to protect them from being inadvertently changed or deleted.

> ✅ **TIP** By default, you can't display, select, or delete hidden system files or the folder structure they're stored in. You can choose to display and work with other hidden files, folders, and drives by selecting that option in the Folder Options dialog box, which is discussed in "Change the File Explorer display options" later in this chapter.

- **Files created by you** These include documents, worksheets, graphics, text files, presentations, audio clips, video clips, and other things that you can open, look at, and change by using one or more apps.

The files that are installed with an app and those it creates for its own use are organized the way the app expects to find them, and you shouldn't move or remove them. However, you have complete control of the organization of the files you create (such as documents and worksheets), and knowing how to manage these files is essential if you want to be able to use your computer efficiently.

Folders

As with files, there are also many different types of folders, but they fall generally into two categories: folders created by Windows or apps and folders created by you to organize your files. Creating folders is covered in "Create and rename folders and files" in Chapter 6, "Manage folders and files."

When Windows 10 was installed on your computer, it created system folders, including these:

- **Program Files folder** Many apps install the files they need in subfolders of the Program Files folder. You might have the option to choose a different folder, but there's rarely a reason to do so. After you install an app, you shouldn't move, copy, rename, or delete its folders and files; if you do, you might not be able to run or uninstall the app.

> **TIP** There are a few valid reasons for deleting app system files, such as deleting the Normal.dot file to reset the Microsoft Word normal template, but if you're working at that level you're probably an expert computer user or following reliable instructions. For more information about using Word to its full potential, see *Microsoft Word 2016 Step by Step* (Microsoft Press, 2015) by Joan Lambert.

- **Users folder** For each user account on the computer, Windows also creates a user account folder in the Users folder. The user account folder contains several subfolders, referred to in this book as your *personal folders*. Some of your personal folders are visible in your user account folder, which is located at C:\Users\[account name].

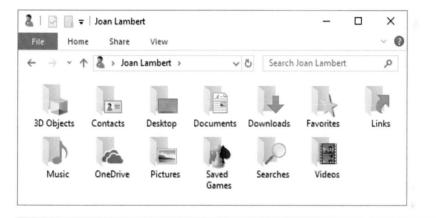

> **TIP** Many of the personal folders can be added as buttons on the left side of the Start menu for quick access; these include Documents, Downloads, Music, Pictures, and Videos. For more information, see "Configure the Start menu" in Chapter 2, "Personalize your working environment."

There is also a hidden folder named AppData that contains information about your user account settings for Windows and for apps that you use. Windows creates the user account folder and its subfolders the first time a user signs in. As you work on your computer and personalize Windows, Windows saves information and settings specific to your user profile in these folders.

In addition to the account-specific folder for each user account that is active on the computer, the Users folder also contains a Public folder, the contents of which are accessible to anyone who is logged on to the computer. The Public folder contains subfolders. Some of these are visible, such as Documents,

Downloads, Music, Pictures, and Videos. The hidden subfolders contain information about settings that are common to all user accounts on the computer. If you want to make files available to anyone who logs on to the computer, you can store them in the Public folders rather than in your personal folders.

> **TIP** If other people have user accounts on your computer, they won't have access to the files in your personal folders unless they have administrative rights or know your password, or if you've shared the folders in a HomeGroup or over the network. To clearly differentiate your personal folders from the public folders, Windows 10 refers to the public folders as Public Documents, Public Downloads, Public Music, Public Pictures, and Public Videos.

- **Windows folder** Most of the critical operating system files are stored in this folder. You can look, but unless you really know what you are doing, don't touch! Most Windows 10 users will never need to access the files in the Windows folder.

Libraries

You can display a collection of folders that you want easy access to in a *library*. Libraries are virtual folders that aren't physically present on the hard drive but that display the contents of multiple folders as though the files were stored together in one location.

The default Windows 10 installation includes seven standard libraries: Camera Roll, Documents, Music, Pictures, Podcasts, Saved Pictures, and Videos. In previous versions of Windows, the libraries included user account folders and their corresponding Public folders, but in Windows 10 the default starting content is your user account folder. Configuring a OneDrive connection on your computer adds your OneDrive Documents, Music, and Pictures folders to the corresponding libraries.

In Windows 10, libraries are hidden by default in File Explorer. You can turn on the display of libraries if you want to use them.

You manage a library from the Manage tab that appears when you select or open a library in the Libraries window. (Tabs that appear only in specific contexts are called *contextual tabs* or *tool tabs*, because they host tools for working with the selected file or folder.)

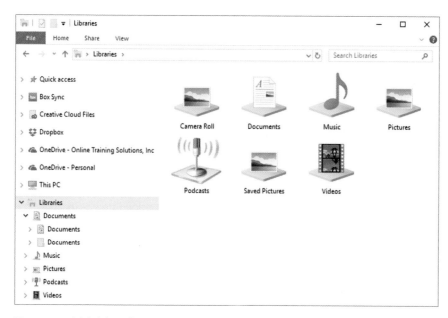

You can add folders from any connected location to libraries, and some apps add folders to libraries for you when you make selections.

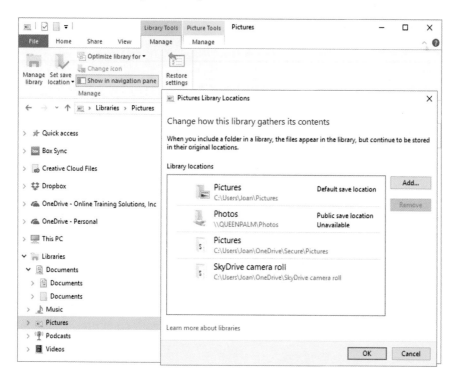

In addition to the standard libraries, you can create your own libraries, and a folder can belong to more than one library. For example, suppose you are working on a Fall Promotion project for a client, Contoso Pharmaceuticals. If you create one library that displays all the folders of your current projects and another library that displays all the folders associated with Contoso, you can include the Fall Promotion folder in both libraries.

If you don't use libraries, you can choose to not display the Libraries node at the root of the Navigation pane.

> **TIP** If you store files locally on your computer rather than in a cloud storage location such as OneDrive, consider storing your private documents, spreadsheets, databases, and similar files in subfolders of your Documents folder, and any files you want to share with other users in subfolders of the Public Documents folder. Similarly, store all your private pictures in Pictures and those you want to share in Public Pictures; and so on for music and video files. Then include the Public folders in the libraries. When you follow this process, backing up your work is a simple matter of backing up only the libraries.

> **SEE ALSO** For more information about how to make any default or custom library available to other users or computers on your network, see "Manage homegroup connections" and "Share files on your network," both in Chapter 8, "Manage network and storage resources."

Get to know File Explorer

Early versions of Windows displayed physical hard drives at the root of the file storage structure. As file management and storage practices have evolved—first to include virtual libraries of folders and now to commonly include OneDrive and other cloud storage locations—File Explorer has also evolved. At the root of the storage structure, File Explorer displays a series of conceptual organizational systems, including the following nodes:

- **Quick Access** Contains links to folders and files that you access frequently or pin here for easy access

- **This PC** Contains links to your user account–specific folders, and to the physical storage locations that are installed in or connected to your computer

- **Libraries** Contains links to virtual collections of folders, which by default are composed of the user account–specific folders and their corresponding OneDrive folders

- **Network** Displays a representation of other computers on your local area network

- **Homegroup** Displays a representation of other computers on your local area network that are joined to the network homegroup

> **SEE ALSO** For information about connecting to network computers and homegroup members, see Chapter 8, "Manage network and storage resources."

5

When you connect your Windows 10 computer to OneDrive or OneDrive for Business cloud storage drives, those drives also appear at the root of the storage structure.

Within the This PC node, File Explorer displays the user-specific file storage folders and the storage devices that are connected to your computer. Storage locations included in This PC include hard drives installed in the computer and storage devices (such as CDs, DVDs, USB flash drives, and external hard drives) that are physically connected to the computer. Each storage drive that is physically connected to the computer is identified by a letter, and in some cases by a description. Your computer's primary hard drive (the one where the operating system is installed) is almost always identified by the letter C.

(By tradition, the letters *A* and *B* are reserved for floppy disk drives, which are all but obsolete and have been superseded by higher-capacity storage media.) If your computer has additional built-in hard drives, they are assigned the next sequential letters, followed by any removable media drives.

> **TIP** You can't assign a specific drive letter to a local drive in File Explorer, but you can name each drive. For information, see the sidebar "Change the computer name" in Chapter 8, "Manage network and storage resources."

To explore your computer's storage system, you can use the This PC window as a convenient entry point. The devices represented in This PC are divided into groups. Internal hard drives (those physically installed in your computer) and external hard drives (those connected to your computer by a cable) are shown first, followed by internal removable storage drives (such as CD and DVD drives) and external removable storage devices (such as USB flash drives), and then storage locations you access through a network connection. For each drive or device, the total storage space and available storage space are given, both as actual measurements and visually as a colored progress bar. The length of the progress bar indicates the portion of the total storage space that is in use. The default bar color is aqua; when less than 10 percent of the storage space on a drive or device remains available, the bar color changes to red.

The File Explorer window layout includes the following elements:

- **The ribbon** This command interface has commands organized in groups on tabs. The File menu and ribbon tabs are covered later in this topic.

- **Navigation pane** This vertical pane is open by default on the left side of the window. It displays a hierarchical view of the physical and virtual storage structures available to the computer. You can browse to folders and files on your computer or network by selecting locations in this pane.

- **Content pane** This primary pane displays the contents of the selected folder as a textual or iconic list. You can't close the content pane.

- **Details pane** This pane displays information about the selected folder or file.

- **Preview pane** This pane displays a preview of the file that is selected in the content pane. The Preview pane can display the contents of image files, Microsoft Word documents, Excel workbooks, PowerPoint presentations, PDF files, and other common file types.

Navigation pane   Content pane   Preview or Details pane   Expand The
                                                                    Ribbon button

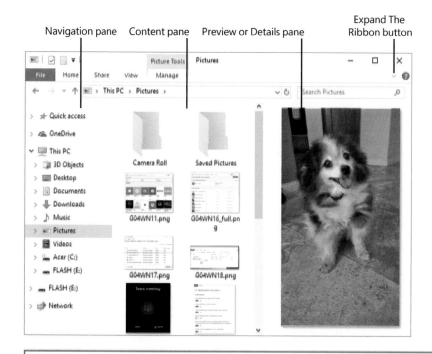

TIP You can display either the Details pane or the Preview pane on the right side of the window, or you can close both. For more information, see "Change the File Explorer display options" later in this chapter.

Work with the standard ribbon tabs

The ribbon in File Explorer includes the File menu, a set of standard tabs, tabs that are displayed for specific folders, and tabs that appear only when specific types of items are selected. These context-sensitive tabs, also called *tool tabs*, host commands that you need only when you select an item of that type. Tool tabs are covered in the "Work with the tool tabs" section later in this topic.

The standard ribbon elements are:

- **File menu** The File menu displays commands in the left pane and a list of recently or frequently displayed folders on the right. You can invoke commands and open specific locations from the File menu.

> **TIP** The most useful of the available commands is Options (labeled Change Folder And Search Options in some Windows versions), which we work with later in this chapter.

You can pin locations to the Frequent Places list by selecting the thumbtack icon. Pinned locations stay at the top of the list and are indicated by angled thumbtacks.

- **Home tab** The Home tab is available when File Explorer is displaying anything other than the This PC, Network, and Homegroup nodes. Commonly used commands are grouped on the Home tab.

- **Share tab** The Share tab provides various ways for you to share a folder or file with other people. These options include sending a copy of a file to other people or sharing its location with other people who are on your network. In addition to sharing options, the Share tab provides commands for printing, burning a file to a disc, and compressing a file.

- **View tab** The View tab hosts the commands that you can use to customize the display of items in the File Explorer window.

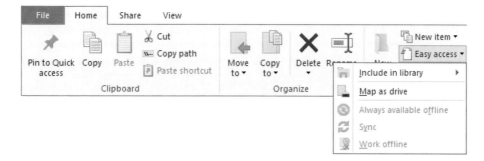

The Home tab provides access to the most commonly used File Explorer commands. Many of them are covered in depth later in this chapter, but some deserve a quick mention, such as the following:

- **Pin to Quick access** This adds the selected folder to the Quick Access list at the top of the Navigation pane. This list is available from within apps and in File Explorer.

- **Easy access** This command displays a menu that offers various ways to make the current location more easily accessible.

- **Open and Edit** When a folder is selected in the content pane, selecting the Open button expands the folder. The Edit button is disabled. When you select an editable file (such as a Word document) in the content pane, both the Open and Edit buttons will open the file. The difference is that when you select the *arrow* next to Open, you get a list of all the programs known to File Explorer that can open this file type, and an option to choose a default one.

- **History** This displays the current file in the File History viewer.

> **SEE ALSO** For information about file version history, see "Back up data" in Chapter 15, "Protect your computer and data."

The View tab provides access to several commands you can use to tailor File Explorer to suit your preferences. Many of these tabs are discussed in greater detail in "Change the File Explorer display options" later in this chapter.

The following commands are the most commonly used:

- **Navigation pane** Select this to display a list of Navigation pane features you can turn on or off, including the display of the pane itself.

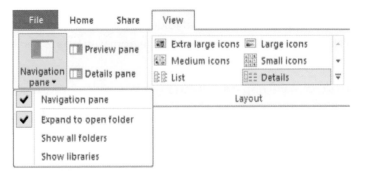

- **Preview pane and Details pane** You can display either of these panes, but only one at a time. The active pane appears on the right side of File Explorer. When the Preview pane is active, selecting a file displays the file content in the preview pane. If the Details pane is active, selecting a file displays its icon and file information such as its size.

- **Layout commands** These commands determine whether the files are displayed as icons of various sizes or one of two types of list.

> **TIP** You can quickly switch between a detailed list and large icons view by using the icons in the lower-right corner of the File Explorer window.

- **Current view commands** Sort By allows you to select the column to sort by. You can also do this by selecting a column title. Select it again to reverse the sort. Select Group By and Add Columns to see the options for each.

- **Show/hide commands** The three check boxes in Show/Hide turn the display of their respective items on and off. You can select one or more items (files or folders) and select Hide Selected Items to mark them as hidden. Then select or clear the Hidden Items check box to display or hide them in the content pane. To unhide the items, first show all hidden items, then select the hidden items, and select Hide Selected Items to turn it off.

> **TIP** When hidden items are displayed in the content pane, the icons of the hidden items are slightly dimmed to differentiate them from items that aren't hidden. The Hide Selected Items button is active when hidden files are selected.

5

- **Options** The Options command displays the Folder Options dialog box, which we discuss in "Change the File Explorer display options," later in this chapter.

Work with the tool tabs

Tool tabs appear on the ribbon when specific storage locations are displayed or specific types of files are selected. Tool tabs are in named groups of one or more tabs that host commands specific to working with the selected file type. (Most groups have only one tab.) A colored tab in the title bar displays the tool tab group name. The tool tab or tabs are below the group tab and to the right of the standard tabs. For example, when you select an image file, the Manage tool tab in the Picture Tools group appears; when you select an audio file, the Play tool tab in the Music Tools group appears; and when you select a compressed folder (a zip file), the Extract tool tab in the Compressed Folder Tools group appears.

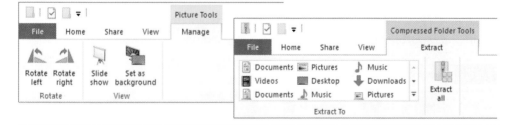

> **TIP** The tool tabs appear when you select multiple files of the same type, but not when you select multiple types of files.

There are theoretically more than 200 tool tabs, each with its own combination of commands. The storage locations that have their own tabs include This PC, Drive, Network, Homegroup, Search, Library, and Recycle Bin. The file types that display tool tabs when you select them include ISO, ZIP, Image, Audio, Video, and Shortcut file types.

For example, when you select This PC in File Explorer, the Home and Share tabs are replaced by the Computer tab. This tab contains links to common functions and tools that you can use to manage your computer. You can point to each command on the Computer tab to display a ScreenTip explaining its purpose.

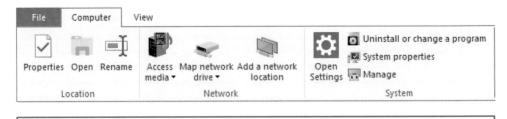

> **TIP** Some of these commands open in a new window and some change what File Explorer displays. This can be confusing. Check for a Back button in the window before selecting Close; otherwise you might close File Explorer.

When you select a hard drive in the Navigation pane, the Manage tool tab in the Drive Tools group appears.

If you have a local network, you can select the icon for it in the Navigation pane. Commands appropriate to the network are displayed on the Network tab.

Even the Recycle Bin has its own tool tab. When you double-click the desktop icon for the Recycle Bin, the Manage tab in the Recycle Bin Tools group appears on the ribbon.

From this tool tab, you can empty the Recycle Bin or restore deleted items.

Work with the Navigation And Search bar

The Navigation And Search bar is displayed just below the ribbon. You can use the commands on this bar to quickly navigate through the folder structure.

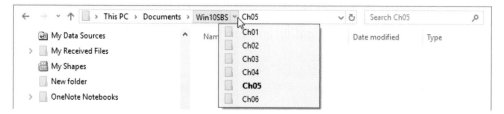

To the immediate right of the folder navigation arrows is the Address bar. The Address bar displays an icon and the friendly path to the current folder. Selecting the folder icon at the left end of the Address bar displays the absolute path from the root drive. Each item in the friendly path has a > after it. If you select a >, the folders within that item are displayed, and you can select one to open it. You can drag the icon to another location, such as the desktop, to create a shortcut to this folder at that location. You can right-click anywhere in the Address bar to display the shortcut menu.

To the right of the Address bar are the Refresh button and the search box. Selecting the Refresh button is the same as pressing the F5 key: it refreshes the display. The search box is one of those special locations that produces a tool tab. Search is discussed in more detail in "Find specific files," later in this chapter.

To start File Explorer

- On the **Start** menu, select **File Explorer**.

- On the taskbar, select the **File Explorer** button.

- Select Win+E.

- Right-click the **Start** button and then on the Quick Links menu, select **File Explorer**.

To display the contents of a folder in File Explorer

- In the **Navigation** pane, select the folder name.

- In the content pane, double-click the folder name.

To expand or collapse a folder in the Navigation pane

- Double-click the folder, or select the > to the left of the folder name.

To move through a list of recent locations

- At the left end of the **Navigation and Search** bar, select the **Back** and **Forward** buttons.

To move directly to a location

1. In File Explorer, on the **Navigation and Search** bar, do either of the following:

   - Select the **Recent locations** button (the **v** between the Forward and Up buttons) to display a menu of recent locations.

   - Select the **Previous Locations** button (the **v** at the right end of the Address box) to display a menu of previous locations.

2. Select the location you want to move to.

> **TIP** You can paste or enter a folder path from the File Explorer Address bar directly into the Address bar in a dialog box to display that location.

To move up one level in the current folder path

- In File Explorer, on the **Navigation and Search** bar, select the **Up** button (the upward-pointing arrow to the left of the Address box).

Work with libraries

The Libraries node that is optionally displayed in the File Explorer Navigation pane is more conceptual than most other folders. Rather than containing files and folders, it points to folders that might exist on your hard drive, on a USB drive, or even on a hard drive on someone else's computer on a network you can access.

 TIP You can control the display of libraries by going to the File Explorer View tab, selecting Navigation Pane, and selecting Show Libraries.

5

Libraries are shortcuts to folders that you can navigate to individually, but that you want quicker access to. For example, the Documents library might include pointers to your private Documents folder, to the Public Documents folder, and to the Documents folder in your OneDrive folder. When you add a file to one of those folders, and it is indexed, it shows up in the Documents library.

You can add folders from any connected location to an existing or new library. Until the library contains at least one folder, it displays a button labeled *Include a folder*.

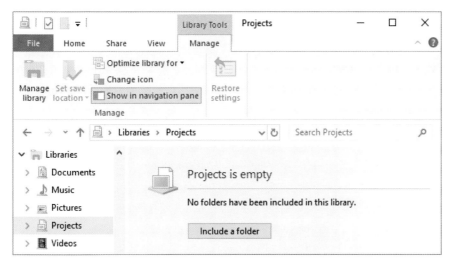

One of the benefits of managing file locations within libraries is that the Libraries node and all the folders it points to are included by default in File History backups.

 SEE ALSO For information about search indexes, see "Find specific files" later in this chapter and "Search your computer and the web" in Chapter 14, "Work more efficiently." For information about File History, see "Back up data" in Chapter 15, "Protect your computer and data."

You can optimize individual libraries for specific file types—either documents, music, pictures, or videos—to set sorting and grouping options specific to that file type. To further personalize the library, you can assign one of over 400 icons to it.

If you no longer use a library, you can delete it without affecting the files and folders it contains, or you can simply hide it so that it doesn't appear in the Navigation pane.

You manage a library and its contents from the Manage tool tab or the library Properties dialog box.

To display or hide the Libraries node in the Navigation pane

- In File Explorer, on the **View** tab, in the **Panes** group, select **Navigation pane**, and then **Show libraries**.

To open a library in File Explorer

- In the **Navigation** pane, select the **Libraries** node. Then in the content pane, double-click the library you want to open.

- In the **Navigation** pane, select the > to the left of the **Libraries** node, and then select the library you want to open.

To open the Properties dialog box for a library

- In File Explorer, right-click the library, and then select **Properties**.

To create a library

1. In the File Explorer **Navigation** pane, do either of the following:

    - Right-click the **Libraries** node.

    - Select the **Libraries** node and then right-click an empty area of the content pane.

2. Select **New**, and then **Library** to create the library with the name active for editing.

3. Enter a name for the new library, and then press Enter. The icon remains neutral until you choose a content type.

> ✓ **TIP** To quickly add the first folder to a new library, open the library in File Explorer, select the Include A Folder button in the content pane to open the Include A Folder dialog box, browse to and select the library you want to include, and then select Include Folder.

To add a folder to a library

1. Do either of the following:

   - Open the library in File Explorer. On the **Manage** tool tab, in the **Manage** group, select **Manage library** to open the Library Locations dialog box specific to the library.

   - Open the **Properties** dialog box for the library.

2. Select **Add** to open the Include Folder In dialog box for the library.

3. Browse to and select the folder you want to include, and then select **Include folder** to add the folder to the library.

4. Select **OK** to close the dialog box.

To optimize a library or folder for a file type

- Open the library's **Properties** dialog box. In the **Optimize this library for** list, select **General items**, **Documents**, **Music**, **Pictures**, or **Videos**. Then select **Apply** or **OK**.

- In File Explorer, display the **Libraries** node, and then select the library you want to optimize. On the **Manage** tool tab, select **Optimize library for**, and then in the list, select **General items**, **Documents**, **Music**, **Pictures**, or **Videos**.

To change the folder icon of a custom library

1. Do either of the following to open the Change Icon dialog box:

   - Open the library in File Explorer. Then on the **Manage** tool tab, select **Change icon**.

   - Open the library's **Properties** dialog box and select **Change library icon**.

2. In the **Change Icon** dialog box, select the icon you want to use, and then select **OK**.

To remove a folder from a library

- Open the library's **Properties** dialog box, select the folder, and select **Remove**. Then select **Apply** or **OK**.

- Open the library's **Library Locations** dialog box, select the folder, and then select **Remove**. Then select **OK**.

To hide a library in the Navigation pane

- In the library's **Properties** dialog box, clear the **Shown in navigation pane** check box. Then select **Apply** or **OK**.

> **TIP** You can hide a folder that is in a system-created library so that the folder appears in the content pane but not in the Navigation pane. To hide a library folder from the Navigation pane only, expand the library and right-click the folder in the Navigation pane, and then select Don't Show In Navigation Pane. To stop hiding the folder, display it in the content pane, right-click it, and then select Show In Navigation Pane.

Change the File Explorer display options

Windows 10 provides many ways to personalize the display of File Explorer to suit the way you work.

Display and hide panes

Each pane of the File Explorer window displays a specific type of information. You can display and hide some panes to show or hide information, or to change the amount of space available in the content pane. For example, if your folders typically contain many files and you are adept at navigating in the Address bar, you might want to turn off the Navigation, Detail, and Preview panes so that the content pane occupies the entire folder window.

5

To display or hide the File Explorer Navigation pane

1. In File Explorer, on the **View** tab, in the **Panes** group, select **Navigation pane**.

2. Select or clear the **Navigation pane** check box to display or hide the pane.

To display or hide the File Explorer Preview pane

- ▪ Select Alt+P.

- ▪ On the **View** tab, select **Preview pane**.

To display or hide the File Explorer Details pane

- ▪ Select Alt+Shift+P.

- ▪ On the **View** tab, select **Details pane**.

> ✓ **TIP** You can change the width of a pane by pointing to its border and, when the pointer changes to a double-headed arrow, dragging in the direction you want to increase or decrease its size. This technique is useful if you want to display more information in one pane without closing the other panes.

Display different views of folders and files

You use commands on the View tab to set the layout, sort order, grouping, and columns that are displayed in the content pane. You can choose to display a check box column (the boxes appear only when you point to or select items), file name extensions, and hidden files.

> ✓ **TIP** The Layout options that you set apply only to the current folder. The Show/Hide settings apply to all folders. You can apply some settings to all folders of the same type in the Folder Options dialog box that is displayed when you select the Options button (not the arrow) at the right end of the View tab.

The standard information displayed for files in Details view includes the file name, date modified, type, and size. You can add a lot more information to the Details view to make it more useful to you. For example, you can display the dimensions of images, the number of pages in a document, or the number of slides in a PowerPoint presentation. Having these types of details available directly from File Explorer can save you a lot of time and effort. Over 300 properties are available for display in File Explorer. Most apply only to specific file types, but many could be useful to you.

When the Details pane is open, it displays detailed information when you select a single file. As you select more files, the Details pane displays the number of items selected, the total size of the files, and other types of information common to the selected files.

8 items selected

Title:	Add a title
Authors:	Add an author
Size:	1.50 MB
Date modified:	9/28/2015 7:28 PM - 9/29/2017 3:40 PM
Tags:	Add a tag
Subject:	Specify the subject
Comments:	Add comments
Date created:	10/2/2017 2:33 PM
Shared with:	HIBISCUS\HomeUsers

If you add a folder to the selection, the Details pane displays only the number of items selected (the folder is counted as one item, regardless of the number of subfolders and files in it) and a stack of icons.

Different views are best suited to different tasks. For example, when you are looking for a specific graphic among those stored in a folder, you might find it useful to be able to see the graphic thumbnails in the content pane.

The available views include the following:

- **Icons** The four Icon views (Extra Large, Large, Medium, and Small) display an icon and name for each folder or file in the current folder. In all but Small Icons view, the icons display either the file type or, in the case of graphic files (including PowerPoint presentations), a representation of the file content.

- **List** This view is like Small Icons view in that it shows the names of the files and folders accompanied by a small icon that represents the file type. The only difference is that the items are arranged in columns instead of in rows.

- **Details** This view displays a list of files and folders, each accompanied by a small icon that represents the item type and its properties, arranged in a tabular format, with column headings. The properties shown by default for each file or folder are Name, Date Modified, Type, and Size. You can hide any of these properties, and you can display a variety of other properties that might be pertinent to specific types of files, including Author and Title.

- **Tiles** For folders, this view displays a medium-size icon and the folder name and type. For files, the icon indicates the file type and is accompanied by the file name, type, and file size.

- **Content** For folders, this view displays an icon, the folder name, and the date. For files, the icon indicates the file type and is accompanied by the file name, type, file size, and date.

> **TIP** In the Extra Large Icons, Large Icons, Medium Icons, Tiles, and Content views, folder icons display representations of the folder content depicted as pages and pictures.

To change the File Explorer folder view

- On the **View** tab, in the **Layout** group, select a layout option.

> **TIP** If you point to one of the view layouts, the content pane temporarily displays that layout.

- Right-click an empty spot in the content pane, point to **View**, and then select a view from the list.

- In the lower-right corner of the content pane, select the **Details** or **Large Icons** button.

> **TIP** You can optimize a folder for a specific view on the Customize tab of the folder's Properties dialog box. Doing so makes that the default view for the folder. You can select a different view at any time by using one of the techniques listed here.

To display folder content as icons

- On the **View** tab, in the **Layout** group, select **Extra Large** icons, **Large** icons, **Medium** icons, or **Small** icons.

To display folder content as a list of items and their properties

■ On the **View** tab, in the **Layout** group, select **Details**.

To add, remove, or rearrange properties in Details view

1. In File Explorer, display the contents of the folder as a detailed list.

2. Do either of the following to open the Choose Details dialog box:

   • On the **View** tab, in the **Current view** group, select **Add columns** and then **Choose columns...**.

   • Right-click any column header, and then select **More...**.

3. In the **Choose Details** dialog box, do any of the following:

   • Select a column name to add or remove its check mark, which adds or removes that column from Details view.

   • Select a column name, and then select **Show** or **Hide** to show or hide that column in Details view.

   • Select a column name, and then select **Move Up** or **Move Down** to move the column higher or lower on the list, which also moves the column to the left or right in Details view.

To resize a column in Details view

- In File Explorer, point to the line between the column heading and the heading to its right, and when the mouse pointer changes to a double-headed arrow, do any of the following:

  - Drag to the left to make the column narrower.

  - Drag to the right to make the column wider.

  - Double-click to make the column resize to fit the widest item in the column.

To resize all columns in Details view to fit the widest item in the column

- On the **View** tab, in the **Current view** group, select **Size all columns to fit**.

To display or hide folder features and content

- In File Explorer, on the **View** tab, in the **Show/hide** group, do any of the following:

  - To turn on or off the display of check boxes when you point to or select an item, select or clear the **Item check boxes** check box.

  - To show or hide each file name extension (for example, .docx), select or clear the **File name extensions** check box.

  - To show or hide hidden items, select or clear the **Hidden items** check box.

Group, sort, and filter folder content

By default, the folders and files in the content pane are displayed in alphabetical order by name, with the subfolders at the top and files below them. You can sort or group the items in a folder or library in any view, by any default or displayed property. The default options include Name, Date Modified, Type, Size, Date Created, Authors, Categories, Tags, and Title. The Sort By and Group By menus display the currently available properties; to sort or group by a hidden property, display the property first to add it to the menu, and then return to the menu to sort or group the folder or library contents.

> **TIP** Changing a folder's layout, type, grouping, or other attribute doesn't affect its appearance in a library. Libraries independently control the appearance of folder content.

If you group folders and files, their overall arrangement changes, but within each group the sort order remains the same. You can change the order of the items in the content pane by sorting them by any of the displayed properties.

> **TIP** If you choose to sort grouped content in ascending or descending order, files and folders are sorted within their groups.

Options for sorting and grouping content are available from the View tab, and also from the shortcut menu that appears when you right-click an empty area of the content pane. Although both options are very similar, the ribbon menus display a few more options.

If a folder contains a lot of files, or contains subfolders of files, you can filter the folder content to display only the files that meet specific conditions. Filtered results include individual files, whether they are at the top level of the folder or within subfolders.

To group folder content

1. On the **View** tab, in the **Current view** group, select **Group by**. If a property has a dot to its left, items in the folder are already grouped by that property.

2. If the **Group by** list doesn't include the property you want to group by, select **Choose columns**, select the property in the **Choose Details** dialog box, and then select **OK**.

3. In the **Group by** list, select the file property you want to group items by.

To ungroup folder content

■ On the **View** tab, in the **Current view** group, select the **Group by** button, and then select **(None)** from the bottom of the list.

To sort files in any view

1. On the **View** tab, in the **Current view** group, select **Sort by**. If a property has a dot to its left, items in the folder are already sorted by that property.

2. If the **Sort by** list doesn't include the property you want to sort by, select **Choose columns**, select the property in the **Choose Details** dialog box, and then select **OK**.

3. In the **Sort by** list, select the file property you want to sort items by.

To sort folder content in Details view

■ Select the column name you want to sort by.

- Selecting the column name once sorts in alphabetical or ascending numerical order.

- Selecting the column name a second time sorts in reverse alphabetical or descending numerical order.

A ^ or v appears in the middle of the column heading to let you know the column is sorted in ascending or descending order.

To filter folder content

1. In File Explorer, display the contents of the folder as a detailed list.

2. Point to a column header until a v appears at its right edge.

3. Select the v to display a list of items you can filter on. (The list content is specific to the properties of the items in the folder.)

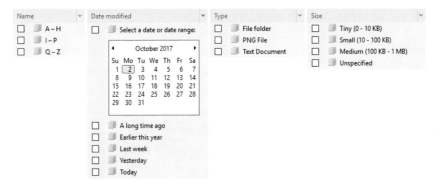

4. Select a check box to show only those items in the list that match the filter.

   Each filter is applied when you select it, so you can immediately see its impact.

 TIP You can repeat steps 3 and 4 to apply filters from other columns to the content pane.

---

5. Click or tap outside the list to close it.

Change folder options

Most of the common folder options you might want to change are included on the File Explorer ribbon. However, some less common ones are available when you select the Options button (not the arrow) at the right end of the View tab.

In the Folder Options dialog box, you can customize folder windows by changing settings on these two tabs:

- **General** On this tab, you can change how you browse folders, whether you select or double-click to open items, and how the Navigation pane behaves.

- **View** On this tab, you can change the default view for all folders and change specific display/hide settings. For example, you can specify whether to show the status bar in File Explorer windows.

TIP When you first start working in Windows 10, the default view for each folder is determined by its type. If you apply the current folder view to all folders of a particular type and then change your mind, you can select Reset Folders on the View tab of the Folder Options dialog box to restore the type-based default views. For information about folder types, see "Work with folder and file properties" in Chapter 6, "Manage folders and files."

To display the Folder Options dialog box from File Explorer

- On the **File** menu, select **Options** or **Change folder and search options**.

- On the **View** tab, select the **Options** button, or select the **Options** arrow and then select **Change folder and search options**.

To change the default File Explorer starting folder

1. In the **Folder Options** dialog box, display the **General** tab.

2. Select the **Open File Explorer to** list, and then select either **Quick access** or **This PC**.

3. Select **OK**.

To change how you select to open an item

1. In the **Folder Options** dialog box, on the **General** tab, do either of the following:

   - Select **Single-click to open an item (point to select)**.

   - Select **Double-click to open an item (single-click to select)**.

2. Select **OK**.

To add a location to your Quick Access list

- Select the folder in File Explorer, and then do either of the following:

   - On the **Home** tab, in the **Clipboard** group, select **Pin to Quick access**.

   - In the content pane, right-click the folder, and then select **Pin to Quick access**.

To hide items in the Quick Access list

1. In the **Folder Options** dialog box, on the **General** tab, do either of the following:

   - Clear the **Show recently used files in Quick access** check box.

   - Clear the **Show frequently used folders in Quick access** check box.

2. Select **OK**.

> **TIP** In Windows 10, a new group called Quick Access was added at the top of the Navigation pane. When this is selected, the content pane on the right displays a collection of your frequently used folders and recent files so that you can quickly return to programs, files, or locations you often need to access. These can be folders on your computer, network computers, or external hard drives.

Find specific files

Windows 10 provides various ways to search everything from a folder on your computer to the web, all from the taskbar search box. File Explorer provides an additional search capability that is limited to files only (that is, it doesn't return apps and web searches). The underlying search engine is the same from all these locations, but the focus of the searches and the way the results are returned varies.

Windows Search

Recent advancements in online and computer search technology have made the instant location of information and files so simple that it's easy to forget how tedious tracking down the same items would have been in the past. The search technology that is built in to Windows 10 is excellent.

Using Windows Search, you can find apps, files, messages, and message attachments on your computer. You don't need to know the name or location of the file or item you want to find; simply enter a word or phrase in the taskbar search box to display a list of matching items, organized by type.

How does Windows Search find items so quickly? Behind the scenes, Windows Search maintains an index of all the keywords in, and associated with, the files stored on your computer—app names, common tasks, and the file names and content (when possible) of documents, audio and video recordings, images, email messages, webpages, and other data files. Windows Search automatically indexes the most common file types (such as documents, text files, and email messages) and doesn't index file types you are less likely to search (such as operating system files). It does not include the system files; such an index would be huge and would slow down the search process.

When you enter a search term, Windows looks for the term in the index instead of searching the actual files on your hard drive.

> **TIP** By default, Windows doesn't index encrypted files, because a search by another computer user could reveal the encrypted data. You can add encrypted files to the search index if you first put in place a full-volume data-encryption solution, such as Windows BitLocker Drive Encryption. For information about changing the file storage locations that are indexed, see "Search your computer and the web" in Chapter 14, "Work more efficiently."

File Explorer Search

File Explorer Search differs from Windows Search in that it is limited to searching for files and displays them in its own familiar interface. So when you get a results list, you can use all the usual commands on the View tab to refine the display.

You initiate a File Explorer Search from the Search box at the right end of the Navigation And Search bar. When you activate this box to enter a search term, the Search Tools group tab appears, providing tools you can use to refine your search.

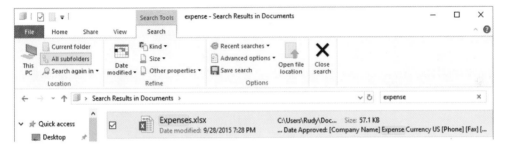

You can save a set of search parameters so that you can display updated results at any time. Saved searches are added to the Favorites group in File Explorer and are also available from your personal Searches folder.

To search for a file in File Explorer

- In the upper-right corner of the File Explorer window, enter a search term in the **Search** box. As you enter the search term, Windows filters the program files, folders, and email messages stored on your computer.

To refine a File Explorer search

- On the **Search** tool tab, in the **Refine** group, select the property by which you want to filter the search results, and then enter the criteria for the filter.

To save a search for later reference

1. On the **Search** tool tab, in the **Options** group, select the **Save search** button. The Save As dialog box displays the content of your personal Searches folder.

2. In the **Save As** dialog box, select **Save** to accept the default name and save the search in the Searches folder.

 TIP Close the Search Results window to return to the original folder.

Key points

- File Explorer is the app in which you display and access the files stored on your computer. Files are organized into folders. Some folders are created by Windows, some by apps, and some by you. You can also create virtual libraries of files.

- You can display additional file properties in File Explorer, and group, sort, and filter files by any displayed property.

- You can limit a search to files and to specific file locations by searching from the File Explorer search box.

Practice tasks

Before you can complete these practice tasks, you need to copy the book's practice files to your computer. The practice files for these tasks are located in the **Win10SBS\Ch05** folder. The introduction includes a complete list of practice files.

Understand files, folders, and libraries

There are no practice tasks for this topic.

Get to know File Explorer

Perform the following tasks:

1. Start File Explorer, and navigate to the practice file folder.

2. Open the **Photos** folder, and then open the **Backgrounds** subfolder.

3. Use the tools on the **Navigation and Search** bar to move up to the **Ch05** folder.

4. In the **Navigation** pane, contract all the expanded storage nodes. Then review the locations in the Navigation pane and ensure you're familiar with each.

5. In the **Navigation** pane, double-click **This PC**. Review the file storage locations that are connected to your computer.

6. On the **View** tab, display the **Navigation pane** menu. If the Navigation pane isn't already configured to display libraries, display them now.

7. Expand the **Libraries** node. Create a new library named **Win10SBS** and ensure that it appears in the Navigation pane.

8. Add the **Backgrounds** subfolder of the **Ch05\Photos** folder to the new **Win10SBS** library.

9. Optimize the **Win10SBS** library for the display of photos. Then assign an icon that you like to the library folder.

10. Hide the **Win10SBS** library from the Navigation pane. Then unhide it.

Change the File Explorer display options

Start File Explorer, and then perform the following tasks:

1. Navigate to the practice file folder and expand its contents in the content pane.

2. Experiment with the settings in the **Panes** group on the **View** tab to hide and redisplay the Navigation pane.

3. Display the **Details** pane. Select a file in the content pane and notice the available details. Select a different type of file, and then select multiple files, noting the details available for each.

4. Display the **Preview** pane and repeat the process in step 3. For each file that displays a preview, observe the preview content and notice the controls available in the Preview pane for scrolling or moving through the preview.

5. Resize the **Preview** pane by dragging its border.

6. Experiment with the settings in the **Layout** group on the **View** tab. Display the content of the practice file folder in each of the eight available layouts. Consider the information provided by each layout and when each would be most or least useful.

7. Display the Details view of the practice file folder content.

8. From the **Add columns** list, navigate to the longer list of columns and select **Dimensions** to add that column to the Details view.

9. Rearrange the columns in the content pane so that the **Dimensions** column is immediately to the right of the **Name** column.

10. Resize all columns to fit the widest item in the column.

11. Remove the **Date Created** and **Dimensions** columns from the Details view.

12. Display item check boxes, file name extensions, and hidden items.

13. Group the items by type.

14. Sort the grouped items alphabetically by name. Then reverse the sort order.

15. Filter the items by using the **Size** filter to display only large items (1-16 MB).

16. Remove the filter, restore the default sort order, and remove the file grouping.

17. Add the **Photos** folder to your Quick Access list.

Find specific files

Display the practice file folder in File Explorer, and then perform the following tasks:

1. Search for a file from the File Explorer search box by using the search term **travel**.

2. Refine the search by narrowing the results to items that are small (between 10 and 100 KB).

3. Save the search for later reference.

4. Return from the **Search Results** folder to the original folder.

Manage folders and files

6

You will find it much easier to locate files and correctly identify them if they are logically organized and given names that clearly describe their contents. You use File Explorer to manage and work with the folders and files that are stored on your computer.

Every file and folder has properties—information that describes the file and its content. Some properties are created automatically by Windows or by the app you create or edit the file in. You can assign other properties that you want.

> **TIP** You can use file properties to automatically populate information within files and in file-management systems such as Microsoft SharePoint. You can display, sort, and group by file properties in File Explorer. For more information, see "Change the File Explorer display options" in Chapter 5, "Explore files and folders."

When managing large files or a lot of files, you can compress them to save space or simply to manage them as one unit.

This chapter guides you through procedures related to creating, renaming, compressing, moving, copying, deleting, and restoring files and folders, and working with folder and file properties.

In this chapter

- Create and rename folders and files
- Compress folders and files
- Move and copy folders and files
- Delete and restore folders and files
- Work with folder and file properties

Create and rename folders and files

Many apps (such as email apps and web browsers) automatically store files in a default location, but most apps allow you to specify storage locations for the files you create. You could save everything in your Documents folder, but that would soon get unwieldy. If you use a logical system for naming and organizing folders and files, you can always find what you need.

One common approach is to store all your private files in subfolders of your Documents folder, and to store all files that you expect to share with others in sub-folders of the Public Documents folder. A benefit of this approach is that Windows can automatically back up these locations to OneDrive or to an external hard drive.

Wherever you store your files, give some thought to a logical naming convention that works for you and within your organization. Here are some things to consider:

- **Unique identification** Ideally, the name of a file or folder will contain all the information that you need to identify it independently of the folder structure you store it in. For example, if you save a purchase order document as 12345. docx in the folder structure Accounting\Documents\Purchase Orders\2017 \October, much of the information is lost when you email the document or otherwise remove it from the folder structure. An informative file name such as PurchaseOrder_12345_2017-10-31 is much more useful and you won't need to store the file in such a complex folder structure.

- **Sort order** File names that incorporate dates will sort in numerical order. To keep them in logical order, enter the date in year-month-day order and use numeric month equivalents. (For example, 2017-10-31 sorts by year, then month, then day, whereas 10-31-2017 sorts by month, then day, then year.)

- **Web addresses** If you store files and folders in the cloud, spaces in the file name or path are converted to the character code *%20*. This presents two problems:

  - When linking to a file online, the path is difficult to parse. For example:

    https://sharepoint.contoso.com/files/purchase%20order%template.docx

  - When downloading files with names that contains spaces, some systems convert the spaces to underscores (_).

  You can avoid these issues by not using spaces in file names.

- **Readability** Long file names, especially those that don't contain spaces, can be difficult to parse. You can maintain descriptive yet readable file names by using internal capitalization (commonly called *camel caps*) or by using underscores or hyphens to separate words. For example:

PayStub_Smith-Jane_2017-10-31

Whatever file naming convention you decide on, use it consistently. If you work within an organization, discuss, agree on, and communicate the naming convention to avoid confusion.

To create a folder

1. In File Explorer, do either of the following:

   - In the content pane, navigate to the location where you want to add the new folder. Then on the **Home** tab, in the **New** group, select **New Folder**.

   - In the **Navigation** pane, right-click the folder to which you want to add the new folder (as a subfolder), point to **New**, and then select **Folder**.

   The default name *New folder* is automatically selected for editing.

2. Enter the name you want to assign to the folder to replace the selected text.

To rename a file or folder in the content pane

1. In the content pane, select the file or folder you want to rename.

2. Do one of the following to activate the name for editing:

   - Select the file or folder again (this equates to a slow double-click).

   - On the **Home** tab, in the **Organize** group, select **Rename**.

   - Right-click the file, and then select **Rename**.

   - Press F2.

3. Enter the new name, and then press Enter.

To rename a file or folder in the Navigation pane

1. Right-click the file or folder, and then select **Rename**.

2. Enter the new name, and then press Enter.

6

Compress folders and files

When you buy a computer these days, it likely comes with a hard drive capable of storing hundreds, if not thousands, of gigabytes (GB) of information. A *gigabyte* is 1 billion bytes, and a byte is a unit of information that is the equivalent of one character. Some of your files will be very small—1 to 2 kilobytes (KB), or 1000 to 2000 characters—and others might be quite large—several megabytes (MB), or several million characters. Small files are easy to copy and move around; large files or large groups of files are more time-consuming to copy and move from one place to another, or to send by email, unless you compress them.

You can compress individual files or entire folders. The result is a compressed folder that is identified by a zipper on its folder icon.

Chapter06.zip

> ✓ **TIP** Compressing is frequently referred to as *zipping*. Compressed folders are also called *zip files*. The term *zip* was adopted by the original file-compression technology developer to indicate that compressed files would move quickly from one location to another.

The reduction in size when you compress a file depends on the compression method and the type of file. Many image file formats are already highly compressed. Microsoft Office file types that end in *x* (.docx, .xlsx, and .pptx, which have been the default file formats since Office 2007) are actually collections of content definition files that have been compressed and given a different extension. Therefore, compressing a folder that contains Word documents or images might have little effect on the folder size.

You open and display the contents of a compressed folder in File Explorer just as you do any other folder. The Extract tool tab on the ribbon indicates that you're displaying the contents of a compressed folder rather than a standard folder.

More button

You can easily add, replace, or remove files within a compressed folder.

To compress one or more files

1. In the content pane, select the file(s) or folder(s) you want to compress.

2. Do either of the following:

   • Right-click any file in the selection, select **Send to**, and then select **Compressed (zipped) folder** to create a compressed folder with the same name as the file you right-clicked.

   • On the **Share** tab, in the **Send** group, select **Zip** to create a compressed folder with the same name as the first selected file.

3. The compressed folder name is selected so that you can change it. Edit the name as necessary, and then press Enter.

To display the contents of a compressed folder

■ In the **Navigation** pane, select the compressed folder.

■ In the content pane, double-click the compressed folder.

To work with files in a compressed folder

■ To add a file or folder, drag it into or onto the compressed folder.

■ To replace a file, drag the new file into the compressed folder and then select **Copy and Replace**.

■ To remove a file or folder, open the compressed folder in File Explorer and then delete the file or folder from the content pane.

To extract all files from a compressed folder

1. Do either of the following:

   • Right-click the compressed folder, and then select **Extract All**.

   • Select or open the compressed folder and then, on the **Extract** tool tab, select **Extract all**.

   The default extraction location is a new folder with the same name as the compressed folder, created in the folder that contains the compressed folder.

	✕
← ▯ Extract Compressed (Zipped) Folders	

   Select a Destination and Extract Files

   Files will be extracted to this folder:

C:\OTSI\Projects\Win10SBSv3\Chapter06	Browse...

   ☑ Show extracted files when complete

2. If you want to extract the files to a folder other than the one indicated in the Files Will Be Extracted To This Folder box, select **Browse** and then, in the **Select a destination** dialog box, navigate to the folder you want.

3. In the **Extract Compressed (Zipped) Folders** dialog box, select **Extract**.

To extract selected files from a compressed folder

1. Open the compressed folder in File Explorer.

2. Select the file or files that you want to extract.

3. Do one of the following:

   • Drag the selection from the content pane to the folder into which you want to extract the files.

   • On the **Extract** tool tab, in the **Extract To** gallery, select the folder you want to extract the selected files to.

   • On the **Extract** tool tab, in the **Extract To** group, select the **More** button, select **Choose location**, and then in the **Copy Items** dialog box, browse to the folder and select **Copy**.

Move and copy folders and files

It is often necessary to move or copy folders and files from one location to another. When you move something to a new location, it is essentially deleted from the original location and copied to the new location. When you copy something to a new location, a copy remains in each location.

Before you move or copy items, you need to select them. There are various ways to select individual or multiple files in the File Explorer content pane. When multiple files are selected, the Details pane indicates the number of items and the total size of the selection. (Because the file sizes in the content pane are rounded up, the total in the Details pane will be more accurate.) If both folders and files are included in the selection, the Details pane indicates the number of items but not the cumulative size. You have the option of displaying check boxes in File Explorer to make it easy to select multiple files.

Select All check box

SEE ALSO For information about the File Explorer Details pane, see "Get to know File Explorer" in Chapter 5, "Explore files and folders."

When you cut or copy a folder or file, the item is stored in a storage area called the *Clipboard* so that you can then paste one or more copies of it elsewhere. In addition to copying files and folders to other locations, you can also make copies of files in the original folder; when you do, File Explorer appends - *Copy* to the original file name to create the new file name.

When you move or copy a folder or file by dragging it, the item is not stored on the Clipboard.

To select all the items in a folder

■ On the **Home** tab, in the **Select** group, select **Select All**.

■ Press Ctrl+A.

■ When item check boxes are shown, select the check box to the left of the first column header.

To select multiple contiguous items

■ Select the first item, hold down the Shift key, and then select the last item in the group you want to select.

 TIP It sometimes helps to group or sort the items to gather the ones you want to select.

To select multiple noncontiguous items

■ Select the first item, and then hold down the Ctrl key and select each additional item.

■ When item check boxes are shown, select the check box to the left of each item you want to select.

To copy selected items to the Clipboard

■ On the **Home** tab, in the **Clipboard** group, select **Copy**.

■ Right-click the selection, and then select **Copy**.

■ Press Ctrl+C.

To cut selected items to the Clipboard

■ On the **Home** tab, in the **Clipboard** group, select **Cut**.

■ Right-click the selection, and then select **Cut**.

■ Press Ctrl+X.

To paste items from the Clipboard

- On the **Home** tab, in the **Clipboard** group, select **Paste**.

- Right-click a blank area in the folder, and then select **Paste**.

- Press Ctrl+V.

To move selected items to a different folder

- On the **Home** tab, in the **Organize** group, select **Move to** and then either select the destination folder or select **Choose location** and browse to the destination folder.

- Cut the files to the Clipboard, navigate to the new folder, and then paste the files into the folder.

- Display the original folder and the new folder in two File Explorer windows. Use the left mouse button to drag the selected items to the new location.

- Display the original folder and the new folder. Use the right mouse button to drag the selected items to the new location. Then select **Move Here** on the menu that appears when you release the mouse button.

To copy selected items to a different folder

- On the **Home** tab, in the **Organize** group, select **Copy to**, and then either select the destination folder or select **Choose location** and browse to the destination folder.

- Copy the files to the Clipboard, navigate to the new folder, and then paste the files into the folder.

- Display the original folder and the new folder in two File Explorer windows. Hold down the Ctrl key and use the left mouse button to drag the selected items to the new location. Release the mouse button, and then release the Ctrl key.

- Display the original folder and the new folder. Use the right mouse button to drag the selected items to the new location. Then select **Copy Here** on the menu that appears when you release the mouse button.

 TIP You can make copies of another item in the same folder; the copies are appended with numbers to give them unique file names.

Delete and restore folders and files

Removing a file from your computer is a two-step process: You first delete the file, which moves it to the Recycle Bin—a holding area on your hard drive from which it's possible to restore an item if you realize you need it. Then you empty the Recycle Bin, which permanently erases its contents. By default, Windows prompts you to confirm the deletion of files and folders. If you prefer, you can turn off this setting.

> **TIP** If you aren't sure whether you will need some files, consider backing them up to a DVD, an external hard drive, or an inexpensive cloud-based storage service such as Microsoft OneDrive.

There are some situations in which deleting something does not send it to the Recycle Bin. The most common are deleting from a shared network drive or an external USB drive.

If you realize immediately that you mistakenly deleted a file, you can often recover it by pressing Ctrl+Z to undo the deletion. If you realize it later, you can usually recover a deleted file or folder by opening the Recycle Bin, locating the item, and restoring it. You can recover a deleted file from the Recycle Bin at any time until you empty the Recycle Bin. You can't open and work with files directly from the Recycle Bin.

You can search the contents of files in the Recycle Bin just as you can search the contents of files in other folders. If you activate the search box when the Recycle Bin is selected, both the Search and Recycle Bin tool tabs are displayed. Assuming that deleted files are listed in the content pane, you can search for any that match the text you enter in the search box.

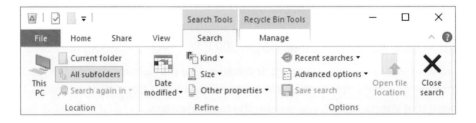

> **TIP** If you want to occasionally bypass the Recycle Bin, you can do so by holding down the Shift key when you press the Delete key or select the Delete button.

To delete an item

1. In the content pane, select the file or folder.

2. Do either of the following:

    *   Press the Delete key.

    *   On the **Home** tab, in the **Organize** group, select **Delete**.

3. In the **Delete File** dialog box that opens, select **Yes** to confirm the deletion and send the file to the Recycle Bin.

 TIP You cannot delete a file by pressing the Backspace key.

To restore a deleted item

1. On the desktop, double-click the **Recycle Bin**.

2. Locate the file you want to restore. If it isn't at the top of the list, here are a couple of tricks:

    *   Sort by Name, Original Location, Date Deleted, or another column, if you know any of that information.

    *   If you remember part of its name, enter that into the search box. This opens the Search tool tab.

3. Select the files you want to recover.

4. On the **Recycle Bin Tools** tool tab, in the **Restore** group, select **Restore the selected items** to return the items to the location from which they were deleted.

To turn off confirmation when deleting items

1. On the desktop, right-click the **Recycle Bin**, and then select **Properties** to display the Recycle Bin Properties dialog box.

2. Clear the **Display delete confirmation dialog** check box.

3. Select **OK** to apply your changes.

6

Recycle Bin size

The Recycle Bin is intended to be a place to temporarily store files that you think you no longer need. Keep in mind, however, that the contents of the Recycle Bin take up space on your hard drive. By default, 10 percent of a drive up to 40 GB in size is allocated to the Recycle Bin, plus 5 percent of any space over 40 GB. If your hard drive is divided into partitions and the Recycle Bin is on a 10 GB partition, only 1 GB is available for deleted files.

When deleting a very large file, Windows might inform you that the file is too large to store in the Recycle Bin and that it will delete it permanently. If you're sure you won't need to recover the file, you can allow Windows to delete the file; if not, you can cancel the deletion. On a small hard drive or drive partition, you might see this "too large" message quite often.

You might need to restrict the amount of space that is used by the Recycle Bin, or you might want to instruct Windows to bypass the Recycle Bin entirely. Both of these options are available from the Recycle Bin Properties dialog box.

To manage the Recycle Bin actions, locate the Recycle Bin on the desktop, right-click it, and then select Properties. Set the maximum size as you see fit, and then select OK to apply your changes.

Work with folder and file properties

Every folder and file has certain properties that describe it or determine how it can be used. Although you can see some of these properties in Details view in File Explorer, you can see the full set by selecting that file or folder in File Explorer and selecting the Properties command on the Home tab.

The Properties dialog boxes for folders and files are similar, but not identical.

View folder properties

The Properties dialog box for a folder typically has four tabs; five if version history is enabled. The tabs are:

6

- **General** The General tab displays the folder's name, some statistics about it, and a few attributes. You can edit the name and the attributes, though it is easier to edit the name in File Explorer.

The Read-only attribute is one that you will change most often. The Read-only attribute can be selected, cleared, or marked with a square box. If the attribute is selected, all the files in the folder and all the subfolders are read-only. If the attribute is cleared, all the files in the folder and all the subfolders are editable.

And if the attribute is marked with a square, the folder and subfolders contain a mix of read-only and editable files.

- **Sharing** Options on this tab control whether a folder is shared.

- **Security** You can use the options on this tab to assign the folder's access permissions to specific users or groups.

- **Previous Versions** If you have enabled File History in Control Panel or PC Settings, all the files in specified folders are backed up periodically. Each backup is separate, so you can view and restore a specific version. You can use this tab to review the contents of the folder after each backup.

> **SEE ALSO** For information about file versions and version history, see "Back up data" in Chapter 15, "Protect your computer and data."

- **Customize** The Properties dialog box for some folder types includes a Customize tab, which has some interesting options that you can set.

Screens Properties	✕

General | Sharing | Security | Previous Versions | **Customize**

What kind of folder do you want?
Optimize this folder for:

Pictures ⌄

☑ Also apply this template to all subfolders

Folder pictures
Choose a file to show on this folder icon.

Choose File...

Restore Default

Folder icons
You can change the folder icon. If you change the icon, it will no longer show a preview of the folder's contents.

Change Icon...

- **Optimize this folder for** On this menu you can set the folder to one of five types: General, Documents, Pictures, Music, or Videos. This setting determines the file layout when you open the folder and whether a tool tab is displayed on the File Explorer ribbon when you select the folder.

- **Folder pictures** Use this setting to assign an image to be displayed for the folder in the Details pane, or when the folder appears in an icon view that is larger than Small Icons.

- **Folder icons** Use this setting to replace the default icon with one that you choose.

File Properties dialog boxes are very similar to those for folders. As with folder Properties dialog boxes, the content depends on the type of file you have selected. The file Properties dialog box includes a Details tab, which isn't present in folder Properties dialog boxes. The information on this tab varies with the file type. The tab also provides an option to remove personal information.

Remove file properties

Selecting the Properties button on the Home tab opens the Properties dialog box for the selected item. If you select the arrow below the Properties button instead of the Properties button itself, you are presented with two options (if you have selected a folder, only the first option is enabled):

- **Properties** Selecting this option displays the Properties dialog box for the selected item and is the same as selecting the Properties button.

■ **Remove Properties** Selecting this displays a dialog box in which you can choose to remove all the properties that can be removed, or only selected ones. One reason to do this is to remove personal information that is stored with some file types.

Remove Properties

Some of these properties might contain personal information.
What personal information might be in a file?

◉ Create a copy with all possible properties removed
○ Remove the following properties from this file:

Property	Value	
Description		
☐ Title	Lab 1	
☐ Subject	Data Analysis in Excel	
☐ Tags	40485; Analyzing and Visual...	
☐ Categories	Course; Lab	
☐ Comments		
Origin		
☐ Authors	Jaime Odell	
☐ Last saved by	Joan Lambert	
☐ Revision number	4	
☐ Version number		
☐ Program name	Microsoft Office Word	

Select All

OK   Cancel

Some file types have no properties that can be removed. Others, such as Word documents, have a long list.

> **TIP** The information displayed in the Remove Properties dialog box varies depending on the type of file selected when you choose the command.

To display the Properties dialog box for a folder or file

1. In File Explorer, select the folder or file you want to display properties for.

2. Do any of the following:

   - Right-click the file or folder, and then on the shortcut menu, select **Properties**.

   - On the **Home** tab, in the **Open** group, select the **Properties** button) not the arrow).

   - On the **Home** tab, select the **Properties** arrow, and then select **Properties**.

To remove personal information from a file

1. In File Explorer, select the file from which you want to remove personal information.

2. Do any of the following:

    • On the **Home** tab, in the **Open** group, select the **Properties** arrow, and then **Remove properties**.

    • In the **Open** group, select the **Properties** button to open the file's **Properties** dialog box, and then on the **Details** tab, select the **Remove Properties and Personal Information** link at the bottom.

    • Right-click the file and select **Properties**, and then at the bottom of the **Details** tab, select **Remove Properties and Personal Information**.

3. In the **Remove Properties** dialog box, do either of the following:

    • Select **Create a copy with all possible properties removed**, and select **OK**.

    • Select **Remove the following properties from this file**, select the properties you want to remove, and select **OK**.

Key points

■ Choose a naming convention for files and folders that works for you and your organization, and apply it consistently.

■ You can compress folders and files to save space or to manage multiple items as a single unit.

■ You can move files and folders between locations in File Explorer, or make multiple copies of files.

■ If you accidentally delete a file, you can restore it from the Recycle Bin. Restoring a file returns it to the location from which it was deleted.

■ You can display, edit, and remove file properties from within File Explorer.

Practice tasks

Before you can complete these practice tasks, you need to copy the book's practice files to your computer. The practice files for these tasks are located in the **Win10SBS\Ch06** folder. The introduction includes a complete list of practice files.

Create and rename folders and files

Display the practice file folder in File Explorer, and then perform the following tasks:

1. In the practice file folder, create a subfolder and name it **MyFiles**.

2. Rename the **MyFiles** folder as **MySBSFiles**.

3. Rename the **Events** document as **Newsletter**.

Compress folders and files

Display the practice file folder in File Explorer, and then perform the following tasks:

1. In the content pane, select the three **Password** files.

2. Save the selected files to a compressed folder, and name it **PasswordPhotos**.

3. Extract the files from the **PasswordPhotos** compressed folder to the **Photos** folder.

Move and copy folders and files

Display the practice file folder in File Explorer, and then perform the following tasks:

1. Select all the items in the folder, and then release the selection.

2. Select three items that are next to each other (listed contiguously) in the folder, and then release the selection.

3. Select three items that are not next to each other in the folder, and then release the selection.

4. Copy the **Expenses** workbook to the Clipboard. Open the **Reports** folder, and paste a copy of the **Expenses** workbook in that folder.

5. Return to the **Ch06** folder. Cut the **Survey** document to the Clipboard, and then paste it into the **Files** subfolder.

Delete and restore folders and files

Display the practice file folder in File Explorer, and then perform the following tasks:

1. Delete the **Photos** folder and all its contents.

2. Navigate to the Recycle Bin. Then restore the **Photos** folder and all its contents.

Work with folder and file properties

Display the practice file folder in File Explorer, and then perform the following tasks:

1. Display the properties of the **Photos** folder.

2. Display the properties of the **Password01** file.

3. Display the properties of the **Expenses** workbook. Determine whether the file is read-only. If it is, change that property.

4. Add your name as one of the properties of the **Expenses** workbook. Then use the commands in the **Remove Properties** dialog box to remove that property from the file.

Part 3

Devices and resources

Manage peripheral devices

7

If your computer is a desktop computer, you'll need to connect a few peripheral hardware devices—such as a monitor, a keyboard, and a mouse—to it before you can use it. Other common peripheral devices are printers, speakers, scanners, fax machines, external storage drives, and external media drives such as DVD drives. Depending on your interests and how you use your computer, you might also use devices such as a microphone, webcam, fingerprint reader, joystick, touchpad, or drawing tablet. The point of all these devices, of course, is to make your computing experience more productive, more enjoyable, and (hopefully) simpler.

Many people now use laptops as their primary computer at home or at work. Laptops have the basic peripherals built in, but you can also connect an external monitor, keyboard, mouse, and other peripherals to your laptop to make it feel more like a desktop environment.

In this chapter, you'll work with a computer's most common external devices—the monitor, mouse, keyboard, printer, speakers, and microphone. In the process, you'll learn about plug-and-play devices, device drivers, and ports.

This chapter guides you through procedures related to installing peripheral devices, locating device information, displaying your desktop on multiple screens, setting up audio devices, changing the way your mouse and keyboard work, and managing printer connections.

In this chapter

- Understand peripheral devices
- Locate device information
- Display your desktop on multiple screens
- Set up audio devices
- Change the way your mouse works
- Change the way your keyboard works
- Manage printer connections

215

Understand peripheral devices

Peripheral devices are things that you can add to your computer to extend its functionality or power, or to serve as an interface between it and human users. There are two general types of peripheral devices:

- **Internal** You install these inside your computer's case and are likely to consider them part of the computer. Internal devices can come in the form of an expansion card, or a new hard drive or DVD drive. For example, you might install an additional video card to improve your computer's graphics capabilities or support multiple displays.

- **External** You attach these to your computer by connecting them to ports on the outside of your computer's case.

Peripheral device terminology

Ports are outlets in your computer's case through which various types of information can pass. Ports come in many shapes and sizes, each designed for a specific purpose. A typical modern computer has a VGA or HDMI port to which you can connect a monitor, an Ethernet port to which you can connect a network cable, and several USB ports to which you can connect a variety of devices. The computer might also support wireless connections through Wi-Fi, Bluetooth, and radio waves (typically used for wireless keyboards and mice).

An older computer might have a DVI monitor port, PS/2 keyboard and mouse ports, a parallel printer port, or an IEEE 1394 port to which you can connect high-speed devices such as digital video cameras. But you probably won't be running Windows 10 on one of these computers.

If you find that you don't have enough ports to connect all the devices you want to use with your computer, you don't have to limit your device choices. Here are three options for expanding your connection capacity:

- **Install extra ports** You can purchase an expansion card with more ports. After turning off your desktop computer and removing its cover, you insert the card into one of the available expansion slots. When you turn the power back on, Windows 10 detects and installs the new ports.

- **Use a hub** You can connect a multiport hub to your computer and then connect multiple devices to the hub, enabling all the devices to share that single connection. Hubs are available for network, USB, and other connection types.

- **Use more wireless devices** A wireless version of almost every external peripheral you might want to use is now available. You can connect to a printer, scanner, fax, keyboard, mouse, or hard drive without using a cable. You can listen to audio and use a microphone without plugging anything into your computer.

Install peripheral devices

Installing a new peripheral device is usually easy and intuitive, because most of these devices are now *plug and play*. Plug and play quite literally means that you can connect devices to the computer and begin using them. Plug-and-play devices include printers, external hard drives, flash drives, fingerprint readers, smart card readers, cameras, and many others.

When you connect a device to your computer, Windows 10 identifies the device and searches through its database of device drivers to locate the appropriate driver for the device. *Device drivers* are files that let Windows communicate with your device. Drivers can be specific to an individual device or to a family of devices (such as all HP LaserJet printers), and they are often specific to a certain version of Windows.

Windows 10 doesn't automatically support all devices (no operating system does), but it natively supports more devices than any previous version. Sometimes old hardware is simply incompatible, or the manufacturer hasn't chosen to provide an updated Windows 10 driver. You can check the compatibility of your current devices or one you are thinking about buying from the Hardware Compatibility Checker at *www.microsoft.com /accessories/support/compatibility*.

If Windows 10 doesn't have a current driver for your device, it asks you to provide the driver. You might have the driver on an installation disc provided by the device manufacturer. Alternatively, Windows can search the internet for the driver, or you can visit the device manufacturer's website.

> **✓ TIP** If your device is in the list of compatible devices in the Hardware Compatibility Checker, allowing Windows 10 to search for the drivers online is almost always the fastest and easiest way to get them.

Some devices come with installation software that expands the devices' capabilities. For example, you might connect an all-in-one printer/scanner/fax/copy machine to your computer and be able to print, fax, and copy without installing additional software. However, to scan documents to electronic files, you might need to install the software provided with the device.

Boost your memory

If you want to upgrade your Windows 10 computer's memory, you can do so without physically installing additional RAM in your computer case. The Windows ReadyBoost feature enables your Windows 10 computer to use a qualifying USB flash drive as a memory-expansion device. For best performance, you should use a USB drive (also referred to as a USB stick or thumb drive) with available space of at least double the amount of memory that is installed in your computer, and preferably four times as much memory. You can use up to eight flash memory devices synchronously (with a total of up to 256 gigabytes [GB] of memory) on one computer—if you have enough ports.

ReadyBoost is easy to use. Insert the USB drive in a USB port, right-click the drive in File Explorer, and select Properties. On the ReadyBoost tab of the Properties dialog box, Windows suggests the amount of flash drive memory you can dedicate to ReadyBoost, and you select the amount you want to use. When ReadyBoost is enabled, Windows 10 creates a file named ReadyBoost.sfcache in the root of the flash memory device.

TIP To use more than 4 GB on a single flash drive, format it with the NTFS file system.

If one or more solid-state drives (SSDs) are connected to your computer, ReadyBoost might be unavailable, because some solid-state drives are faster than flash memory devices and are unlikely to benefit from ReadyBoost.

Locate device information

You can display information about the devices that are connected to your computer from the Devices page of the Settings window. On this page, Windows 10 displays information about printers, scanners, projectors, the mouse or touchpad, the keyboard, Bluetooth and USB devices, and other devices that are connected to the computer.

The information that is available from this page is specific to the hardware and peripheral devices that are connected to your computer either directly or through a network.

> **SEE ALSO** Display connections are managed from the System page of the Settings window. For information about displays, see "Customize device display settings" in Chapter 12, "Manage computer settings," and "Display your desktop on multiple screens" later in this chapter.

You can add devices to your system by selecting the Add button at the top of the appropriate settings pane and following the steps described in the wizard to install the compatible device drivers on your computer. You can remove the connection to a device by selecting it in the list and then selecting Remove Device. Doing so doesn't delete the device's drivers from your computer, so if you add the device again later, the process is a bit simpler.

Adding a device means more than just connecting to the device physically or wirelessly; it means that Windows has confirmed that the drivers are correct and it can communicate with the device. What you are really adding it to is the list of available devices that are displayed when you choose to do something that requires a device. For example, when the Print dialog box is displayed, all the available printers are listed so you can choose the one you want. When you remove a device, you're just removing it from that list.

When a device isn't working properly, you can get information about the device and its drivers, and often troubleshoot the problem, from the Device Manager window.

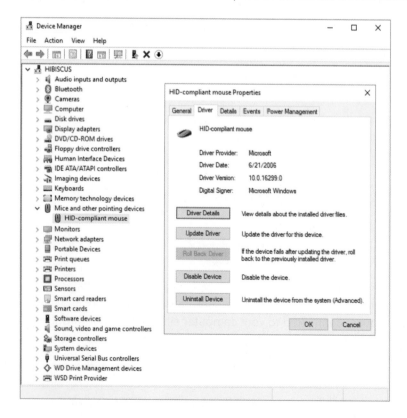

You can double-click any device to display its Properties dialog box, in which you can explore detailed information about any device.

You can also display information about the hardware, software, and components that form your computer system, in the searchable System Information window.

To open the Settings window

- Select the **Start** button, and then select **Settings** on the menu.

> ✓ **TIP** When the Settings window opens, its icon is displayed on the taskbar. To make it easier to open this window in the future, you can right-click that icon and select Pin To Taskbar.

To display information about installed devices

1. Do either of the following to start Device Manager:

   - Right-click the **Start** button and then, on the **Quick Link** menu, select **Device Manager**.

   - Enter **Device Manager** in the taskbar search box, and then select the **Device Manager** Control Panel app.

> ✓ **TIP** There are various ways to do almost everything in Windows 10. These procedures introduce different approaches. Always feel free to explore each approach more fully on your own.

2. In the **Device Manager** window, expand any category to display the devices in that category that are installed on your computer.

3. To display information about a specific device, double-click the device (or right-click the device, and then select **Properties**).

 IMPORTANT Don't change any of the settings unless you have the experience necessary to anticipate the consequences of the change.

To display information about hardware, software, and components

1. Enter system information in the taskbar search box and then, in the search results, select the **System Information** desktop app.

2. In the **System Information** window, expand any category to display information about the system components that are installed on your computer.

Display your desktop on multiple screens

A basic computer system includes one display that shows your Windows desktop. This is sufficient for many computing experiences. However, in some situations, you might find it convenient, or even necessary, to extend your desktop across multiple displays or duplicate your desktop on a secondary display (such as a remote monitor or video projector screen). You can easily add one, two, or more displays to your computer system.

You can physically connect as many displays as you have ports available; ports can be provided by video cards, a multiport video card, or USB ports. Windows 10 also natively supports Miracast—a wireless technology you can use to project a screen image from your Windows 10 device to a television, projector, or other device that also supports Miracast. Miracast does not require a wireless network or use your network bandwidth. Many modern internet-connected televisions support screen casting, so you can, for example, use this technology to play a slideshow or video (with audio) on televisions throughout your house during a get-together. (Or, for the video gamers in the house, to display your championship game on the big screen so your friends don't have to watch over your shoulder.) No special app is required.

You connect the display to the computer by using a cable with the appropriate port connectors on it, or, if you are using Miracast, wirelessly. If you don't have a cable with connectors that match the available ports, you can use an adapter to match the cable connector type to the port type. You then inform Windows where the displays are physically located so you can easily move on-screen objects between displays.

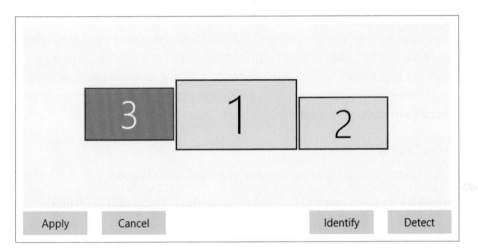

When you physically connect a secondary display to your computer, Windows 10 detects the device and, if your computer system already has the necessary drivers, automatically extends the desktop to the newly connected display.

After connecting the display, you can change the way Windows displays information on the devices. Options include:

- **Duplicate these displays** The same content appears on both displays. This is useful when you are giving a presentation and are not facing the screen (for example, when standing at a podium facing an audience) or want to have a closer view of the content you're displaying.

- **Extend these displays** Your desktop expands to cover both displays. The Windows Taskbar appears only on the screen you designate as the primary display.

- **Show desktop only on** Content appears only on the selected display. This is useful if you are working on a laptop or tablet that is connected to a second, larger display.

When you are working on a computer that is connected to two displays, Windows designates one as the primary display and the other as the secondary display. The Welcome screen and taskbar automatically appear on the primary display, as do most app windows when they first open. You can set the taskbar to appear on one or all displays, and drag selected windows between displays. You configure these settings separately, from the Taskbar pane of the Personalization settings page.

By default, Display 2 appears to the right of Display 1. When you move the mouse pointer horizontally from screen to screen, it should leave the right edge of the left screen and enter the left edge of the right screen at vertically the same point. If your displays are not physically the same size, are set to different screen resolutions, or are not placed level with each other, you can change the alignment of the displays so that the pointer moves cleanly between them.

To open the Display settings pane

- In the **Settings** window, select **System**, and then select **Display**.

- Right-click an empty area of the desktop, and then select **Display settings**.

> ✅ **TIP** If a technical problem involving the connection between your computer and one display occurs when your desktop is extended across two or more displays, you might find yourself in the situation of having windows open on the inactive displays. To retrieve a hidden window, press Alt+Tab until the window you want to move is selected in Task view, and then press Shift+Win+Right Arrow (or Left Arrow) to move the active window to the next display.

To extend or duplicate your desktop across multiple displays

- In the **Display** settings pane, select an option from the **Multiple displays** list (which is available only if a second display is connected), and then select **Apply**.

> ✅ **TIP** If you later want to change the Multiple Display settings, you can do so quickly by pressing Win+P. A Project pane slides out from the right side of your main display, offering the same options to extend or duplicate the display.

To extend your screen to a TV or remote display by using a Miracast connection

1. Make sure the remote display is turned on and the dongle is connected (if applicable).

2. Display the **Display** settings pane.

3. In the **Multiple displays** sections, select **Connect to a wireless display**.

   The Connect pane slides out from the right side of your screen and displays a list of wireless display and audio devices within range. Select the device you want to connect to.

> ✅ **TIP** Wireless screen extensions are not made automatically, so they are a bit more effort to initially establish and must be reestablished each time you restart your computer. (Wired connections are restored with the previous settings each time you restart.) After setting up the connection, you can customize the display settings.

7

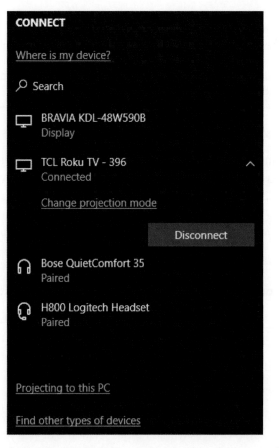

4. Accept any connection prompts that appear on the remote screen.

   The remote screen displays a message telling you that it is connecting to the computer. After the connection is made, the desktop extends to the remote screen, and you can arrange the displays as you want.

To ascertain which screen is the primary display

■ In the **Display** settings pane, below the **Select and rearrange displays** preview area, select **Identify** to show the numbers from the display icons on the screens that they represent.

To change which display is designated as the primary

1. In the **Display** settings pane, in the **Select and rearrange displays** preview area, select the secondary display.

2. In the **Multiple displays** area, select the **Make this my main display** check box, and then select **Apply**.

To adjust the relative position of the displays

1. In the **Display** settings pane, drag the rectangle representing Display 2 to the location you want it to be in relation to Display 1. Try to align the display rectangles so that the arrangement resembles the alignment of the physical displays.

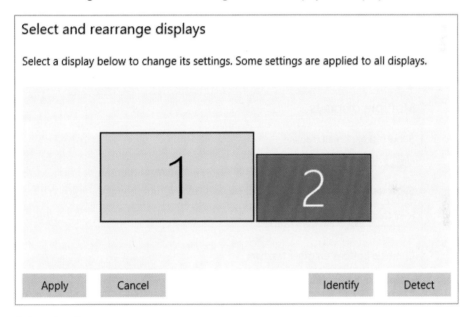

2. Select **Apply**.

> ✓ **TIP** After rearranging the display icons, you can judge whether the displays are appropriately aligned by moving the pointer between the screens. Ideally, the pointer will remain on the same horizontal or vertical plane when you do so.

> 🔍 **SEE ALSO** For information about changing screen resolution and increasing the size of on-screen elements, see "Customize device display settings" in Chapter 12, "Manage computer settings."

To specify the position of the taskbar on multiple displays

1. Right-click an empty area of the taskbar, select **Taskbar settings** to display the Taskbar pane of the Personalization settings page, and then scroll to the **Multiple Displays** section.

> ⚠ **IMPORTANT** The controls in the Multiple Displays section are active only when multiple displays are connected to your computer.

2. In the **Multiple displays** section of the **Taskbar** settings pane, do either of the following:

   - If you want to extend the taskbar across the screens, turn on **Show taskbar on all displays**.

   - In the **Show taskbar buttons on** list, select the location where you want to display the working taskbar content.

Multiple displays

Show taskbar on all displays

🔘 On

Show taskbar buttons on

All taskbars ⌄

Combine buttons on other taskbars

Always, hide labels ⌄

Set up audio devices

Computers are no longer devices used primarily to produce traditional business documents such as letters, reports, and worksheets. You can use your computer for multimedia activities such as listening to music, watching movies, or playing games, and you can create sound-enhanced documents such as presentations and videos. Even if you're not likely to work with these types of files, your productivity might be diminished if you cannot hear the sound effects used by Windows 10 to alert you to events such as the arrival of email messages. And you'll need speakers and a microphone if you want to participate in video conferences or use your computer to place telephone calls.

Expand your laptop or tablet with peripheral devices

Laptops and tablets are useful when you want to be able to move around with your computer—from room to room, from work to home, or from city to city.

Although laptops can offer fast computing and large-capacity hard disks, you might have to deal with a smaller screen, a smaller keyboard, and a touchpad or stylus instead of a standard mouse. Many "ultra-light" laptops don't have internal CD or DVD drives.

Carrying a full-size monitor, keyboard, and mouse when you travel with your portable computer is not always convenient, but adding full-size peripherals is a great way to improve your computing experience when you're using your laptop in your office or at home. If you use a laptop so that you have a seamless transition between work and home, you can set up a monitor, keyboard, and mouse at each location for a relatively small sum of money. You then have the best of both worlds—mobile computing and a full-size setup.

Instead of connecting your hardware devices to your laptop through a USB port or wirelessly, you could connect the devices to a docking station or USB hub, and then connect your computer to that whenever you want to use the devices.

When you attach an external monitor to your laptop, you might at first see the same content on both displays, or the content might appear only on the laptop display. To change which display shows your desktop, use the techniques described in "To change which display is designated as the primary" earlier in this topic.

7

If you want to use external audio input and output devices, you can connect them to your computer either through the audio jacks, through USB ports, or through Bluetooth or wireless connections. USB-connected microphones generally produce cleaner audio because the processing is done externally to the PC, so the sound isn't subject to as much electronic interference. This is particularly important in text-to-speech conversion.

Desktop computers have audio output jacks (usually found on the back of the computer case) and might also have dedicated headphone jacks (either on the front or on the back of the case). Laptop computers have headphone jacks and microphone jacks, or on rare occasions one jack that handles both output and input.

> ✓ **TIP** The audio output jack might be indicated by a small speaker icon, an arrow symbol, or the words Audio or Audio/Out. On desktop computer cases that feature standard component color-coding, the audio output jack is light green, the headphone jack is light orange, and the audio input jack is pink. This color-coding simplifies the process of locating the correct jacks. Some audio device connection cables are color-coded to match.

With the rapid evolution of internet-based communications, digital video, and speech-to-text technologies, microphones are being used more commonly with business and home computer systems. Microphones come in a variety of types, such as the following:

- Freestanding microphones

- Headset microphones with built-in headphones that allow more private communication and consistent recording quality

- Boom microphones with a single headset speaker

If you will be recording a lot of speech or using the Windows Speech Recognition feature, consider investing in a good-quality microphone. To get the highest quality sound, it's critical that you choose the type of microphone that fits your needs. Headset and boom microphones maintain a constant distance between the microphone and your mouth, which helps to maintain a more consistent sound level than a stationary microphone.

The Speech Recognition feature in Windows 10 includes a very capable speech recognition engine. After you set up speech recognition, you can use it to control your computer and enter text into most apps where you would normally type it. Windows 10 also features Cortana, a service that is designed to be your new digital assistant and can respond to your voice instructions.

> 🔍 **SEE ALSO** For information about configuring your Windows 10 computer for Cortana, see Chapter 9, "Get assistance from Cortana," and for speech recognition, see "Manage speech settings" in Chapter 12, "Manage computer settings."

When you connect an audio device to your Windows 10 computer, a notification might appear briefly and then be stored with other notifications in the Action Center.

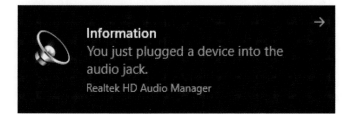

Information
You just plugged a device into the
audio jack.
Realtek HD Audio Manager

To switch between audio playback devices

1. In the notification area of the taskbar, right-click the **Sound** icon (labeled with a speaker), and then select **Playback devices** to display the Playback tab of the Sound dialog box.

2. Select the speakers, headphones, or other playback device you want to use, and then select **Set Default**.

To manage audio playback device settings

- On the **Playback** tab of the **Sound** dialog box, select the device you want to manage, and then select **Properties** to display settings that you can configure manually.

Or

1. On the **Playback** tab of the **Sound** dialog box, select the device you want to manage, and then select **Configure** to start the Speaker Setup wizard.

> **TIP** A configuration appears twice in the list if the audio channel has multiple speaker-arrangement options.

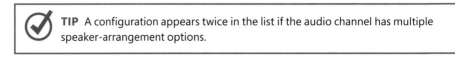

2. On the **Choose your configuration** page, select the appropriate audio channel, and select **Test**. Then select each speaker in the speaker setup diagram.

    An image representing sound waves appears next to each speaker as the wizard plays a sound through that speaker. If a sound is not audible each time the sound waves appear, or if the sound plays through a speaker other than the one indicated in the wizard, verify that the speakers are properly connected and test again.

3. Select **Next** to display the Select Full-Range Speakers page.

4. In some configurations, the front left and right speakers, or the surround speakers, are full-range speakers that produce the entire audio range and include a subwoofer unit to enhance bass output. If your speaker configuration includes full-range speakers, select the check box for those speakers. Then select **Next**.

5. On the **Configuration complete** page, select **Finish**, and then select **OK** to close the Sound dialog box.

To switch between audio recording devices

1. In the notification area of the taskbar, right-click the **Sound** icon, and then **Recording devices** to display the Recording tab of the Sound dialog box.

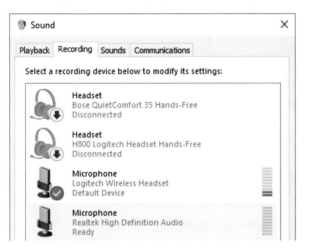

2. Select the microphone, headset, or other recording device you want to use, and then select **Set Default**.

To manage audio recording device settings

- On the **Recording** tab of the **Sound** dialog box, select the device you want to manage, and then select **Properties** to display settings that you can configure manually.

Or

1. On the **Recording** tab of the **Sound** dialog box, select the device you want to manage, and then select **Configure** to open the Speech Recognition window of Control Panel.

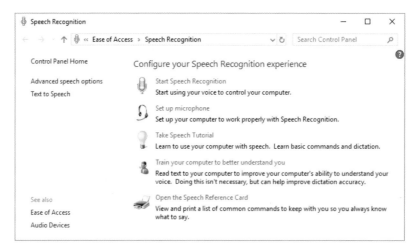

2. In the **Speech Recognition** window, select **Set up microphone** to start the Microphone Setup Wizard.

× Microphone Setup Wizard

What type of microphone is Microphone (Logitech Wireless Headset)?

◉ **Headset Microphone**
Best suited for speech recognition, you wear this on your head.

○ **Desktop Microphone**
These microphones sit on the desk.

○ **Other**
Such as array microphones and microphones built into other devices.

Next   Cancel

3. Select the type of microphone you are using, and then select **Next**.

> **TIP** You can return to the previous wizard page at any time by selecting the arrow in the upper-left corner of the wizard.

4. On the **Set up your microphone** page, follow the instructions to correctly position the microphone, and then select **Next**.

5. On the **Adjust the volume** page, read the microphone test paragraph aloud in your normal speaking voice. Or, just for fun, you might try singing a couple of lines from your favorite song! Any audio input delivered at the volume you'll usually use when using the microphone will work.

As you speak (or sing), the volume gauge moves in response to your voice.

> **TIP** If the volume gauge does not move, your microphone might be incorrectly connected, malfunctioning, or incompatible with your computer. If this happens, hold the microphone close to your mouth and speak loudly; if the recording meter moves slightly, the connection is good, and the problem is compatibility between your microphone and your computer. You might be able to solve this problem by downloading new device drivers from the microphone manufacturer's website, or it might be simpler to replace the microphone.

6. When you finish reading the paragraph, select **Next**.

7. If it seems necessary to repeat the input sample, do so. When you're satisfied with the results, select **Next** on each page until the wizard confirms that the microphone is set up. On the last page of the wizard, select **Finish**.

Change the way your mouse works

In the beginning, a computer mouse consisted of a shell with one clickable button and a rubber ball on the bottom that correlated your mouse movements with a pointer on the screen. Nowadays, mice come in many shapes and sizes, employing a variety of functions, buttons, wheels, and connection methods.

Windows 10 offers enhanced wheel support that allows for smooth vertical scrolling and, on some mice, horizontal scrolling. Check the manufacturer's documentation to see whether your mouse can take advantage of this technology. Even if it can't, you can still customize your mouse settings in various ways to optimize the way it works with Windows.

You can change the function performed by each of the buttons and the wheel, if your mouse has one, in addition to the appearance of the pointer in its various states, and its functionality. If you want, you can allow the appearance of the mouse pointer in Windows 10 to be controlled by the visual theme.

> **TIP** If you have a high-tech mouse, it might come with software you can install that extends its functionality beyond what the Settings window or Control Panel offer. Similarly, some mice and keyboards include custom management interfaces that augment or override the Windows settings. Look in the packaging for a CD/DVD or instructions for installing the software from the manufacturer's website.

To set basic button and wheel options

1. In the **Settings** window, select **Devices**, and then select **Mouse**.

2. Configure any of the following settings:

   - To specify the normal functionality of the mouse buttons, in the **Select your primary button** area, select **Left** or **Right**.

     If you select Right, you would select the right mouse button to select an item and select the left one to display a shortcut menu.

     > **TIP** This setting is useful if you are left handed, if you have injured your right hand, or if you want to switch your mousing hand to decrease wrist strain.

- To set the distance scrolled when you move the scroll wheel, from the **Roll the mouse wheel to scroll** list, select either **Multiple lines at a time** or **One screen**. When you select Multiple Lines At A Time, you can specify how many lines to scroll at a time by dragging the slider.

Dragging the slider displays the number of lines in a small box above the slider. This number is approximate and varies depending on where the text is and how it is formatted.

- To scroll an inactive window when you point to it, turn on **Scroll inactive windows when I hover over them**.

To change additional mouse button settings

1. At the bottom of the **Mouse** settings pane, select **Additional mouse options** to open the Mouse Properties dialog box.

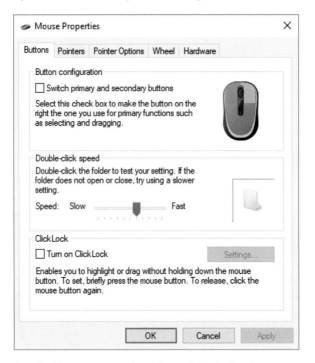

2. On the **Buttons** tab, do either of the following:

   - In the **Double-click speed** area, double-click the folder image to test the speed at which Windows registers a double-click. Then, if necessary, drag the **Speed** slider to adjust the speed. (If you have changed the default primary button, use the right mouse button to double-click the folder and to drag the slider.)

   - To drag without holding down the mouse button, in the **ClickLock** area, select the **Turn on ClickLock** check box.

3. Select **Apply** to apply the changes but leave the dialog box open, or **OK** to apply the changes and close the **Mouse Properties** dialog box.

To change the appearance of the entire set of mouse pointers

1. In the **Mouse Properties** dialog box, select the **Pointers** tab.

2. In the **Scheme** list, select a different scheme to display the set of pointers associated with that scheme.

3. Select **Apply** to apply the changes and keep the dialog box open, or **OK** to apply the changes and close the Mouse Properties dialog box.

To change an individual pointer icon

1. In the **Mouse Properties** dialog box, display the **Pointers** tab.

2. In the **Customize** list, select any pointer icon, and then select **Browse**. The Browse dialog box opens, displaying the contents of the Cursors folder. (*Cursor* is another name for pointer.)

3. In the **Browse** dialog box, double-click any pointer icon to replace the one you selected in the Customize list.

> **TIP** You can restore the selected pointer to the default for the original scheme at any time by selecting Use Default.

4. If you want to add a shadow to your pointers, select the **Enable pointer shadow** check box.

5. Select **Apply** to apply the changes and keep the dialog box open, or **OK** to apply the changes and close the Mouse Properties dialog box.

To change the mouse pointer functionality

1. In the **Mouse Properties** dialog box, select the **Pointer Options** tab.

2. Make any of the following changes:

- To change the pointer speed, in the **Motion** section, drag the slider.

- To speed up dialog-box operations, in the **Snap To** section, select the **Automatically move pointer to the default button in a dialog box** check box.

- To make the pointer more visible on the screen, in the **Visibility** section, select or clear any of the three check boxes.

3. Select **Apply** to apply the changes and keep the dialog box open, or **OK** to apply the changes and close the Mouse Properties dialog box.

To change how the mouse wheel works

1. In the **Mouse Properties** dialog box, select the **Wheel** tab.

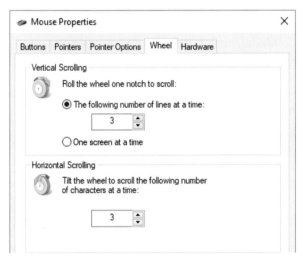

7

Here you can set the scroll distance just as you can in the Settings window. If you set this in either location, the change is reflected in the other location the next time you open it.

2. To control how much of the screen scrolls with each roll of the mouse wheel, in the **Vertical Scrolling** section, do either of the following:

- Select **The following number of lines at a time,** and then enter or use the arrows to select the number of lines you want to scroll.

- Select **One screen at a time.**

3. If your mouse supports horizontal scrolling, in the **Tilt the wheel to scroll the following number of characters at a time** box, enter or select the number of characters you want to scroll horizontally when you tilt the mouse wheel to the left or right.

4. Select **Apply** to apply the changes and keep the dialog box open, or **OK** to apply the changes and close the Mouse Properties dialog box.

Change the way your keyboard works

Regardless of the type of keyboard you have, all keyboards work in the same general way: Pressing each key or key combination generates a unique key code that tells the computer what to do. Pressing a key or key combination that gives a command always carries out that command.

You can change the keystrokes that Windows receives from a keyboard to those of another language. Chapter 12, "Manage computer settings," reviews procedures for installing languages and switching among installed keyboards.

In the Typing pane of the Devices page of the Settings window, you can change settings that control the following text input features:

- **Spelling** Choose whether to automatically correct and/or highlight misspelled words.

- **Typing** Show text suggestions as you type, add a space when you insert suggested text, and add a period after you insert two spaces.

- **Touch keyboard** Play key sounds as you type, capitalize the first letter of each sentence, turn on All Caps when you double-tap the Shift key, add the standard keyboard layout as a touch keyboard option, and automatically show the touch keyboard in windowed apps when there is no keyboard attached to your device.

You can configure options on the Speed tab of the Keyboard Properties dialog box, which is accessible from Control Panel or search, to change the speed at which you must press and release a key to input a single character.

To configure text input settings

1. Open the **Settings** window, select **Devices**, and then select **Typing** to display spelling, typing, and touch keyboard options.

⚙ Typing

Spelling

Autocorrect misspelled words
⬤ On

Highlight misspelled words
⬤ On

Typing

Show text suggestions as I type on the software keyboard
⬤ On

Add a space after I choose a text suggestion
⬤ On

Add a period after I double-tap the Spacebar
⬤ On

Touch keyboard

Play key sounds as I type
⬤ On

Capitalize the first letter of each sentence
⬤ On

Use all uppercase letters when I double-tap Shift
⬤ On

Show the touch keyboard when not in tablet mode and there's no keyboard attached
⬤ Off

2. Turn on or off each toggle button to configure the settings as you want them.

7

To change the key repeat delay and blink rate

1. Do either of the following to open the Keyboard Properties dialog box:

   - Display an Icons view of Control Panel, and then select **Keyboard**.

   - Enter **keyboard** in the taskbar search box, and then select the **Keyboard** Control Panel app.

2. To adjust how long you can hold down a key before Windows repeats its character, drag the **Repeat delay** slider.

3. To adjust the rate at which Windows repeats a character while you hold down its key, drag the **Repeat rate** slider.

   > **TIP** You can test the Repeat Delay and Repeat Rate settings in the box at the bottom of the Character Repeat area.

4. To adjust how fast the cursor blinks, drag the **Cursor blink rate** slider.

5. Select **Apply** or **OK**.

Manage printer connections

Previous editions of this book provided many pages of information about connecting printers to your computer. The good news is that modern printer connections are incredibly simple to complete.

If you have only one computer and one printer, you can connect them directly, by using a physical cable, or over a network. When you do, Windows searches for the printer driver. If you have an installation disc for your printer, you can install the printer drivers from the disc. However, the installation disc might contain out-of-date drivers. The more dependable option is to have Windows download the current list of printers that are supported by the drivers that are available through Windows Update. You can choose your printer in the list and immediately install the latest driver (this is an example of "plug and play").

Printer driver discs frequently include printer management apps that provide an interface to information about your printer; you can also get that information by entering the IP address and port the printer is connected to into a browser window. If your computer doesn't have an optical drive for the installation disc (which is becoming quite common with laptops and all-in-one computers), you can install the printer management software from the printer manufacturer's website.

7

You manage installed printers from the Printers & Scanners pane of the Devices settings page.

Home	**Printers & scanners**
Find a setting	**Add printers & scanners**
	+ Add a printer or scanner
Devices	
Bluetooth & other devices	**Printers & scanners**
Printers & scanners	ABS PDF Driver v400
Mouse	Adobe PDF
Typing	Fax
Pen & Windows Ink	Microsoft Print to PDF
AutoPlay	Microsoft XPS Document Writer
USB	HP Color LaserJet
	RingCentral Internet Fax
	Send To OneNote 2016
	☐ Let Windows manage my default printer
	When this is on, Windows will set your default printer to be the one you used most recently at your current location.

Your computing environment might include one or more printers that are connected directly to the network through a wired or wireless network connection. These printers are called *network printers*. Network printers aren't connected to any computer and are available on the network whenever they are turned on.

> **SEE ALSO** For information about sharing printers and other resources with a homegroup, see "Share files on your network" in Chapter 8, "Manage network and storage resources."

If Windows is unable to locate and automatically connect to a remote printer, you can help to identify it by providing either the path to the printer, if it's connected to another computer, or the IP address, if it's a network printer.

To install a local plug-and-play printer

1. In the **Settings** window, select **Devices**, and then **Printers & scanners**. The Printers & Scanners pane displays a list of the currently installed printers.

2. Connect the printer to the appropriate port on your computer.

3. Connect the printer to a power outlet, and then if necessary, turn it on.

   Windows 10 locates and installs the appropriate device driver while displaying a progress bar in the Printers area. If the printer appears in the Printers section of the Printers & Scanners pane, your printer is installed and ready to use.

> ⚠️ **IMPORTANT** If the printer wasn't recognized or the drivers weren't properly installed, continue with the next procedure.

To manually install a local printer

1. Display the **Printers & scanners** settings pane.

2. At the top of the pane, select **Add a printer or scanner**. Windows searches for any available printers that aren't yet installed on your computer.

Add printers & scanners

↻ Refresh

🖨 HP2CE486 (HP Officejet 5740 series)
Printer, Ink-jet printer, Scanner, Fax

Show Wi-Fi Direct printers

The printer that I want isn't listed

---

3. If the list includes the printer that you want to install, select it to have Windows locate and install the appropriate device driver.

4. If the search didn't locate the printer you want to add, select **The printer that I want isn't listed** to start the Add Printer wizard.

> **TIP** A printer that is connected directly to your computer is called a *local printer*. A printer that is available to you through your network is called a *network printer* or *remote printer*.

5. On the first page of the **Add Printer** wizard, select **Add a local printer or network printer with manual settings**, and then select **Next**.

6. On the **Choose a printer port** page, select the port to which your printer is connected from the **Use an existing port** list. Then select **Next** to display the Install The Printer Driver page.

> **IMPORTANT** It's likely that the correct port will already be selected. If not, the installation instructions from your printer manufacturer will tell you which port you should use. Some manufacturers supply helpful drawings to guide you.

7. Do either of the following:

   - If your printer model is listed, select it.

   - If your printer is not listed, or if you want to be sure you have the latest driver, select **Windows Update**. Windows Update retrieves the current set of Windows 10 printer drivers from its online database and updates the Manufacturer and Printers lists. There are a lot of printer drivers, so this process can take a couple of minutes. In the updated list, select your printer.

8. Select **Next** to display the Type A Printer Name page.

> ⚠ **IMPORTANT** The Printers list is actually a list of drivers, rather than printers. Many printer drivers support multiple printers, and the supported printers might not all be in the Printers list. If the list doesn't include your specific printer model, select a model with a similar name. Alternatively, download the necessary drivers from the manufacturer's website, return to the Install The Printer Driver page, and select Have Disk to install the printer manually.

9. On the **Type a printer name** page, change the printer name or accept the suggested name. Then select **Next**.

   A progress bar indicates the status of the driver installation. When the installation is complete, the Printer Sharing page appears.

10. On the **Printer Sharing** page, choose whether to share the printer through your computer with other printers on your network. Then select **Next**.

   > **TIP** To share a printer with other network computer users, the Network Discovery and File And Printer Sharing settings must be turned on for the current network profile. For information, see "Share files on your network" in Chapter 8, "Manage network and storage resources."

   The Add Printer wizard confirms that you've successfully added the printer. If you chose to share the printer, it is now available to other network computer users.

11. On the last page of the **Add Printer** wizard, select **Print a test page**. Your printer might require an additional step or two here to print the page. After Windows 10 sends the test page to the printer, a confirmation message box appears.

12. In the confirmation message box, select **Close**. Then in the **Add Printer** wizard, select **Finish**. An icon for the newly installed local printer appears in the Printers area of the Printers & Scanners window.

To display information about printer status

1. Display the **Printers & scanners** settings pane.

2. Select the printer you want to display status information for, and then in the pane that opens, select **Open queue**.

   The printer-specific window displays information about the printer status and active print jobs. You can manage settings and print jobs from the Printer menu.

To manage printer settings

- In the **Printers & scanners** settings pane, select the printer, and then select **Manage** to open a window that contains printer-specific configuration options.

Virtual printers

Some apps install printer drivers that you can use to "print" content to their default file type. Most notably, virtual printer drivers allow you to print to a PDF file, a text file, an XPS file, or Microsoft OneNote. When you install an app that has this capability, it usually automatically installs the appropriate driver and adds the virtual printer to the printer list.

You can print to a virtual printer just as you do to a real printer. Virtual printers are available in apps in the same locations as other printers.

Key points

- You can connect peripheral devices to your computer, either through a cable or wirelessly through a USB or Bluetooth connection, to extend its capabilities. Keyboard and mice are the most common peripheral devices. Other examples are external monitors, drives, printers, smart card readers, and fingerprint readers. You can display information about the devices connected to your computer in Device Manager.

- You can connect a Windows 10 computer to multiple displays through physical connections, or you can connect wirelessly to display devices (such as televisions) that support Miracast.

- You can connect a variety of audio output and input devices to your computer and easily switch between devices to fit the requirements of a specific situation.

- Whether you use a wired or wireless mouse, you can specify which button is the primary mouse button and the speed of action that constitutes a double click. If your mouse has a scroll wheel, you can specify the number of lines the screen content moves when you scroll.

- You can set keyboard options to correct many common typing errors.

- Windows 10 has built-in drivers for most device connections, which makes it easy to connect to a local or network printer.

7

Practice tasks

No practice files are necessary to complete the practice tasks in this chapter.

Understand peripheral devices

There are no practice tasks for this topic.

Locate device information

Perform the following tasks:

1. Open the **Settings** window and display the **Devices** settings page. Review each pane of the page. Identify the devices that you can currently configure from this page.

2. Open **Device Manager** and familiarize yourself with the categories of installed devices. Then do the following:

   - If any device displays a warning symbol, open its **Properties** dialog box and on the **Driver** tab, select the **Update Driver** button to search for a new device driver.

   - Select each of the options on the **View** menu to display other ways of locating devices. Then return to the Devices By Type view.

3. If you want to, open the **System Information** window to locate technical information about the hardware, software, and components in your computer system.

Display your desktop on multiple screens

Perform the following tasks:

- If you have multiple displays connected to your computer, do the following:

   - In the **Settings** window, select **System**, and then select **Display**. From the **Display** settings pane, identify the monitors by number.

   - If you want to, change the screen that is designated as the primary display.

- Experiment with extending and duplicating the display. Consider the circumstances under which you might want to use each of these settings.

- If your desktop is extended across displays, adjust the relative position of the displays, and then move the pointer across the displays and notice the effect.

- In the **Settings** window, select **Personalization**, and then **Taskbar**. In the **Multiple displays** section, try each of the taskbar settings. Choose the one you like best, and then select **OK**.

Set up audio devices

Perform the following tasks:

1. Open the **Sound** dialog box.

2. Configure the settings for the playback device you want to use, manually or by using the wizard.

3. Configure the settings for the recording device you want to use, manually or by using the wizard.

Change the way your mouse works

Perform the following tasks:

1. Display the **Mouse** settings pane. Review the settings that you can manage in this pane, and configure them as you want them.

2. At the bottom of the **Mouse** settings pane, select **Additional mouse options**. In the **Mouse Properties** dialog box, review the settings that you can manage, and configure them the way you want them. Then select **Apply**.

3. Compare and contrast the settings in the open **Mouse** settings pane with those in the open **Mouse Properties** dialog box. Then close the dialog box.

Change the way your keyboard works

Perform the following tasks:

1. Display the **Typing** settings pane. Review the settings that you can manage in this pane, and configure them as you want them.

2. From Control Panel (or taskbar search), open the **Keyboard Properties** dialog box. Review the settings that you can manage in the dialog box, and configure them the way you want them. Then select **Apply**.

3. Compare and contrast the settings in the open **Typing** settings pane with those in the open **Keyboard Properties** dialog box. Then close the dialog box.

Manage printer connections

Perform the following tasks:

1. Display the **Printers & scanners** settings pane, and review the physical and virtual printers that are available in the window.

2. If you have a printer installed, display the printer-specific configuration options. Review the available options and configure them the way you want them. Then close the window.

Manage network and storage resources

8

In the early days of Microsoft, Bill Gates envisioned a future with "a computer on every desk and in every home." Today, the business world couldn't function without computers, and terms such as "information worker" are commonly used to describe people who spend most of the day working on computers. Computers make it possible for an increasing number of people to successfully run small businesses with large presences, to maximize productivity by working from home, to have learning resources at their fingertips (literally), and to stay connected to information all the time, from any location.

As more apps and resources become available as online services, an internet connection is increasingly important to the computing experience. Your computer connects to the internet through a network that provides and safeguards the connection. Windows 10 uses network connection security profiles to govern the way your computer interacts with other computers and devices on the network. On a local network, you can connect directly to other computers or manage the connection through a homegroup—a password-protected security group that defines the sharing of specific information and devices with other homegroup member computers.

This chapter guides you through procedures related to managing network connections, managing homegroup connections, and sharing files on your network.

In this chapter

- Manage network connections
- Manage homegroup connections
- Share files on your network

Manage network connections

A *network* is a group of computers that communicate with each other through a wired or wireless connection. A network can be as small as two computers or as large as the internet. In the context of this book, the term *network* refers primarily to the connection between computers in one physical location that are connected to each other, and to the internet, through a network router.

> ⚠ **IMPORTANT** This chapter assumes that you are connecting to an existing, functioning network. This chapter does not include instructions for setting up or configuring networking hardware. When setting up a network infrastructure, be sure to follow the instructions provided by the hardware manufacturer.

Connect to a network

If your computer is a desktop computer, you'll probably connect it to only one network: your home or office network. However, you might connect a laptop or mobile device to networks in many locations for the purpose of connecting to the internet: at home, at work, at a friend's or relative's house, at a public library, at a coffee shop—some highway rest areas even offer free internet access! You can't connect a device directly to the internet, so wherever you want to connect to the internet, you will first need to connect to a network.

Connecting your computer to a network requires two things:

- Your computer must have an active network adapter. This is usually in the form of a network interface card that is part of the internal workings of the computer, but you can purchase external network adapters that connect to a USB port on your computer. A network adapter can be for a wired network or a wireless network. Many laptops and desktop computers have both. If a computer has a wired network adapter, it has an external Ethernet port that the cable connector fits into. This looks a bit like a wide telephone cable port.

- The environment you're in must have a network. This could be a wired network that you connect to directly or through a switch box, a wireless network that you connect to through a router, or a wireless network connection that you share from a phone or other device that connects to a cellular network.

If your computer has an enabled network adapter, whether or not it is actively connected to a network, a connection icon appears in the notification area at the right end of the Windows Taskbar. The connection icon indicates whether your network adapter is an Ethernet adapter or a wireless adapter and whether it is currently connected to a network.

The white arcs on the wireless connection icon indicate the strength of the wireless network signal that the computer is currently connected to. When the computer is configured for a connection but not connected to a network, different versions of the basic network connection icon indicate the network status, as follows:

- A white starburst indicates that a connection is available.

- A white X on a red background indicates that no network is available.

Selecting the network connection icon displays information about the current network connection status and any available wired networks, VPN connections, wireless networks, and Wi-Fi Direct devices.

Each network connection has a name; it might be a generic name provided by the network router or a specific name assigned by the network owner. The icon to the left of the network name indicates the connection type and, for wireless connections, the signal strength. The word or words below the network name provide additional information about the network.

Right-clicking the connection icon in the notification area displays a shortcut menu of commands that you can use to diagnose network connection problems and display the Network & Internet settings page.

When you physically connect your computer to a network by using an Ethernet cable, Windows 10 automatically creates the network connection. To connect to a wireless network for the first time, you need to make the connection.

Network vs. internet connections

Connecting a computer to a network does not automatically connect the computer to the internet; it connects the computer to the network router or hub that sits between the computer and the internet. Additional action might be necessary to connect to the internet.

For example, when you connect to a corporate network, the network management system might scan the security settings on your computer and require that you install updates before it permits a connection. When this happens, the connection will be noted as Limited, and you must disconnect from the connection, perform the required action, and then reconnect.

When connecting to a free, pay-per-use, or subscription-based public network (such as one at an airport, restaurant, coffee shop, library, or hotel), you might have immediate internet access. Frequently, though, you will be required to provide information, credentials, or payment to connect from the public network to the internet. You might be prompted to provide this information when the connection is established. If you connect to a network but then find that you can't connect to the internet, start a new instance of the web browser to display the organization's connection page, and then provide the required information. (It might be necessary to refresh the page to force the display of the gateway page.)

The purpose of connecting a computer to a network is usually to connect beyond the network to the internet, but it might also be to access devices (such as printers) or information (such as files) on other computers that are connected to the same network. On a computer running Windows 10, connecting a computer to a network doesn't automatically allow users to access folders on other computers on the network. If you want to do so, you must first turn on network discovery. The network discovery feature enables the computer to "see and be seen by" other computers on the network that also have this feature turned on. Simply turning on network discovery doesn't automatically expose the information stored on your computer to other computers. You configure the sharing of specific folders individually on each computer. This helps to ensure that you don't accidentally share information that you don't want to.

> **SEE ALSO** For information about sharing individual folders and Public folders, see "Share files on your network" later in this chapter.

To connect to an available wired network

1. Plug one end of an Ethernet cable into the port on the network router or a switch box that is connected to the router.

2. Plug the other end of the cable into the Ethernet port on your computer.

To connect to an available wireless network

1. In the notification area of the taskbar, select the wireless connection icon to display a list of available connections.

2. In the connection list, select the network you want to connect to, to display the connection options.

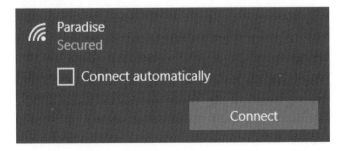

3. If you want the computer to automatically connect to this network when it's available, select the **Connect automatically** check box.

> **TIP** Automatic connection is appropriate when you are connecting to a home network or another network that you trust. It works less well when connecting to a public network that has a gateway access page. If your computer establishes a connection, it might appear that you have internet access when you don't. And you might not realize that you don't have a connection until you notice a dozen unsent messages in your email outbox.

4. Select **Connect**. If the network prompts you to enter credentials or a password (such as a WEP encryption key or WPA password), do so.

> **TIP** Wired Equivalent Privacy (WEP), Wi-Fi Protected Access (WPA), and Wi-Fi Protected Access II (WPA2) are security protocols that govern the credentials passed from a computer to a wireless network when establishing a connection. WPA2 is the most current of these.

To turn on network discovery

1. Open File Explorer.

2. In the **Navigation** pane, select the **Network** node. If network discovery is turned off, Windows displays an informative message. Select **OK** to dismiss the message window. The information remains visible on a banner below the ribbon, and the Network folder is empty.

3. Select the banner, and then select **Turn on network discovery and file sharing** to display the Network Discovery And File Sharing message box.

    If your user account doesn't have administrative permissions on the computer, a User Account Control window opens and requires the entry of administrative credentials. Do either of the following:

    *   Enter the password for the displayed account, and then select **Yes**.

    *   Select **More choices**, choose a different account, enter the password for that account, and then select **Yes**.

    Because Windows 10 automatically designates new connections as Public networks, you must specify whether to permit network discovery on all Public networks.

    Network discovery and file sharing   ✕

    Do you want to turn on network discovery and file sharing for all public networks?

    → No, make the network that I am connected to a private network
    Network discovery and file sharing will be turned on for private networks, such as those in homes and workplaces.

    → Yes, turn on network discovery and file sharing for all public networks

    [Cancel]

    ⚠ **IMPORTANT** You almost certainly do NOT want to select the Yes option in this dialog box. Doing so would keep the network connection Public and allow computers on other Public network connections to gain access to your computer.

4. Unless you specifically want to allow computers on Public networks to connect to your computer, select **No, make the network that I am connected to a private network** to change the network connection type to Private, turn on network sharing, and display a list of the network resources you can now access.

8

To disconnect from a wired network

- Remove the cable from the Ethernet port on your computer or from the network connection point.

- Disable the network adapter.

 SEE ALSO For information about disabling network adapters, see "Troubleshoot network connections" later in this topic.

To disconnect from a wireless network

1. In the notification area of the taskbar, select the wireless connection icon.

2. At the top of the list of network connections, select the network that is designated as Connected.

3. Select **Disconnect**.

 TIP Unless you're connecting to a wireless network that accesses the internet over a cellular network, moving out of range of the network broadcast will automatically disconnect you.

Display information about networks and connections

After you connect to a network, you can display information such as which computers, printers, and other devices are connected to it. In File Explorer, the Network window displays the devices on your network that the current Public or Private security profile settings allow the computer to detect, and the devices that support the network infrastructure, such as the network router.

TIP Your Network window will show the devices on your network rather than those shown in the images in this book.

From the Network window, you can access information and devices in different ways. For example:

- The Computer section of the Network window displays other computers on the network. Double-click a computer to display the folders that are shared with you on that computer. Right-click a computer to display the shortcut menu, which has options for displaying content, creating shortcuts, or starting a Remote Desktop Connection session.

> **SEE ALSO** For information about sharing files and folders on a network, see "Share files on your network" later in this chapter.

- The Displays section shows network display devices that are available through a Miracast connection.

> **SEE ALSO** For information about connecting to wireless displays, see "Display your desktop on multiple screens" in Chapter 7, "Manage peripheral devices."

- The Media Devices section displays media servers on the network. Double-click a device to display its default media interface, which might be Windows Media Player or a proprietary app for the operating system that is installed on the device.

- The Network Infrastructure section displays wired and wireless routers on the network. Double-click a router to display its web management interface in your default web browser.

- The Printers and Scanners sections display devices that support printing and scanning; if a device supports both, it appears in both sections. Double-click a device to display its web management interface, if it has one, in your default web browser.

Most of the device shortcut menus include options for displaying device webpages or properties. You can change the display of devices in the Network window from the View tab. In Details view, you can display properties such as the discovery method, MAC address, and IP address.

> **SEE ALSO** For more information about working with File Explorer views, see "Change the File Explorer display options" in Chapter 5, "Explore files and folders."

Information about your current network connection is available in the Status pane of the Network & Internet settings page.

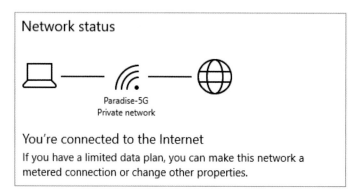

Similar information is available in the Network And Sharing Center. Some settings can be accessed more directly from this window.

Network and Sharing Center

Control Panel > Network and Internet > Network and Sharing Center

Search Control Panel

View your basic network information and set up connections

Control Panel Home

Change adapter settings

Change advanced sharing settings

View your active networks

Paradise-5G
Private network

Access type: Internet
HomeGroup: Available to join
Connections: Wi-Fi (Paradise-5G)

See also

HomeGroup

Infrared

Internet Options

Windows Defender Firewall

Change your networking settings

Set up a new connection or network
Set up a broadband, dial-up, or VPN connection; or set up a router or access point.

Troubleshoot problems
Diagnose and repair network problems, or get troubleshooting information.

Beyond the general network connection information, you can also display useful information about the connection speed and data transfer to and from the computer from the status dialog box of each adapter. (The speed varies with the signal quality, but also depends on other factors.) Each connection is linked to a network adapter; the connection information is available from the adapter information.

8

Wi-Fi Status

General

Connection

IPv4 Connectivity:	Internet
IPv6 Connectivity:	Internet
Media State:	Enabled
SSID:	Paradise-5G
Duration:	15:50:00
Speed:	300.0 Mbps
Signal Quality:	

Details...   Wireless Properties

Activity

Sent — Received

Bytes:	12,298,044	239,554,036

Properties   Disable   Diagnose

Close

If you're interested in the details of your network activity, that information is available to you from the Data Usage and Usage Details panes. Windows 10 provides you with information about the amount of data transfer by connection type and by app in the past 30 days.

Data usage

Overview
Total: 101.89 GB

■ Wi-Fi: 48 MB
■ Ethernet: 101.84 GB

From the last 30 days

⚙ Usage details

Show usage from:

Ethernet	⌄

Reset usage stats

☁	OneDrive.exe	25.85 GB

e	Microsoft Edge	25.17 GB

▥	System	18.29 GB

o☑	OUTLOOK.EXE	7.78 GB

To display network device information in the Network window

1. Open File Explorer.

2. In the **Navigation** pane, select **Network**.

> ✓ **TIP** If network discovery is off, an error message appears when you select Network. For information about this, see "Connect to a network" earlier in this topic.

To display network connection information in Settings

- Right-click the **Start** button and then on the **Quick Links** menu, select **Network Connections**.

- Open the **Settings** window, select **Network & Internet**, and then select **Status**.

- In the notification area of the taskbar, select the network icon, and then select **Network & Internet settings**.

- In the notification area of the taskbar, right-click the network icon, and then select **Open Network & Internet settings**.

To display network connection information in the Network And Sharing Center

- Display the **Status** pane of the **Network & Internet** settings page. Near the bottom of the pane, select **Network and Sharing Center**.

- Open Control Panel in Category view. In the **Network and Internet** category, select **View network status and tasks**.

- Open Control Panel in an Icons view, and then select **Network and Sharing Center**.

To display detailed information about the current network connection

- Display the **Status** pane of the **Network & Internet** settings page. Near the bottom of the pane, select **View your network properties**.

To display network connection speed and data transfer information

1. Open the **Network and Sharing Center**.

2. In the **View your active networks** section, to the right of **Connections**, select the network adapter name.

To display data usage by app

1. In the **Settings** window, select **Network & Internet**.

2. Select **Data usage** to display the total amount of data transferred in the past 30 days, broken down by connection type.

3. In the **Data usage** pane, select **View usage details** to display the amount of data transferred by each app over the current type of connection.

4. On the **Usage details** page, to show app usage for a different connection type, select the **Show usage from** list, and then select **Wi-Fi** or **Ethernet**.

To display the status of all installed network adapters

- Display the **Status** pane of the **Network & Internet** settings page. In the **Change your network settings** section, select **Change adapter options**.

- Open the **Network and Sharing Center**. In the left pane, select **Change adapter settings**.

To display details of a specific network adapter

1. Open the **Network Connections** window.

2. Do one of the following:

   - Double-click the network adapter you want to display information for.

   - Select the network adapter to activate the toolbar buttons. Then, on the toolbar, select **View status of this connection**.

> ⚠ **IMPORTANT** If the Network Connections window isn't wide enough to display all the buttons related to a selected adapter on the toolbar, chevrons (>>) appear at the right end of the toolbar. Select the chevrons to display the remaining commands.

Configure network connection security

Each time you connect your computer to a network that you haven't previously connected to, Windows 10 associates the network connection with one of two security profiles, Private or Public, and then assigns the security settings configured for that profile to the network connection.

> ✓ **TIP** Previous versions of Windows prompted you to designate whether the network was at work, at home, or in a public place for the purpose of configuring appropriate security settings for the environment. Windows 10 has only Private and Public network security profiles.

The network security profiles include the following settings:

- **Network discovery** Determines whether the computer can see and be seen by other computers connected to the network.

- **File and printer sharing** Determines whether network users can access folders and printers that you configure for sharing from the computer.

- **HomeGroup connections** Determines whether user account credentials are necessary to connect to computers that are joined to your homegroup. Available only for the Private network security profile.

- **Public folder sharing** Determines whether network users can access files that are stored in the Public account folders on your computer.

- **Media streaming** Determines whether network users can access music, videos, and pictures that are stored in your media library.

- **File sharing connections** Determines the security requirements for devices that connect to your computer's file sharing connections.

- **Password protected sharing** Determines whether shared files are available to any network user or only to those users with user accounts on your computer.

You can review and configure the settings for the individual security profiles and the security settings that apply to all network connections in the Advanced Sharing Settings window. The window has three sections of settings: Private, Guest Or Public, and All Networks. You can expand or hide each section separately.

The settings that are applied to all network connections are available in the All Networks section at the bottom of the window. These include settings for sharing Public folders, streaming media, protecting file-sharing connections, and specifying the type of credentials that are required to access the computer from another computer on the network.

All Networks

Public folder sharing

When Public folder sharing is on, people on the network, including homegroup members, can access files in the Public folders.

- ○ Turn on sharing so anyone with network access can read and write files in the Public folders
- ● Turn off Public folder sharing (people logged on to this computer can still access these folders)

Media streaming

When media streaming is on, people and devices on the network can access pictures, music, and videos on this computer. This computer can also find media on the network.

Choose media streaming options...

File sharing connections

Windows uses 128-bit encryption to help protect file sharing connections. Some devices don't support 128-bit encryption and must use 40- or 56-bit encryption.

- ● Use 128-bit encryption to help protect file sharing connections (recommended)
- ○ Enable file sharing for devices that use 40- or 56-bit encryption

Password protected sharing

When password protected sharing is on, only people who have a user account and password on this computer can access shared files, printers attached to this computer, and the Public folders. To give other people access, you must turn off password protected sharing.

- ● Turn on password protected sharing
- ○ Turn off password protected sharing

The settings that are applied to Guest or Public networks are intended for the types of networks that you might connect to in a public place, such as an airport or coffee shop, only for the purpose of connecting your computer to the internet. You don't have a need to access information on other computers that are connected to a Public network, and it isn't a good idea to allow those other computers to access information on your computer. When you connect to any network that you don't explicitly trust, configure the connection as a Public network to protect your privacy. The Public network profile connects your computer to the network without exposing it to other network users.

```
Guest or Public                                                              ⌃

    Network discovery

        When network discovery is on, this computer can see other network computers and devices and is
        visible to other network computers.

            ○ Turn on network discovery
            ⦿ Turn off network discovery

    File and printer sharing

        When file and printer sharing is on, files and printers that you have shared from this computer can
        be accessed by people on the network.

            ○ Turn on file and printer sharing
            ⦿ Turn off file and printer sharing
```

Windows 10 assumes that every network you connect to is Public until you tell it otherwise. Before you can access network resources you must either change the network connection type (from Public to Private) and turn on network discovery, or create a homegroup.

> **SEE ALSO** For more information about homegroups, see "Manage homegroup connections" later in this chapter.

The settings that are applied to Private networks are intended for networks such as the network in your home or small business. If you connect computers and devices that only you use and control to the network and want to share information among the computers (for example, if you want to insert a picture stored on one computer into a document you're creating on a different computer), the Private network security profile is the one for you.

If you share your network credentials with people who visit your home so that they can connect their laptops or other devices to the internet through your network, be aware that assigning the Private network security profile to a computer will expose any information you choose to share from that computer with anyone you provide the network credentials to, should they choose to look for it.

> **SEE ALSO** For more information about sharing network resources with other people, see the sidebar "Wireless network security" later in this topic.

8

Private (current profile)

Network discovery

When network discovery is on, this computer can see other network computers and devices and is visible to other network computers.

◉ Turn on network discovery
 ☑ Turn on automatic setup of network connected devices.
○ Turn off network discovery

File and printer sharing

When file and printer sharing is on, files and printers that you have shared from this computer can be accessed by people on the network.

◉ Turn on file and printer sharing
○ Turn off file and printer sharing

HomeGroup connections

Typically, Windows manages the connections to other homegroup computers. But if you have the same user accounts and passwords on all of your computers, you can have HomeGroup use your account instead.

◉ Allow Windows to manage homegroup connections (recommended)
○ Use user accounts and passwords to connect to other computers

The Private network security profile connects your computer to the network and con-figures the network profile to include network discovery, file and printer sharing, Public folder sharing, media streaming, and password-protected sharing. Your computer is visible to other computers and devices on the network. You don't necessarily have per-mission to access these computers or devices, but you know they're connected to the network, and other network members know that your computer is also connected.

> **TIP** If you're running Windows 10 on a computer in an enterprise environment, the computer and its network settings are likely managed by the IT department, and you won't have to concern yourself with these settings. You're more likely to encounter this situation when connecting a laptop or mobile device to a network, or if you have multiple computers on a home network.

You can change the settings for the Private security profile, the Public security profile, or all networks. When you do so, Windows automatically applies the new settings to all network connections.

Network discovery is controlled by the network security profile—it is off for Public networks and on for Private networks. You can change the security profile for a specific network that you're connected to. For example, if you connect to a wireless network at a friend's house and want to allow your friend to copy files from your computer over the network, you can change the network connection from Public to Private. (And when you finish, you can change it back so that the next time you connect to the network, your shared folders are protected.)

⚙ **Paradise-5G**

Connect automatically when in range

🔘 On

Network profile

○ Public
Your PC is hidden from other devices on the network and can't be used for printer and file sharing.

◉ Private
For a network you trust, such as at home or work. Your PC is discoverable and can be used for printer and file sharing if you set it up.

8

To open the Advanced Sharing Settings window

1. Open the **Network and Sharing Center**.

2. In the left pane, select **Change advanced sharing settings**.

Or

1. Display the **Network & Internet** settings page, and then select the connection type (either **Wi-Fi** or **Ethernet**).

2. In the **Related settings** section of the pane, select **Change advanced sharing options**.

To identify the security profile assigned to the current connection

1. Open the **Advanced Sharing Settings** window.

2. Review the three security profile headings. The phrase *current profile* appears in parentheses after the name of the active security profile.

Wireless network security

If you have a wireless network router, it is important that you secure the network properly to prevent unauthorized users from connecting to it and gaining access to the computers on your network.

When you set up your wireless router, be sure to follow the instructions that come with it. For the initial setup, you'll usually be required to connect the router directly to a computer (by using an Ethernet cable) and run a setup program. After the router is set up, you can usually connect to it wirelessly by using its IP address on your network. During the setup process, you can do several things to increase the security of your wireless network, such as:

■ Change the administrative password from the default password shared by all routers of that type to a unique, strong password. (Some manufacturers use the same password for all routers, and some use blank passwords.)

■ Secure the network with an appropriate level of encryption. Establish a WEP key or WPA password to prevent unauthorized users from connecting to your wireless network.

Your router configuration might offer multiple levels of WEP encryption, controlled by the length of the WEP key. A 10-character WEP key provides 64-bit encryption, and a 26-character key provides 128-bit encryption.

WPA encryption is a far more secure encryption standard than WEP encryption. If you have a gigabit network router (which transmits data at 1,000 kilobytes per second (KBps), as opposed to the standard 100 KBps), you should use WPA encryption. WPA encryption supports gigabit data transmission; WEP encryption does not.

When creating a security key or password, use a combination of letters and numbers that you can remember—for example, a series of significant dates. If the key is particularly long or difficult, you might want to keep a printed copy of it handy for when visitors want to connect their devices to your wireless network. Better yet, set up a Guest network that is isolated from the network that you connect your computers to. Guests can then access the internet without also being able to locate or attempt to access the computers on your regular network.

To display or hide settings for a specific security profile

- Select the circled v or ^ at the right end of the security profile heading.

To modify the settings for a network security profile

1. Open the **Advanced sharing settings** window.

2. Expand the security profile that you want to change.

3. Make your changes and then, at the bottom of the window, select **Save changes**. If you're signed in with a standard user account, Windows prompts you to provide administrative credentials.

4. If the **User Account Control** dialog box opens, select an administrative user account and enter its password, or have the person who owns the account do it for you.

To change the security profile assigned to a network connection

1. Display the **Network & Internet** settings page.

2. Display the settings pane that applies to the adapter you want to configure (**Wi-Fi** or **Ethernet**), and then at the top of the pane, select the specific connection to display its information.

3. In the **Network profile** section of the adapter page, select **Public** to hide the computer from other network devices, or **Private** to make the computer discoverable.

> **TIP** Computers running Windows 10 can easily coexist on a network with computers running earlier versions of Windows. Other computers and devices on the network do not affect the available network security profiles or their settings. However, network security profiles and homegroups aren't available on a computer running a version of Windows earlier than Windows 7.

Troubleshoot network connections

A network of any size includes several components that affect the network connection. Your network might include one or more wired routers, wireless routers, hubs, or switches. These hardware devices, the cables that connect them, and the external connection to your internet service provider (ISP) can all develop problems or entirely quit functioning. A large organization usually has one or more network technicians (if not an entire IT department) who maintain the organization's hardware and keep the internal and external network connections running smoothly. In a small to medium organization, or in a household, it helps if you know enough about your network to be able to function as your own network technician. This book provides information specifically about managing the network connections on a Windows 10 computer.

As mentioned earlier in this topic, the network adapter is the hardware on your computer's end of a network connection. A computer typically has one or two network adapters. You can monitor and manage network adapters and their current connections from the Network Connections window of Control Panel. This window displays connectivity information for each network adapter and for each dial-up or virtual private network (VPN) connection on your computer. A red X on an adapter icon indicates that the adapter is disabled or disconnected.

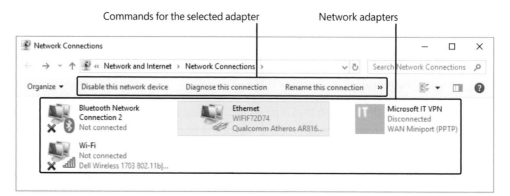

When you experience a network or internet connection problem, first determine whether the problem occurs only on your computer, or also on other computers on your network. You can frequently resolve connection issues by taking one of these simple actions:

- If the problem occurs on only one computer, reset the network adapter or restart the computer.

- If computers can connect to the network but not to the internet, restart the router that connects your network to your ISP.

When you experience a connection problem beyond these simple issues, either when connecting to the internet or when connecting to another computer on your network, you can use one of the handy troubleshooting tools included with Windows 10. These troubleshooting tools (referred to as *Troubleshooters*) can help you identify and resolve problems. Individual troubleshooters are available from the relevant settings panes. The entire collection of Troubleshooters (for Programs, Hardware and Sound, Network and Internet, and System and Security) is available from Control Panel.

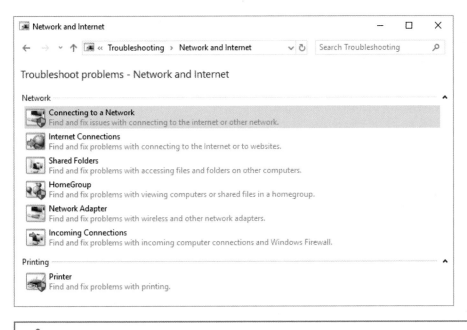

! **IMPORTANT** The following procedures require administrative permission.

To disable a network adapter

1. Open the **Network Connections** window.

2. Select the adapter you want to disable.

3. On the toolbar, select **Disable this network device**. The icon and words that represent the disabled adapter change from color to gray, and the word *Disabled* appears below the adapter name.

To enable a network adapter

1. In the **Network Connections** window, select the adapter you want to enable.

2. On the toolbar, select **Enable this network device**. The icon and words that represent the disabled adapter change from gray to color. If the adapter is configured to automatically connect to a network, it does so.

To reset a network adapter

1. In the **Network Connections** window, disable the adapter.

2. After the process of disabling the adapter completes, enable the adapter.

To display network troubleshooting tools

- In the **Settings** window, select **Update & Security**, and then select **Troubleshoot**.

To run a Troubleshooter

1. In the **Troubleshoot** settings pane, select the Troubleshooter you want to run, and then select **Run the Troubleshooter**. The Troubleshooter starts, scans your system, and then leads you through a diagnostic process.

   If the Troubleshooter finds an issue, it prompts you to apply or skip the recommended fix. When the troubleshooter completes, it reports its progress.

   If the Troubleshooter doesn't identify any specific issues, it offers you the option to explore additional options.

2. Select **Close the troubleshooter** to quit the process, **View detailed information** to display more information about the applied fix, or **Explore additional options** to display a list of pertinent resources.

Manage homegroup connections

When your computer is connected to a Private network, network computer users can connect to resources on other computers either through the network or through a homegroup. You can think of a homegroup as a private network that allows secure access to specific resources, such as files that are stored on the computers that are joined to it. Only one homegroup can exist on a local network; it exists as long as it has at least one member. (If your environment has multiple networks, each can have one homegroup.) The homegroup doesn't have a name, a designated administrator, or a management interface.

> ⊘ **TIP** Homegroups were introduced in Windows 7 and are not accessible to computers running earlier versions of Windows or a non-Windows operating system.

When a homegroup exists on a Private network, other computers on that network can join the homegroup. The only information you need to join the homegroup is the homegroup password, which Windows generates randomly when the homegroup is created. If the homegroup password isn't readily available, it's quite simple to locate.

8

Use this password to add other computers to your homegroup

Before you can access files and printers located on other computers, add those computers to your homegroup. You'll need the following password.

Write down this password:

TC86JP1q3p

Print password and instructions

The randomly generated homegroup passwords aren't easy to remember. If you want to, you can change the password. It's best to do so immediately after you create the homegroup because changing the password disconnects any computers that joined by using the original password. Alternatively, you can have Windows validate your identity when joining multiple computers to the homegroup by using your user account credentials.

You can create and manage homegroup connections from two separate places:

- The HomeGroup window of Control Panel, which displays commands as links

- The Homegroup node in File Explorer, which displays commands on a ribbon and sends you to Control Panel to manage homegroup settings

You can create or join a computer to a homegroup when you are signed in with a Standard or Administrator user account. When you start the process of connecting a computer to a homegroup, Windows 10 tells you whether a homegroup already exists on the network.

Homegroup membership is on a per-computer basis, not a per-user basis. (In other words, the computer joins the homegroup, not the user.) When any user of a computer that has multiple user accounts joins the computer to a homegroup, the computer is joined to the homegroup on behalf of all its users. However, each user has control over the resources that he or she shares with other homegroup members. By default, all libraries other than the Documents library are selected for sharing.

SEE ALSO For information about libraries, see "Understand files, folders, and libraries" in Chapter 5, "Explore files and folders." For information about changing the resources shared with your homegroup, see "Share files on your network" later in this chapter.

On a multiple-user computer, if another user joins your computer to a homegroup, it doesn't share any of your user account folders. You can specify your homegroup resource sharing settings at any time from either homegroup window. When another user has shared the computer, a message appears in the homegroup window. Each user sets individual sharing settings.

> ⚠ Steve Lambert has joined your computer to a homegroup. You haven't shared any libraries with your homegroup. Click the link below to change what you are sharing. Don't shut down or restart your computer until sharing is finished.

The only resource sharing setting that is common to all user accounts of a homegroup member computer is the Printers & Devices setting, which controls access to the Devices And Printers folder. When any user shares or excludes this folder from the shared homegroup resources, the printer is shared or excluded on behalf of the computer rather than the user.

If at any time you decide that you no longer want to share resources with other homegroup members, you can remove your computer from the homegroup with no adverse effects. It is not necessary to disconnect from the network. If you have any problems with the homegroup, Windows 10 has a built-in troubleshooting tool that can help you to diagnose and fix homegroup problems.

8

> 🔍 **SEE ALSO** For more information about Troubleshooters, see "Troubleshoot network connections" earlier in this chapter.

To open the Homegroup window in File Explorer

- In the Navigation pane of File Explorer, select the **Homegroup** node. If a homegroup already exists on the network, the window contains a Join Now button. If no homegroup exists, the window contains a Create A Homegroup button.

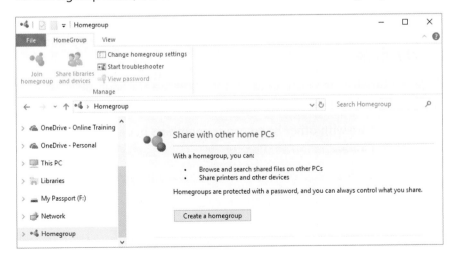

To open the HomeGroup window of Control Panel

- In Category view of Control Panel, under **Network and Internet**, select **Choose homegroup and sharing options**.

- In Large Icons view or Small Icons view of Control Panel, select **HomeGroup**.

- In File Explorer, right-click the **Homegroup** node, and then select **Change HomeGroup settings**.

- In File Explorer, open the **Homegroup** window. Then on the **HomeGroup** tab, select **Change homegroup settings**.

  If a homegroup already exists on the network, the window contains a Join Now button. If no homegroup exists, the window contains a Create A Homegroup button.

To create a homegroup

1. Open the **HomeGroup** window of Control Panel or the **Homegroup** window in File Explorer.

2. Select **Create a homegroup** to start the **Create a Homegroup** wizard. On the first page of the wizard, select **Next**.

3. On the **Share with other homegroup members** page of the wizard, do the following for each folder or library:

   - To share the resource, select **Shared** in the adjacent **Permissions** list.

   - To keep the resource private, select **Not shared** in the adjacent **Permissions** list.

> **SEE ALSO** For information about changing the resources you've shared through a homegroup, see "Share files on your network" later in this chapter.

4. Select **Next** to create the homegroup and display the homegroup password.

5. If you want to print the password, do the following:

   a. On the **Use this password to add other computers to your homegroup** page of the wizard, select **Print password and instructions**.

   b. On the **View and print your homegroup password** page of the wizard, select **Print this page**.

   c. In the **Print** dialog box, select a printer, and then select **Print**.

6. If you don't want to print the password, manually record it in a convenient location (write it down or save a screen clipping in Microsoft OneNote).

7. Select **Finish** to display your homegroup sharing settings and options for working with the homegroup.

To display the password for an existing homegroup

- Sign in to any computer that is joined to the homegroup, and then do any of the following:

  - Open the **HomeGroup** window of Control Panel, and then select **View or print the homegroup password**.

  - In File Explorer, right-click the **Homegroup** node, and then select **View the HomeGroup password**.

  - In File Explorer, display the **Homegroup** node. Then on the **HomeGroup** tab, select **View password**.

> **TIP** If you don't have an account on another network computer, you might have to ask another person to sign in to a computer that is connected to the homegroup and retrieve the password for you.

8

To change a homegroup password

1. Make sure that any computer that has already joined the homegroup is active (turned on and not asleep).

2. Display the **HomeGroup** window of Control Panel. In the **Other homegroup actions** section, select **Change the password** to start the **Change your Homegroup Password** wizard. If you're logged in as a Standard user, provide the credentials of an Administrator account when prompted to do so.

> **TIP** You can't change the password from the Homegroup window in File Explorer.

3. On the **Changing the homegroup password will disconnect everyone** page of the wizard, read and heed the warning. Then when you've prepared the homegroup-joined computers, select **Change the password**.

4. On the **Type a new password for your homegroup** page of the wizard, do one of the following, and then select **Next**:

   - Accept the new randomly generated password.

   - Select the Refresh button (labeled with circling arrows) to generate a new random password.

   - Enter the password that you want to use.

5. If necessary, record the new password somewhere. Then on the **Your home-group password was successfully changed** page of the wizard, select **Finish**.

To discard the password requirement for a homegroup

1. Open the **Network and Sharing Center**.

2. In the left pane, select **Change advanced sharing settings**.

3. In the **Advanced sharing settings** window, expand the **Private** security profile.

4. In the **HomeGroup connections** section of the profile, select **Use user accounts and passwords to connect to other computers**.

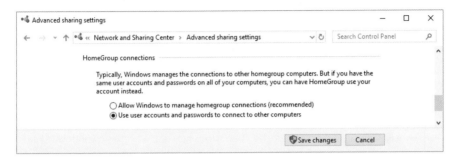

5. Select **Save changes**, and then sign out of Windows to apply your changes to the homegroup.

To join a computer to an existing homegroup

1. If you haven't already joined a computer to the homegroup when logged in with the current user account, obtain the homegroup password.

 TIP The homegroup doesn't require an existing user to enter the password when joining additional computers to the homegroup.

2. Do either of the following:

   • Open the **HomeGroup** window of Control Panel.

   • Open the **Homegroup** window in File Explorer.

3. Select **Join now** to start the **Join a Homegroup** wizard. On the first page of the wizard, select **Next**.

4. On the **Share with other homegroup members** page, designate each folder or library as **Shared** or **Not shared**, and then select **Next**.

   SEE ALSO For information about changing the resources you've shared through a homegroup, see "Share files on your network" later in this chapter.

5. If the wizard displays the **Type the homegroup password** page, enter the password you obtained in step 1, and then select **Next**.

6. On the **You have joined the homegroup** page of the wizard, select **Finish**.

8

To connect to homegroup resources

1. In the **Navigation** pane of File Explorer, expand the **Homegroup** node to display the user accounts that have shared resources through the homegroup.

2. Expand each user account to display the computers or devices the user has shared resources from.

3. Expand each computer or device to display the specific shared folders, libraries, and devices. Devices that are offline or sleeping aren't shown.

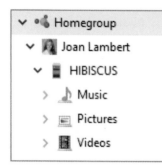

4. Select any user account, device, or shared item to display its contents in File Explorer.

To disconnect all other computers from a homegroup

- Change the homegroup password.

To reconnect computers to a homegroup after changing the password

1. On each computer, display the **HomeGroup** window of Control Panel.

2. Select **Type new password** to start the **Update Your Homegroup Password** wizard.

3. Enter the new password, select **Next**, and then select **Finish**.

To remove a computer from a homegroup

1. Display the **HomeGroup** window of Control Panel.

2. Select **Leave the homegroup** to start the Leave The Homegroup wizard.

3. On the first page of the wizard, select **Leave the homegroup**.

4. When the wizard confirms that the computer has successfully been removed from the homegroup, select **Finish**.

> **TIP** Changing the network security profile for a connection from Private to Public also removes a computer from a homegroup. If you use this method and then later change the connection type back to Private, your computer will automatically rejoin the homegroup.

To delete a homegroup

- Remove each member computer from the homegroup.

To run the HomeGroup troubleshooter

- Open the **HomeGroup** window of Control Panel and then, in the **Other home-group actions** section, select **Start the HomeGroup troubleshooter**.

- In File Explorer, right-click the **Homegroup** node, and then select **Start the HomeGroup troubleshooter**.

- In File Explorer, open the **Homegroup** window. Then on the **HomeGroup** tab, select **Start troubleshooter**.

Share files on your network

If you have more than one computer in your organization, you might find it convenient to share files and file storage locations with other people on your network. And if you have more than one computer in your household, you might want to share resources with family members, whether or not your computer is joined to a homegroup. For example, you might:

- Share project-related files with specific team members.

- From your laptop, work on a file that is stored on your desktop computer.

- Share household management documents with your family members.

- Collect all your family photos in one place by having all your family members save their digital photos to a shared external hard drive.

8

Change the computer name

When your computer was initially set up by the original equipment manufacturer (OEM) it was assigned a default name, probably based on its make or model. The name might be one that helps you to identify the computer, such as *ACER* or *DELL*, or something less obvious such as *FVPAD89*. When network discovery is turned on, the computer name is displayed in the Network node of File Explorer and to other network users.

The name isn't really important, as long as it is unique within your local network. However, you might want to assign a name that makes it easier for you and other network users to identify it—such as *OfficePC*, *GuestLaptop*, or *GamingPC*—or that follows a themed naming convention you have for your network—such as *Hibiscus*, *Plumeria*, and *Sunset* on a network named *Paradise*.

IMPORTANT You must be signed in with an Administrator account to rename your computer.

To rename your computer, follow these steps:

1. In the **Settings** window, select **System**, and then **About**. The About pane displays your current computer name, operating system version and product ID, and hardware information.

2. In the **About** pane, below your current computer name, select **Rename this PC** to open the Rename Your PC dialog box.

Rename your PC

Rename your PC

You can use a combination of letters, hyphens, and numbers.

Current PC name: DESKTOP-H9TKKO1

[   ]

[Next]   [Cancel]

3. In the input box below your current computer name, enter the new name. The name can include uppercase and lowercase letters, numbers (0-9), and hyphens, but no other symbols. Then select **Next**.

   IMPORTANT Selecting Next commits you to the selected name. You can't change the name again until after you restart the computer.

   After a short process, the dialog box displays a restart notice. You can restart the computer now or later; the name change takes effect after the restart. Until then, the PC name in the About pane of the Settings window reflects the planned change.

Device specifications

Device name   DESKTOP-H9TKKO1
                (PLUMERIA after restart)

8

There are several ways to share files with users (including yourself) who are logged on to other computers in your network. To share files by using any of these methods, you must first make sure network discovery and file and printer sharing are turned on so that your computer and any resources you choose to share are visible to other network computers and devices. Network discovery and file and printer sharing are turned on by default for Private network connections.

> **TIP** When network discovery is on, your computer is visible in the Navigation pane of File Explorer and in the Network window. When file and printer sharing is on, any resources you choose to share from the computer are also visible in the Network window.

When you share a folder, you can specify the people (in the form of user accounts or groups of users) you are sharing the folder with and what each person (or group) can do with the folder contents. The permission level options are:

- **Read** The user can open a file from the shared folder but cannot save any changes to the file in the shared folder.

- **Read/Write** The user can open and edit a file and save changes to the file in the shared folder.

The default permission level is Read. If you want to allow a network user or group of users to modify shared files, you must explicitly assign the Read/Write permission level.

> **IMPORTANT** Files and printers that you share are available only when your computer is on, and not when it is in Sleep mode.

Files that you store in the Public folders (Public Documents, Public Downloads, Public Music, Public Pictures, and Public Videos) are accessible to any user logged on to your computer. If you choose to share the Public folders on your computer with other computers on your network, their contents are visible to any user connected to your network. Public folder sharing with other network computer users is turned on by default for Private and Public network connections.

If you frequently connect to public networks, consider carefully whether you want to share the contents of your computer's Public folders with strangers. If not, you can easily turn off this feature to safeguard your privacy.

> 🔍 **SEE ALSO** For more information about Public folders, see Chapter 5, "Explore files and folders." For information about the Network And Sharing Center, see the "Connect to a network" section in the topic "Manage network connections" earlier in this chapter.

When your computer is a member of a homegroup, you can share files with other homegroup members while still keeping the files hidden from computers that aren't homegroup members. (Remember that computers, rather than users, are the home-group members.) When you first create or join your computer to a homegroup, you have the option of sharing the built-in Documents, Pictures, Music, and/or Videos libraries. The choices you make at that time are not binding; you can change the library selections at any time. You can add or remove libraries from the shared home-group resources at any time. Files that you store in a library that you share with your homegroup, whether in your personal folders or the Public folders, are accessible to any user logged on to a computer that is a member of the homegroup.

Regardless of whether your computer is a member of a homegroup, you can share a folder or library with users of other computers on your network. You can control access to the shared folder or library by specifying the user accounts or groups of users that can access the shared resource and assigning a specific level of access for each user account or group.

You can share an entire storage drive—either a disc drive that is built in to your computer, or an external storage device such as a freestanding hard drive or a USB flash drive. For example, you might share an internal hard drive on which you store only project-related resources with all the computers on your work network so that your coworkers have access to them, or you might share an external hard drive with all the computers on your home network so that all your family members can save digital photos in one place for safekeeping.

8

To configure your computer to share files with other network computer users

1. Open the **Network and Sharing Center**.

2. In the left pane, select **Change advanced sharing settings**.

3. In the **Advanced sharing settings** window, expand the **Private** profile, and then do the following:

   - In the **Network discovery** section, select **Turn on network discovery**.

   - In the **File and printer sharing** section, select **Turn on file and printer sharing**.

4. At the bottom of the **Advanced sharing settings** window, select **Save changes**. (If you didn't make any changes, select **Cancel**.)

To prevent network users from accessing your Public folders

1. Open the **Advanced sharing settings** window.

2. Expand the **All Networks** profile.

3. In the **Public folder sharing** section of the profile, select **Turn off Public folder sharing**. With this setting off, the Public account folders on your computer can be accessed only from your computer, and not from the network.

4. At the bottom of the **Advanced sharing settings** window, select **Save changes**.

To change the resources that you're sharing with a homegroup

1. Do either of the following to start the **Change Homegroup Sharing Settings** wizard:

    • Display the **HomeGroup** window of Control Panel, and then select **Change what you're sharing with the homegroup**.

    • Display the **Homegroup** window in File Explorer. On the **HomeGroup** tab, select **Share libraries and devices**.

2. On the **Share with other homegroup members** page of the wizard, do the following for each folder or library, and then select **Next**:

    • To share the resource, select **Shared** in the adjacent **Permissions** list.

    • To keep the resource private, select **Not shared** in the adjacent **Permissions** list.

3. On the **Your sharing settings have been updated** page of the wizard, select **Finish**.

> **TIP** Custom libraries that you create on your computer aren't among those listed in the wizard. You can share a custom library by following the procedure for sharing individual folders and libraries.

> **SEE ALSO** For more information about homegroups, see "Manage homegroup connections" earlier in this chapter.

To share a folder or library through a homegroup

1. Do one of the following to display a menu of user accounts on network-connected computers, and other sharing options:

   - In File Explorer, right-click the folder or library you want to share, and then select **Give access to**.

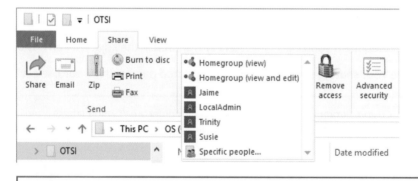

   - In File Explorer, display the folder or library you want to share. On the **Share** tab, select the **More** button at the bottom of the **Share with** gallery scroll bar.

TIP If the computer is not joined to a homegroup, the Give Access To menu and Share With gallery have Create Or Join A Homegroup options instead of Homegroup options. When a folder is shared, the menu and gallery include a Remove Access option.

2. On the **Give access to** menu or in the **Share with** gallery, select the level of access that users of homegroup-joined computers will have to the folder:

- To allow homegroup users to display the folder and open (but not edit) files stored in the folder, select **Homegroup (view)**.

- To allow homegroup users to edit files stored in the folder, select **Homegroup (view and edit)**.

To share a folder or library with one person

- Display the **Give access to** menu or **Share with** gallery for the folder, and then select the user account name or email address of the person you want to share the folder with.

To share a folder or library with everyone on your network

1. Display the **Give access to** menu or **Share with** gallery for the folder, and then select **Specific people...** to start the Network Access wizard.

2. In the **Network access** wizard, select the **v** at the right end of the empty box to display a list that includes people and groups you can share the folder with.

3. In the list, select **Everyone**. Then select **Add**.

4. If you want to allow network users to edit files stored in the folder, select the arrow in the **Permission Level** column adjacent to **Everyone**, and then select **Read/Write**.

5. In the **Network access** wizard, select **Share**. After sharing the folder, the window displays the shared folder's information. You can quickly share a link to the folder with other people by selecting the **e-mail** link.

6. To close the **Network access** wizard, select **Done**.

> ✓ **TIP** When you select a shared file or folder in File Explorer, the Details pane displays a list of the people or groups the folder is shared with.
>
> If you collaborate with a team of people on a document, working with the document in a shared folder entails the risk of one person overwriting another person's changes, even if you restrict access to the folder. To eliminate this risk, you need to use a system with version control. If your organization uses Microsoft SharePoint, you can store the document in a document library so that only one person at a time can check out and work on the document.

To stop sharing a folder or library

- In File Explorer, right-click the folder, select **Give access to**, and then select **Remove access**.

- In File Explorer, display the folder or library you want to stop sharing. On the **Share** tab, in the **Share with** group, select **Remove access**.

To make shared resources available without user account access

1. Display the **Advanced sharing settings** window.

2. Expand the **All Networks** profile.

3. In the **Password protected sharing** section, select **Turn off password protected sharing**.

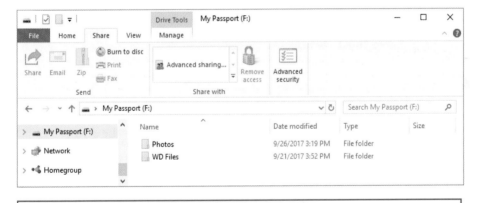

4. At the bottom of the **Advanced Sharing Settings** window, select **Save changes**.

To share a drive

1. In File Explorer, do one of the following to open the drive Properties dialog box:

   - Display the drive you want to share. On the **Share** tab, in the **Share with** gallery, select **Advanced sharing...**.

   - Right-click the drive you want to share, and then select **Properties**.

   - Right-click the drive you want to share, select **Give access to**, and then select **Advanced sharing...**.

TIP Remember that if the shared drive is removable, it is shared only until it is removed.

2. In the **Properties** dialog box for the drive, select the **Sharing** tab, and then select **Advanced Sharing**. If Windows prompts you to enter administrator credentials, do so.

8

3. In the **Advanced Sharing** dialog box, select the **Share this folder** check box.

4. The **Share name** box displays the drive letter of the drive you're sharing. If you want to replace the drive letter with a more user-friendly name to distinguish it from other network drives, enter the name in this box.

> **My Passport (F:) Properties** ✕
>
> **Advanced Sharing** ✕
>
> ☑ Share this folder
>
> Settings
>
> Share name:
>
> | eBook collection |
>
> [Add] [Remove]
>
> Limit the number of simultaneous users to: [20 ▲▼]
>
> Comments:
>
> [   ]
>
> [Permissions] [Caching]
>
> [OK] [Cancel] [Apply]
>
> To change this setting, use the Network and Sharing Center.
>
> [OK] [Cancel] [Apply]

5. Select **Permissions** to display the share permissions for the drive.

6. If the group or user you want to share with is not listed in the **Group or user names** box, select **Add**, and then do the following:

   a. In the **Select Users or Groups** dialog box, enter the name of the user, group, or computer you want to share the drive with, and then select **Check Names**. You can enter multiple names, separated by semicolons.

    TIP To display a list of users and groups you can share with, select Advanced and then, in the secondary Select Users Or Groups dialog box that opens, select Find Now.

b. After Windows indicates a valid name by underlining it, select **OK** to return to the **Permissions** dialog box.

7. In the **Group or user names** box, select the user account or group you want to share the drive with.

8. In the **Permissions for** list, select the check boxes of the permission levels you want to grant to the user account or group.

8

9. Select **OK** in the **Permissions** dialog box and in the **Advanced Sharing** dialog box. Then close the drive's **Properties** dialog box.

Key points

- A network consists of two or more computers that communicate with each other through a wired or wireless connection. Network connections are made by network adapters installed in or connected to your computer. You can view detailed information about the adapters, the active network connections, and the data being transferred through the connections.

- You can change the name of your computer to make it more easily identifiable on your network.

- You can share files that are stored in libraries among computers on your network by creating a password-protected homegroup from one computer and joining other computers to it. Each computer user can select the libraries she or he wants to share with other homegroup users.

- You can share folders outside of libraries with your homegroup, with everyone on your network, or with specific users.

Practice tasks

Before you can complete these practice tasks, you need to copy the book's practice file folder to your computer. The practice file folder for these tasks is the **Win10SBS\Ch08** folder. The introduction includes a complete list of practice files.

Manage network connections

Complete the following tasks:

1. In the notification area of the taskbar, point to the network icon to display information about your current network connection status.

2. Select the network icon to display a list of available networks.

3. If your computer is not currently connected to a network and one is available, select that network name, and connect to it.

4. Near the bottom of the network pane, select **Network & Internet settings**.

5. In the **Status** pane of the **Network & Internet** settings page, review the information about your active network connection.

6. In the **Change your network settings** section, select **Network and Sharing Center**. To the right of **Connections**, select the connection name to display its status. Notice the information about the connection speed, duration, and activity. Then close the **Status** dialog box and **Network and Sharing Center**.

7. In the **Change your network settings** section, select **Change adapter options** to display the network adapters available on your computer. Notice the adapter types that are available and whether each is enabled, disabled, or connected.

8. Select any adapter, and then if necessary, display additional commands that don't fit on the toolbar. Notice that you can enable or disable the adapters and diagnose, rename, or change the settings of the current connection.

9. Return to the **Network and Sharing Center**. In the left pane, select **Change advanced sharing settings** to display the sharing options for the different network profiles.

10. Note the type of network that your computer is currently connected to. Review the settings for that network security profile.

11. Display the network troubleshooting tools. Review the available troubleshooters, and run one that interests you.

12. Open the **Settings** window. Select the **Network & Internet** category, and then display the **Data usage** pane.

13. Review the historical information about data transfers by connection type.

14. In the **Data usage** pane, select **View usage details** and then the individual connections to display the amount of data transferred by each app.

15. When you finish, close the open windows.

Manage homegroup connections

Complete the following tasks:

1. Open the **HomeGroup** window of Control Panel.

2. Determine whether your computer is currently part of a homegroup. If it isn't, determine whether a homegroup is available to join.

3. If your computer is not connected to a homegroup, do either of the following:

   - If no homegroup is available, create a homegroup.

   - If a homegroup is available, join the homegroup.

   Or

   If your computer is connected to a homegroup, do any of the following that interest you:

   - Display the homegroup password.

   - Display the homegroup resources in File Explorer.

   - Disconnect from the homegroup.

Share files on your network

Complete the following tasks:

1. Open the **Advanced sharing settings** window.

2. Review the **Private** network security profile settings, and verify that network discovery and file and printer sharing are turned on, so that your computer can detect and connect to other computers on private networks.

3. In the **Advanced sharing settings** window, expand the **All Networks** profile.

4. In the **Public folder sharing** section of the profile, turn on or off the sharing of Public folders from your computer. (Choose the option you want.)

5. Save your changes and close the **Advanced sharing settings** window.

6. Open File Explorer and locate the practice file folder for this book.

7. Select the **Ch08** folder to select it. On the **Share** tab, notice your options for sharing the folder with other people. If you want to, follow the procedure for sharing the folder with everyone on your network.

8. If you have access to another computer on the network, verify that the folder is available from that computer.

9. On your computer, stop sharing the **Ch08** folder.

10. When you're done, close File Explorer.

Get assistance from Cortana

Cortana is an exciting feature of Windows 10 that can really help you to do things more efficiently. Touted as "your personal assistant," Cortana can monitor your online activity and provide helpful reminders. Cortana interacts with Bing Search to locate information, and also enables you to conduct searches and perform tasks on your computer by giving verbal commands.

The sidebar "Hey, Cortana!" in Chapter 1, "Get started using Windows 10," introduced Cortana. If you've been using Windows 10 for a while, you might have already experimented with Cortana as a verbal interface to your computer. It's a convenient technique, and after you become accustomed to using it, you'll probably find a lot of uses for it.

This chapter guides you through procedures related to configuring Cortana settings and connections, specifying the types of information you want Cortana to track, and managing the information Cortana collects.

In this chapter

- Configure Cortana settings
- Configure Cortana connections
- Configure information tracking
- Manage Cortana information and notifications

Configure Cortana settings

Earlier releases of Windows 10 required users to perform a few processes to set up Cortana on the computer, but now the service is running from the get-go. On a new Windows 10 computer, Cortana leads you through the computer setup process verbally, which is a great way to get used to interacting with the computer by using voice commands. (In case you've been wondering, Cortana's name is pronounced "Cortonn-uh" rather than "Cor-tann-uh." But after you train it to recognize your voice, it responds to your preferred pronunciation.) You can also install the Cortana app on your Android, iOS, or Windows phone.

Cortana is easy to use and interact with through the keyboard and verbally. You can keep Cortana in a listening mode to respond to a verbal cue, or you can activate it manually. Here are some of the methods you can use to activate Cortana:

- When on the Lock screen or signed in, say "Hey Cortana" to activate Cortana's listening mode.

- When signed in, activate the taskbar search box to bring up the on-screen user interface, or press Win+C to activate Cortana's listening mode. (If Win+C doesn't work for you, you can enable it in the Cortana settings.)

You configure Cortana activation, permissions, and notifications settings from the Cortana settings page, and you separately configure the information that you want to track on the Cortana Notebook page. You have the option of providing a name for Cortana to address you by.

One of the fun and useful features of Cortana is that you can give commands verbally. You can manually cue Cortana to listen, or you can configure Cortana to listen for the verbal cue "Hey, Cortana." When you provide verbal input to Cortana, the search box displays the detected input, and then evaluates and refines it to match logical searches or commands. The input and recalculation is displayed in the search box. It's quite interesting to watch the logical revision of the perceived input.

The Cortana input interface can be hidden, or hidden on the taskbar in one of two ways: as the Cortana icon, or as the search box. When it is in the form of a search box, the Cortana icon at the left end indicates that Cortana is configured, and a microphone icon at the right end indicates that Cortana is configured to accept audio input.

To display the Cortana settings page

- Open the **Settings** window and select **Cortana**.

- Open the Cortana pane, and then in the lower-left corner, select the **Settings** icon.

To configure Cortana to respond to a voice prompt

1. If you plan to use an external microphone or headset, connect it to the computer and set it as the default recording device.

     SEE ALSO For information about configuring a microphone in Windows 10, see "Set up audio devices" in Chapter 7, "Manage peripheral devices."

2. Display the **Cortana** settings page.

3. In the **Hey Cortana** section of the **Talk to Cortana** pane, turn on **Let Cortana respond to "Hey Cortana"**.

    ### Hey Cortana

    Let Cortana respond to "Hey Cortana"

    ◖◗ On

    ☐ Keep my device from sleeping when it's plugged in so I can always say "Hey Cortana" (unless I turn it off myself)

    Cortana uses more battery when this is on.
    ◉ Respond when anyone says "Hey Cortana"

    ○ Try to respond only to me
    Learn how I say "Hey Cortana"

    ---

4. If you want Cortana to always monitor for a voice prompt, select the **Keep my device from sleeping...** check box.

5. If you want Cortana to ignore voice prompts from other people, select **Try to respond only to me** or, if the option is unavailable, do the following:

    a. Select **Learn how I say "Hey Cortana"** to start the Cortana-specific voice recognition wizard, which takes you through a quick six-phrase exercise.

    b. When you're ready to start speaking the phrases, select **Start**. Cortana prompts you to speak the first phrase. As you speak, the taskbar search box displays what Cortana hears you say. When it understands you, it moves to the next phrase.

> **TIP** Instead of speaking a phrase immediately after Cortana prompts you to, wait for the audio signal and the Cortana icon to flash before you begin. Otherwise, you'll have to repeat yourself.

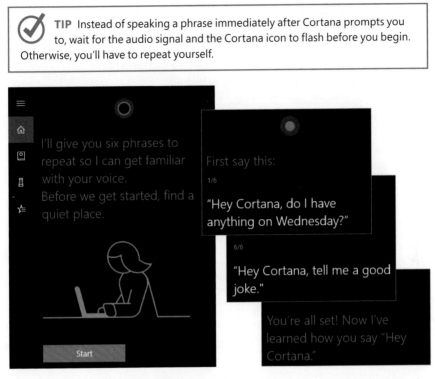

c. Speak each of the six phrases, using different inflections to provide a good sample of how you might sound when you verbally cue Cortana. When you finish, close the Cortana pane, and then speak the cue Hey Cortana to test that it activates the search box.

To turn on the Cortana keyboard shortcut

1. Display the **Cortana** settings page.

2. In the **Keyboard shortcut** section of the **Talk to Cortana** pane, turn **Let Cortana listen for my commands...** to activate the Win+C keyboard shortcut.

To configure Cortana listening mode on the Lock screen

1. Display the **Cortana** settings page.

2. In the **Lock Screen** section of the **Talk to Cortana** pane, turn on or off **Use Cortana even when my device is locked**.

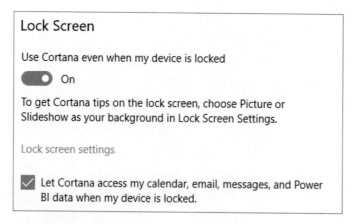

3. When Lock screen listening is turned on, select or clear the **Let Cortana access my calendar...** check box to control access to your information from the Lock screen.

> **TIP** Cortana's Lock screen listening mode doesn't affect the display of Cortana tips on the Lock screen. You can turn these on when you set a picture or slide-show as your Lock screen background.

To display or hide Cortana on the taskbar

1. Right-click a blank area of the taskbar or the taskbar search box.

2. On the shortcut menu, select **Cortana**, and then select **Hidden**, **Show Cortana icon**, or **Show search box**.

Cortana availability

At the time of the 2017 Fall 2017 Creators Update, Cortana is available in the following locations and languages.

Country/region	Language
Australia	English (Australia)
Brazil	Portuguese (Brazil)
Canada	English (Canada) and French (Canada)
China	Chinese (Simplified)
France	French (France)
Germany	German (Germany)
India	English (India)
Italy	Italian (Italy)
Japan	Japanese
Mexico	Spanish (Mexico)
Spain	Spanish (Spain)
United Kingdom	English (United Kingdom)
United States	English (United States)

To use Cortana, your device must be configured so that the country or region, device language, and speech language match as shown in the table.

TIP When Cortana isn't available, you can still use the taskbar search feature, which works in all locations and languages. For more information about taskbar search, see "Search your computer and the web" in Chapter 14, "Work more efficiently."

9

Configure Cortana connections

Activating the taskbar search box displays the Cortana home page. Cortana might offer you specific information or query suggestions here. From the menu in the upper-left corner of the home page, you can go to the other information pages— Notebook, Devices, and Collections—and to the Cortana settings page.

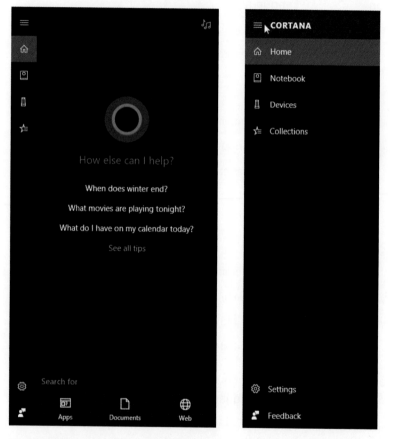

The Notebook is Cortana's central information portal.

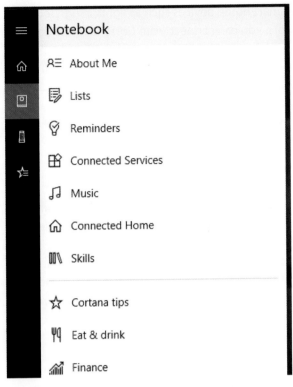

The Cortana Notebook is divided into two sections. The top section contains the lists and reminders that Cortana is tracking for you, and these three menus on which you configure your personal information:

- **About Me** Change the name or nickname Cortana uses for you, save favorite locations (such as home and work) that Cortana can use when providing information, and specify the Microsoft account you want Cortana to associate your information with.

- **Connected Services** Connect Cortana to your Office 365 account, or to a Dynamics CRM, Knowmail, LinkedIn, Outlook.com, Skype, or Wunderlist account.

- **Music** If you have a music service subscription, provide the connection information to Cortana so it can stream music from the service to your devices. At the time of this writing, Cortana supports Groove Music and Spotify subscriptions.

- **Connected Home** If you use smart home devices such as lights, plugs, locks, thermostats, and water monitors, you can connect from Cortana to the device controller services. At the time of this writing, Cortana supports the Hue, Insteon, Nest, Samsung SmartThings, and Wink controllers.

> ✅ **TIP** On the Cortana Devices page, you can manage any connected Cortana devices that you have on your network. At the time of this writing, available devices include computers and phones with the app installed, and a Harmon Kardon speaker that has Cortana built in. Microsoft is experimenting with Cortana connections that are built in to cars, and other devices are presumably in development.

- **Skills** These are apps and routines that Cortana can use to provide you with information and services. A wide variety of skills are available. For example, Cortana can order a pizza from Domino's, make a restaurant reservation through OpenTable, fetch a recipe from FoodNetwork, get information about a sports team, provide a weather report or trivia fact, and much more. The full catalog of skills is available from *www.microsoft.com/en-us/cortana/skills/all*. The skills are free to use, but you must provide permission to Cortana the first time that you use each skill.

If you sign in to your Windows 10 devices with a Microsoft account and synchronize settings across your devices, you need to set up Cortana to connect to services on only one device. The settings automatically sync with your other devices to get you up and running quickly.

To change or provide a name for Cortana to use for you

1. Open the Cortana pane. In the upper-left corner, do either of the following to display the Notebook page:

   - Select the menu button, and then **Notebook**.

   - Select the **Notebook** icon.

2. At the top of the **Notebook** page, select **About Me**.

3. In the **About me** pane, select **Change my name**.

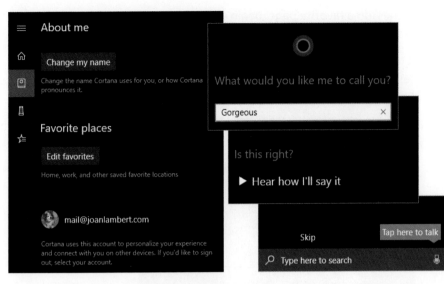

4. On the **What would you like me to call you?** page, enter the name or nickname you want Cortana to use when addressing you, and then at the bottom of the pane, select **Enter**.

> ⚠️ **IMPORTANT** The rest of this procedure requires that your device have working audio input and output devices. Make sure that your speakers, microphone, headset, or other audio devices are connected and working before you continue.

5. On the **Is this right?** page, select **Hear how I'll say it**. Listen to the pronunciation, and then do one of the following:

   - If Cortana pronounces the name correctly, select **Sounds good**.

   - If you want to modify the pronunciation, select **That's wrong**. Then select the microphone icon in the taskbar search box, speak the name, and follow the prompts for further refining the pronunciation by providing phonetic prompts, if necessary.

To save locations for Cortana to reference

1. Open the Cortana pane and select the **Notebook** icon.

2. In the upper section of the **Notebook** page, select **About Me**.

3. In the **Favorite places** section, select **Edit favorites**.

4. At the bottom of the **Places** pane, select the **Add** button (+).

9

5. In the **Add a favorite** pane, begin entering an address or location name in the search box.

6. If the address or location you want to enter comes up in the search results, select it. Otherwise, complete the address entry in the search box and press Enter.

7. In the **Nickname** box, enter a name by which you'd like to be able to find the location.

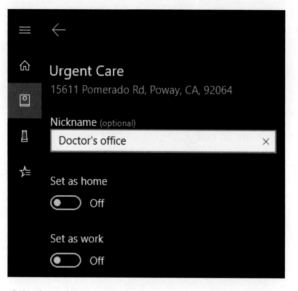

8. If the location is your home, turn on **Set as home**.

9. If the location is your workplace, turn on **Set as work**.

10. Select **Save** (🖫) to save the location.

To manage your saved locations

1. Display the **Notebook** page. In the upper section of the page, select **About Me**.

2. In the **Favorite places** section, select **Edit favorites**.

3. In the **Places** pane, review the locations that have been saved or associated with your account.

4. To modify location details, right-click the location, and select **Edit**. Then enter a nickname for the location, or specify it as your Home or Work.

5. To delete a location, right-click the location, and select **Delete**.

To connect to an information service

1. Display the **Notebook** page. In the upper section of the page, select **Connected Services**.

2. If the service you want to connect to doesn't appear in the list on the **Connected Services** page, select **Add a service** and then select the service.

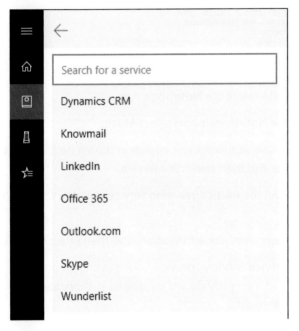

3. On the service-specific page, read the information, and then select **Connect**.

4. In the **Connecting to a service** window, provide your existing credentials for the selected service and then provide any requested authorization for Microsoft to access your information and save your connection information.

> **TIP** The permissions are specific to the service you're connecting to, so they'll vary based on the service.

9

When the connection is complete, the Connect button changes to a Disconnect button.

To connect to a music streaming service

1. Open the Cortana pane and select the **Notebook** icon.

2. In the upper section of the **Notebook** page, select **Music**.

3. If the service you want to connect to doesn't appear in the list on the **Music** page, select **Add a service** and then select the service.

4. On the **Music** page, turn on the music streaming service that you want to con-figure a connection to.

5. On the service-specific page, read the information, and then select **Connect**.

6. In the **Connecting to a service** window, provide your existing credentials for the selected service and then provide any requested authorization for Microsoft to access your account.

To connect to a smart device controller service

1. Open the Cortana pane and select the **Notebook** icon.

2. In the upper section of the **Notebook** page, select **Connected Home**.

3. On the **Connected Home** page, turn on **Enable Connected Home**.

4. On the **Connected Home** page, select the smart device controller service you want to connect to.

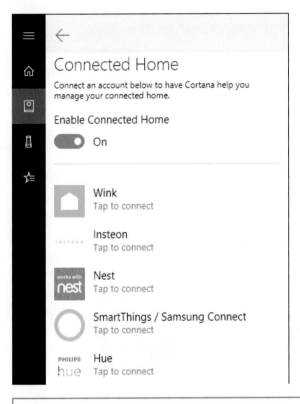

> ⚠ **IMPORTANT** The rest of this procedure requires that you have an existing account with a supported smart device controller service.

5. On the service-specific page, read the information, and then select **Connect**.

6. In the **Connecting to a service** window, provide your existing credentials for the selected service, and then provide any requested authorization for Microsoft to access your connected devices.

To enable a Cortana skill

1. Open the Cortana pane and select the **Notebook** icon.

2. In the upper section of the **Notebook** page, select **Skills**.

3. On the **Manage Skills** page, select **Learn more...** to open the Cortana Featured Skills webpage. Near the top of the page, you can switch between featured skills and all skills, or filter the skills for those that apply to iOS, Android, or Windows, or to the Invoke speaker.

4. Locate a skill that interests you. An example of the verbal cue for each skill is shown below the skill name; if a skill has multiple examples, pointing to the example displays arrows on the left and right sides of the card. Select the arrows to move between examples.

Jaguars Fan

"Hey Cortana, ask Jaguars Fan how are the Jaguars doing?"

LEARN MORE

Currency conversion

"Hey Cortana, what's $5 in Euros"

LEARN MORE

5. To enable a skill, do either of the following:

   • Speak the verbal cue on the card.

   • Select the card to display more information, and then select **Try Now**.

   Then in the skill-specific Cortana pane that opens, select **Yes** to provide permission for Cortana to use the skill.

Configure information tracking

The lower section of the Cortana Notebook page contains the information categories described in the following table. Each category has options for configuring Cortana to track information of that type.

Category	Options
Cortana tips	On/off: All tip suggestions, Tip cards, Tip notifications, Skills notifications
	Option: Notify me what Cortana can do (available only on Android and iPhone)
Eat & drink	On/off: Eat & drink cards, Restaurant recommendations, Lunch Conflict Experience
	Set: Cuisine preferences, Times you normally eat lunch, Ambience
Finance	On/off: Finance cards
	Set: Stocks you're tracking
Getting around	On/off: Traffic, time, and route notifications
	Options when driving: Traffic updates to my calendar events, Notify me when it's time to go to my calendar events, Traffic updates to my favorite places, Notify me when it's time to go to work or head home
	Options when using public transit: Transit updates to my calendar events, Notify me when it's time to go to my calendar events, Transit updates to my favorite places, Notify me when it's time to go to work or head home, Notify me when the last ride is leaving, Show me taxi choices when it's time to leave
	Set: Your preferences for getting around
Meetings & reminders	On/off: Meeting & reminder cards & notifications, Meeting prep, Daily timeline, Related documents, Show reminders on Cortana home, Email assistance
News	On/off: News cards, Local news - Stories happening near you, Headline news - Today's top stories, Recommended stories - News based on your interests, News topic cards, News category cards, Popular now - Stories people are searching for
	Set: Teams, news topics, and news categories you're tracking

9

Category	Options
On the go	On/off: All on the go cards; Offer suggestions when I leave work, leave home, arrive home, or arrive at work; When I'm far from home and work, show me helpful information
Packages	On/off: Package tracking cards
	Option: Notifications for your packages
	Set: Packages you're tracking
Pick up where I left off	On/off: Help me pick up where I left off
Shopping	On/off: All shopping cards, Coupons, Grocery card
Special days	On/off: Celebrate special days
Sports	On/off: All sports cards & notifications, Score updates for your teams, Show upcoming games and matches
	Set: Teams you're tracking
Suggested reminders	On/off: All reminder suggestion cards
	Option: Notify me when something I mentioned doing is coming up
Travel	On/off: Travel cards & notifications
Weather	On/off: Weather cards & notifications, Nearby Forecast, Forecast for your cities
	Set: Cities you're tracking, Temperature units

 IMPORTANT When you change an option, you must select Save at the bottom of the category pane to save your change.

To configure your Cortana information preferences

1. Display the **Notebook** page. In the lower section of the page, select the category you want to configure.

2. In the category pane, turn on or off each setting. When individual settings are available, select the check box, setting name, or **Add** link as appropriate, and then provide the requested information.

   Most options permit only one choice, but some options permit multiple choices.

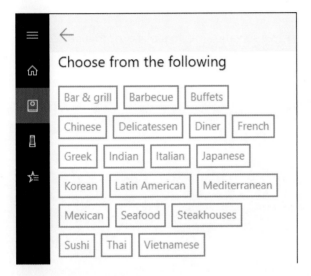

3. If you make changes in a category, select the **Save** button at the bottom of the category pane before leaving the pane.

4. Select the **Back** arrow in the upper-left corner of the pane to return to the Notebook, where you can select a different category.

Add reminders

Cortana can remind you about upcoming appointments and travel plans it finds in your electronic information, but you can also set specific reminders in Cortana. This is particularly convenient if you have Cortana on all your compatible devices, so you can get reminders wherever you are. On a device that has GPS, Cortana can provide reminders based on your location—for example, when you get home, Cortana can remind you to do the laundry, and when you arrive at your local grocery store, Cortana can remind you to buy bread.

You can link each reminder to a specific time, to a place, or to a person or company that is in your contact list; mark the tasks as complete; and look back through your completed task history.

You add reminders from the Reminders pane of Cortana, or you can simply say "Hey, Cortana, remind me to..." Cortana interprets your request in the form of a reminder.

Cortana prompts you for any missing information, and then asks you to approve the reminder. You can say *Yes* or select Remind to set the reminder, say *No* or select Cancel to cancel the reminder, or edit the reminder information in the pane and then complete the process.

Manage Cortana information and notifications

While you use your Cortana-enabled devices, Cortana collects and analyzes information about where you are, who you communicate with, your schedule, packages that are on their way to you, tasks you say you will complete, websites you visit, and so on. All this information enables Cortana to offer helpful advice and answers. If you would prefer that Cortana not collect specific types of information, you can turn off information collection for a specific category of information on a device-by-device basis.

Location

 On

When you let Cortana collect and use your location and location history, Cortana can remind you at places you choose, help you find directions, and keep you posted on what's up nearby.

Contacts, email, calendar & communication history

 On

Cortana can help keep you on time and prepared for meetings, suggest reminders to help you follow up on your commitments, help track your packages and flights, and more when you let Cortana collect and use information like your contacts, calendar details, and content and communication history from messages and apps.

Browsing history

 On

If you let Cortana collect and use your browsing history, Cortana can offer personalized suggestions and help you pick up where you left off on Microsoft Edge websites.

You can also manage the information that Cortana provides by filtering out adult content from search results, including or excluding cloud storage content, and including or excluding information gleaned from your app history, settings history, and search history on your devices—not only those that are running Cortana, but any that you sign in to with the account Cortana is connected to.

9

After you install the Cortana mobile app on your phone, Cortana can notify you on your computer about phone calls that you miss, text messages that you receive, app notifications issued on your phone, and low battery status. These notifications appear in the Cortana section of the Action Center. This convenient inter-device messaging enables you to review and respond to text messages from within the Action Center.

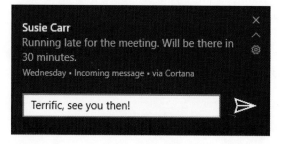

By default, inter-device notifications are also stored in the cloud so they can be managed across multiple devices that you sign in to.

To manage information previously saved by Cortana

1. Display the **Cortana** settings page, and select **Permissions & History**.

2. In the **Permissions** section, do any of the following:

   - To review the types and sources of personal information that Cortana collects, select **Change what Cortana knows about me in the cloud**.

     > **TIP** You can review the information saved by other services by selecting Change What Cortana Knows About Me In The Cloud, and then selecting other links such as Bing Maps and Search History Page from the Personal Information pane.

   - To clear the information saved by Cortana, select **Change what Cortana knows about me in the cloud**, and then at the bottom of the **Personal Information** pane, select **Clear**.

3. In the **History** section, if you want to clear the app and settings information that Cortana has saved on this device, select **Clear my device history**.

To manage Cortana's access to information

1. Display the **Cortana** settings page, and select **Permissions & History**.

2. In the **Permissions** section of the **Permissions & History** pane, select **Manage the information Cortana can access from this device**.

3. In the **Permissions** section of the **Manage the information...** page, turn on or off any of the following:

   - **Location**

   - **Contacts, email, calendar & communication history**

   - **Browsing history**

4. If you turn off any of the options, follow these steps to delete the existing information:

   a. Open Cortana and select the **Notebook** icon.

   b. In the Cortana Notebook, select **About Me**, and then at the bottom of the page, select your account.

   c. In the **Account** window, select **Sign out**.

To manage Cortana search settings

1. Display the **Cortana** settings page, and select **Permissions & History**.

2. In the **SafeSearch** section, select **Strict** or **Moderate** to designate the types of adult content you want to filter out of search results, or **Off** if you don't want to filter content.

> ## SafeSearch
>
> ○ Strict - Filter out adult text, images, and videos from my web results
>
> ◉ Moderate - Filter adult images and videos but not text from my web results
>
> ○ Off - Don't filter adult content from my web results
>
> ## Cloud Search
>
> Windows Cloud Search
>
> ⬤ On
>
> Show my cloud content in Windows Search

3. In the **Cloud Search** section, if you want to exclude files stored in Microsoft OneDrive and other cloud content from search results, turn off **Windows Cloud Search**.

To manage device and search history settings

1. Display the **Cortana** settings page, and select **Permissions & History**.

2. In the **History** section, do any of the following:

   - To include or exclude app and setting information, turn on or off **My device history**.

   - To include or exclude search terms and results, turn on or off **My search history**.

To configure Cortana notifications about your phone

1. Display the **Cortana** settings page, and select **Notifications**.

2. To manage notifications about missed phone calls, text messages, app notifications, and low battery warnings on your phone, turn on or off **Send notifications between devices**.

3. When phone notifications are turned on, select **Manage notifications** to open the Manage Notifications pane in Cortana. In this pane, you can see the status of the Upload Notifications From This PC To The Cloud setting. To change the setting, select it in the pane and then, in the setting-specific pane, turn it on or off.

> **TIP** You can get more information about how Cortana and Windows handle your personal information from the More Details pane of the Cortana settings page. You can manage your privacy settings from the Privacy settings page. For more information, see "Configure privacy settings" in Chapter 15, "Protect your computer and data."

Key points

- Cortana is a helpful personal assistant that you can take with you on any device. It monitors your activities and provides useful related information and reminders.

- You can use Cortana to manage connected smart home devices and interact with many companies and services.

Practice tasks

No practice files are necessary to complete the practice tasks in this chapter.

Configure Cortana settings

If Cortana is available on your computer, perform the following tasks:

1. Display the Cortana **Notebook** page. In the **About Me** pane, provide any information that you want Cortana to have, but haven't yet saved—for example, a nickname to personalize its communications with you, or your work address.

2. Display the **Cortana** settings page. From the **Talk to Cortana** pane, configure Cortana to respond to verbal cuing, and set the other options in the pane as you want them.

3. Experiment with giving Cortana commands, such as "Hey, Cortana. Start Word," and asking questions, such as "Hey, Cortana. What's the weather?"

Configure Cortana connections

Perform the following tasks:

1. Review the options in the **Connected Services**, **Music**, and **Connected Home** panes. If you have accounts with any of the available services, configure a connection to them.

2. Return to the Cortana **Notebook** page. Display the skills that you can configure for Cortana. Review the skill cards and select one that interests you to see more information about it. If you want to, configure Cortana to connect to one or more of the available skills.

Configure information tracking

Perform the following tasks:

1. Configure your Cortana information preferences.

2. Review the information shown on the Cortana home page.

Manage Cortana information and notifications

Perform the following tasks:

1. In the **Permissions & History** pane, review the types of information that Cortana collects about you, and consider how that can be of service to you.

2. In the **Notifications** pane, review the notification options that are available for you to manage. If you want to make any changes to these, do so.

Safely and efficiently browse the internet

Some businesses and government agencies totally isolate their computers from any direct connection to the public internet, for security and privacy reasons. But for the average person, internet access is one of the primary reasons for having a computer.

Many apps connect to the internet without any external input, but the primary method for individuals to interact on the internet is through an internet browser. Regardless of the browser you use, the internet browsing experience has many common characteristics.

The Microsoft Edge browser, which was released with Windows 10, was designed from the ground up for speed and security. It offers many interesting and useful features. Since its initial release, it has had many updates, and independent tests have found it to be the best-performing browser for running modern web applications, more effective than Chrome or Firefox at blocking malware downloads and phishing attacks, and more power-efficient than Chrome or Firefox when streaming high-definition video.

This chapter guides you through procedures for displaying websites in Microsoft Edge; finding, saving, and sharing information; managing Microsoft Edge settings; configuring browser security settings; maintaining browsing privacy; and troubleshooting browsing issues.

In this chapter

- Display websites in Microsoft Edge

- Find, save, and share information

- Manage Microsoft Edge settings

- Configure browser security settings

- Maintain browsing privacy

- Troubleshoot browsing issues

About Microsoft Edge

Microsoft Edge is a *universal app*, which means it will run on many different devices—not only on your computer, but also on tablets, phones, Xbox gaming systems, HoloLens headsets, and Surface Hub devices. This is a bigger deal than it might seem—universal apps have only recently become an achievable reality. The benefit for app developers is that they can learn one coding system, create only one version of each app, sell it to consumers on multiple platforms, and provide support for only one source code project. The benefit to consumers is that they can purchase one app that is of better quality and use it across multiple platforms. (For example, a Bejeweled game that you can play on your computer, phone, and tablet, with your progress following you across all the devices.) Universal apps are a win-win situation for everyone.

Microsoft Edge is installed as part of the Windows 10 operating system and is automatically set as the default browser. This means that you can use any browser you want, but when you select a link in an app, it automatically opens in Microsoft Edge. The initial version released with Windows 10 was a little rough around the edges, but since that time, Microsoft Edge has become a great browser. It's fast, secure, has a sleek interface, and features some cool tools. In short, there's a lot to like about it.

If you updated your computer from another version of Windows to Windows 10, any browsers you had installed on your system are still installed and available for use. Internet Explorer is also available; it's hidden in the app list in the Windows Accessories folder, but if you want to use it (or any other browser), you can create a Start menu or taskbar shortcut.

SEE ALSO For information about creating app shortcuts, see "Create and manage app shortcuts" in Chapter 3, "Work with shortcuts and tiles."

If you give Microsoft Edge a try and find that it isn't going to work for you, you can change the default browser to any other that you have installed. For information about setting default apps, see "Specify default apps" in Chapter 14, "Work more efficiently."

Display websites in Microsoft Edge

The Microsoft Edge user interface is simple and clean. The browser was designed to be secure, but also to provide a minimal interface with relatively few distractions.

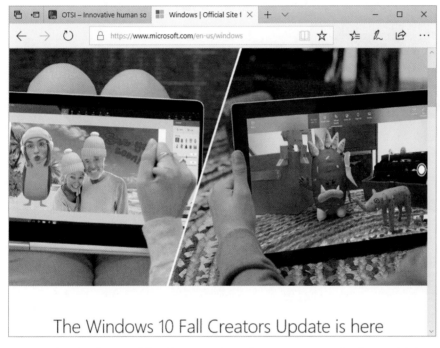

The Windows 10 Fall Creators Update is here

Microsoft Edge has a tabbed browser interface so you can display multiple webpages in one window. When you start the browser, it displays either the Start page, a new tab, the most recent tab set, or a home page (or pages) that you specify. New tabs display your choice of a blank page, links to the websites that you frequently visit, or website links and newsfeed content.

The Microsoft Edge controls are on a simple toolbar below the page tabs.

In addition to the standard browser view experience, Microsoft Edge supports playing audio in the background of webpages (for example, the sound of birds shown in some

Bing background images) and has a Reading view that hides the distracting elements and displays the current webpage as it might appear in an e-book reader, so you can concentrate on the content.

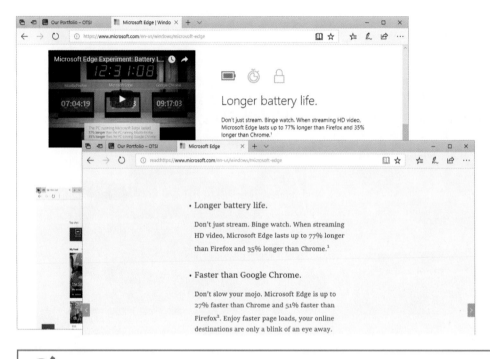

> ✓ **TIP** When Reading view is active, the Reading view button in the toolbar is blue. When Microsoft Edge displays a webpage that doesn't support Reading view, the button is dimmed.

Reading view becomes available only after Microsoft Edge loads all the webpage content, including advertisements. Reading view is available only for some webpages because it displays primarily text content. It doesn't display all the content on the page—and the standards by which it chooses content aren't entirely clear. It isn't available for website home pages, online commerce sites, or webpages that don't contain much text.

> ✓ **TIP** If you own a website that doesn't display well in Reading view, check the Microsoft Edge Reading View webpage at *docs.microsoft.com/en-us/microsoft-edge/dev-guide /browser/reading-view* to identify possible causes.

If a webpage includes audio content, a speaker icon appears on the page tab when the audio is playing. This makes it much easier to locate the source of unwanted audio output. If you can't hear the audio and want to, you might need to turn up your speaker volume or change your audio playback device.

The Microsoft Edge version released with the Fall 2017 Creators Update of Windows 10 also supports the filling out of PDF forms in the browser window.

To start Microsoft Edge

- On the taskbar, select the **Microsoft Edge** button (labeled with a stylized **e**).

- On the **Start** menu, in the app list, jump to the **M** section, and then select **Microsoft Edge**.

To display the Settings And More menu

- In the upper-right corner of the Microsoft Edge window, below the **Close** button (the **X**), select the **Settings and more** button (**...**).

To open a new browser tab

- At the top of the Microsoft Edge window, to the right of the rightmost tab, select the **New tab** button (the **+**).

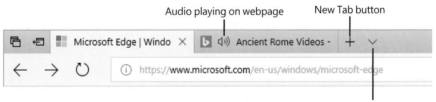

Audio playing on webpage   New Tab button

Show Tab Previews button

- Press Ctrl+T.

10

To preview all open webpages

- At the top of the Microsoft Edge window, to the right of the New Tab button, select the **Show tab previews** button (the **v**).

To display a webpage

1. Select the Address bar to activate it.

2. Enter a URL or search term into the **Search or enter web address** box, and then press Enter or select a webpage from the list that appears below the Address bar.

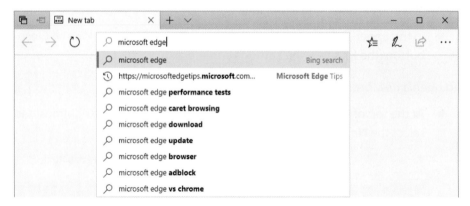

To display webpages on separate Microsoft Edge tabs

- Right-click a link, and then select **Open in new tab**.

- Right-click a tab, and then select **Duplicate**. In the duplicate tab, navigate to a new webpage.

To display webpages in separate Microsoft Edge windows

- Right-click a link, and then select **Open in new window**.
- Drag an existing tab away from the original Microsoft Edge window to display it in its own window. (Releasing the tab creates the new window.)
- Right-click a tab, and then select **Move to new window**.
- On the **Settings and more** (...) menu, select **New window**.
- On the **Settings and more** (...) menu, select **New InPrivate window**.

> **SEE ALSO** For information about InPrivate browsing, see "Maintain browsing privacy" later in this chapter.

To move between webpages visited on a tab

- At the left end of the active tab toolbar, select the **Back** or **Forward** button.
- Hold down the Shift key and then scroll the mouse wheel.

To refresh the display of a webpage

- At the left end of the active tab toolbar, select the **Refresh** button.
- Press F5.
- Right-click any tab, and then select **Refresh all**.

To switch the display of a webpage to and from Reading view

- In the Address bar, select the **Reading view** button.

> **TIP** You can configure the Reading view background color and type size. For more information, see "Manage Microsoft Edge settings" later in this chapter.

10

Find, save, and share information

A web search for specific information sometimes leads to webpages that contain a lot of content. It can be difficult to locate the information you're looking for on the webpage. You can quickly highlight all instances of a search term on the current webpage, and scroll to spot them or cycle through them in order.

After you find the information you're looking for, you can annotate (draw and write on) a snapshot of the webpage by using the Add Notes tool, and then save or share the annotated webpage.

Typed notes   Handwritten notes

You can share webpages or their content with other people, or save them for your own reference. The Share pane displays the apps you can use to share the webpage.

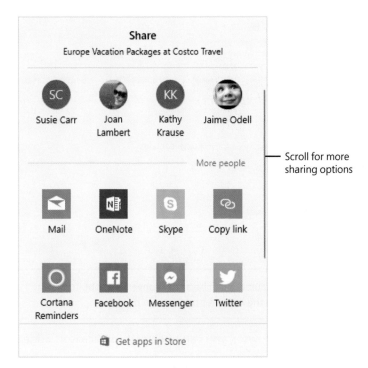

Scroll for more sharing options

You can share a screenshot of the webpage, or you can send, post, or save information from the webpage and a link to it. Your sharing options depend on the apps that are installed on your computer and the user account you're signed in to Windows with. Some common options include the Cortana, Facebook, Mail, Messenger, OneNote, Skype, and Twitter apps.

> **SEE ALSO** For information about Cortana, see Chapter 9, "Get assistance from Cortana."

You can easily keep track of and return to sites of ongoing interest. If you think you will want to return to a webpage, you can add it to one of your lists:

- Add articles and blogs that you want to read later to your Reading list.

- Add sites that you want to store for long-term reference to your Favorites list. You can organize favorites in folders and optionally display them on the Favorites bar for quick access.

10

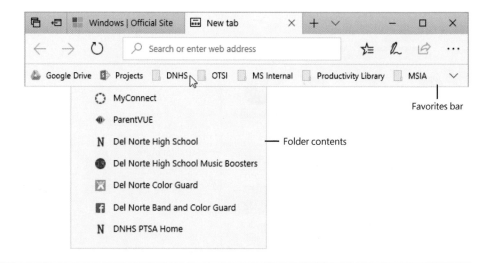

Favorites bar

Folder contents

> ✓ **TIP** The Favorites bar is hidden by default but can be a very convenient tool. To display it, follow the instructions in "To display the Favorites bar" later in this topic.

If you've built a Favorites list in another browser, you can transfer it to Microsoft Edge.

You can also pin websites to the Start screen or taskbar so that you can easily access them.

If you have multiple webpages that you use together, such as a timecard site, payroll site, and employee pension site, or if you want to save a set of tabs that you're working with and come back to them later, you can "set them aside" and easily open all of them at one time. You can set aside multiple sets of tabs. Restoring the tabs removes them from the saved tab sets, so if you want to use them again, you should save them in your Favorites.

To find text on a webpage

1. Display the webpage in Microsoft Edge.

2. Do either of the following to display the Find On Page toolbar:

   - Press Ctrl+F.

   - On the **Settings and more** (…) menu, select **Find on page**.

3. Begin entering your search term in the search box.

As you enter characters, every instance of matching text on the webpage is highlighted. The number of instances found on the page appears to the right of the search box.

| Find on page | microsoft teams | × | 1 of 7 | ‹ › | Options ⌄ | × |

Match whole word

Match case

4. After you enter as much of the search term as is necessary to return a manage-able number of results, you can scroll through the page content to review the highlighted instances of the search term, or select the **Next** or **Previous** buttons to move among the results.

5. To further restrict the search, select **Options** on the **Find on page** toolbar, and then select **Match whole word** or **Match case**.

To annotate a webpage

1. On the Microsoft Edge toolbar, select the **Add Notes** button (the pen). The browser converts the page to a screenshot and displays an annotation toolbar at the top of the page.

2. Select the buttons on the toolbar to activate any of the following functions:

    *   Draw with a pen (select from 30 ink colors and 24 widths).

    *   Highlight (select from 6 ink colors and 53 widths).

    *   Erase (freehand or all markup).

    *   Add a typed note.

    *   Clip part of the image.

    *   Draw with your finger or a stylus instead of the mouse.

    *   Save the marked-up page to OneNote, your Favorites list, or your Reading list.

    *   Share the marked-up page through any of the installed apps that support content sharing.

10

To share a webpage

1. At the right end of the Microsoft Edge toolbar, select the **Share** button to open the Share pane on the right side of your screen. The Share pane displays people you frequently share information with, and the apps you can use to share the webpage.

2. Do either of the following:

   - At the top of the **Share** pane, select the person you want to share the page with, or select **More people** and then find and select the person. Then select the sharing method you want to use.

   - At the bottom of the **Share** pane, select the method you want to use to share the page. Then follow the process appropriate to that method to share the page on your feed or with specific people.

To save a webpage for later reference

1. Select the **Add to favorites or reading list** button (the star) at the right end of the Address bar, or press Ctrl+D.

2. At the top of the pane, select either **Favorites** or **Reading list**.

3. In the **Name** box, edit the page name that will be displayed in the list, if you want to.

4. If you're saving the page to your Favorites list and you have organized your favorites in folders, select **Save in** to display the storage folders, and select or create a folder.

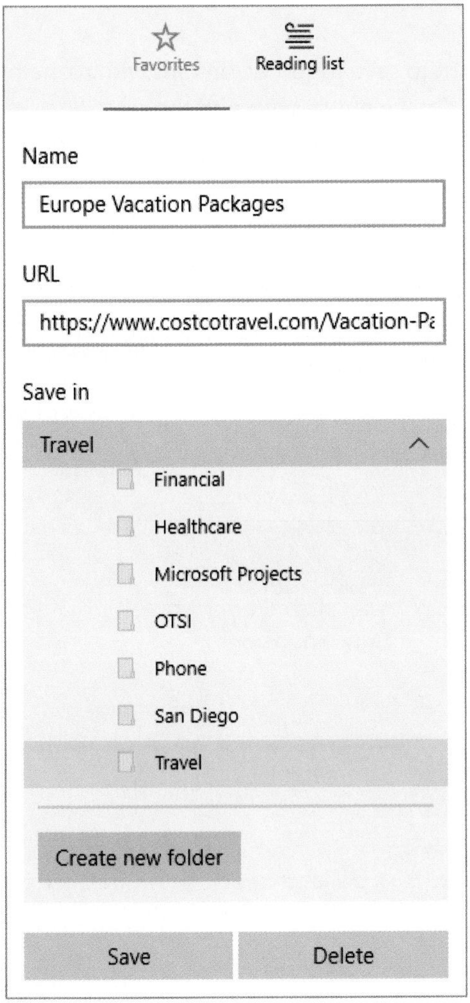

☆
Favorites

≋
Reading list

Name

Europe Vacation Packages

URL

https://www.costcotravel.com/Vacation-Pa

Save in

Travel ∧

☐ Financial

☐ Healthcare

☐ Microsoft Projects

☐ OTSI

☐ Phone

☐ San Diego

☐ Travel

Create new folder

Save   Delete

5. Select **Save**.

10

To set aside tab sets

1. Open the webpages that you want to save together, on tabs within one browser window. Close any tabs that you don't want to save with the set.

2. Near the upper-left corner of the window, select the **Set these tabs aside** button.

To restore tab sets

1. In the upper-left corner of the Microsoft Edge window, select the **Tabs you've set aside** button.

2. In the **Tabs you've set aside** pane, locate the tab set you want to open. In the upper-right corner of the tab set, select **Restore tabs**.

To import your Favorites list from another browser to Microsoft Edge

1. At the bottom of the **Settings and more (...)** menu, select **Settings**.

2. In the **Settings** pane, under **Import favorites and other info**, select **Import from another browser** to display a list of installed browsers that have saved favorites.

«   Import info from another browser   ⊣⊐

Import your info

We'll bring over your favorites, browsing history, and other data from another browser.

◉ Internet Explorer

Favorites, browsing history, cookies, passwords, form data, and settings.

○ Chrome

Bookmarks, browsing history, cookies, passwords, and settings.

[Import]

Import or export a file

Favorites can be imported or exported as HTML files.

[Import from file]

[Export to file]

---

3. Select the browser you want to import favorites from, and then select **Import**. Repeat for each browser you want to import your favorites from.

To display your Favorites list, Reading list, browsing history, or file downloads

1. On the Microsoft Edge toolbar, select the **Hub** button. The Hub displays the most recently accessed pane when it opens.

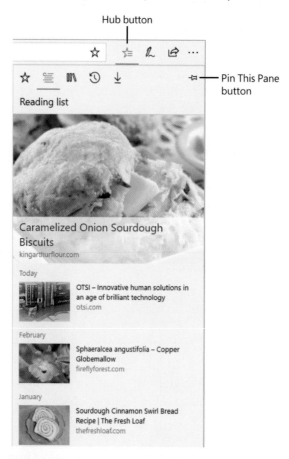

2. At the top of the **Hub**, select the **Favorites**, **Reading list**, **Books**, **History**, or **Downloads** button to display that list.

To pin the Hub to the browser window

1. Display any list in the Hub.

2. In the upper-right corner of the Hub, select the **Pin this pane** button (the pushpin).

To read articles from your Reading list

1. On the Microsoft Edge toolbar, select the **Hub** button.

2. At the top of the Hub pane, select the **Reading list** button.

3. Select the article you want to read, to display it in the current tab.

To remove a webpage from your Reading list

1. Display the **Reading list** in the Hub.

2. Right-click the page you want to remove, and then select **Delete**.

To organize your Favorites list

1. Display the **Favorites list** in the Hub.

2. Do any of the following:

    - To move a saved page into a folder, drag the page to the folder.

    - To move a saved page or folder onto the Favorites bar, drag it to the **Favorites Bar** folder.

    - To rename a saved page or folder, right-click it and select **Rename**. Then edit the entry or enter a new name, and press Enter to save the change.

    - To sort your saved favorites, right-click any folder or page and then select **Sort by name**. Folders appear at the top of the list, followed by pages.

    - To change the URL associated with a saved page, right-click the page and then select **Edit URL**. In the box that opens, edit the URL and then press Enter to save the change.

To display the Favorites bar

1. At the bottom of the **Settings and more (...)** menu, select **Settings**.

2. In the **Settings** pane, turn on **Show the favorites bar**.

3. If you have a lot of favorite sites and want to fit more of them on the Favorites bar, turn on **Show only icons on the favorites bar** to display only site icons and not names.

10

To pin a webpage to the Start menu or taskbar

- On the **Settings and more (...)** menu, select **Pin this page to Start** or **Pin this page to the taskbar**.

To print the current webpage

1. In Microsoft Edge, on the **Settings and more (...)** menu, select **Print** to preview the page in the Print dialog box.

2. If the webpage will print on multiple pages, a Next arrow appears above the preview to the right of the page number. Move through the pages to verify that they will print as you want them.

3. In the **Printer** list, select the printer or app you want to print to.

4. Configure any additional print settings, and then select **Print**.

Manage Microsoft Edge settings

All browsers provide a way to set options and default behavior. The settings in Microsoft Edge are well organized and, for the most part, straightforward. You manage Microsoft Edge settings from the Settings And More menu that expands from the upper-right corner of the browser window.

Settings And More button

The Microsoft Edge settings panes are quite bland and don't have icons to visually differentiate between settings, so it can be slightly difficult to locate specific settings.

You configure most of the Microsoft Edge settings in the Settings pane and the Advanced Settings pane. We don't cover configuration processes for *all* the individual settings in this section, but they're easy to locate and most have simple On/Off toggle buttons.

You can specify the page or pages that Microsoft Edge displays when it starts, and you can specify, to some extent, the content of new tabs that you open. The options include:

- A blank page, which displays only a search box.

- Top sites, which displays up to eight tiles that link to sites that you visit most frequently.

- Top sites and suggested content, which displays site tiles and news feeds.

By default, Microsoft Edge uses the Bing search engine. If you prefer to use a different search engine, you can easily specify any search engine that uses OpenSearch technology.

You can have Microsoft Edge save passwords and form entries, and automatically enter them for you. It can be very convenient to not have to manually enter your address into online forms, but before agreeing to save a password, consider whether you want this information to be available to someone else who might use your computer and user account. You should never save a password on a computer that has a shared user account, such as a public computer at a school or library.

To display the Settings And More menu

- In the upper-right corner of the Microsoft Edge window, below the **Close** button (the **X**), select the **Settings and more** button (...).

To set or change your home page or starting content

1. At the bottom of the **Settings and more** (...) menu, select **Settings**.

2. In the **Settings** pane, expand the **Open Microsoft Edge with** list, and then do one of the following:

   - Select **Start page** to display news feeds from MSN.

   - Select **New tab page** to display a new tab showing either a blank page, your frequently visited sites, or top sites and suggested content.

   > **SEE ALSO** For information about setting the content for new tabs, see the procedure "To specify the content of new tabs" later in this topic.

   - Select **Previous pages** to display the tabs that were open when you last closed Microsoft Edge.

- Select **A specific page or pages** to have Microsoft Edge display one or more specific pages when it starts.

Settings	📌
Choose a theme	
Light ⌄	
Open Microsoft Edge with	
Start page	
New tab page	
Previous pages	
A specific page or pages	

3. If you chose **A specific page or pages**, do any of the following:

   - To specify the first home page, select the **Enter a URL** box, enter the web-page address, and then select the adjacent **Save** button (💾).

   > **TIP** To include the Microsoft Edge Start page in a home page set, enter *about:start* as the URL, or to include a blank page, enter *about:blank*.

   - To specify additional home pages, select **+Add new page**, enter the web-page address, and then select the adjacent **Save** button.

   - To modify a home page address, point to the URL, select the **Edit** button (the pencil) that appears, edit the address, and then select the adjacent **Save** button.

   - To remove a page from a set of home pages, point to the webpage address, and then select the **Delete** button (the **X**) that appears.

   > **TIP** If you set a home page or home pages, display the Home button on the Microsoft Edge toolbar so you can return to your home page by selecting the button. To display the button, turn on Show The Home Button at the top of the Advanced Settings pane.

4. Open a new Microsoft Edge window to display your selected configuration.

10

To specify the content of new tabs

1. At the bottom of the **Settings and more (...)** menu, select **Settings**.

2. In the **Settings** pane, expand the **Open new tabs with** list, and then do one of the following:

    -   Select **Top sites and suggested content** to display thumbnails of the sites you visit often and a current newsfeed.

    -   Select **Top sites** to display only thumbnails of sites you visit often.

    -   Select **A blank page** to display the simplest page, without any distracting content.

Open Microsoft Edge with

A specific page or pages	⌄

▭ http://otsi.sharepoint.com/	✕
▭ https://windows.microsoft.com/	✕

Top sites and suggested content

Top sites

A blank page

3. Open a new tab to test your selected setting.

To customize your suggested content (news feed)

1. Set the new tab content to **Top sites and suggested content** (referred to in some places as **Top sites and my news feed**).

2. Open a new tab in Microsoft Edge.

3. At the right end of the **Top sites** heading, select the **Customize** button (the cog) to display your suggested sites/news feed customization options.

4. In the **Information cards** section, turn on the topics you want to display.

5. Select **Save** to apply your changes.

To change your default search engine

1. Open Microsoft Edge and go to the webpage of the search engine you want to use (for example, to use Google Search, go to *www.google.com*).

> **TIP** Microsoft Edge supports OpenSearch search engines. For a full list of OpenSearch search engines, visit *www.opensearch.org/Community /OpenSearch_search_clients*.

2. At the bottom of the **Settings and more** (...) menu, select **Settings**.

3. At the bottom of the **Settings** pane, select **View advanced settings**.

4. In the **Privacy and services** section of the **Advanced settings** pane, below **Search in the address bar with**, select **Change search engine** to display the search engine options.

5. In the **Change search engine** pane, select the search engine you want to use, and then select **Set as default**.

> ⚠ **IMPORTANT** If the Change Search Engine pane doesn't include the search engine you want to use, be sure that you completed step 1.

To save and manage passwords and form entries

1. At the bottom of the **Settings and more (…)** menu, select **Settings**.

2. At the bottom of the **Settings** pane, select **View advanced settings**. Then in the **Advanced settings** pane, locate the **Privacy and services** section.

3. Do any of the following:

   - To save and autofill passwords that you enter in password boxes in the Microsoft Edge browser, turn on **Offer to save passwords**.

     > ⚠ **IMPORTANT** This option doesn't automatically save every new password you enter; it displays a message box offering to do so.

   - To stop saving passwords, turn off **Offer to save passwords**.

- To review the sites that you've saved passwords for, select **Manage passwords** to open the Manage Passwords pane.

Select any website to display and edit the saved user name and password, or point to a website and select the **Clear** button (the **X**) that appears on the right side of the pane to delete the saved user name and password.

- To save form entries that you enter in the Microsoft Edge browser (so the browser can automatically enter them for you in other forms), turn on **Save form entries**.

- To stop saving form entries, turn off **Save form entries**.

> ⚠️ **IMPORTANT** The information you save will be used to automatically fill forms in the future. This is convenient, but it might also be a security risk. Some less-than-scrupulous websites add hidden form fields to collect information that you don't know you're providing.

> ✅ **TIP** Another interesting password management tool is Credential Manager, which you can open from the taskbar search box or an Icons view of Control Panel.

To delete saved information

1. At the bottom of the **Settings and more (...)** menu, select **Settings**.

2. In the **Clear browsing data** section of the **Settings** pane, select **Choose what to clear** to display the types of data you can clear.

« Clear browsing data

- ☑ Browsing history
- ☑ Cookies and saved website data
- ☑ Cached data and files
- ☑ Tabs I've set aside or recently closed
- ☐ Download history
- ☐ Form data
- ☐ Passwords
- ☐ Media licenses
- ☐ Website permissions

  Manage permissions

Clear

Always clear this when I close the browser

◉◯ Off

Change what Microsoft Edge knows about me in the cloud

Clear Bing search history

Learn more

3. In the **Clear browsing data** pane, select the check boxes of the types of browsing data you want to purge. Then select the **Clear** button.

 IMPORTANT Clearing a browsing data category doesn't stop Microsoft Edge from collecting data; you must turn off data collection separately.

Anatomy of a website address

The words, letters, numbers, and symbols that appear in the Address bar of your web browser window when you connect to a webpage might look like a logical address or like a bunch of nonsense. Every character has a specific purpose. Here's a breakdown of a typical webpage address and a description of what each part does. The webpage address is *http://movies.msn.com /showtimes/today.aspx?zip='92127'*.

Protocol	Subdomain	Domain name	Folder	Page	Query
http	movies	msn.com	showtimes	today.aspx	?zip='92127'

The *protocol* tells your web browser what type of connection to make to the destination site. The most common protocol is *http* (Hypertext Transfer Protocol, the protocol that delivers information over the World Wide Web). Another common web protocol is *https* (HTTP over a secure connection). In a URL, the protocol is followed by a colon and two forward slashes (*://*).

TIP There are dozens of protocols for many different types of communication, including internet connections, email delivery, file sharing, local and remote network connections, and a plethora of others. Some of the more familiar protocols include ADSL, DHCP, DNS, FTP, HTTPS, IMAP, IP, ISDN, POP3, SMTP, SOAP, TCP, and Telnet.

The *domain name* is the base address of the site. The top-level domain (TLD), such as *.com*, is part of the domain name. Each domain name is purchased and registered by an organization or individual and is assigned to an Internet Protocol (IP) address representing the location of the site content on a server. Domain names and IP addresses are managed by ICANN (the Internet Corporation for Assigned Names and Numbers), a nonprofit corporation based in California. Although ICANN is an American corporation, it manages internet-related tasks worldwide in cooperation with international agencies.

TIP Top-level domains (TLDs) are governed by an international organization. Each TLD has a specific meaning: generic TLDs (such as .com and .net) are available to anyone, sponsored TLDs (such as .edu, .gov, and .travel) belong to private agencies or organizations, and two-letter country code TLDs are intended to represent the country or region of origin or use of a site's content. Country code TLDs are frequently used for other purposes, however; for example, the TLD .am is assigned to Armenia, and .fm is assigned to the Federated States of Micronesia, but many radio stations have website addresses ending in these TLDs.

When you go to a website, your computer connects to the internet to find out the IP address currently assigned to the domain name. Then it connects to the server located at that IP address and displays the content located on that server. Because the alphabetic domain name leads to the less-obvious IP address, the domain name is sometimes referred to as a *friendly name*.

If an address includes a *subdomain*, it points to a specific site, usually one of a group of sites presented under the umbrella of one domain name. The sites represented by the subdomains don't have be of the same type or reside in the same location. For example, Contoso Corporation might have the registered domain name *contoso.com*, a public website at *http://www.contoso.com* and the subdomains *sharepoint,* for its collaboration site at *http://sharepoint.contoso.com; mail,* for its web email server at *http://mail.contoso.com; and shopping,* for a secure online shopping cart application at *https://shopping.contoso.com.*

A *folder name* indicates the location in the website structure of the page on the screen. In the same way that you store files within a logical folder structure on your hard drive, a website administrator might arrange files in a logical structure within the site. Single forward slashes (/) separate folders from other address elements, in the same way that single backward slashes (\) separate folders in the File Explorer Address bar.

The *page name* represents the specific file containing the content and code that generates the information displayed on the screen; it includes a file name extension indicating the file type. Common page name extensions include .htm for HTML files containing static content, and .aspx for Active Server Pages (ASP pages) displaying dynamic content gathered from a database or other source within a framework governed by code in the file.

An HTML page name might include a bookmark, preceded by a pound sign (#), indicating a specific location in a file. An ASP page name might include a query, preceded by a question mark (?), indicating the search term that generated the page content. In the example given at the beginning of this sidebar, the query *?zip='92127'* is intended to return show times for movies playing in the geographical area identified by the ZIP Code 92127.

When you connect to a simple website address, Microsoft Edge uses the protocol to establish the communication method, connects to the server hosting the domain or subdomain, and then displays the page designated by the website administrator as the home page for the site.

10

To configure your Reading view settings

1. Display a webpage in Reading view.

2. Do either of the following to display the Reading view Options menu:

   - Click or tap near the top of the page to display the menu bar, which is hidden by default. Then on the menu bar, select the **Options** button.

   - Press Ctrl+Shift+O.

Reading view is active   Options button

And, more innovative features

Windows 10

Text size

Page theme

3. To adjust the text size, do any of the following:

   - In the **Text size** section of the **Options** menu, select the **Make smaller** or **Make bigger** button.

   - Press Ctrl+Minus sign to decrease the text size, or Ctrl+Plus sign (Ctrl+Equal sign also works, if the Plus sign is above that on your keyboard) to increase the text size.

   > **TIP** You can use the keyboard shortcuts without opening the Options menu.

4. To change the page background and font colors, in the **Page theme** section of the **Options** menu, select the **Light**, **Sepia**, or **Dark** button.

Educate kids about online safety

In November 1998, the US Congress passed the Children's Online Privacy Protection Act (COPPA), which requires that operators of US-based online services or websites obtain parental consent before collecting, using, disclosing, or displaying the personal information of children under the age of 13. COPPA went into effect on April 21, 2000, and is governed by regulations established by the Federal Trade Commission.

Many children have internet access at home, at school, and at friends' houses. On their own computers, you can protect children from exposure to objectionable content by setting up their user accounts as Child accounts and configuring the Family Safety settings at age-appropriate levels. However, it's important to proactively educate children about online safety and computer security.

The Federal Trade Commission provides helpful information for parents and teachers about computer security, phones, social networks, virtual worlds, texting, video games, parental controls, and COPPA at *consumer.ftc.gov/topics /kids-online-safety*.

SEE ALSO For more information about Child accounts and Family Safety, see "Create and manage user accounts" in Chapter 11, "Manage user accounts and settings."

10

Configure browser security settings

It is difficult (at least for some of us) to imagine how we would survive without constant access to the internet. The internet has become a primary source of information and services. But it can be hard to know whether the information is accurate and the services are benign: some people use the internet to try to steal information from other people, or damage their computers, through malicious attacks on computer systems.

The security of Microsoft Edge is constantly monitored and managed by Microsoft. Windows Defender updates are released frequently to safeguard your computer against newly discovered threats, or source code issues through which someone who really wants to could exploit the browser. There are bad people who launch malicious attacks, and good people who fix problems; between those two groups, there are people who have the challenging job of finding potential problems before the bad guys do, so the good guys can fix them. All these people are smart and dedicated to playing their roles in the threat lifecycle.

Malware can present itself in many forms—you can find it, or it can find you. Some of the problems that the browser can guard against include:

- Unsafe websites that are phishing websites or that contain malicious software.

- Pop-up windows that display false information and links to malicious software. These frequently are crafted to look like Windows warning messages.

Taking care of Microsoft Edge is the responsibility of Microsoft. Protection generally lags slightly behind the threat, so there is no guarantee that Microsoft or any other company can protect you from all threats. Being aware while browsing the internet is the responsibility of each individual. This topic describes measures that you can take to be safe and secure while browsing the internet.

Protect yourself from phishing and malicious sites

One of the special security features of Microsoft Edge is the Windows Defender SmartScreen filter. It runs in the background of your browsing session and monitors websites, webpages, and downloads for known issues or suspicious content. SmartScreen warns you if it identifies (or suspects) a security problem, such as:

- If you visit a website that has been reported as an unsafe website.

- If you visit a webpage that has characteristics that might indicate a security risk.

- If you download an app that is known to be unsafe.

- If you download an app that isn't known to be unsafe, but also hasn't been downloaded by many people.

SmartScreen is on by default in Microsoft Edge. The only management option is whether it is on or off. If your computer is centrally managed by your organization, the option might be unavailable. If it is, the Advanced Settings pane will include the message *Some settings are managed by your organization*, and the SmartScreen setting text and toggle button will be gray.

You can also turn on SmartScreen for Store apps that pass URLs, from the Privacy page of the Settings window.

To turn SmartScreen on or off

1. At the bottom of the **Settings and more** (...) menu, select **Settings**.

2. At the bottom of the **Settings** pane, select **View advanced settings**.

3. At the bottom of the **Advanced settings** pane, turn on or off **Help protect me from malicious sites and downloads with Windows Defender SmartScreen**.

To report an unsafe website to Microsoft

1. On the **Settings and more** (...) menu, select **Send feedback**.

2. In the **Feedback & reporting** pane, select **Report unsafe site**.

3. On the **Report a website** page, verify that the URL shown in the **Website you are reporting** section is that of the website you want to report.

4. Select any of the following check boxes:

   - **I think this is a phishing website**

   - **I think this website contains malicious software**

5. At the bottom of the page, enter the characters from the image into the box to verify that you are a person rather than a computer. Then select **Submit**.

Block pop-up windows

Pop-up windows are secondary web browser windows that open in front of (or sometimes behind) the window you're working in when you go to a website or select an advertising link. The content of these windows might be informational—for example, a new window might open when you select a link for more information or when you sign in to a secure site—or in some cases might be irritating or malicious—for example, when browsing the internet for information, you might display a page that causes several advertisements to pop up behind it. However, pop-up windows frequently display annoying advertisements, adware (fake warning messages containing links to product sites), spyware (malicious software that can collect personal information from your computer), or other types of content you did not invite and probably don't want.

If a suspicious pop-up window does open, it's best to not select any buttons in it; instead, you can usually close the window from the taskbar, from Task View, or from Task Manager. You can also configure your browser to block pop-up windows from opening. When a site does try to display a pop-up window, the browser alerts you, and

10

you can choose to provide a one-time or permanent exception for that site. If you later change your mind, you can review and remove specific exceptions in Microsoft Edge.

To block pop-up windows

1. At the bottom of the **Settings and more (...)** menu, select **Settings**.

2. At the bottom of the **Settings** pane, select **View advanced settings**.

3. Near the top of the **Advanced settings** pane, turn on **Block pop-ups**.

To clear pop-up window exceptions that you've granted

1. At the bottom of the **Settings and more (...)** menu, select **Settings**.

2. At the bottom of the **Settings** pane, select **View advanced settings**.

3. In the **Website permissions** section of the **Advanced settings** pane, select **Manage**.

4. In the **Manage permissions** pane, the word *Pop-ups* indicates each site that you've allowed pop-up windows on. Point to any site that you want to remove from the list, and then select the **Clear** button (the **X**) that appears.

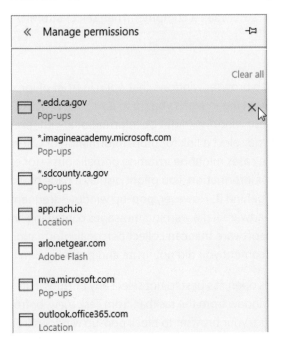

Maintain browsing privacy

Internet browsers keep track of the websites you visit so that you can return quickly to them from your browsing history list. They also track the credentials you sign in to websites and services with, so they can resupply them to the site without bothering you. This can cause conflicts if you have multiple user names for the same site—for example, if you have two different Microsoft accounts, or two different Microsoft Office 365 accounts.

Some sites temporarily save credentials and other information that you provide, in session variables that expire after some period of time. To ensure that your information isn't available to other people who connect to the site from the same computer, take care to sign out of secure sites instead of just closing the browser window.

You can restrict Microsoft Edge from tracking your browsing and credentials by using an InPrivate browsing session. This opens a separate browser window that doesn't carry forward any credentials that are currently in use. The browsing that you do in this window is not tracked—the pages and sites do not appear in your browsing history, and temporary files and cookies are not saved on your computer.

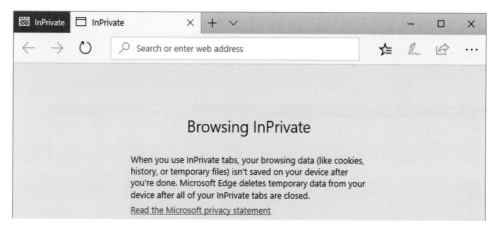

The InPrivate browsing session lasts only as long as the window is open. Any browsing that you do in other browser windows is recorded as usual.

InPrivate browsing is a useful tool for information workers who have multiple Office 365 accounts; you can ensure that Microsoft Edge uses the correct credentials for a browsing session by starting from an InPrivate window.

You can increase the security of an InPrivate browsing session by disabling toolbars and extensions in those sessions. This setting is turned on by default in Microsoft Edge.

To start an InPrivate browsing session

- On the taskbar, right-click the Microsoft Edge button, and then select **New InPrivate window**.

- In Microsoft Edge, on the **Settings and more** (**...**) menu, select **New InPrivate window**.

- Press Ctrl+Shift+P.

Troubleshoot browsing issues

If Microsoft Edge is unable to support site requirements, it displays a link so that you can switch to Internet Explorer. If you think Microsoft Edge is having difficulty with a site, you can switch to the other browser from within Microsoft Edge (and transfer your session information at the same time), or you can have Microsoft Edge act as though it's a different browser (emulate the browser), even one that doesn't usually run on your computer or device. Microsoft Edge can emulate many different browsers, not only those installed on your computer.

Undock button

If you have difficulty navigating a webpage by using the mouse, you can use caret browsing instead. Caret browsing enables you to use standard navigation keys on your keyboard—Home, End, Page Up, Page Down, and the arrow keys—to select text and move around on a webpage.

The concept of caret browsing has been available for years. Like many things associated with accessibility, it can be useful to almost anyone.

To switch the display of a site from Microsoft Edge to Internet Explorer

- In Microsoft Edge, on the **Settings and more (...)** menu, select **Open with Internet Explorer**.

To emulate a different browser

1. In Microsoft Edge, on the **Settings and more (...)** menu, select **F12 Developer Tools**.

2. In the **F12 Developer Tools** window, select the **Emulation** tab.

3. In the **Mode** section of the tab, in the **User agent string** list, select the browser (or browser and platform, if appropriate) that you want Microsoft Edge to emulate.

4. If you want to move the F12 Developer Tools window away from the browser window so you can see more of the content, select the **Undock** button near the right end of the window title bar.

> **TIP** Watch the webpage as you select a browser to emulate. The page will refresh and might look a little or a lot different, depending on your selection.

To turn on or off caret browsing

1. In Microsoft Edge, press **F7**.

2. In the **Turn on caret browsing?** or **Turn off caret browsing?** dialog box, do the following:

   a. If you want Microsoft Edge to automatically turn on or off caret browsing when you press F7, select the **Don't ask me again when I press F7** check box.

   b. Select **Turn on**.

> **IMPORTANT** After you select the Don't Ask Me Again When I Press F7 check box, the Turn On/Off Caret Browsing? dialog box will not open again, so you can skip this step.

10

To use caret browsing

- Select or tap in a text area on the webpage to set the initial insertion point. Then do any of the following:

  - Press the arrow keys to move the insertion point one character or line at a time.

  - Press the Home, End, Page Up, and Page Down keys to move greater distances.

  - Hold down the Ctrl key and press Home or End to move to the beginning or end of the page.

  - Hold down the Shift key and press the navigation keys to select text.

Key points

- Microsoft Edge is a fast and secure browser with a clean and simple user interface that has tabbed browsing. You can display websites in the standard view or cut down on distractions by using Reading view. You can annotate webpages, and fill out PDF forms in the browser window.

- You can save websites or webpages that you want to return to later by adding them to your Favorites list or your Reading list.

- You can organize sites in your Favorites list within folders, and put the sites you access most frequently on the Favorites bar.

- You can set aside entire sets of tabs to return to later.

- You can specify the page or pages that Microsoft Edge displays on startup, and also specify the information that appears on new tabs.

- Windows Defender SmartScreen helps to protect you from unsafe websites and downloads. It's turned on by default.

- InPrivate browsing is a useful feature if you're juggling multiple sets of credentials or don't want Microsoft Edge to save information from your browsing session.

- If Microsoft Edge doesn't display a website correctly, you can quickly open the current browsing session in Internet Explorer, or use the Developer Tools to emulate the experience of a different browser.

- If you have difficulty navigating the content of a webpage by using the mouse, you can turn on caret browsing and use the keyboard instead.

Practice tasks

No practice files are necessary to complete the practice tasks in this chapter.

Display websites in Microsoft Edge

Perform the following tasks:

1. Start Microsoft Edge and display the msn.com site. Select an article title on the page to display an article. Notice whether the article opens in the same tab or in a new tab.

2. If the article opened in the same tab, the Back button is now available. Select the **Back** button to return to the first page, and the Forward button becomes available. Select the **Forward** button to return to the new article.

> ✓ **TIP** If the article opened in a new tab, try the Back and Forward buttons later, when the Back button is available.

3. In the new article, right-click a link, and then select **Open in new tab**. Right-click another link, and then select **Open in new window**. Note the differing results.

   You now have two Microsoft Edge windows open. The first window has at least two page tabs, and the second window has one page tab.

4. Arrange the Microsoft Edge windows side by side, and drag one tab from the first window to the second window, to move the page between windows.

5. In either window, to the right of the rightmost tab, select the **New tab** button to open a new tab. Note the content of the tab, which will be one of the following:

   - A "blank" page that displays a search box

   - A page that displays eight squares, some or all of which might contain tiles that represent websites

   - A page that displays eight site tile spaces and news articles

   In a later exercise, you'll configure this page to display different content.

6. In the Address bar, enter Windows 10 to display a list of search suggestions (and possibly sites, if you've visited any Windows 10 sites). Enter microsoft after *Windows 10* to further refine the search term list.

7. Select the highlighted search term directly below the Address bar to search for *Windows 10 microsoft*, and to display a page of search results.

8. On the Microsoft Edge toolbar, to the right of the Address bar, notice the **Reading view** button. Note whether the button is active (with a dark outline) or inactive (with a pale outline).

9. On the search results page, locate the result that represents the primary Windows page of the Microsoft website. Select the link to display the Windows home page.

10. On the Microsoft Edge toolbar, note whether the **Reading view** button is active. If the button isn't active, select a link to display another page until you find one that does support Reading view.

11. On the Microsoft Edge toolbar, select the **Reading view** button to display the current page in Reading view. Note the background color of the page.

    In a later exercise, you'll change the Reading view color scheme.

12. Scroll the page to determine the content that is displayed in Reading view.

13. Select the **Reading view** button again to return to the standard view of the page. Locate the information from Reading view on the page and note the page elements that Reading view did not display.

14. Close the browser windows, selecting the option to close all tabs when prompted to do so.

Find, save, and share information

Perform the following tasks:

1. Start Microsoft Edge and display the website of your company, your school, an organization you belong to, or another organization whose website content you're familiar with. (If you can't think of another website, display the Windows website at windows.microsoft.com.)

2. Display the Find On Page toolbar. In the search box, start entering a word or phrase that appears multiple times on the page. As you enter each character, notice that the number of results changes.

3. Modify the search to include only results that aren't part of other words. Note whether the number of results changes. Then remove the filter.

4. Modify the search to include only results that have the same letter casing that you entered. Note whether the number of results changes. Then remove the filter.

5. From the **Find on page** toolbar, display the first search result, and then move to the second search result. Then scroll the page and notice that all search results are highlighted.

6. On the Microsoft Edge toolbar, select the **Add Notes** button to display the annotation toolbar. Point to each of the buttons on the toolbar to display the button name.

7. On the annotation toolbar, select the **Pen** button. Use the pen tool to circle something on the page, and then to underline something else.

8. On the annotation toolbar, select the **Add a typed note** button. Select the text next to the circle you drew in step 7, and then enter **Good idea!** in the note window that appears.

9. On the annotation toolbar, select the **Eraser** button. Then swipe anywhere on the underline you drew in step 7 to erase it. Notice that swiping anywhere on the line erases the entire line.

10. Experiment with other annotation techniques. When you finish, select the **Share** button near the right end of the annotation toolbar to display the Share pane and the apps you can use to share the webpage.

11. Share either the webpage or a screenshot of the webpage by using one of the available options.

12. Exit the annotation toolbar.

13. Save the current webpage to your Reading list.

14. Display your Reading list in the **Hub** pane, and then display your browsing history. Review the webpages that you've visited today.

15. Pin the current webpage to the Start menu. Then close the browser window and locate the Start menu tile for the webpage.

Manage Microsoft Edge settings

Perform the following tasks:

1. Set your Microsoft Edge home page to either **MSN**, **Bing**, or **Custom**. If you choose Custom, specify a webpage of your choice.

2. Without closing the **Settings** pane, display the **Open new tabs with** list, and then select a tab content option. (Choose something different from the content you noted in step 5 of the first practice task.)

3. Display the **Advanced settings** pane, turn on the display of the Home button, and then configure the Home button to display the same page you designated as your home page. (Use **msn.com** for MSN or **bing.com** for Bing.)

4. Click or tap anywhere on the webpage to close the Advanced Settings pane. Then on the Microsoft Edge toolbar, select the **Refresh** button to update the Home button settings.

5. Select the **Home** button and verify that it displays the home page you chose in step 2.

6. Select the **New tab** button, and verify that it displays the content you chose in step 3.

7. Follow the procedure for importing your Favorites list from another browser into Microsoft Edge. If another browser is available, import those favorites. Then display the **Hub** pane and verify that your Microsoft Edge Favorites list includes the imported entries.

8. Close the browser window.

Configure browser security settings

Perform the following tasks:

1. Start Microsoft Edge and display the **Advanced Settings** pane.

2. Near the top of the **Advanced settings** pane, verify that the option to block pop-up windows is turned on.

3. Locate the **Privacy and service**s section of the pane. Review and consider the settings you can configure. At the bottom of the section, verify that the option to use SmartScreen is turned on.

4. Perform any other procedures from the "Configure browser security settings" topic of this chapter that interest you. When you finish, close the browser windows.

Maintain browsing privacy

Perform the following tasks:

1. Start Microsoft Edge and display any website that you sign in to by using credentials. (If you can't think of another website, display your Microsoft OneDrive site at **onedrive.live.com**.) Sign in to the website.

2. Open a new tab and display the same website you chose in step 1. Notice that it recognizes your credentials and signs you in.

3. From the **Settings and more** (...) menu, open a new InPrivate browsing window. In the InPrivate window, display the same website you chose in step 1. Notice that it doesn't automatically sign you in.

4. Close the browser windows.

Troubleshoot browsing issues

Perform the following tasks:

1. Start Microsoft Edge and display a website of your choice.

2. From the **Settings and more** (...) menu, display the **F12 Developer Tools** window. Move or resize the window so you can see the website.

3. On the **Emulation** tab, choose a different browser to emulate. Notice any differences in the display of the website.

4. Choose a browser that is on a different platform, and notice differences in the display of the website.

5. Close the **F12 Developer Tools** window, and then close the browser window.

Part 4

Behind the scenes

Manage user accounts and settings

Computers have become an integral part of our lives. We store personal and business information on them, and use them to access financial and social information online. That information might be protected by a password, but the password could easily be accessible to any other person who is using your computer. To protect your privacy and the integrity of your information, it is important to control who can sign in to your computer or tablet, and what they can do when they're signed in.

Computer access is managed through user accounts. Each user of a computer, regardless of age, should sign in with his or her own account. Each user account has access to a private file storage area and user interface customizations, and to a shared public file storage area. Accounts designated as Child accounts have additional safeguards that are designed to protect them from content that isn't age appropriate.

When you sign in to your computer, you have a myriad of options available for doing so. User accounts can be protected by passwords, but users can choose alternative sign-in credentials such as PINs, picture passwords, and biometric identification through fingerprint or facial recognition.

This chapter guides you through procedures related to creating and managing user accounts, managing account pictures and passwords, customizing your sign-in options, and synchronizing settings across computers.

In this chapter

- Understand user accounts and permissions
- Create and manage user accounts
- Manage account pictures and passwords
- Customize your sign-in options
- Synchronize settings across computers

Understand user accounts and permissions

Windows 10 requires at least one user account. You specify that account when you're completing the installation processes, or the first time the computer starts after Windows 10 has been installed. Windows 10 designates this first account as an Administrator account so that the account can be used to manage the computer. It isn't possible to sign in to the computer without a user account.

The words "user" and "account" are used frequently in this book, and particularly in this chapter. Here's a summary of the uses of those terms:

- A *user* is the person who is using the computer.
- A *user account* is an account that a person uses to sign in to a computer.

Each user account is either:

- A *Microsoft account*, which is any email address that has been registered with the Microsoft account service.
- A *local account* that exists only on a single computer and is not associated with a specific email address.

You can use your Microsoft account to sign in to multiple computers, websites, and services by using the same email address and password. By signing in with your Microsoft account credentials, you can share settings and files among all your devices. Any device you sign in to with this account has access to the same settings and information. Signing in with a local account places limits on the applications you can purchase or download from the Store, and might limit your access to Microsoft OneDrive. Because almost any email account can also be set up to be a Microsoft account, it's a good idea to take advantage of the extra benefits that allows.

Every user account is also classified as either:

- An *Administrator account*
- A *Standard User account*

This classification provides a specific level of permission to manage system actions on the computer. The next section of this topic explains what each of these types of accounts can do.

A user account can also be one of the following:

- A *Child account* that is monitored by using Family Safety

- An *Adult account* that can manage Family Safety settings for Child accounts

These are optional designations that make the user account holder part of your family group. The sidebar "Manage and monitor family safety settings" later in this chapter discusses family groups.

> ⚠ **IMPORTANT** The information in this chapter applies to computer user accounts, and not to network domain user accounts.

User profiles

Windows provides the ability to share one computer among multiple users, or for one user to have multiple accounts for different purposes. To do this, each user account (whether a Microsoft account or a local account) is associated with a user profile that describes the way the computer environment (the user interface) looks and operates for that user. This information includes simple things such as the desktop background, desktop content, and Windows color scheme. It also includes personal and confidential information, such as saved passwords and your internet browsing history.

Each user profile includes a personal folder that is not generally accessible by other people who are using the computer, in which you can store documents, pictures, media, and other files that you want to keep private.

11

The Windows 10 system of user profiles allows more than one person to use the same computer while providing the following safeguards:

- **Each user's information is stored separately** You prevent standard users from reading or altering your documents, pictures, music, and other files by storing them in subfolders that are automatically set up within your user account folder. For example, if you manage your family's financial records on a home computer that your children use to do their homework, the children log in with separate accounts and don't have access to confidential information or the ability to change your files. Administrators can access all user accounts.

- **Each user's working environment is protected** You can personalize your environment in various ways, without worrying about other people making changes to your personal settings.

- **Each user's app usage is unique** Each user runs separate instances of each app on the computer. For example, you can set up Outlook to connect to your accounts, and other computer users can set up Outlook to connect to their accounts, but they cannot also connect to your accounts. Each user's data is stored and managed separately.

User account permissions

The system actions that a user can perform are governed by the type of account he or she signs in with. An Administrator account has higher-level permissions than a Standard User account, which means that an Administrator account owner can perform tasks on your computer that a Standard User account owner cannot.

Standard User account credentials allow a user to do things that affect only his or her account, including:

- Change or remove the password.

- Change the user account picture.

- Change the theme and desktop settings.

- View files stored in his or her personal folders and files in the Public folders.

Administrator account credentials are necessary to do things such as:

- Create, change, and delete accounts.

- Change settings that affect all the computer's users.

- Change security-related settings.

- Install and remove apps.

- Access system files and files in other user account profiles.

Tasks that require administrator permission are indicated in windows and dialog boxes by a Windows security icon that is shaped like a shield.

 User Accounts
🛡 Change account type

If you have an Administrator account—even if you're the only person who will be using your computer—it's a good idea to create and use a Standard User account for your day-to-day computing. There is a much higher risk of serious damage to a computer system if malware infiltrates your computer (or a malicious person gains control of it) when you're signed in as an administrator than there is when you're signed in as a standard user. Through an Administrator account, the person or app has access to all system files and settings, whereas a Standard User account doesn't have access to certain functions that can permanently damage the system.

Family accounts

Many children use computers for educational or entertainment purposes. Each child should have a unique Microsoft account that you designate as a Child account. For each Child account, you (and other adults you designate as family members) can do the following:

- Monitor web browsing history, app use, and game use.

- Block websites that contain adult content, or allow young children to visit only specific websites.

- Restrict the usage of apps and games to only those that meet specific age ratings.

- Monitor screen time, and restrict computer usage to only specific times or to a specific number of hours per day.

- Manage payment options and monitor purchases in the Windows Store and Xbox Store.

You can monitor children's activity on every computer or device they sign in to with their Microsoft accounts.

You can check on your child's recent computer usage on the Family page of your Microsoft account website (at *account.microsoft.com*) at any time, and you can opt to receive weekly reports summarizing your child's computer use.

 SEE ALSO For more information about monitoring and managing children's computer activity, see the sidebar "Manage and monitor family safety settings" later in this chapter.

11

User Account Control

User Account Control (UAC) protects your computer from changes to Windows system settings by requiring that an administrator expressly permit certain types of changes. Each area of the Windows interface that requires administrator permission is labeled with a security icon. When you attempt to access or change protected Windows settings, a User Account Control message box appears, asking for confirmation that Windows should continue the operation. The message box varies depending on your account and the action.

If you're signed in with an Administrator account, you can simply select Yes to continue the operation. If you're signed in with a Standard User account, the message box displays a list of the Administrator accounts on the computer. To continue the operation, you select one of the Administrator accounts, enter its password in the box that appears (or have the account owner do it for you), and then select Yes.

> **TIP** If an Administrator account doesn't have an associated password, you can continue the operation by simply selecting that account and then selecting Yes. This is one of the reasons it's important that each Administrator account on the computer has a password.

Windows doesn't save the credentials you enter in the User Account Control message box; they are valid for this operation only. Anyone who doesn't have access to administrator credentials can't perform the operation, which effectively prevents non-administrators from making changes you haven't authorized.

UAC has four levels of control. Only the first two are available when you're signed in with a Standard User account, even if you have access to administrator credentials:

- **Always notify me** This is the default setting for a Standard User account. When a user or app initiates a change that requires administrator credentials, the desktop dims and the User Account Control message box opens. You must respond to the message box before you can take any other action.

- **Notify me only when apps try to make changes to my computer** This is the default setting for an Administrator account. When an app initiates a change that requires administrator credentials, the desktop dims and the User Account Control message box opens. You must respond to the message box before you can continue.

- **Notify me only when apps try to make changes to my computer (do not dim my desktop)** When an app initiates a restricted action, the User Account Control message box opens. The restricted action will not be performed until you respond to the message box, but you can perform other tasks while it is open.

- **Never notify me** This is the equivalent of turning off UAC. Any user or app can make any changes to the computer without restriction.

With the default setting, Windows 10 prompts for administrator credentials when a user or app initiates an action that will modify system files. There's not a lot of reason to change the User Account Control setting, but you can.

To change the User Account Control setting

1. Do one of the following to open the User Account Control Settings window:

    - On the taskbar or in the **Settings** window, enter **UAC** in the search box and then, in the search results list, select **Change User Account Control settings**.

    - Display Control Panel in an Icons view. Select **User Accounts**, and then **Change User Account Control settings**.

11

- Display Control Panel in Category view. Select **User Accounts**, **User Accounts**, and then **Change User Account Control settings**.

> ✅ **TIP** The security icon to the left of the command indicates that administrator credentials are required to complete this operation.

2. Click or tap above or below the slider, or drag it, to set UAC to the level you want, and then select **OK**.

3. In the **User Account Control** message box that appears, enter administrator credentials if necessary, and then select **OK**.

> ✅ **TIP** You must be signed in with an Administrator account to select either of the two lowest settings. If you select Never Notify, you must restart your computer to finish turning off UAC.

Manage user accounts in the Computer Management console

Some user account management tasks can be completed from the Family & Other People settings pane. On a computer running Windows 10 Pro or Windows 10 Enterprise, additional tasks can be performed in the Users node of the Computer Management console.

TIP The Local Users And Groups folder referenced in this sidebar is available in the Computer Management console only in Windows 10 Pro and Windows 10 Enterprise. It is not available in Windows 10 Home.

To open the Computer Management console, do any of the following:

- Right-click the **Start** button, and then on the **Quick Links** menu, select **Computer Management**.

- On the **Start** menu, in the app list, expand the **Windows Administrative Tools** folder, and then select **Computer Management**.

- Enter computer management in the taskbar search box, and then select the **Computer Management** desktop app.

To open the Users node, follow these steps in the left pane of the Computer Management console:

1. Expand the **System Tools** folder and the **Local Users and Groups** subfolder.

2. Select the **Users** folder.

Create and manage user accounts

An administrator can give other people access to the computer in one of three ways:

- Create a user account that is linked to an existing Microsoft account.

- Create a user account that is linked to an email address, and register that account as a Microsoft account.

- Create a local account that isn't linked to a Microsoft account.

Every user account has an associated name and can have a picture and a password. Any user can change the following details for his or her account:

- **Account name** You can change the display name that appears on the Welcome screen and Start menu.

- **Account picture** You can change the picture that identifies you on the Welcome screen and Start menu.

- **Password** You can create or change the password.

If you have administrator credentials, you can change these properties for any user account. You can also change the account type from Administrator to Standard User (provided that at least one Administrator account remains on the computer) or vice versa.

You create computer accounts and designate permission levels from the Family & Other People pane of the Accounts page of the Settings window.

> ⚠ **IMPORTANT** Only administrators can create user accounts—if you're signed in with a Standard User account, your Accounts pane list will not include Family & Other People.
>
> When you create a user account, you must designate whether the user is part of your family group. All types of user accounts are visible in the Family & Other People pane. However, the processes for managing family accounts and non-family accounts differ, so the following sections cover them separately to avoid confusion.

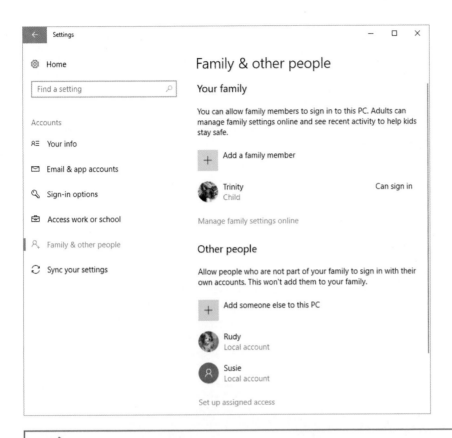

> ✓ **TIP** You manage other user accounts from this pane, so the lists don't include the account you're signed in with.

When you first add a user account, it is identified in lists by its email address or by the name you give it. If your computer is running Windows 10 Pro or Windows 10 Enterprise, you can change the user account name (and delete user accounts) from the Users node of the Computer Management console.

If a person is not going to sign in to a specific computer again, it's a good idea to delete his or her user account. This will clean up the user account lists and recover the hard-drive space that is used by that user's data. If you don't want to delete the user account data, you can disable the account instead of deleting it.

Manage and monitor family safety settings

Microsoft Family Safety is an impressive system for safeguarding against young family members accidentally accessing inappropriate content on the internet. It allows you to place restrictions on their computer usage and provides you with reports that you can use to spot problems. Family Safety was introduced with Windows 7, and has evolved with each version of Windows. If you've used it in the past, it's a good idea to revisit it now to make sure the settings are up to date for the way your children use the computer.

Originally, Family Safety was an app through which you could register specific computer user accounts. It was necessary to register a child on each computer he or she used, and Family Safety reported separately on each local account. Since then, Family Safety has evolved into an online service that can monitor your child's activity on each device he or she signs into that is running Windows.

The key to the successful use of Family Safety is for each child to sign in to Windows 10 computers and devices with his or her own Microsoft account, and for parents to designate the account as a Child account. Family Safety monitors and reports on the websites children visit, the apps they use, the games they play, and the time they spend signed in to the computer.

Create and manage family user accounts

You can designate a user account as belonging to a family member. When you do, the account is added to your family group. Adults in the family group can manage family safety settings online.

You can change the display name of a family user account to use something other than that person's email address

For the safety of your children, all family user accounts must be associated with Microsoft accounts. You can't create a local account in the Your Family group, or an account linked to an email address that isn't yet registered as a Microsoft account.

 IMPORTANT You must sign in to the computer with an Administrator account to perform any of the following procedures.

You can review usage and modify settings on the Family page of your Microsoft Account site, or directly through *familysafety.microsoft.com*, and opt to receive weekly activity reports by email. From the Family page, you can choose to block or allow specific websites or content by rating so that children have access to only age-appropriate information.

11

To create a family user account

1. In the **Settings** window, select **Accounts**, and then select **Family & other people**.

2. In the **Your family** section of the **Family & other people** settings pane, select **Add a family member** to start the wizard.

3. On the **Add a child or an adult** page, select **Add a child** or **Add an adult**, and then enter the person's Microsoft account address in the **Enter their email address** box. If the person doesn't have an email address, or has an email address that isn't yet registered as a Microsoft account, select **The person I want to add doesn't have an email address**, and then skip to the procedure "To create or register a Microsoft account" later in this topic.

4. After you enter the email address, select **Next**. The wizard searches the Microsoft account database for the email address.

5. If the email account is already registered as a Microsoft account, select **Confirm** on the **Add this person?** page to add the person to your family group and create a user account for him or her on the computer.

Or

If the email account isn't already registered as a Microsoft account, the wizard displays a warning.

Add a child or an adult?

Enter the email address of the person you want to add. If they use Windows, Office, Outlook.com, OneDrive, Skype, or Xbox, enter the email address they use to sign in.

○ Add a child

◉ Add an adult

   Adults will be able to manage requests and change kids' settings

| steve@fourthcoffee.com | ✕ |

Looks like this isn't a Microsoft account. Try another email or sign up for a new one.

The person I want to add doesn't have an email address

If the warning appears, do either of the following:

- Enter a registered email address, select **Next**, and then select **Confirm** to create the account.

- Select **sign up for a new one**, and then skip to the procedure "To create or register a Microsoft account" later in this topic.

When you register an adult family account, the person receives an email message and must select a link in the message and then sign in to his or her Microsoft account to confirm membership in the family group.

Joan would like you to join their family as an adult.

After you accept, you can

- Give kids money so they can shop in Windows and Xbox stores without a credit card.
- See activity reports about what kids do on devices, including buying apps and searching the web.
- Set age limits for rated content like apps, games, videos, movies and TV.
- Set time limits for how long kids can use devices.
- Connect with your family anywhere with Skype.
- Find children in the family on a map, when they have Windows 10 mobile phones.

Accept Invitation

To decline the invitation, delete or ignore this email.

To learn more, visit https://account.microsoft.com/family

Until the family membership is confirmed, the person can sign in to the computer but the account status is shown as *Adult, Pending*.

To create or register a Microsoft account

1. On the **Let's create an account** page, provide the requested information, and then select **Next**.

2. If you want to, clear the check boxes permitting Microsoft to send and track information for marketing purposes. Then select **Next**.

3. On the final page of the wizard, select **Finish**.

11

To change the display name of a family user account

> ⚠ **IMPORTANT** This procedure can be performed only on computers running Windows 10 Pro or Windows 10 Enterprise. The Computer Management\Local Users And Groups folder in which this procedure is performed is not available in Windows 10 Home.

1. On a computer running Windows 10 Pro or Windows 10 Enterprise, display the **Users** node of the **Computer Management** console.

> 🔍 **SEE ALSO** Instructions for navigating to the Users node of the Computer Management console are in the sidebar "Manage user accounts in the Computer Management console" earlier in this chapter.

2. Do either of the following:

   - To change the full name that appears in the user account lists, double-click the account name to open the **Properties** dialog box. Then enter or update the name in the **Full name** box, and select **Apply** or **OK** to make the change.

   - To change the short name by which Windows identifies the account, right-click the account name in the **Users** list, and select **Rename** to activate the name for editing. Then enter the short name you want, and press Enter to complete the change.

To disable a family user account

1. On the **Accounts** page of the **Settings** window, select **Family & other people**.

2. In the **Your family** section of the **Family & other people** pane, select the account you want to disable to display your options for managing the account.

3. On the account tile, select **Block**. Windows displays a confirmation request.

4. In the **Block this person from signing in?** box, select **Block**.

To enable a disabled family user account

1. On the **Accounts** page of the **Settings** window, select **Family & other people**.

2. In the **Your family** section of the **Family & other people** pane, select the account you want to enable to display your options for managing the account.

3. On the account tile, select **Allow**. Windows displays a confirmation request.

4. In the **Allow this person to sign in?** box, select **Allow**.

To delete a family user account

> ⚠ **IMPORTANT** This procedure can be performed only on computers running Windows 10 Pro or Windows 10 Enterprise. The Computer Management\Local Users And Groups folder in which this procedure is performed is not available in Windows 10 Home.

1. Ensure that the user has moved or copied personal files from the user account folders and uninstalled or deactivated any apps that require this to free up the user license.

> ⚠ **IMPORTANT** To preserve any files that are saved in the user account folders, back up the folder C:\Users\[UserName] (where [UserName] is the account name of the user).

11

2. On a computer running Windows 10 Pro or Windows 10 Enterprise, display the **Users** node of the **Computer Management** console.

> (Q) **SEE ALSO** Instructions for navigating to the Users node of the Computer Management console are in the sidebar "Manage user accounts in the Computer Management console" earlier in this chapter.

3. Right-click the user account you want to delete, and then select **Delete**. A message box displays a warning.

4. In the message box, select **Yes** to delete the account and all its files.

Create and manage non-family user accounts

Accounts in the Other People section of the Family & Other People settings pane are not associated with your family safety group. These accounts can certainly belong to members of your family, but they can't be part of your family safety settings group. Local computer accounts can be created only in the Other People section.

> (!) **IMPORTANT** You must sign in to the computer with an Administrator account to perform any of the following procedures.

To create a non-family user account that is linked to an existing Microsoft account

1. In the **Settings** window, select **Accounts**, and then select **Family & other people**.

2. In the **Other people** section of the pane, select **Add someone else to this PC** to start the wizard.

3. On the **How will this person sign in?** page, enter the Microsoft account address in the **Email or phone** box, and then select **Next**. The wizard confirms that the email address is a registered Microsoft account.

> ## Good to go!
>
> To log in the first time, jaime@contoso.com will need to be connected to the internet.

4. Select **Finish** to complete the process.

To create a local user account

1. On the **Accounts** page of the **Settings** window, select **Family & other people**.

2. In the **Other people** section of the pane, select **Add someone else to this PC** to start the wizard.

3. At the bottom of the **How will this person sign in?** page, select **I don't have this person's sign-in information**.

4. At the bottom of the **Let's create your account** page, select **Add a user without a Microsoft account** to get to the interface for creating a local account.

Microsoft account   ×

Create an account for this PC

If you want to use a password, choose something that will be easy for you to remember but hard for others to guess.

Who's going to use this PC?

Penny

Make it secure.

••••••••

••••••••

My nickname

Next   Back

11

5. Enter a user name. If you don't want to create a password for the local account, leave the rest of the boxes blank. Otherwise, enter the password (two times) and an optional password hint. Then select **Next** to create the account.

> ⚠ **IMPORTANT** If you don't implement a password, anyone can sign in to your computer by selecting your user account and then selecting Sign In. Your data is especially vulnerable if you travel with your computer or use it in a public place. The password hint appears on the Welcome page if you can't remember your password.

To disable a non-family user account

> ⚠ **IMPORTANT** This procedure can be performed only on computers running Windows 10 Pro or Windows 10 Enterprise. The Computer Management\Local Users And Groups folder in which this procedure is performed is not available in Windows 10 Home.

1. On a computer running Windows 10 Pro or Windows 10 Enterprise, display the **Users** node of the **Computer Management** console.

> 🔍 **SEE ALSO** Instructions for navigating to the Users node of the Computer Management console are in the sidebar "Manage user accounts in the Computer Management console" earlier in this chapter.

2. Double-click the account you want to disable.

3. In the **Properties** dialog box, select the **Account is disabled** check box. Then select **OK**.

To enable a disabled non-family user account

1. On a computer running Windows 10 Pro or Windows 10 Enterprise, display the **Users** node of the **Computer Management** console.

2. Double-click the account you want to enable.

3. In the **Properties** dialog box, clear the **Account is disabled** check box. Then select **OK**.

To delete a non-family user account

1. Ensure that the user has moved or copied personal files from the user account folders and deactivated any apps that require deactivation to free up the user license.

    > ⚠️ **IMPORTANT** To preserve any files that are saved in the user account folders, back up the folder C:\Users\[UserName] (where [UserName] is the account name of the user).

2. Display the **Settings** window, select **Accounts**, and then select **Family & other people**.

3. In the **Other people** section of the **Family & other people** pane, select the account you want to delete, to display your options for managing the account.

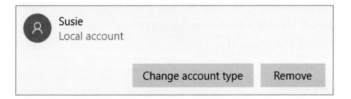

4. On the account tile, select **Remove**. Windows displays a confirmation request.

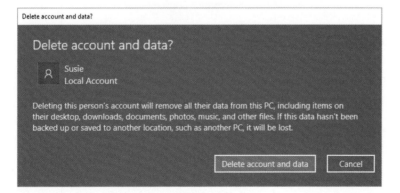

5. In the message box, select **Delete account and data**. Windows deletes the account and then returns to the Family & Other People pane.

Manage settings for any user account

Windows 10 has two built-in accounts, *Administrator* and *Guest*, that don't have passwords assigned. When Windows creates the first user-specific Administrator account, it disables the default Administrator account. The Guest account is inactive by default (and disabled on computers that are part of a domain. You can activate the Guest account to give someone temporary, limited access to your computer without having to create a user account for that person.

Another method of giving someone limited access is to restrict the account so that it can access only one app. Access restriction works only with Store apps that are already installed on your computer.

When creating a family or non-family user account, if you don't supply an email address, the wizard displays a page on which you can create a new outlook.com email address or register an existing email address as a Microsoft account. The email address that you provide will receive a confirmation email message; you must respond to it to activate the account.

Let's create your account

Windows, Office, Outlook.com, OneDrive, Skype, Xbox. They're all better and more personal when you sign in with your Microsoft account.* Learn more

After you sign up, we'll send you a message with a link to verify this user name.

joan@fourthcoffee.com

Get a new email address

•••••••••••••••••••••••••

United States

July   31   1979

*If you already use a Microsoft service, go Back to sign in with that account.

Add a user without a Microsoft account

To activate the built-in Guest account

- On a computer running Windows 10 Pro or Windows 10 Enterprise, do the following:

    a. Display the **Users** node of the **Computer Management** console.

    b. Double-click the disabled **Guest** account.

    c. In the **Properties** dialog box, clear the **Account is disabled** check box, and then select **Apply** or **OK**.

- On a computer running Windows 10 Home, do the following:

    a. In the taskbar search box, type cmd. In the search results, right-click the **Command Prompt** desktop app, and then select **Run as administrator**.

    b. In the command prompt window that opens, enter net user guest / active:yes, and then press Enter.

    c. Close the command prompt window.

To grant administrative permissions to an account

1. In the **Settings** window, select **Accounts**, and then select **Family & other people**.

2. Select the account you want to modify, to display your options. Then select **Change account type**.

3. In the **Account type** list, select **Administrator**. Then select **OK**.

To revoke administrative permissions

1. On the **Accounts** settings page, display the **Family & other people** pane.

2. Select the account, and then select **Change account type**.

3. In the **Account type** list, select **Standard User**. Then select **OK**.

To restrict an account to one Store app

> ⚠️ **IMPORTANT** This procedure can be performed only on computers running Windows 10 Pro or Windows 10 Enterprise. The Assigned Access feature is not available in Windows 10 Home.

1. On the **Accounts** settings page, display the **Family & other people** pane.

2. At the bottom of the pane, select **Set up assigned access**.

3. In the **Choose which account will have assigned access** section, select **Choose an account** (or, if the pane already displays a restricted account, select the account). Then, in the **Choose an account** pane that opens, select the Standard User account that you want to restrict.

4. In the **Choose which app this account can access** section, select **Choose an app** (or if the section already contains an app, select it) and then in the **Choose an app** pane that opens, select the app you want to assign.

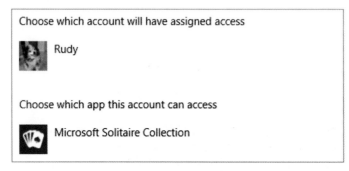

Choose which account will have assigned access

Rudy

Choose which app this account can access

Microsoft Solitaire Collection

5. If the user you assigned access to is currently signed in to the computer, sign the user out to complete the access assignment process.

> **TIP** When you sign in to Windows 10 with an assigned access account, you have access only to the assigned app. To sign out of an assigned access account, press Ctrl+Alt+Del.

To switch from a Microsoft account to a local account

1. On the **Accounts** settings page, display the **Your info** pane.

2. In the area below your user picture, select **Sign in with a local account instead**.

3. In the **Switch to a local account** window, enter your Microsoft account password to confirm your identity, and then select **Next**.

4. Provide a user account name for the local account. If you don't want to use a password, leave the rest of the entries blank. Otherwise, fill in the password and password hint entries.

5. Select **Next**, and then select **Sign out and finish** to return to your profile.

To connect a local account to a Microsoft account

1. Display the **Your info** settings pane, and select **Sign in with a Microsoft account instead**.

2. On the **Make it yours** page, enter the email address of the Microsoft account you want to sign in with, and then select **Next**.

3. On the **Enter password** page, enter your Microsoft account password, and then select **Sign in**.

4. If your local user account has a password, enter it on the **Sign in to this device using your Microsoft account** page, and then select **Next**.

   A code will be sent to the Microsoft account email address, or you can open the list below the question about how you want to get the code, and choose to receive it in a text message. After you receive the code, return to this process and enter it in the box provided. Then select **Finish**.

   > **TIP** The verification code arrives quickly and is valid for only a short time, so check your email or text messages for the code and finish the account creation process promptly. If the code expires before you complete the process, you can select Back on the code page and request another code.

5. Select **Sign out and finish** to return to your profile.

Manage account pictures and passwords

As previously discussed, you can sign in to Windows 10 by using a Microsoft account or a local account.

Each user account has an associated user account picture that is shown on the Welcome screen, at the top of the Start menu, on app and browser window title bars when you're signed in, and in other places. If you sign in to Windows with your Microsoft account credentials, Windows displays the user account picture that is associated with that account. If you sign in by using a local account, you can associate a picture with that account on that computer. Until you associate a picture with either type of account, the computer account displays a placeholder account picture (a head-and-shoulders icon) wherever the account picture would usually appear. Selecting your user account button displays all active user accounts.

You can easily add or change an account picture, regardless of whether you're signed in with a Microsoft account or a local account, on any computer you sign in to.

Previous versions of Windows provided many Standard User account picture options, depicting a variety of animals, sports, and interests. Windows 10 doesn't provide any account pictures, but does offer the option of taking a picture if your computer has a webcam. You can use .bmp, .gif, .jpg, or .png files as user account pictures. The original image can be any size or shape, but Windows 10 displays the user account picture as a circle, so when selecting a picture, keep in mind that it will be cropped to a square and then have its corners cut off.

All Microsoft accounts have passwords. If you sign in to Windows or any website with your Microsoft account credentials, you use the same password wherever you sign in. (The user account name and password, together, are referred to as *credentials*.) Local accounts can have or not have passwords. If you don't store or access personal information on your computer, a password is not essential. However, it's never a bad idea to have a password. You can add a password to a local account or change the password, and you can change your Microsoft password. Changing your Microsoft account password changes it across all computers, sites, and services.

If you're going to take the trouble to protect your user account with a password, choose one that no one is likely to guess. A strong password is at least eight characters long, does not contain names or dictionary words, and contains at least one uppercase character, one lowercase character, one number, and one punctuation mark.

> ⚠️ **IMPORTANT** If you change your Microsoft account password and then sign in to a computer that hasn't been able to connect over the internet to the Microsoft account site since before you changed the password, the computer won't be able to verify your new password and will prompt you to sign in with the last password you used on that computer.

When you assign a password to a local user account, you can also save a password hint. Windows displays the password hint on the Welcome screen after you enter an incorrect password.

Each computer user manages his or her own account picture and password. The information in this section assumes that you're working with your own account.

11

To display the Your Info settings pane

- On the left side of the **Start** menu, select your user account button, and then select **Change account settings**.

- In the **Settings** window, select **Accounts**, and then select **Your info**.

  The content of the Your Info pane varies based on whether you're signed in with a Microsoft account or a local user account, and what pictures have been associated with the account on the computer.

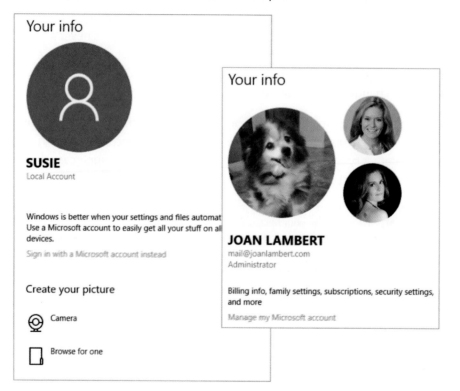

To assign an existing picture to your user account

1. Locate and review the photo. If necessary, edit it to ensure that it displays well in the circular format.

2. Display the **Your info** settings pane, and then do one of the following:

   - If you want to select a previously used image, select the image in the **Create your picture** section.

   - If you want to select an image that isn't shown in the **Create your picture** section, select **Browse for one**. In the **Open** dialog box, locate and select the image you want to use, and then select **Choose picture**.

To capture and set a user account picture

1. Display the **Your info** settings pane.

2. In the **Create your picture** section, select **Camera**.

3. If Windows Camera prompts you to permit it to access your location, select **Yes** or **No**.

4. Adjust the camera, yourself, and your background as necessary, and then select the **Take Photo** button (the camera icon) to take the picture.

5. If Microsoft Photos prompts you to allow it to access your contacts, select **Yes** or **No**.

6. In the **Photos** window, do any of the following, and then select **Done**:

   - Drag the photo within the defined square to center the image you want within it.

   - Drag any corner of the crop box to change the size of the square.

To set or change your Microsoft account picture

1. Display the **Your info** settings pane.

2. Select **Manage my Microsoft account** to display your Microsoft Account home page.

3. Select **Your info** on the menu bar, or select your account picture.

4. On the **Your info** page, select **New picture**.

5. In the **Open** dialog box, locate and select the picture you want to use, and then select **Open**.

6. On the **Your info** page, drag any of the picture handles to resize the circle, and drag the circle to change the part of the picture that is displayed. The crosshairs mark the center of the picture.

11

To add a local user account password

1. In the **Settings** window, select **Accounts**, and then select **Sign-in options**.

2. In the **Password** section, select **Add**.

3. On the **Create a password** page, enter and reenter the password you want to use. Enter a password hint if you want to be able to display one from the Welcome page, and then select **Next**.

4. Select **Finish**.

To change or delete a local user account password

1. In the **Settings** window, select **Accounts**, and then select **Sign-in options**.

2. In the **Password** section, select **Change**.

3. On the **Change your password** page, enter your current password, and then select **Next**.

4. On the second **Change your password** page, do either of the following, and then select **Next**:

   - To change your password, enter and reenter the password you want to use. Enter a password hint if you want to be able to display one from the Welcome page.

   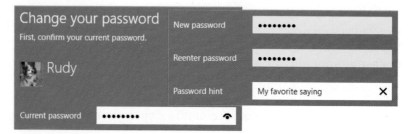

   - To delete your password, leave the three boxes empty.

5. On the final **Change your password** page, select **Finish**.

To change a Microsoft account password

1. Display the **Sign-in options** settings pane.

2. In the **Password** section, select **Change** to open a Microsoft Account window.

3. In the **Making sure it's you** dialog box, if your user account has a PIN, enter the PIN for identity verification.

4. On the **Please reenter your password** page, enter the password for the account, and select **Sign in**.

5. On the **Help us protect your info** page, choose a phone number or email address at which you want to receive a one-time security code. Enter the last four digits of the phone number, or the email address, in the verification box, and then select **Next**.

6. Check your phone's text messages, or your email account, for the security code, and then enter it on the **Enter the code you received** page.

7. On the **Set a new password** page, enter your current password and then enter and reenter the new password.

> ⚠ **IMPORTANT** The new password must be one that you haven't used before. The password reset system will not permit you to enter a password that you've used previously.

If you're uncertain whether you entered the password correctly, select the eye icon at the right end of the input box to temporarily display the password.

8. When you're satisfied with the new password, select **Next**.

9. On the page confirming the password change, select **Finish**.

   In addition to the onscreen confirmation, Microsoft sends a confirmation email message to your Microsoft account email address and to any email addresses that you provided as secondary contacts for the Microsoft account.

11

Customize your sign-in options

Each user manages the password and sign-in options for his or her account. This topic addresses actions you can take for your own user account, not for other people's user accounts.

If (and only if) your sign-in account has a password, you can create alternative sign-in options on each computer you log in to. These sign-in options include the following:

- **Personal identification number (PIN)** A number (from 4 to 127 digits long) or alphanumeric phrase that you enter in place of your password.

- **Picture password** An image of your choice on which you perform a specific combination of gestures. Windows divides the picture into a 100x100 grid and looks for your selected gesture pattern in the appropriate grid coordinates. You can perform the gestures directly on a touchscreen or by using a mouse.

> ⚠ **IMPORTANT** Some critics say that a picture password isn't very secure because people generally do the obvious thing on any picture. For example, on a picture of a person, people tap the eyes and draw a line across the mouth. When you set up a gesture-based password, try to do something less obvious.

- **Windows Hello** Biometric identification through fingerprint, facial, or iris recognition. This feature is available only on computers that have biometric identification hardware such as a built-in or external fingerprint reader.

After you set up a PIN or picture password sign-in option, the Welcome page changes to offer your new option by default. There is also a Sign-In Options link on the page, so if you forget your PIN or the specific gestures of your picture password, you can sign in at any time by using your password.

When you have a fingerprint reader, facial recognition camera, or other biometric identification hardware installed on your computer, the Windows Hello section of the Sign-In Options settings pane includes an option to set up biometric recognition. Otherwise, it includes the message "Windows Hello isn't available on this device." If you don't have built-in biometric identification hardware but would like to use Windows Hello, you can purchase a USB fingerprint reader and insert it into the computer's USB port.

> ⚠️ **IMPORTANT** The options available to you in the Sign-In Options settings pane are specific to your computer configuration and, in a business environment, may be subject to restrictions set by your system administrator.

😃 Windows Hello

Sign in to Windows, apps and services by teaching Windows to recognize you.

Learn more about Windows Hello

Fingerprint

Set up

🔑 Password

Change your account password

Change

⠿ PIN

Create a PIN to use in place of passwords. You'll be asked for this PIN when you sign in to Windows, apps, and services.

Add

🖼 Picture password

Sign in to Windows using a favorite photo.

Add

11

When you have multiple sign-in options configured for your account, the Welcome screen displays the most recently configured sign-in option by default. You can switch to a different sign-in option from the Welcome screen.

IMPORTANT You can perform the following procedures only for your own account (or the account that is currently logged in).

To create a PIN

1. On the **Accounts** settings page, select **Sign-in options**.

2. In the **Sign-in options** pane, in the **PIN** section, select **Add**.

3. In the **Please reenter your password** window, enter the password for your account, and then select **Sign in**.

4. In the **Set up a PIN** window that opens, do one of the following:

   - If you want to use a numeric PIN (as indicated by the term *personal identification number*), enter a number that is from 4 to 127 digits long in the **New PIN** and **Confirm PIN** boxes.

   - If you want to use a combination of numbers, letters, and symbols in your PIN, select the **Include letters and symbols** check box, and then enter an alphanumeric phrase in the **New PIN** and **Confirm PIN** boxes.

   You can select the eye icons to check your entries.

Windows Security ⮾

Set up a PIN

Create a PIN to use in place of passwords. Having a PIN makes it easier to sign in to your device, apps, and services.

| ••••••• |
| ••••••• |

☐ Include letters and symbols

| OK | Cancel |

5. In the **Set up a PIN** window, select **OK**.

   If your computer system meets certain conditions, you will be prompted to complete the process in a secondary window.

6. Select **Set up PIN**. In the next window, enter the verification code you receive from Microsoft and select **Next**. Then select **OK** to create your PIN and make the PIN sign-in option available from the Welcome screen.

To change a PIN

1. In the **Sign-in options** settings pane, in the **PIN** section, select the **Change** button.

2. In the **PIN** box, enter your current PIN to validate your credentials.

3. Enter the new personal identification number (at least four digits long) in the **New PIN** and **Confirm PIN** boxes, and then select **OK**.

11

To configure Windows Hello fingerprint authentication

1. In the **Sign-in options** settings pane, in the **Windows Hello** section, select **Set up** to start the Windows Hello setup wizard, and then select **Get started**.

> ✓ **TIP** In the Windows Hello section of the Sign-In Options settings pane, the option to configure biometric identification is available only if your computer system includes a compatible fingerprint reader or facial recognition camera.

The Windows Hello Setup wizard that starts prompts you to provide a series of sample fingerprint swipes.

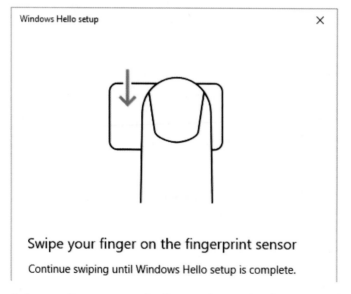

2. Swipe any finger across the fingerprint reader (from top to bottom, as indicated). Keep the finger flat and steady as you swipe. After the reader detects a usable fingerprint reading, it prompts you to swipe the same finger again, until it gets about four good readings.

Swipe again

3. After Windows registers the fingerprint, you can immediately add another fingerprint by selecting **Add another finger** and repeating step 2.

4. If you haven't yet set up a PIN, Windows Hello prompts you to do so. (If you close the wizard without setting up a PIN, the fingerprint isn't saved.)

To create a picture password

1. Locate the picture you want to use. Choose a picture that includes objects you can use to correctly position your gestures.

2. In the **Sign-in options** settings pane, in the **Picture password** section, select **Add** to start the Picture Password wizard. The wizard has a background picture of purple flowers in a field of green.

3. In the **Create a picture password** dialog box, enter your account password, and then select **OK** to verify your identity.

4. The wizard demonstrates the three permissible gestures (tap, line, and circle) against the floral background. After you're familiar with the gestures, select **Choose picture**.

5. In the **Open** dialog box, browse to and select the picture you want to use, and then select **Open** to replace the wizard background picture. Drag the picture to adjust it in the available space, and then select **Use this picture**.

11

6. Decide on a combination of three taps, lines, and/or circles you'll be able to consistently remember, and then perform them on the picture. The wizard changes the number in the left pane as you perform each gesture.

7. Repeat the three gestures when the wizard prompts you to do so, and then select **Finish**.

To change authentication methods on the Welcome screen

1. On the Welcome screen displaying your user account name, select **Sign-in options** to display an icon for each sign-in method you have configured.

2. Select the icon for the sign-in method you want to use.

Synchronize settings across computers

In addition to controlling sign-in options, each user who signs in with Microsoft account credentials can choose whether to synchronize settings across all the computers he or she signs in to with those credentials. This is a very cool feature after you have it set up the way you want it and get used to it. You can synchronize the following groups of settings:

- **Theme** Desktop background, colors, and sounds

- **Web browser settings** Favorite sites and recent searches

- **Passwords** Passwords that you've saved for specific websites

- **Language preferences** Installed language packs, regional date and time settings, and keyboard language

- **Ease of Access settings** Narrator and other accessibility tools

- **Other Windows settings** Your Start menu app list, shared printer list, mouse cursor size and color, File Explorer settings, and notification preferences

To configure setting synchronization across computers

1. In the **Settings** window, select **Accounts**, and then select **Sync your settings**.

2. In the **Sync your settings** pane, turn on **Sync settings** to activate synchronization on this computer.

← Settings	— □ ✕
⚙ Home	**Sync your settings**
Find a setting 🔍	**Sync your settings**
Accounts	Sync Windows settings to other devices using joan@fourthcoffee.com.
R≡ Your info	How does syncing work?
✉ Email & app accounts	Sync settings
🔑 Sign-in options	🔘 On
🗂 Access work or school	**Individual sync settings**
👤 Family & other people	Theme
🔄 Sync your settings	🔘 On
	Internet Explorer settings
	🔘 On
	Passwords
	🔘 On
	Language preferences
	🔘 On
	Ease of Access
	🔘 On
	Other Windows settings
	🔘 On

11

> ⚠ **IMPORTANT** The sync settings are available only when you're signed in with a Microsoft account. If you're signed in with a local user account, the settings will be unavailable (gray).

3. Consider the computers that you sign in to with the current Microsoft account credentials. Then, in the **Individual sync settings** section, do the following:

- Turn on each setting that you want to synchronize to and from this computer.

- Turn off each setting that you want to maintain independently on this computer.

Key points

- Each person who uses the computer should sign in to his or her own user account.

- Each user account is either a Microsoft account or a local account and a Standard User or Administrator account. Secondary accounts added to the computer are either Family or Other (non-family) accounts. Family accounts are either Child or Adult accounts. Each of these designations controls some aspect of the rights and permissions associated with the account.

- When you first set up your Windows 10 computer, you sign in with a Microsoft account or create a local user account. You can create additional user accounts and specify the rights and permissions of the accounts. Other settings for each user account, such as the picture, password, and alternative sign-in options, are managed by the person who signs in with the user account.

- You have the option of not assigning passwords to local user accounts. Accounts that have passwords can also have numeric or alphanumeric PINs, biometric validation that relies on fingerprint or retinal scan recognition, and picture passwords that require the user to draw three gestures on a background.

- One of the greatest benefits of signing in to your Windows 10 computer with a Microsoft account is that you can synchronize your desktop theme, passwords, language settings, Ease Of Access settings, favorite websites, and web searches across multiple Windows computers and devices.

Practice tasks

Before you can complete these practice tasks, you need to copy the book's practice files to your computer. The practice files for these tasks are located in the **Win10SBS\Ch11** folder. The introduction includes a complete list of practice files.

Understand user accounts and permissions

There are no practice tasks for this topic.

Create and manage user accounts

Display the Family & Other People settings pane, and then perform the following tasks:

1. Create a local user account with the name **Riley** that is not part of your family group.

2. If your computer is running Windows 10 Pro or Windows 10 Enterprise, disable the account and verify that it no longer appears in the **Family & other people** settings pane.

3. Activate the built-in **Guest** account.

4. If you disabled the **Riley** account, enable it for use in the next practice task.

5. Verify that the **Riley** and **Guest** accounts appear in the **Family & other people** settings pane.

6. Check the permissions for the **Riley** account, and make sure that it is a Standard User account.

Manage account pictures and passwords

Perform the following tasks:

1. From the user account menu at the top of the **Start** menu, switch to the **Riley** account, and sign in to the computer.

2. Display Riley's account information in the **Your info** settings pane.

3. Add an account picture to Riley's account. Choose one of the **Account** pictures in the practice files folder.

4. Add a password to Riley's account.

5. Lock the computer, and sign in as Riley, using the password.

Customize your sign-in options

Perform the following tasks:

1. Sign in using the **Riley** account you created in the preceding task, or if you want to configure your own sign-in options, sign in using your account.

2. Display the sign-in options that are available for the account.

3. Create a PIN that you can use instead of the current password to sign in to the computer.

4. Lock the computer.

5. Dismiss the lock screen, and then sign in by using the PIN.

6. If your computer has a biometric identification system that is compatible with Windows Hello, create a Windows Hello sign-in authentication. Then lock the computer, dismiss the lock screen, and sign in by using Windows Hello.

7. Create a picture password that you can use to sign in to the computer. Use one of the **Password** pictures in the practice file folder.

8. Lock the computer.

9. Dismiss the lock screen. On the Welcome screen, select the **Sign-in options** link and notice the icons that represent the available authentication methods.

10. Sign in by using the picture password. If you want to, change the picture password to use a picture of your own.

Synchronize settings across computers

Perform the following tasks:

1. Display the **Sync your settings** pane. Review the elements that you can synchronize among computers and consider which of these would be useful or not useful. (If you're signed in as Riley, you won't be able to modify the sync settings because it is a local account.)

2. If you have a Microsoft account and want to modify the sync settings for that account, sign in using your own account, return to the **Sync your settings** pane, and modify the settings to fit your needs.

3. If you're signed in as Riley, sign out and then sign in with your own account. Then remove the Riley account from your computer.

Manage computer settings

In Windows 10, the management of computer settings is gradually migrating from the more complex Control Panel to the seemingly simple Settings window. This migration supports the development of Windows 10 as a cross-platform system that operates equally gracefully on large (desktop computer) and small (mobile device) display screens. The Settings window organizes function-specific pages into 13 categories that, due to the simplification of the category titles, aren't always self-explanatory. The organization of the settings isn't entirely different from that in Windows 8.1, Windows 7, and earlier versions of Windows, but it's different enough that users of any previous version of Windows are likely to need a bit of time to get used to it. Most settings that remain in Control Panel can be reached through links from the Settings window panes.

In previous chapters, you worked with user interface settings. In this chapter, you work with settings that control the underlying behavior of the computer.

This chapter guides you through procedures related to managing date and time settings, regional and language settings, and speech settings, and for customizing the display of on-screen content.

In this chapter

- Manage date and time settings
- Manage regional and language settings
- Manage speech settings
- Customize device display settings

Manage date and time settings

Your computer system has an internal clock that keeps track of the date and time (down to time increments as small as nanoseconds—billionths of a second), even when the computer is turned off. By default, Windows 10 displays this system date and time in the notification area at the right end of the taskbar, and most of us refer to that information frequently.

The taskbar clock doesn't display the time down to the nanosecond. But programmatically, when a system tool or app captures the time or a time duration, it will typically be accurate to between 1 millisecond and 100 nanoseconds, depending on the hardware platform and the programming language. This accuracy can be very important in some cases. Communication and calendaring software coordinates with the internal clock to keep us on time and on task, but more importantly, system tools and apps use that clock to monitor and manage events on your computer.

To help keep the date and time that your computer references accurate, the clock is set to automatically synchronize with an internet time server every seven days. (You can set the time manually if you can't synchronize with a server.) Internet-based time servers transmit the current Coordinated Universal Time to your computer. This time is known as *UTC* (for *Universal Time Coordinated*), an acronym based on a compromise that allows the use of the same abbreviation in all languages. UTC is a standard based on International Atomic Time and roughly equivalent to Greenwich Mean Time (GMT), which is kept at the Royal Observatory in Greenwich, England. Time zones around the world are expressed by the number of hours they are ahead of or behind UTC/GMT. Computers that aren't located in the UTC/GMT time zone must be set to the correct time zone to display the correct time. If your computer is in a region that participates in daylight saving time, you also need to indicate that fact, so that your computer adjusts from standard time to daylight saving time and back again on the appropriate days. Many computers now have built-in GPS functionality that can provide an accurate location to the computer so that you don't have to adjust your computer.

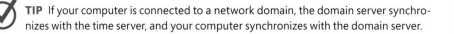 **TIP** If your computer is connected to a network domain, the domain server synchronizes with the time server, and your computer synchronizes with the domain server.

When you install Windows 10, it prompts you to select a time zone. If you move or travel with your computer, you can easily change the time zone.

If you want to be able to quickly check the time, day, and date in other locations, you can configure Windows to display up to three clocks; for example, if you work in a regional office, you might also want to keep track of the time at your company headquarters. The taskbar displays the primary clock. You can display additional clocks in a ScreenTip or in the calendar pane.

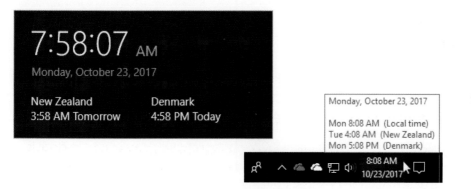

If you need to display time in more than three locations, you can do so on the World Clock page of the built-in Alarms & Clock app.

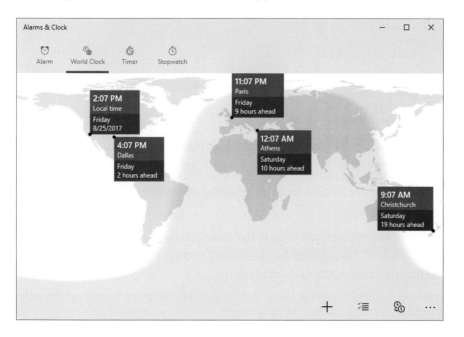

12

You can manage the date, time, time zone, daylight saving time, and date and time formats in the Date & Time pane of the Time & Language settings page.

Date & time

Set time automatically

⬤ On

Set time zone automatically

⬤ Off

Change date and time

Change

Time zone

(UTC-08:00) Pacific Time (US & Canada)   ⌄

Adjust for daylight saving time automatically

⬤ On

Show additional calendars in the taskbar

Don't show additional calendars   ⌄

Formats

First day of week: Sunday
Short date: 10/23/2017
Long date: Monday, October 23, 2017
Short time: 1:03 PM
Long time: 1:03:50 PM
Change date and time formats

To display the current time and date

■ The taskbar displays the time and the date. To display additional information, do either of the following:

- Point to the time or date to display the day of the week, the month, the day, and the year.

- Select the time or date to display the current time to the second, the day and date, and the calendar for the current month. (Your First Day Of Week setting determines the first column.)

1:34:20 PM
Monday, October 23, 2017

October 2017					∧	∨
Su	**Mo**	**Tu**	**We**	**Th**	**Fr**	**Sa**
1	2	3	4	5	6	7
8	9	10	11	12	13	14
15	16	17	18	19	20	21
22	**23**	24	25	26	27	28
29	30	31	1	2	3	4
5	6	7	8	9	10	11

To display the Date & Time settings pane

- On the taskbar, right-click the current date or time, and then near the top of the shortcut menu, select **Adjust date/time**.

- In the **Settings** window, select **Time & Language**, and then select **Date & time**.

To manually set the system date and time

1. Display the **Date & time** settings pane.

2. To stop the computer from synchronizing with a time server, turn off **Set time automatically**.

3. Select **Change** to display the Change Date And Time pane.

12

Change date and time

Change date and time

Date

October ⌄ | 23 ⌄ | 2017 ⌄

Time

1 ⌄ | 34 ⌄ | PM ⌄

Change | Cancel

4. In the **Change date and time** pane, set the date and time as you want them, and then select **Change** to apply your changes.

To manually synchronize with an internet time server

1. Open Control Panel, and then do either of the following to open the Date And Time dialog box:

    - In Category view, select **Clock, Language, and Region**, and then select **Date and Time**.

    - In Small Icons or Large Icons view, select **Date and Time**.

2. In the **Date and Time** dialog box, select the **Internet Time** tab, and then select **Change settings** to open the Internet Time Settings dialog box.

    > **TIP** The shield adjacent to the Change Settings command indicates that this action requires administrator-level permissions. For information about user account permissions, see "Understand user accounts and permissions" in Chapter 11, "Manage user accounts and settings."

3. Select the **Synchronize with an Internet time server** check box, and then expand the **Server** list to display the available servers.

    > **TIP** The internet time servers available in your Server list might differ from those shown here. The default internet time server is *time.windows.com*, which is maintained by Microsoft. Servers with *nist* in their names are maintained by the National Institute of Standards and Technology (NIST) at various locations around the United States. At the time of this writing, NIST is upgrading the servers and networks that support the internet time service; this will result in new addresses for some servers and the discontinuation of others. The global address for all NIST servers is *time.nist.gov*.

4. In the **Server** list, select the server you want to synchronize with, and then select **Update now** to try to connect to the server and update your system time. A message below the server list lets you know whether the clock was successfully synchronized.

> **TIP** If the synchronization fails, and you have an active internet connection, select Update Now again to resubmit the synchronization request to the server.

5. After the clock successfully synchronizes, select **OK** in the **Internet Time Settings** dialog box, and again in the **Date and Time** dialog box.

To change the time zone

1. Display the **Date & time** settings pane.

2. Turn off **Set time zone automatically**.

3. Select the **Time zone** list to display a list of the time zones. Notice that there are multiple time zone descriptions per time zone.

Set time zone automatically

⬤◯ Off

Change date and time

(UTC-09:00) Coordinated Universal Time-09

(UTC-08:00) Baja California

(UTC-08:00) Coordinated Universal Time-08

(UTC-08:00) Pacific Time (US & Canada)

(UTC-07:00) Arizona

(UTC-07:00) Chihuahua, La Paz, Mazatlan

(UTC-07:00) Mountain Time (US & Canada)

(UTC-06:00) Central America

(UTC-06:00) Central Time (US & Canada)

4. In the **Time zone** list, select any time zone that matches your region's variance from UTC. Then check the taskbar clock to confirm that the system time has changed.

5. If your location participates in daylight saving time, turn on **Adjust for daylight saving time automatically**.

To change date and time formats

1. Display the **Date & time** settings pane. The Formats section displays the current settings for the first day of the week, short date, long date, short time, and long time.

2. In the **Formats** area, select **Change date and time formats** to display the Change Date And Time Formats pane.

The First Day Of Week options, which control the display of weekly and monthly calendars, are simply the days of the week. The other lists use abbreviations to represent numeric and alphabetic expressions of the month, day, year, hour, minute, second, and 12-hour time notation.

12

3. In the **Change date and time formats** pane, select the setting you want for the first day of the week and the short and long date and time expressions.

   Changes to the Short Time and Short Date are immediately reflected on the taskbar. Changes to the Long Date are reflected in the ScreenTip that appears when you point to the taskbar time or date.

   > 🔍 **SEE ALSO** For information about changing date and time formats to those of a specific location or language, see "Manage regional and language settings" later in this chapter.

To configure Windows to display multiple clocks

1. Display the **Date & time** settings pane. At the bottom of the pane, select **Add clocks for different time zones** to display the Additional Clocks tab of the Date And Time dialog box.

2. For each additional clock you want to display, select the **Show this clock** check box, select a time zone in the corresponding list, and then enter a display name to identify the time on calendars.

3. Select **OK** in the **Date and Time** dialog box to implement your changes.

To display secondary clocks

- Point to the taskbar clock to display the additional clocks in a ScreenTip.

- Select the taskbar clock to display the calendar pane with the information for the additional time zones at the top.

Manage regional and language settings

Windows 10 was initially released in 190 countries/regions and 111 languages. At the time of this writing, the operating system is "fully localized" in 39 location-specific language variations, shown in the following table.

Arabic (Saudi Arabia)	Bulgarian (Bulgaria)	Chinese (Simplified, China)
Chinese (Hong Kong)	Chinese (Traditional, Taiwan)	Croatian (Croatia)
Czech (Czech Republic)	Danish (Denmark)	Dutch (Netherlands)
English (United Kingdom)	English (United States)	Estonian (Estonia)
Finnish (Finland)	French (France)	French (Canada)
German (Germany)	Greek (Greece)	Hebrew (Israel)
Hungarian (Hungary)	Italian (Italy)	Japanese (Japan)
Korean (Korea)	Latvian (Latvia)	Lithuanian (Lithuania)
Norwegian, Bokmål (Norway)	Polish (Poland)	Portuguese (Brazil)
Portuguese (Portugal)	Romanian (Romania)	Russian (Russia)
Serbian (Latin, Serbia)	Slovak (Slovakia)	Slovenian (Slovenia)
Spanish (Spain, International Sort)	Spanish (Mexico)	Swedish (Sweden)
Thai (Thailand)	Turkish (Turkey)	Ukrainian (Ukraine)

12

Regional variations of these languages are available as Language Interface Packs, which provide a translated version of the most widely used dialog boxes, menu items, and help content. At the time of this writing, 140 Language Interface Packs are available.

Install and manage languages and language features

The Windows display language is used by the operating system to label user interface elements (such as dialog box titles, settings, and button names). When you upgrade to Windows 10, the default Windows display language stays the same as before the upgrade. If you want or need to work with features in a language other than the current Windows display language, you can change the system language, switch between languages, or simply install the other language to make its features available on your computer. Other apps can check the system language and use features that are installed with the language. For example, installing a language that uses characters other than those in the default language installs fonts that support those characters. You can use those fonts when creating documents in Microsoft Word, Adobe InDesign, Silhouette Studio, or any other app that pulls a font list from Windows. Windows and installed apps fetch content based on your region and language settings. At the time of this writing, 140 languages, plus dialects, are available.

Some system languages include enhanced language-specific features such as spelling, text prediction, alphabet-specific fonts, handwriting recognition, optical character recognition, speech recognition, text-to-speech, and Cortana support. You can install some of these options separately from the language pack. The Optional Features list shows installed supplemental font features.

> ⚠ **IMPORTANT** At the time of this writing, the interactive Cortana service is available in 13 countries/regions—Australia, Brazil, Canada, China, France, Germany, India, Italy, Japan, Mexico, Spain, the United Kingdom, and the United States—but can translate phrases in 40 languages. When the system language is set to one that Cortana doesn't speak, the feature is automatically disabled. The standard search feature is available when Cortana isn't.

Installing a language makes the keyboard layout for that language available. If you connect a physical keyboard with the layout and character set that is typically used with that language, switching the keyboard language enters the correct characters (as labeled on the keyboard) when you press the keys. If you don't have a physical keyboard that is configured for a language, switching the keyboard language makes your existing keyboard function as though it were labeled in that language. It also makes the on-screen keyboard available in that language. There are often other options available; they vary by language.

> ✓ **TIP** To display the touch keyboard icon on the taskbar, right-click or press and hold a blank area of the taskbar, and then select Show Touch Keyboard Button. Although this is called the *touch* keyboard, you can also use your mouse to select the keys.

After you install a language, it is available from the Settings window and from the notification area of the taskbar. You can easily switch languages from the taskbar.

> ⚠ **IMPORTANT** If you synchronize settings across multiple computers through your Microsoft account, installing a language on one computer triggers the installation of that language on your other computers, and switching languages on one computer makes the same change on your others. If your keyboard begins to generate keystrokes other than you think it should, check the notification area of the taskbar to make sure that you haven't inadvertently changed the language.

You can manage the country or region of record and the system language in the Region & Language pane of the Time & Language settings page.

⚙ # Region & language

Country or region

Windows and apps might use your country or region to give you local content

United States	⌄

Languages

You can type in any language you add to the list. Windows, apps and websites will appear in the first language in the list that they support

 + Add a language

 English (United States)
Windows display language

Related settings

Additional date, time, & regional settings

12

To display the Region & Language settings pane

- In the **Settings** window, select **Time & Language**, and then select **Region & language**.

To specify your country or region for local content

1. Display the **Region & language** settings pane.

2. Select the **Country or region** list, and then select the location you want Windows and installed apps to consider your home location.

> ✓ **TIP** Many websites discern your location based on the IP address of your internet connection. The location you select in the Region & Language pane does not affect the location that is conveyed by the IP address.

To install an additional system language

1. Display the **Region & language** settings pane. The Languages section displays the currently installed languages. (There is only one until you add a language.)

2. In the **Languages** section, select **Add a language** to display the list of languages you can install. The name of each language is shown first in that language and then in your current system language.

Add a language		
Type a language name...		
Afrikaans Afrikaans	Shqip Albanian	Elsässisch Alsatian
አማርኛ Amharic	العربية Arabic	Հայերեն Armenian
অসমীয়া Assamese	Азәрбајҹан дили Azerbaijani (Cyrillic)	Azərbaycan dili Azerbaijani (Latin)
বাংলা Bangla	Башкорт Bashkir	Euskara Basque
Беларуская Belarusian	Босански Bosnian (Cyrillic)	Bosanski Bosnian (Latin)
Brezhoneg Breton	Български Bulgarian	မြန်မာစာ Burmese

3. Scroll the list and select the language you want to install. If Windows has multiple versions of that language available, select the dialect you want from the secondary screen.

Deutsch

Type a language name...

Deutsch (Österreich)
German (Austria)

Deutsch (Deutschland)
German (Germany)

Deutsch (Liechtenstein)
German (Liechtenstein)

Deutsch (Luxemburg)
German (Luxembourg)

Deutsch (Schweiz)
German (Switzerland)

Windows displays a notification and installs the language from Windows Update, or adds the language to the language list and notifies you that you need to install a language pack.

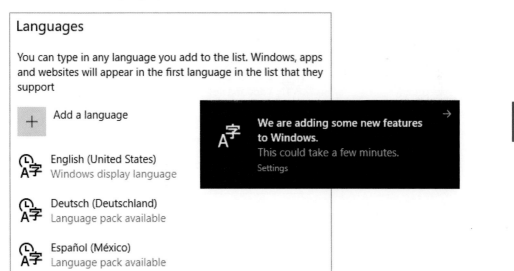

12

To install a language pack

1. In the **Languages** area of the **Region & language** settings pane, select a language that has an available language pack.

2. In the pane that expands, select **Options** to display the Language Options pane.

3. At the top of the **Language options** pane, in the **Download language pack** area, select **Download** to download and install the language pack. You can also track the installation progress from the Region & Language settings pane.

To configure language options

1. In the **Languages** area of the **Region & language** settings pane, select an installed language and then, in the pane that expands, select **Options** to display the Language Options pane.

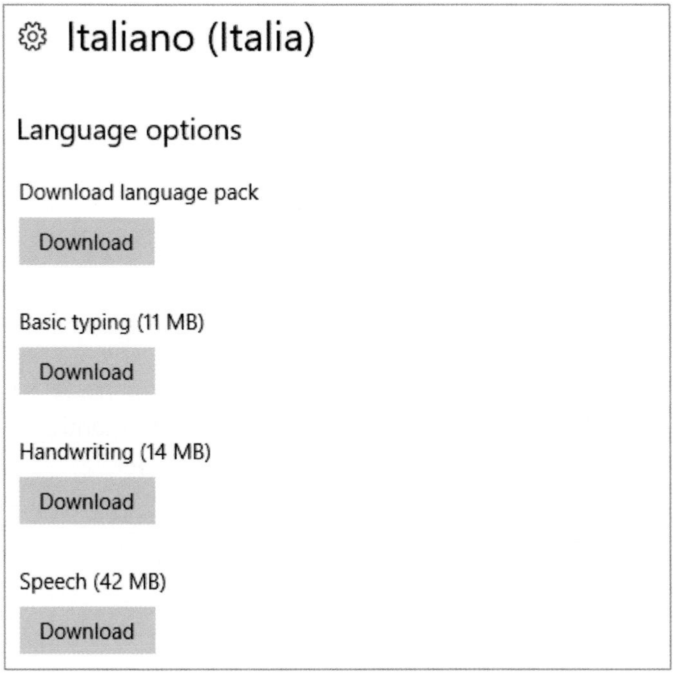

⚙ Italiano (Italia)

Language options

Download language pack

Download

Basic typing (11 MB)

Download

Handwriting (14 MB)

Download

Speech (42 MB)

Download

2.   Peruse the available options and download or configure any you want to use.

To display the installed supplemental font features

1.   In the **Settings** window, select **Apps**, and then select **Apps & features**.

2.   In the **Apps & features** section of the **Apps & features** pane, select **Manage optional features**.

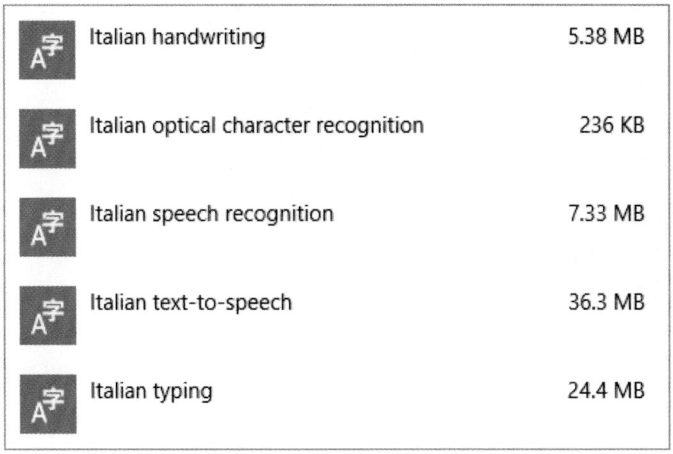

12

A⅀	Italian handwriting	5.38 MB
A⅀	Italian optical character recognition	236 KB
A⅀	Italian speech recognition	7.33 MB
A⅀	Italian text-to-speech	36.3 MB
A⅀	Italian typing	24.4 MB

To change the Windows display language

1. In the **Languages** area of the **Region & language** settings pane, select a language that is not labeled *Windows display language* and then, in the pane that expands, select **Set as default**. The change takes effect immediately in some system areas, such as the date and time displayed on the taskbar.

2. Sign out of Windows, and then sign back in to completely implement the display language change.

To remove a system language

- In the **Languages** section of the **Region & language** settings pane, select the language you want to remove and then, in the pane that expands, select **Remove**.

To change the keyboard language

1. Install the system language of the keyboard you want to use.

2. Do either of the following:

   - On the taskbar, to the left of the clock, select the keyboard language button to expand the available keyboard list.

   - Press Win+Spacebar to cycle through the installed keyboard languages.

Configure regional settings

You can modify numeric formats to those of another country/region without installing a language. You can modify settings for only your user account, or also for the Welcome screen, system accounts (such as the Guest account), and new user accounts on the computer.

To change date and time formats to those of a specific region

1. Display the **Date & time** settings pane. In the **Related settings** area, select **Additional date, time, & regional settings** to display the Clock, Language, And Region category of Control Panel.

2. In the **Region** category, select **Change date, time, or number formats** to display the Formats tab of the Region dialog box. The default format is *Match Windows display language*.

3. Select the **Format** list, and then select the language and country or region that you want to use for the standard date and time formats.

12

> ✅ **TIP** You can make changes to the date and time formats by selecting Additional Settings. You can reset customized settings to the defaults for the language and location at any time.

4. In the **Region** dialog box, select **OK** to apply your changes and close the dialog box.

To copy regional settings to Windows system screens and new user accounts

1. Display the **Region** dialog box, and then select the **Administrative** tab.

2. In the **Welcome screen and new user accounts** section, select **Copy settings** to display the current settings.

3. At the bottom of the **Welcome screen and new user accounts settings** dialog box, select one or both check boxes to specify the settings that you want to change. Then select **OK**.

4. Restart the computer to implement the changes.

Manage speech settings

Many people talk to their computers, but the time has finally come when doing so represents more of an efficiency than an eccentricity. If your Windows 10 computer is configured to run one of the system languages that supports speech recognition, you can now accomplish even more by speaking to your computer, through the Cortana user interface. You can also configure your computer to respond to verbal commands, and you can dictate content into apps.

> **TIP** At the time of this writing, speech recognition is available for only the following languages: English (United States, United Kingdom, Australia, Canada, and India), French, German, Japanese, Mandarin (Chinese Simplified and Chinese Traditional), and Spanish. For more information about Cortana, see Chapter 9, "Get assistance from Cortana."

You can make the best use of speech recognition if you have a good-quality microphone. Most computers and devices have built-in microphones, but you can also purchase reasonably priced headset microphones that maintain a constant distance between the microphone and your mouth and block out external distractions. They also tend to pick up fewer keyboard and mouse noises than built-in microphones that are close to those interface elements.

Dictate content to your computer

The Fall 2017 Creators Update includes specific improvement in dictation features. You can easily dictate text into any text field by pressing Win+H to open the dictation toolbar, and then speaking the text you want to write.

You can tap the microphone on the dictation toolbar to turn dictation on and off, or you can give verbal commands, such as *select, clear, delete, go after* (or before), *move to, move forward* (or *back*) *to, go up* (or *down*) *to, tap, press, start,* and *stop.* To turn off dictation, say "stop dictation." A full list of commands and a guide for entering symbols are available from *support.microsoft.com /help/4042244.*

12

If you're having trouble getting Cortana to understand verbal commands, you can run the Speech troubleshooter to configure your microphone. Additional speech configuration tools are available from the Speech Recognition page of Control Panel. If you intend to dictate content into an app that supports it, it's worthwhile to invest time in the speech tutorial and the speech recognition voice training. If you use a good microphone and enunciate properly, speech recognition works well. It won't outpace a fast, accurate typist, but if you are a "hunt and peck" typist, this might help you churn out your next novel.

Configure your Speech Recognition experience

Start Speech Recognition
Start using your voice to control your computer.

Set up microphone
Set up your computer to work properly with Speech Recognition.

Take Speech Tutorial
Learn to use your computer with speech. Learn basic commands and dictation.

Train your computer to better understand you
Read text to your computer to improve your computer's ability to understand your voice. Doing this isn't necessary, but can help improve dictation accuracy.

Open the Speech Reference Card
View and print a list of common commands to keep with you so you always know what to say.

As you interact with Cortana, Windows 10 monitors your spoken, handwritten, and typed input in addition to your messages and appointments. (This feature was originally called *Getting to know you* but is now referred to simply as *speech services and typing suggestions*.) From this information, Cortana can adjust the speech recognition patterns, create a local user dictionary, and serve up content that is pertinent to the things it detects happening in your life. Speech services and typing suggestions are on by default and are required to use Cortana voice commands. If you're not using Cortana, you can turn off speech services and typing suggestions in the Windows 10 privacy settings.

 SEE ALSO For more information about Cortana, see Chapter 9, "Get assistance from Cortana."

Your computer can talk back to you, too. By using text-to-speech technology, it can read printed content to you, or provide verbal cues for the visual aspects of the user interface (for example, reading button labels or dialog box options to you). The English-language version of Windows 10 has three default voice options—a female voice identified as Zira and two male voices identified as David and Mark. You can listen to a sample of each voice. Adding language packs can also add male and female voices with language-specific names and samples.

Under the best of conditions, this technology is amazing, and seems almost like artificial intelligence. Under the worst of conditions, it is at least mildly funny. Between those extremes it can range from mildly useful to mildly annoying.

You can manage the speech language, text-to-speech, and microphone settings in the Speech pane of the Time & Language settings page.

To display the Speech settings pane

- In the **Settings** window, select **Time & Language**, and then select **Speech**.

To run the Speech troubleshooter

1. Display the **Speech** settings pane.

2. In the **Speech language** section, expand the **Choose the language...** list, and then select the language that you speak and want the computer to recognize.

> **TIP** The list includes only the system languages that are installed on your computer that support speech recognition. To make one of these languages available that isn't your default, you must first install the language pack. For more information, see "Manage regional and language settings" earlier in this chapter.

12

Choose the language you speak with your device

English (United States)

German (Germany)

Italian (Italy)

Spanish (Mexico)

☐ Recognize non-native accents for this language

3. To give the computer the best chance of understanding you, select the **Recognize non-native accents for this language** check box.

4. Prepare your microphone:

   - If you have a headset microphone, put it on and adjust the microphone so that it's directly in front of your mouth, with two to three finger-widths of space between your lips and the microphone.

   - If you have a freestanding microphone, position it so that it is in front of you when you're facing the computer screen.

   - Be sure that the microphone is turned on and connected to the computer.

   - Close the door and turn off or remove any loud things from the area.

5. In the **Microphone** section of the **Speech** pane, select **Get started** to start the Speech wizard. (This button used to start a microphone setup wizard, but that has been replaced with a microphone/speaker troubleshooter.)

6. To troubleshoot the microphone, select **Cortana can't hear me** and then on the **Which of these devices...** page, select the microphone you prepared in step 4.

7. On the **Set up your microphone** page, select **Set up the mic**. After reading the instructions on the **Mic Calibration** page, select **Next**. The wizard provides a sentence for you to speak.

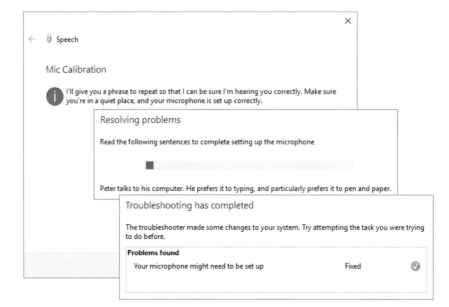

8. Read aloud the sentence below the progress bar, speaking in the voice that you will normally use when dictating text, giving verbal commands, or speaking to Cortana. When the wizard has a sufficient sample to properly adjust the microphone levels, it moves to the next page.

9. Select **Close** to complete and exit the wizard.

To display additional speech configuration tools

- Display Control Panel in Category view. Select the **Ease of Access** category, and then select **Speech Recognition**.

- Display Control Panel in Large Icons view or Small Icons view, and then select **Speech Recognition**.

To change the voice and speed of the computer's text-to-speech narrator

1. Display the **Speech** settings pane.

2. In the **Text-to-speech** area, expand the **Voice** list to display the currently available voices.

> Text-to-speech
>
> Change the default voice for apps
>
> Voice
>
> | Microsoft David |
> | Microsoft Zira |
> | Microsoft Mark |
>
> Speed
>
> ————————————————○————————————————
>
> Listen to voice sample
>
> Preview voice

3. In the **Voice** list, select the voice you want to set as the default.

4. On the **Speed** slider, set the speed you think you'll be comfortable with. (The slider represents speeds from very slow on the left to very fast on the right.)

5. Set your speakers to a comfortable level, and then select **Preview voice**.

6. Adjust your settings as necessary until the preview voice clip is at a speed you can understand.

12

To turn off speech services and typing suggestions

1. Do either of the following to display the **Speech, inking, & typing** privacy settings pane:

   - Display the **Speech** settings pane. In the **Related settings** area, select **Speech, inking, & typing privacy settings**.

   - In the **Settings** window, select **Privacy**, and then select **Speech, inking, & typing**.

2. Read the feature description and be certain that you don't want to use the dictation or Cortana features. (You can still use the Ease Of Access Speech-to-Text app.)

> ## Getting to know you
>
> Use your voice to do things like talk to Cortana or Store applications, and use your typing history and handwriting patterns to create a local user dictionary that makes better suggestions for you. Microsoft will use your voice input to make cloud-based speech services work even better.
>
> When this is switched off, you can't speak to Cortana, and your typing and inking user dictionary will be cleared. Speech services that don't rely on the cloud, like Windows Speech Recognition, will still work. Typing suggestion and handwriting recognition using system dictionary will also continue to work.
>
> Turn off speech services and typing suggestions

3. Select **Turn off speech services and typing suggestions**.

Customize device display settings

Windows 10 was designed to run on a diverse array of devices with displays of many different sizes, shapes, and orientations.

When you purchase a computer monitor, all-in-one computer, laptop, tablet, or smartphone, one of the things you consider is its size, or display area, which is measured like a television screen: diagonally in inches. As important as the physical size, though, is the screen resolution the monitor supports, which is measured in pixels and is expressed as the number of pixels wide by the number of pixels high. *Pixels* are the individual dots that make up the picture displayed on your screen. Each pixel displays one color; depending on your screen resolution, the images shown on the screen might consist of from 500,000 to several million individual dots of color.

When personal computers first became popular, most computer monitors could display only 640 pixels horizontally and 480 pixels vertically (a screen resolution of 640 × 480). Nearly all screen displays now support a screen resolution of no less than 1024 × 768 pixels, and many newer screens support a resolution of 3840 × 2160 pixels (referred to as *4K*) or even higher. In effect, as the screen resolution increases, the size of each pixel decreases, and more information can be shown in the same display area. In other words, as the screen resolution increases, so does the amount of information that is shown on the screen—but all the information appears smaller.

Most computer systems provide a choice of at least two screen resolutions, but you might have many more choices. Some people prefer to work at a lower screen resolution so that everything on the screen appears larger; others prefer to fit as much information on the screen as they possibly can. Recent statistics indicate that more than 95 percent of internet users have their screen resolution set to 1024 × 768 or greater. At the time of this writing, the most widely used screen resolution is 1366 × 768 pixels, which is a common laptop screen resolution.

Originally, most monitors had a 4:3 aspect ratio, with the screen 4 units wide and 3 units high. These 4:3 displays are now referred to as *standard displays*. Many monitors now have *widescreen displays* intended to improve the experience of viewing movies on the computer by displaying them at a 16:9 aspect ratio, which is also the standard for high-definition television and ultra-high-definition television. These resolutions might be available on your computer regardless of the native aspect ratio of your actual monitor. The popular 1366 × 768 computer screen resolution is a widescreen display. Tablets and smartphones rotate to support both horizontal and vertical displays.

12

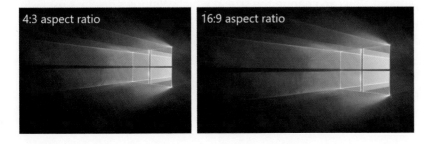

449

> **TIP** To guarantee clear display of the official Windows 10 desktop background, Microsoft provides nine high-resolution versions of it at different vertically and horizontally oriented sizes. These files are available from the C:\Windows\Web folder.

In the original release of Windows 10, the screen resolution was deemed an "advanced" display setting—possibly because most people like to set it and forget it—and was not as easily accessible as in earlier versions of Windows. Fortunately, that decision was revisited, and in the Fall 2017 Creators Update, the screen resolution setting is back on the Display pane of the System setting page. Screen resolution capabilities are hardware specific.

Scale and layout

Change the size of text, apps, and other items

| 100% (Recommended) | ∨ |

Custom scaling

Resolution

| 2560 × 1440 (Recommended) | ∨ |

Orientation

| Landscape | ∨ |

> **TIP** The maximum resolution is the highest resolution supported by your monitor or the highest resolution supported by the graphics card installed in your computer, whichever is lower.

Windows 10 offers an additional option for increasing the size of user interface elements. Instead of changing the size of everything on the screen (by changing the screen resolution), you can change the size at which Windows displays user interface elements. The default setting is 100%, and you can increase the size in 25-percent increments. The maximum increase depends on the screen size and resolution.

You can temporarily magnify part or all of your on-screen content by using the Magnifier tool. For information about Magnifier, see "Configure Windows accessibility features" in Chapter 13, "Manage power and access options."

Smaller handheld devices such as tablets and smartphones are designed to support the rotation of on-screen content as the device rotates, but this capability isn't generally built into laptops or desktop monitors (although there are specialized monitors that support rotation). If you have a device that supports monitor rotation, you can easily configure Windows 10 to change the orientation of on-screen content. The default orientation is Landscape (with the screen wider than it is high). Other options include Portrait, flipped Landscape, and flipped Portrait.

> **SEE ALSO** For information about manually and automatically adjusting the screen brightness and color tone, see Chapter 13, "Manage power and access options."

To display the Display settings pane

- Open the **Settings** window. Select **System**, and then select **Display**.

- Right-click an empty area of the desktop, and then select **Display settings**.

To change the screen resolution

1. Display the **Display** settings pane.

2. In the **Scale and layout** section, expand the **Resolution** list to display the screen resolutions that are supported by the computer graphics card and the monitor.

> **TIP** When you change the screen resolution, try to choose one that has the same aspect ratio as your actual monitor. If *(Recommended)* appears after a screen resolution, this will be the largest screen resolution at the native aspect ratio. You might be able to discern the aspect ratio visually from the preview boxes; if not, you can do the math to identify the aspect ratio. The available resolutions depend on your graphics card and monitor.

12

```
Resolution

2560 × 1440 (Recommended)        ↖
2048 × 1152
1920 × 1440
1920 × 1200
1920 × 1080
1680 × 1050
1600 × 900
1440 × 900
1366 × 768
```

3. In the list, select the screen resolution you want, to temporarily apply the setting. Windows displays a Keep These Display Changes? message box.

4. If you like the new screen resolution, select **Keep changes**. Otherwise, select **Revert** (or wait 15 seconds) to return to the previous screen resolution.

To change the scale of user interface elements

1. Display the **Display** settings pane.

2. In the **Scale and layout** section, expand the **Change the size of text, apps, and other items** list, and then select the scale you want. The change takes effect immediately in the Settings window and on the taskbar.

3. To apply the change to all apps, sign out of Windows and then sign back in.

> ✓ **TIP** It is possible to set a custom scaling level, but this is not recommended. If you're interested in this, select Custom Scaling in the Scale And Layout section of the Display settings pane, enter a scale from 100 to 500, and then select Apply.

To change the orientation of on-screen content

1. In the **Display** settings pane, select the **Orientation** list, and then select **Landscape**, **Portrait**, **Landscape (flipped)**, or **Portrait (flipped)**.

2. Windows temporarily changes the screen orientation and displays a Keep These Display Changes? message box. If you like the new screen orientation, select **Keep changes**. Otherwise, select **Revert** (or wait 15 seconds) to return to the previous orientation.

Key points

- Your computer's internal clock can be synchronized to an internet time server or set manually.

- Windows 10 supports many languages. You can install language packs to support the use of alternative keyboard layouts, speech-recognition languages, and menu and option labels.

- You can interact with your computer by talking to it, and it can read content back to you. You can choose from multiple computer voices and adjust the speed to fit your pace.

- You can change the screen resolution and orientation, and the scale of the content, to best suit your current working conditions.

12

Practice tasks

No practice files are necessary to complete the practice tasks in this chapter.

Manage date and time settings

Perform the following tasks:

1. From the taskbar, experiment with different methods of displaying the current time and date.

2. Display the calendar, and from there display the **Date & time** settings pane.

3. Change the time zone to another, and notice that the clock immediately changes. Examine other content on your computer that has time stamps, such as email messages, and determine how the time zone change affects that content. Then set the time zone to the one you're in.

4. Configure Windows to display date and time information for an additional time zone. Choose a time zone that is far away from your own, preferably on the other side of the date line. Then experiment with the different methods of displaying the secondary clock.

5. Configure Windows to display the clocks that you want to have available.

Manage regional and language settings

Display the Region & Language settings pane, and then perform the following tasks:

1. Check that the correct country or region is specified for local content.

2. If you want to, install an additional system language. If the language requires a language pack, install the language pack.

3. If you install an additional language, notice that the language button appears in the notification area of the taskbar. Select the button to display the keyboard language options. Experiment with the other keyboard if you want, to try to locate keys that enter different characters than those shown on your keyboard.

4. Experiment with any other features that are discussed in the "Manage regional and language settings" topic that you're interested in. When you finish, configure the settings on your computer for the way you want to work.

Manage speech settings

Display the Speech settings pane, and then perform the following tasks:

1. Preview the voices that are available for the computer's text-to-speech narrator. Choose the voice you like best, and then adjust its speed so you can best understand it.

2. Complete the process of setting up your microphone, if you haven't previously done so.

3. Display the additional speech configuration tools available from Control Panel. If you're interested in more precisely configuring the computer for speech recognition, complete at least one of the configuration processes.

Customize device display settings

Display the Display settings pane, and then perform the following tasks:

1. Experiment with the **Change the size of text, apps, and other items** slider to determine the largest possible magnification you can apply to your display by using this feature. If you want to, apply the **125%** setting, and then sign out and back in to your computer to get the full effect of the setting.

2. Display the screen resolution options supported by your computer system. If you want to, temporarily apply a different screen resolution and examine the effect. If you find another screen resolution that you prefer, keep it.

Manage power and access options

Your power settings determine how long your computer will sit idle before reducing power consumption by turning off the screen or going into sleep mode.

One factor in your computer's power usage that you can control is the screen brightness. A brighter screen uses more power. You can manage the screen brightness independently or as part of a power plan.

Screen brightness, in addition to the color of the light coming from the screen, can cause eyestrain and sleeplessness. The Night Light feature introduced with the Fall 2017 Creators Update of Windows 10 can help mitigate the negative effects of spending too much time in front of your computer screen.

Microsoft takes wellness and accessibility seriously, and this is apparent in the company's early and continued commitment to the Windows Ease Of Access features that provide alternative methods for information input and output. Anyone can use these features to enhance their computing experience.

This chapter guides you through procedures related to changing the screen brightness, configuring power options for corded and battery-powered computers, and configuring Windows accessibility features.

In this chapter

- Change the screen brightness
- Configure power options
- Configure Windows accessibility features

Change the screen brightness

You might have heard the term *blue light* for the light that shines from a television, computer, or mobile device screen. Health professionals advise that people should avoid blue light for an hour before going to bed, because it can contribute to sleeplessness.

When you're working in a dark room, a brighter screen can cause more eyestrain than a dimmer screen. You can adjust the screen brightness, and you can now also change the color tone from blue light to warmer colors, by using the Night Light feature.

You can turn the Night Light feature on and off manually, or schedule it to turn on and off automatically.

To change the screen brightness

- Display the **Action Center**, expand the **Quick Actions** section if it's collapsed, and then select **Brightness** to cycle through screen brightness settings in 25-percent increments.

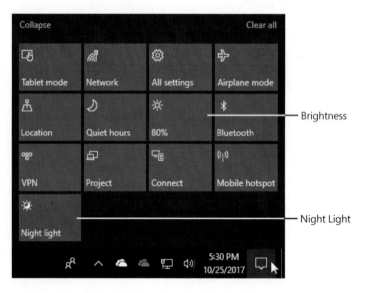

- Open the **Settings** window. Select **System**, and then **Display**. In the **Brightness and color** section, drag the **Change brightness** slider, or click or tap on either side of the slide box, to adjust the screen brightness to a percentage of the maximum level configured for your screen.

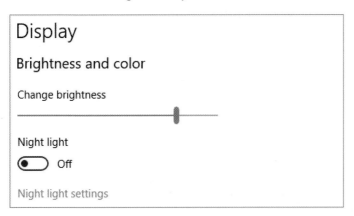

The brightness changes immediately, so you can slowly move the slider until the screen is exactly as bright as you want it in your current lighting conditions.

To turn Night Light on or off

- Display the **Action Center**, expand the **Quick Actions** section if it's collapsed, and then select **Night light**.

- In the **System** settings window, select **Display**. In the **Brightness and color** section, turn on **Night light**.

To configure Night Light screen color

1. In the **System** settings window, select **Display**.

2. In the **Brightness and color** section, select **Night light settings**.

3. On the **Night light settings** page, drag the **Color temperature at night** slider, or click or tap on either side of the slide box, to adjust the color.

13

⚙ **Night light settings**

Screens emit blue light, which can keep you up at night. Night light displays warmer colors to help you sleep.

Turn off now

Color temperature at night

Schedule

Schedule night light

⬤ Off

To configure automatic Night Light start and end times

1. In the **Brightness and color** section of the **Display** system settings pane, select **Night light settings**.

2. In the **Schedule** section of the **Night light settings** pane, turn on **Schedule night light**, and then do either of the following:

   • To link the on and off times to your local sunset and sunrise, select **Sunset to sunrise**.

   • To schedule specific on and off times, select **Set hours**, and then set the **Turn on** and **Turn off** times.

Schedule

Schedule night light

⬤ On

◉ Sunset to sunrise (6:04 PM – 7:02 AM)

○ Set hours

> ⚠️ **IMPORTANT** If Sunset To Sunrise is unavailable, select Location Settings, and in the Location pane of the Privacy settings page, turn on Location Service. Then select the Back button in the upper-left corner of the Settings window to confirm that Sunset To Sunrise is turned on.
>
> If your Sunset To Sunrise schedule shows times from 12:00 AM to 12:00 AM, leave and then return to the Night Light Settings page to update the sunset and sunrise times.

Configure power options

Reducing power consumption is obviously of higher priority if your device is running on battery power. On battery-powered computers, such as laptops and tablets, you can separately configure settings that are in effect when the device is plugged in and when it runs on battery power.

The screen brightness can have a significant effect on the length of time a battery charge powers a computer. In the previous topic, you learned about independently adjusting the screen brightness. You can also manage it as part of a power plan.

Each Windows 10 computer has a set of built-in power plans that define three settings:

- When to turn off the display
- When to put the computer to sleep
- How bright to make the display

The built-in power plans vary based on the computer type and manufacturer, but usually include the following:

- **Power Saver** This power plan prioritizes power conservation over performance. The screen is less bright and computer processes turn off earlier.

- **High Performance** This power plan prioritizes the user experience over power conservation. The screen is brighter and the computer remains idle for a longer time before turning off processes.

- **Balanced** This power plan uses less power than High Performance and has higher performance values than Power Saver.

You can choose a preconfigured power plan, modify individual elements of a power plan, or even create your own. Creating a custom plan is similar to editing an existing plan, but you name and save it so you can easily apply it at any time. If you decide you no longer need a custom power plan, you can delete it.

13

To configure the power management settings

1. Open the **Settings** window. Select **System**, and then select **Power & sleep**. The Power & Sleep pane displays the current length of inactive time you want the computer to wait before it turns off the screen and then goes to sleep.

> **TIP** A laptop or other battery-powered computer has separate "on battery power" and "when plugged in" lists; a desktop computer has only the "when plugged in" lists.

2. In the **Screen** section of the **Power & sleep** pane, in each available list, select a time from **1 minute** to **5 hours**, or **Never**, to indicate the period of inactivity after which you want the screen to turn off (but the computer to continue running).

3. In the **Sleep** section of the **Power & sleep** pane, in each available list, select a time from **1 minute** to **5 hours**, or **Never**, to indicate the period of inactivity after which you want the computer to enter Sleep mode.

> **TIP** The Sleep timeout must be equal to or greater than the Screen timeout. Setting the Sleep value to less time than the Screen value lowers the Screen value to match; setting the Screen value to more time than the Sleep value raises the Sleep value to match.

The power setting changes take effect immediately.

To choose a built-in power-management plan

1. Display the **Power & sleep** settings pane.

2. In the **Related settings** section of the pane, select **Additional power settings** to open the Power Options window of Control Panel.

3. If **Show additional plans** appears below the plan descriptions, select it to display hidden power plans.

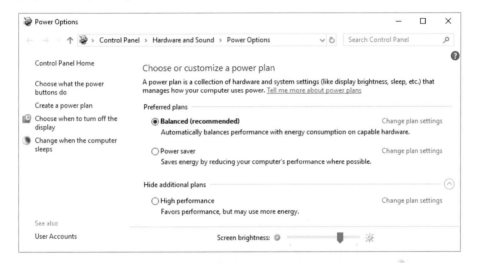

4. To compare plan settings, select the **Change plan settings** link to the right of each plan name, peruse the settings, and then select the **Back** button to return to the Power Options window.

5. In the **Power Options** window, select the preconfigured power option you want.

To modify an existing power plan

1. Open the **Power Options** window of Control Panel.

2. Select **Change plan settings** to the right of the plan that you want to modify, to open the Edit Plan Settings window for the plan.

13

> **TIP** A laptop or other battery-powered computer has separate "on battery power" and "when plugged in" lists; a desktop computer has only the "when plugged in" lists.

3. For each available power source, do the following:

   - To the right of **Turn off the display**, select a time from **1 minute** to **5 hours**, or **Never**, to indicate the period of inactivity after which you want to turn off the screen when the computer is running on that power source.

   - To the right of **Put the computer to sleep**, select a time from **1 minute** to **5 hours**, or **Never**, to indicate the period of inactivity after which you want the computer to enter Sleep mode when it is running on that power source.

   - To the right of **Adjust plan brightness**, move the slider to indicate how bright you want the screen to be when the computer is running on that power source.

4. In the **Edit Plan Settings** window, select **Save change**s to apply your changes to the power plan and return to the Power Options window. If you modified the currently active plan, changes to the brightness are immediately apparent.

> **TIP** If you decide you don't like the screen brightness you set, you can change it at the bottom of the Power Options window. The change will be applied to the current plan and automatically saved with it.

System power settings

Windows 10 has default behaviors for entering sleep mode, waking up, and shutting down. If you find that these defaults aren't working for you, you can change the options. (Changes require approval from an Administrator account.)

There are three sets of settings that you can change:

- **Shutdown action triggers** These settings are related to the Power and Sleep buttons (the physical buttons) on your computer. Not all computers have Sleep buttons, but many do; they're usually located on the keyboard and labeled with something that indicates sleep such as "zzz" or a moon. On a laptop, you can also specify what happens when you close the lid. The following table describes the shutdown actions that can occur when you press the Power or Sleep button, or close the laptop lid.

Shutdown action	Power button	Sleep button	Close the lid
Do nothing	Y	Y	Y
Turn off the display	Y	Y	Not optional
Sleep	Y	Default	Y
Hibernate	Y	Y	Y
Shut down	Default	N	Y

- **Password requirement** By default, when your computer comes out of sleep mode, Windows displays the Lock screen. Users whose accounts are protected by passwords must enter their passwords to sign in. You can turn off this requirement.

- **Shutdown settings** This category is a bit of a catchall. You can control whether the Power menu includes the Sleep and Hibernate commands, and whether the user account menu includes the Lock command.

In general, if things are working well for you, it's best to leave them as they are. But if you want to make changes, you can do so from the System Settings page of Control Panel. In Category view, select Hardware And Sound, and then in the Power Options group, select Change What The Power Buttons Do. Most of the options are unavailable to change until you select Change Settings That Are Currently Unavailable and provide Administrator account credentials.

13

To create a custom power plan

1. Open the **Power Options** window of Control Panel.

2. In the left pane, select **Create a power plan** to open the Create A Power Plan window.

3. Select one of the default plans as the starting point for your new plan, then provide a name for your custom power plan. Then select **Next** to display the Edit Plan Settings window.

4. For each available power source, select times in the **Turn off the display** list and the **Put the computer to sleep** list, and move the **Adjust plan brightness** slider to indicate how bright you want the screen to be when the computer is running on that power source.

5. In the **Edit Plan Settings** window, select **Create** to create the custom power plan and return to the Power Options window.

To edit advanced settings of an existing power plan

1. Open the **Power Options** window of Control Panel.

2. Select **Change plan settings** to the right of the plan that you want to modify.

3. At the bottom of the **Edit Plan Settings** window, select **Change advanced power settings** to open the Power Options dialog box.

4. If the plan shown at the top of the **Power Options** dialog box is not the one you want to modify, expand the list, and select the plan you want to customize.

5. Scroll through the available settings and select the expand button (+) to expand any category of interest.

6. If the settings you want to change are unavailable (dimmed), you can select the **Change settings that are currently unavailable** link above the list and provide administrator permission, if necessary, to make the changes.

7. If you change settings, select **Apply** or **OK** to apply the changes.

13

Make your battery last longer

The Battery Saver feature is available only on battery-powered devices (such as laptops). Battery Saver conserves battery power (and thereby extends battery life) by regulating background activity and hardware settings.

In the Battery system settings pane, the Battery progress bar indicates the remaining battery charge; the note below the bar indicates whether the battery is currently discharging or charging.

Battery

Overview

70%

Estimated time remaining: 2 hours

Battery usage by app

Battery

Overview

64%

Estimated time to full charge: 0 hour 51 minutes

Battery usage by app

TIP The Battery settings pane is available only on battery-powered devices.

To reset a power plan to its defaults

1. Open the **Power Options** window of Control Panel.

2. Select **Change plan settings** to the right of the plan that you want to restore.

3. At the bottom of the **Edit Plan Settings** window, select the **Restore default settings for this plan** link, and then select **Yes** in the **Power Options** message box that opens.

Windows automatically turns the Battery Saver feature on when the battery charge falls below 20 percent, but you also have the option of turning it on whenever the device is running on battery power. To manually start Battery Saver, display the Battery settings pane, and then turn on Battery Saver Status Until Next Charge. This setting is available only when the computer is running on battery power, not when it's plugged in.

To modify the battery charge level at which Battery Saver turns on, select the Turn Battery Save On Automatically... check box, and then move the slider to select the charge level you want.

☑ Turn battery saver on automatically if my battery falls below:
───────────────────────────────── 30%
Battery saver status until next charge
◉⎯ Off
☑ Lower screen brightness while in battery saver

To delete a custom power plan

1. Open the **Power Options** window of Control Panel.

2. Apply any power plan other than the one you want to delete.

3. Select **Change plan settings** to the right of the plan that you want to delete.

4. At the bottom of the **Edit Plan Settings** window, select the **Delete this plan** link, and then select **OK** in the **Power Options** message box that opens.

 TIP You can delete only custom power plans. You can't delete built-in power plans.

Configure Windows accessibility features

Are the words on the screen too small to read easily? Do you wish the icons were larger? Does it take you a while to locate the cursor because it is so skinny? Windows 10 has accessibility features that make it easier for you to get information from the computer (output features), and other features that make it easier for you to provide information to the computer (input features).

Windows 10 includes a group of tools (collectively known as *Ease Of Access features*) that are specifically designed to help people interact with the computer by making content easier to access or providing alternative input and output methods. The tools include the following:

- **Closed captions** Text narrations of audio content that display as videos play.

- **High Contrast** Color schemes that make individual user interface elements stand out on the screen.

- **Magnifier** A panel that magnifies the screen under the mouse pointer up to nine times. You can move and resize the magnification panel.

- **Narrator** A text-to-speech tool that reads menu commands, dialog box options, and other screen features out loud, telling you what options are available and how to use them. It also reads your keystrokes to you as you type them, and tells you the pointer location on the screen as you move the mouse.

> **SEE ALSO** For information about high-contrast themes, see "Apply and manage themes" in Chapter 2, "Personalize your working environment."

When you turn on an accessibility feature, it remains on until you turn it off.

If you sign in to multiple computers by using your Microsoft account credentials, you can configure the accessibility settings on one computer, and then have Windows 10 synchronize the settings across all computers.

> **SEE ALSO** For information about synchronizing Ease Of Access settings across devices, see "Customize your sign-in options" in Chapter 11, "Manage user accounts and settings."

You can turn on the High Contrast, Magnifier, Narrator, On-Screen Keyboard, Sticky Keys, or Filter Keys features from the Welcome screen, before you sign in to Windows. When you're signed in to Windows 10, you can manage most of the accessibility features from the Ease Of Access settings page.

Accessibility features are also still available from the Ease Of Access Center in Control Panel. If you're unsure which features would be helpful to you, you can answer a series of questions, and Windows will recommend accessibility settings based on your answers.

13

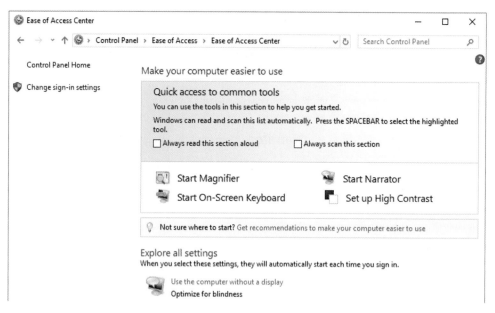

Many of the accessibility features have keyboard shortcuts, but those aren't of much use when you're working on a device that doesn't have an external keyboard. To simplify the process for users of tablets and other handheld Windows 10 devices, you can configure Windows 10 to launch Magnifier, Narrator, or the On-Screen Keyboard when you press the external Windows button and Volume Up button on those devices.

To display Ease of Access settings

- To display the Ease Of Access settings page, do either of the following:

  - Open the **Settings** window, and then select **Ease of Access**.

  - Press Win+U.

- To display the Ease Of Access Center

  - Display Control Panel in category view, select **Ease of Access**, and then select **Ease of Access Center**.

To get accessibility setting recommendations from Windows

1. Display the **Ease of Access Center**.

2. Select the **Get recommendations to make your computer easier to use** link.

3. On the **Eyesight**, **Dexterity**, **Hearing**, **Speech**, and **Reasoning** pages, select the check box for each statement that applies to you, and then select **Next**.

4. On the **Recommended settings** page, review the accessibility options that Windows recommended in response to your selections. Select or clear any additional check boxes that you want to, and then select **Apply** or **OK**.

To configure a device hardware shortcut for an accessibility tool

1. Display the **Ease of Access Center**.

2. In the **Explore All Settings** section, select **Make touch and tablets easier to use**.

3. In the **Launching common tools** section, expand the list, and then select the accessibility tool that you want to start when you press the Windows button and Volume Up button on your device.

4. In the **Make touch and tablets easier to use** window, select **Apply** or **OK** to implement the change.

High-contrast settings

A high-contrast theme displays text and background colors that might be easier to see and cause less eyestrain. When you apply a high-contrast theme, it affects all the content that you display on your screen. Some content, such as a busy webpage image, is not visible when a high-contrast theme is applied. Windows comes with four high-contrast themes. You can preview and modify the color palettes of each of the high contrast themes in the Settings window.

13

It takes Windows a bit longer (about 10 seconds) to apply a high-contrast theme than it does to make other changes. Windows displays a *Please wait* screen while it applies the theme.

To preview and apply a high-contrast theme

1. Open the **Settings** window, select **Ease of Access**, and then select **High contrast**.

2. In the **High contrast** settings pane, expand the list, and then select one of the four high-contrast themes to preview the theme colors that are assigned to the background, text, hyperlinks, disabled text, selected text, and button text.

3. Select the theme you want, and then select **Apply**.

To apply the most recent or default high-contrast theme

- To reapply the most recent high-contrast theme (or to apply High Contrast #1 if you haven't yet applied a high-contrast theme), press left Alt+left Shift+Print Screen, and then select **Yes** in the message box that appears.

To modify the High Contrast settings

1. Do one of the following to display Ease Of Access Center:

   - In the taskbar search box, enter **ease**, and then select **Ease of Access Center**.

   - In Category view of Control Panel, select **Ease of Access**, and then **Ease of Access Center**.

   - In Large Icons or Small Icons view, select **Ease of Access Center**.

2. In the **Quick access to common tools** section, select **Set up High Contrast** to open the Make The Computer Easier To See window.

3. In the **High Contrast** section, select or clear the check boxes for the keyboard shortcut, warning message, and sound alert.

Make the computer easier to see
When you select these tools, they will automatically start each time you sign in.

High Contrast
   Choose a High Contrast theme
   ☑ Turn on or off High Contrast when left ALT + left SHIFT + PRINT SCREEN is pressed
      When using keyboard shortcuts to turn Ease of Access settings on:
      ☑ Display a warning message when turning a setting on
      ☑ Make a sound when turning a setting on or off

To revert to a regular contrast theme

- Press left Alt+left Shift+Print Screen.

- In the **High Contrast** settings pane, select **None** in the **Choose a theme** list, and then select **Apply**.

- Open the **Personalization** window of Control Panel, and select the theme you want to apply.

   Windows displays a *Please wait* screen while it applies the theme.

13

Magnifier settings

You can use the Magnifier tool to magnify all or part of the screen up to 1600 percent of its usual size. For digital artists, in addition to people with vision problems, this can be very useful. Magnifier has three magnification modes:

- **Full Screen** Magnifies the entire screen. This is the default mode until you change it.

- **Lens** Magnifies a rectangular portion of the screen behind the pointer. By default, the lens is 30 percent of the width and height of the screen. You can set each dimension to from 10 percent to 100 percent of the screen size.

- **Docked** Splits the screen vertically into two panes, one with the standard view and one with magnification. The magnification pane displays the content at the pointer location. You can change the height of the magnification pane.

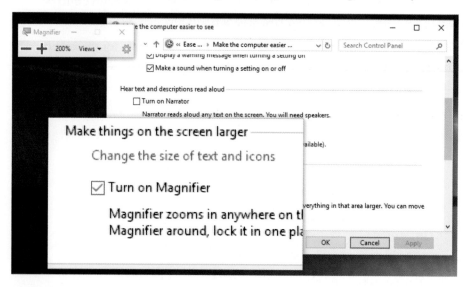

Magnifier has many configurable options, including:

- The zoom level, from 125 to 1600 percent.

- The zoom level increments, from 25 percent to 400 percent.

- The tracking options, which by default follow the pointer, keyboard focus, text insertion point, or Narrator cursor.

- Automatic start options.

- Optional color inversion and bitmap smoothing.

- The appearance of the on-screen Magnifier menu.

When Magnifier is running, you control its settings from the Magnifier menu window. When the window is not in use, it can collapse to a magnifying glass (if you select this option). You redisplay the menu by selecting the magnifying glass.

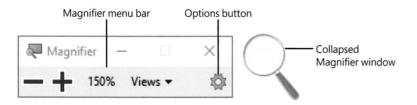

To turn on Magnifier

- Press Win+Plus sign (on the numeric keypad) or Win+Equal sign (on the numeric key row above the letters).

- On the **Ease of Access** settings page, select **Magnifier**. Then in the **Magnifier** settings pane, turn on **Magnifier**.

- In the **Ease of Access Center**, in the **Quick access to common tools** section, select **Start Magnifier**.

To turn off Magnifier

- On the **Magnifier** menu bar, select the **Close** button (the **X**).

- In the **Magnifier** settings pane, turn off **Magnifier**.

- Press Win+Esc.

To change the Magnifier mode

- On the **Magnifier** menu bar, select **Views**, and then select **Docked**, **Full screen**, or **Lens**.

- In the **Magnifier** settings pane, in the **Magnifier mode** section, expand the list, and then select **Docked**, **Full screen**, or **Lens.**

- Press any of the following keyboard shortcuts:

  - To display the Docked view of Magnifier, press Ctrl+Alt+D.

  - To display the Full Screen view of Magnifier, press Ctrl+Alt+F.

  - To display the Lens view of Magnifier, press Ctrl+Alt+L.

13

To change the Magnifier Lens size

1. With Magnifier turned on or off, use any of the above methods to set the Magnifier mode to Lens.

2. Display the **Magnifier** settings pane. In the **Magnifier mode** section, drag the scroll boxes below and to the right of the **Change lens size** preview.

To change the Magnifier level of magnification

- On the **Magnifier** menu bar, select the **Plus sign (+)** or **Minus sign (-)**.

- In the **Magnifier** settings pane, select the plus sign or minus sign adjacent to the current magnification zoom level.

- Press Win+Plus sign or Win+Minus sign.

  The magnification changes in the increments that are set in the Magnifier Options dialog box. The default increment is 100%.

To change the Magnifier magnification increment

1. Display the **Magnifier** settings pane.

2. In the **Magnifier options** section, expand the **Zoom level increments** list, and then select **25%, 50%, 100%, 150%, 200%, or 400%**.

To change the appearance of the inactive Magnifier menu bar window

- In the **Magnifier** settings pane, in the **Magnifier options** section, select or clear the **Collapse to magnifying glass icon** check box.

To automatically start Magnifier

- In the **Magnifier** settings pane, in the **Magnifier options** section, do either of the following:

  - To automatically start Magnifier when you sign in to Windows, select the **Start Magnifier after sign in** check box.

  - To automatically start Magnifier after Windows starts, from the Lock screen, select the **Start Magnifier automatically before login for all users** check box.

> ⊘ **TIP** You can start Magnifier manually from the Lock screen by selecting the Ease Of Access icon and then Magnifier.

To invert the colors of the magnified area to their color spectrum opposites

- In the **Magnifier options** section of the **Magnifier** settings pane, select the **Invert colors** check box.

Narrator and Audio Description settings

Windows 10 includes two tools that can provide descriptions of visual content: Narrator and Audio Descriptions.

Narrator reads out loud the labels, descriptions, and instructions for on-screen elements. For example, when you select a category in the Settings window, Narrator might tell you the name of the category, how many category options there are, and that you can

13

double-click to open the category pane. You can select from multiple Narrator voices and adjust the speed of the voice to match your listening speed. You can also specify the interface items that you want Narrator to identify for you.

For those people who sign in to multiple computers with Microsoft accounts, and synchronize settings across those computers, here's a warning: turning on Narrator on one computer turns on Narrator on all the computers, and you'll have to turn it off individually on each computer. This might be exactly what you want, but be prepared, if you're signed in to four separate computers around the house, that things can get a bit noisy. If you want to turn on Narrator (or any of the Ease Of Access tools) on only one computer, turn off the synchronization of Ease Of Access settings on that computer first.

> **SEE ALSO** For more information about synchronizing settings among computers, see "Customize your sign-in options" in Chapter 11, "Manage user accounts and settings."

Audio Descriptions are spoken descriptions of video content that are provided with the video. In the television and movie industries, these supplemental audio tracks (also referred to as *video descriptions*) are often provided with special versions of films that are called Descriptive Video Service (DVS) versions. Sometimes the audio is provided by professional voiceover performers reading scripted descriptions of the film activity, and other times it's simply a recording of the actors and director watching the film and talking about it.

In Windows 10, you can turn on the Audio Description feature, and if a video has an audio description, it will play with the video. No additional configuration is possible.

To turn on Narrator

- On the **Ease of Access** settings page, select **Narrator**. Then in the **Narrator** settings pane, turn on **Narrator**.

- In the **Ease of Access Center**, in the **Quick access to common tools** section, select **Start Narrator**.

To select a Narrator voice

1. Display the **Narrator** settings pane.

2. In the **Voice** section, expand the list, and then select the voice you want.

3. Drag the **Speed** and **Pitch** sliders to adjust the Narrator voice until you can understand it best.

> ✅ **TIP** If you've installed additional languages, the Voice list includes voices for those languages with language and region designations. For more information about installing languages, see "Manage regional and language settings" in Chapter 12, "Manage computer settings."
>
> You configure the Narrator voice separately from the text-to-speech voice, so changing one doesn't change the other. For information about configuring text-to-speech settings, see "Manage speech settings," also in Chapter 12.

To configure audio narration options

1. Display the **Narrator** settings pane, and scroll to the **Sounds you hear** section.

   Sounds you hear

   Read hints for controls and buttons

   ⬤○ On

   Amount of contextual reading for controls and buttons

2 - Read only immediate context ⌄

   Order of contextual reading for controls and buttons

Before ⌄

   Characters you type

   ⬤○ On

   Words you type

   ⬤○ On

   Lower the volume of other apps when Narrator is speaking

   ⬤○ On

   Play audio cues

   ⬤○ On

2. Turn on the features you want Narrator to read aloud.

13

To configure visual narration options

1. Display the **Narrator** settings pane, and scroll to the **Cursor and keys** section.

> ### Cursor and keys
>
> Highlight the cursor
>
> ⬤◯ On
>
> Have insertion point follow Narrator
>
> ⬤◯ On
>
> Activate keys on touch keyboard when I lift my finger off the keyboard
>
> ◯⬤ Off

2. Turn on the features you want Narrator to display.

To turn on Audio Description for videos

1. In the **Ease of Access Center**, select **Make the computer easier to see**.

2. In the **Hear text and descriptions read aloud** section, select the **Turn on Audio Description** check box. Then select **Apply** or **OK** to apply the change.

Keyboard and mouse settings

The traditional method of entering text into an app or other computer interface is by typing it on an external keyboard. However, mobility problems can make typing difficult. Windows 10 includes a variety of tools to help with entering text, including the following:

- **Filter Keys** Causes Windows to ignore brief or repeated keystrokes, or slows the repeat rate.

- **Mouse Keys** Enables you to move the cursor around the screen by pressing the arrow keys on the numeric keypad.

- **On-Screen Keyboard** Displays a visual representation of a keyboard on which you can tap individual keys by using your finger, tablet pen, or other pointing device.

- **Speech Recognition** Allows you to control Windows, control running apps, and dictate text by speaking into a microphone.

> **SEE ALSO** For information about speech recognition, see "Manage speech settings" in Chapter 12, "Manage computer settings."

- **Sticky Keys** Makes it easier to use the keyboard with one hand by making the Ctrl, Shift, and Alt keys "stick down" until you press the next key.

- **Toggle Keys** Sounds an audio signal when you press the Caps Lock, Num Lock, or Scroll Lock key. A high-pitched sound plays when the keys are activated, and a low-pitched sound plays when the keys are deactivated.

The mouse is an integral part of most desktop computer experiences. By default, the mouse pointer is represented by a small arrow that moves around the screen as quickly as you move the mouse, and sometimes fades out of sight when the mouse is still. It can be difficult not only to find the pointer, but also to track its progress across the screen. If you're working in a screen-presenting situation—for example, sharing your screen in an online meeting, or presenting content on a large screen in a conference room, it is even more difficult for your audience members to follow the mouse movements because they aren't controlling the mouse.

You can simplify things for yourself and for other people by enlarging the pointer and changing its color. If you have difficulty moving the mouse, you can opt to control it by using the numeric keypad.

In addition to these Ease Of Access features, you can configure other useful mouse features such as "mouse trails" that can be very helpful. For information about keyboard and mouse configuration options that aren't related to the Ease Of Access features, see Chapter 7, "Manage peripheral devices."

To turn on keyboard accessibility features

1. In the **Settings** window, select **Ease of Access**, and then select **Keyboard**.

2. In the **Keyboard** settings pane, turn on any of the following options:

   - On-Screen Keyboard

   - Sticky Keys

   - Toggle Keys

   - Filter Keys

> ✓ **TIP** You can also display a taskbar icon for the On-Screen Keyboard by right-clicking an empty area in the taskbar and selecting Show Touch Keyboard Button. You can then select that icon to display the keyboard when you need it.

13

3. In the **Other Settings** section of the **Keyboard** pane, turn on the accessibility options you want for keyboard shortcuts.

Other Settings

Enable shortcut underlines

⬤◯ Off

Display a warning message when turning a setting on with a shortcut

◯⬤ On

Make a sound when turning a setting on or off with a shortcut

◯⬤ On

To configure mouse accessibility features

1. In the **Settings** window, select **Ease of Access**, and then select **Mouse**.

2. In the **Mouse** settings pane, select the pointer size and color you want.

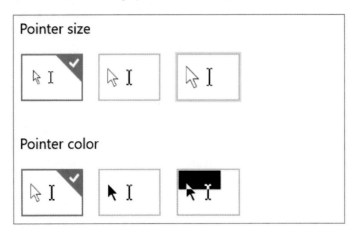

3. To start Mouse Keys, turn on **Use numeric keypad to move mouse around the screen**.

4. When Mouse Keys is turned on, turn on or off **Hold down Ctrl to speed up and Shift to slow down** and **Use mouse keys when Num Lock is on**.

Mouse keys

Use numeric keypad to move mouse around the screen

On

Hold down Ctrl to speed up and Shift to slow down

Off

Use mouse keys when Num Lock is on

Off

Key points

- You can control the brightness of your screen manually or automatically. A dimmer screen saves power and causes less eyestrain.

- The Night Light feature changes the screen light to warmer tones to lessen eye-strain and the increase in brain activity caused by blue light–emitting devices.

- Turning off the screen and putting your computer to sleep are two ways to conserve power when you're not actively using the computer. You can specify the length of inactivity after which Windows should automatically take these actions. On a battery-powered device, you can configure separate settings for when the computer is plugged in and when it's running on battery.

- Windows 10 has many accessibility features that help users to interact with the computer.

13

Practice tasks

No practice files are necessary to complete the practice tasks in this chapter.

Change the screen brightness

Perform the following tasks:

1. Display the Action Center, and then cycle through your brightness changes.

2. Adjust the screen brightness to suit your current working environment.

3. Turn on Night Light.

4. Experiment with the Night Light color temperature setting to understand the difference between colors on the warm and cool ends of the spectrum.

5. Turn off Night Light.

6. If you want to, configure Night Light to turn on automatically from sunset to sunrise. If necessary, turn on **Location Settings** to support this.

Configure power options

Perform the following tasks:

1. Display the **Power & sleep** settings pane, and configure the screen and sleep times as you want them. If your computer is running on battery power, configure the settings for when the computer is plugged in and when it is running on battery power.

2. Open the **Power Options** window of Control Panel. If **Show additional plans** appears near the bottom of the window, select it to display any hidden power-management plans.

3. Display the settings for each plan on your computer, and consider which is best for you.

4. Modify a built-in power plan. Then reset the plan to its defaults.

5. If none of the power-management plans fits your needs, create a custom plan. Otherwise, apply a standard plan.

Configure Windows accessibility features

Display the Ease Of Access Center, and then perform the following tasks:

1. Complete the **Get recommendations to make your computer easier to use** wizard to familiarize yourself with the situations in which you might benefit from using the various accessibility tools.

2. Locate a webpage that contains text and graphic elements, and display it in your default internet browser.

3. Apply a high contrast theme. Look for differences in the user interface elements and in the webpage content.

4. Start Narrator, and then configure Narrator to use the voice and speech cadence that you prefer.

5. Display a webpage, the **Start** screen, the **Settings** window, any category page, and then any apps or files you want, to gain experience with the information Narrator provides. (Wait each time as Narrator provides you with information.)

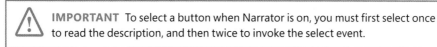 **IMPORTANT** To select a button when Narrator is on, you must first select once to read the description, and then twice to invoke the select event.

6. Exit Narrator, and display the **Ease of Access** settings page.

7. Start Magnifier, and experiment with using it to view different screens and documents. Then exit Magnifier.

8. Display the touch keyboard, and experiment with navigating around Windows and entering text without using an external keyboard. Then close the touch keyboard.

9. Display the Ease Of Access Center, and explore other settings that interest you. Select the links, and try out these features:

   • Turn on **Sticky Keys**, and experiment with using it to enter text that contains capital letters.

   • Turn on **Mouse Keys**, and practice using it to move the cursor around on the screen.

   • Turn on **Filter Keys**, and try using it with an app of your choice.

10. Exit any running accessibility tools.

Work more efficiently

Many features of Windows 10 are designed to help you do things faster and more efficiently—or in some cases to do them for you.

The Action Center is a central location for reviewing notifications from many sources, including Windows, Cortana, email, and even text messages sent to your mobile phone. It also contains action buttons that provide shortcuts to settings that you access often.

Another interesting development is virtual desktops, which provide a way for multitaskers to organize apps in separate views of the desktop. This isn't a feature that all Windows 10 users will use, but it's certainly handy for people who want to compartmentalize tasks.

Two other topics discussed in this chapter are configuring your settings so that files always open in the app you want them to, and finding helpful information in Task Manager.

This chapter guides you through procedures related to configuring Quick Action buttons, searching your computer and the web, specifying default apps, organizing apps on multiple desktops, monitoring apps and system tasks, and managing app startup.

In this chapter

- Configure Quick Action buttons
- Search your computer and the web
- Specify default apps
- Organize apps on multiple desktops
- Monitor apps and system tasks
- Manage app startup

Configure Quick Action buttons

The Windows 10 Action Center is a full-height pane that slides out from the right side of your screen when you select its taskbar icon. After Windows displays notifications about recent events on your computer, such as incoming email messages, security and maintenance alerts, and updates, those notifications are available from the Action Center for your review. The Action Center icon displays a count of your unread messages.

Collapsed Quick Action area Action Center pane

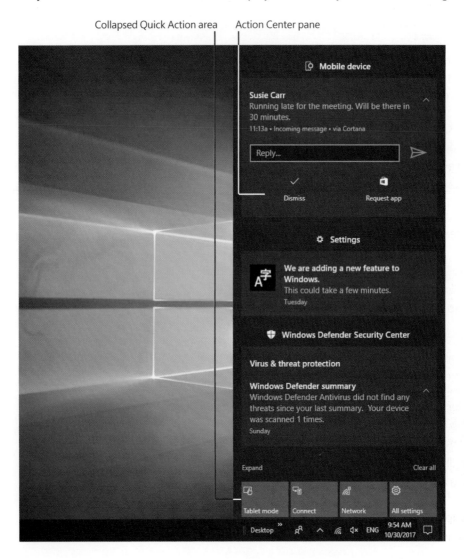

In addition to notifications, the Action Center displays several rows of Quick Action command tiles at the bottom of the pane. The top row is always visible when the pane is open; you can expand or collapse the remaining rows.

Chapter 1, "Get started using Windows 10," includes procedures for previewing, opening, and removing messages in the Action Center. Chapter 2, "Personalize your working environment," provides procedures for managing the color and transparency of the Action Center pane. Chapter 4, "Work with apps and notifications," covers procedures for configuring app notifications that appear in the Action Center, and for temporarily turning off notifications by turning on Quiet Hours.

This topic covers the action buttons available at the bottom of the Action Center pane. By default, this section is collapsed to display only the top row of buttons.

The top row is always available

You can choose which of the action buttons appear in this row (and are available when the other action buttons are hidden).

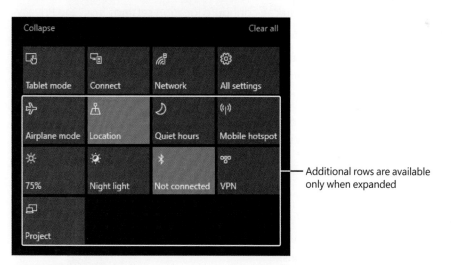

Additional rows are available only when expanded

14

When expanded, the section contains about a dozen action buttons, depending on the functions that are available on your computer or device.

The action buttons provide quick access to the following Windows 10 tools and settings:

- **Airplane mode** Available only on portable computers and tablets, airplane mode turns off all wireless connections from your device, including Wi-Fi, Bluetooth, and cellular data if you have that service. The action button turns this feature on or off.

- **All settings** Opens the Settings window.

- **Battery Saver** Available only on battery-powered devices, Battery Saver is a feature introduced in Windows 10 that reduces background activity to extend the time the device can run on the battery charge. You can turn on Battery Saver at any time; Windows turns it on automatically when the battery charge drops below 20% or the setting you specify. The action button turns this feature on or off.

- **Bluetooth** Turns the Bluetooth connection on or off.

- **Brightness** Cycles through 25%, 50%, 75%, and 100% screen brightness settings.

- **Connect** Searches for wireless display and audio devices (including those that support Miracast connections).

- **Location** Available only on devices with built-in GPS, this action button turns location services on or off. You can configure location settings from the Privacy page of the Settings window.

- **Mobile Hotspot** Makes an internet connection through your device available over Wi-Fi or Bluetooth to other devices.

- **Network** Displays the list of available networks with a link to the Network & Internet Settings window and the Wi-Fi, Airplane Mode, and Mobile Hotspot action buttons (if applicable to your device).

- **Night Light** Changes the screen light to a warmer color temperature.

- **Project** Controls the display of desktop content on multiple screens. You can choose from PC Screen Only, Duplicate, Extend, and Second Screen Only.

- **Quiet hours** Turns on or off the Quiet Hours feature, which temporarily disables sound and banner notifications.

- **Tablet mode** Available only on touchscreen devices, Tablet mode makes the device interface more touch-friendly by enlarging user interface elements and hiding taskbar buttons. You can configure Tablet mode settings from the System page of the Settings window.

- **VPN** Starts a virtual private network (VPN) connection or walks you through the configuration of a connection if one doesn't already exist.

- **Wi-Fi** Available only on mobile devices. Turns the wireless network connection on and off.

Buttons that represent features that are simply on or off are a different color (when the feature is turned on) from those that open apps or configure settings. You can add and remove action buttons in the Quick Action area so that the actions you need are easily available.

> **SEE ALSO** For more information about the Settings window, see "Explore Windows settings" in Chapter 1, "Get started using Windows 10." For more information about the Quiet Hours feature, see "Manage app notifications" in Chapter 4, "Work with apps and notifications." For more information about the screen brightness, see "Change the screen brightness" and "Configure power options" in Chapter 13, "Manage power and access options." For more information about Battery Saver, see the sidebar "Make your battery last longer," also in Chapter 13.

A final thing to note about the Action Center is that you can hide its taskbar icon if you want to free up space on your taskbar (or always use the keyboard shortcut). The Action Center is always available regardless of whether the taskbar icon is visible.

To display the Action Center pane

- At the right end of the taskbar, select the **Action Center** icon, which is empty or filled, depending on whether you have unread messages.

- Press Win+A.

- On a touchscreen device, swipe in from the right edge of the screen.

14

To display all current action buttons

1. Display the **Action Center** pane.

2. At the bottom of the pane, select **Expand**.

To add and remove action buttons in the Quick Action area

1. Open the **Settings** window. Select **System**, and then select **Notifications & actions**.

2. In the **Quick actions** section of the **Notifications & actions** settings pane, select **Add or remove quick actions** to display a list of the action buttons available on your computer.

3. In the **Add or remove quick actions** list, turn on the buttons that you want to display in the Quick Action area, and turn off the buttons that you want to hide.

4. Select the **Back** button to return to the Quick Actions preview pane. In the pane, drag the buttons to rearrange them. Position the four buttons that you will use most often in the top row.

To display or hide the Action Center taskbar icon

1. In the **Settings** window, select **Personalization**, and then select **Taskbar**.

2. In the **Notification area** section of the **Taskbar** pane, select **Turn system icons on or off**.

3. Turn on Action Center to display the taskbar icon, or turn it off to hide it.

Search your computer and the web

The technology that supports rapid searching through massive amounts of information has improved tremendously over the past few years. We can probably thank cloud computing and the proliferation of massive data centers for this technology, which has worked its way down to the personal computer level.

Chapter 1, "Get started using Windows 10," included procedures for searching for settings from the Settings window search box. Chapter 5, "Explore files and folders," included procedures for searching for files from the File Explorer search box. Both of these processes search the content on your computer (or the storage location you're displaying in File Explorer). To speed up these search processes, Windows indexes information on your computer hard drive, and complex processes in the Microsoft cloud index information in your OneDrive storage folders. You can refine the indexing parameters to include or exclude specific storage locations; for example, if you have folders in which you store duplicate backups or older versions of files, you can remove those from the indexing process so that search results reflect only the current files.

Search storage locations and the web

When you're searching for a broader range of information, you can do so from the taskbar search box. Windows 10 search can quickly locate items on your computer, in connected storage locations, and across the web. You can filter the search results by category. When your search locates the item, app, or information you want, select the search result to open, start, or display it.

14

If you're looking for online search results, such as you'd get from searching directly in a web browser, select See Web Results to display Bing web search results in your default browser.

To search for anything

- Activate the taskbar search box, and then enter the search term.

- If Cortana is enabled, select the microphone icon in the search box, and then speak the search term.

- If Cortana is configured for voice cuing, say **Hey, Cortana** followed by your search request.

> **TIP** When speaking a search term, you can quickly filter contents by specifying parameters such as file type and contents. For example, if you search for *Find PowerPoint presentations on my computer that contain Contoso and Sales*, the search results include a snapshot of the content that includes your specified search terms.

To specify the file type you want to search for

- Activate the taskbar search box, select **Apps**, **Documents**, or **Web**, and then enter your search term.

To filter search results in the search results pane

- At the top of the search results pane, select the **Apps**, **Documents**, or **Web** icon to filter by that category.

- At the top of the search results pane, select **Filters**, and then select **All**, **Apps**, **Documents**, **Folders**, **Music**, **Photos**, **Settings**, **Videos**, or **Web** to filter on the type and locations shown.

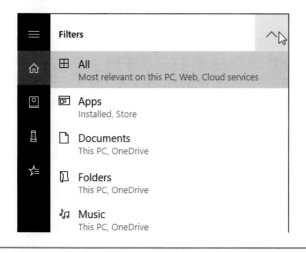

> **TIP** If you're getting search results that you find offensive, you can configure the SafeSearch settings to control the level of adult content that is filtered from or allowed through in search results. For more information, see "Manage Cortana information and notifications" in Chapter 9, "Get assistance from Cortana."

14

Manage File Explorer search processes

Chapter 5, "Explore files and folders," provided an introduction to File Explorer and to searching for files by using Windows Search and File Explorer Search.

Searching is often the fastest way to locate a file or settings pane on your computer. This is primarily because you're searching the index rather than all the available content and metadata.

The search engine is fast, but you can improve the efficiency of your search by applying a bit of logic and forethought. Here are some hints to help you rapidly locate the files you need:

- The search index includes all the common locations in which users store files. If you want to improve the search time in other locations, either add them to the indexed locations, or add them to Libraries, which is automatically included in the index.

- When searching in File Explorer, select a specific folder in which to start your search, or restrict the search to likely locations, such as Libraries.

- If a simple search from the File Explorer window doesn't locate the item you are looking for, you can perform more advanced searches in the Search Results folder. Your search criteria can include the date a file was created, its size, part of its name or title, its author, and any tags you might have listed as properties of the file.

> **SEE ALSO** For information about file properties, see "Work with folder and file properties" in Chapter 6, "Manage folders and files."

If search processes don't return all the pertinent results, or return old results that no longer lead to the correct location, you might need to do a bit of maintenance work. You can change some basic search parameters, and adjust the indexing options and the locations that are being indexed to increase the efficiency of your searches. Ensure that the index includes the locations where you frequently store files.

From the Advanced Options dialog box, you can also do the following things, which require administrator permission:

- Include encrypted files in the index.

- Add a type of file to the index.

- Change the indexing level for a type of file.

- Change the location of the index file.

- Restore the default settings.

- Rebuild the index file from scratch.

If you continue to have trouble, you can run the indexing troubleshooter to look for problems and recommend solutions.

14

To filter File Explorer search results

1. Perform a search.

2. On the **Search** tool tab, select one of the following:

   - **Kind** In the list that appears, select the appropriate kind if it is listed.

   - **Other Properties** Select one of the options: *Name* is a good choice if you know part of the name. If you are sure about the start of the name, enter that. If you are sure only that some characters are somewhere in the name, enter ~= and the characters. For example, if the search term is *name:~=dog*, the search will return all files with the letters "dog" anywhere in the name.

   - **Date Modified and Size** You can specify parameters for either of these options, if you know that information.

3. If you want to further refine the search, you can enter criteria directly into the search box; for example, *kind:=music*, *datemodified:last week*, or *authors:joan*. You can also use Boolean operators such as AND and OR, for example, *authors:joan AND authors:steve*.

To set File Explorer search options

1. In File Explorer, display the **View** tab and then at its right end, select **Options**.

2. In the **Folder Options** dialog box, select the **Search** tab. Only a few options are available, but their settings can impact the time required to perform a search in File Explorer.

3. Make any changes you want, and then select **OK**.

To change the locations that are being indexed

1. Perform a search.

2. On the **Search** tool tab, in the **Options** group, select **Advanced options**, and then select **Change indexed locations**.

3. In the **Indexing Options** dialog box, add or exclude specific locations (folders). Then select **Close**.

To change advanced indexing options

1. Perform a search.

2. On the **Search** tool tab, in the **Options** group, select **Advanced options**, and then select **Change indexed locations**.

3. In the **Indexing Options** dialog box, select **Advanced**.

4. In the **Advanced Options** dialog box, configure the options on the **Index Settings** and **File Types** tabs.

14

5. Select **OK** and then select **Close** to return to File Explorer.

To rebuild the index

1. Perform a search.

2. On the **Search** tool tab, in the **Options** group, select **Advanced options**, and then select **Change indexed locations**.

3. In the **Indexing Options** dialog box, select **Advanced**.

4. In the **Advanced Options** dialog box, select **Rebuild**. Then in the **Rebuild Index** message box, select **OK**.

> ⚠ **IMPORTANT** Rebuilding the index can take quite a while. You might want to put it off until a time when you don't need the full attention of your computer for a few hours.

Specify default apps

When you open a file by using any of the standard methods, Windows opens it in the default app for that type of file (as specified by the file name extension). The default app might be set when you install an app, or you can set it in Windows independently of the app. In File Explorer, the default app is often apparent from the icon that is associated with the file.

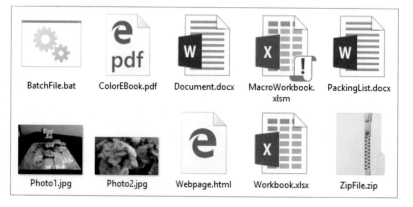

If you uninstall the app that is set as the default for a file type, or don't have an app that associates itself with that file type, Windows will prompt you to choose the app you want to use to open the file. You can select an installed app, or install an app from the Store.

> ✓ **TIP** In some cases, you have the option of browsing to an app executable file. This option is necessary only if the app hasn't provided a list of file extensions it can associate, or a problem prevents Windows from detecting the app/file type association.

A clean installation of Windows 10 automatically sets a lot of defaults for you. When it comes to setting default apps, if Microsoft has an app that will open a type or class of file, it generally assigns that as the default app.

During an upgrade from an earlier version of Windows, Windows 10 might leave the defaults as you previously set them or, if there is a change in the apps (for example, the change from Internet Explorer to Microsoft Edge as the default browser) it might change them.

Windows 10 provides several ways for you to change these default settings. You can match category to apps, apps to file types, or file types to apps. As with many Windows configuration processes, there are simple and complicated ways of going about this that provide varying levels of control.

The simplest method for assigning default apps is by category. In the Default Apps pane, you can choose a default email app, map app, music player, photo viewer, video player, and web browser. You can choose from the apps that are already installed on your computer, or display a list of Store apps that you can install.

Each of the categories is associated with a specific set of file types, but you don't interact with those directly.

14

Another way you can assign default apps is by file type. The Choose Default Apps By File Type pane displays a long list of file extensions, and you can set the default app for each. It isn't necessary to assign a default app to every type of file. The list is not based on the files that are installed on your computer—you might never encounter some of these file types. This method is useful if you set the default app for a category—for example, a photo viewer—and then want to specify a different default app for only one type of photo file.

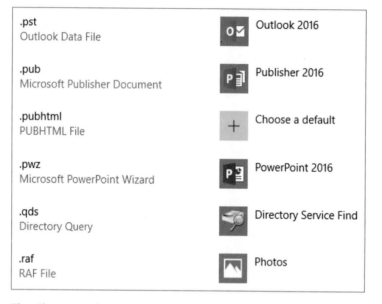

The Choose Default Apps By File Type list is sorted alphabetically by file extension. You can't sort it by default app (which might be somewhat useful).

Another way to assign default apps is by protocol. Protocols aren't something that most of us think about frequently (if at all), but the word might be familiar to you from *Hypertext Transfer Protocol*, the full name of the HTTP protocol that is used to connect to most websites. The Choose Default Apps By Protocol pane displays a long list of protocols. Unlike the file extension list, each protocol is assigned to a default app.

From the protocol list, you can assign default apps to different protocols that are associated with the same general kind of file. This creates a relationship between the protocol and the app in the Windows Registry. A file type is also associated with a protocol. So when you double-click a file, Windows can get the file protocol and then locate the default app in the registry.

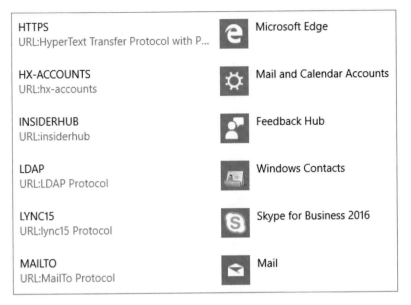

Another way to assign a default app is when you're opening a file. You can specify a non-default app to open the file with, and at that time, you can also specify whether to set the non-default app as the default for that type of file. Using this method, you're setting default apps for files that you definitely work with.

Another way to assign default apps is by assigning file types and protocols for each app.

To open a file in the default app from File Explorer

- Double-click the file.

- Right-click the file, and then select **Open**.

- Select the file. Then on the **Home** tab, in the **Open** group, select the **Open** button.

To open a file in a non-default app

- In File Explorer, do either of the following:

  - Right-click the file, select **Open with...**, select **More apps** if the app you want to use isn't shown, and then select the app you want.

  - Select the file. On the **Home** tab, in the **Open** group, select the **Open** arrow, and then in the list, select the app you want.

- Start the app. Then from within the app, browse to and open the file.

To specify the default app for a type of file

1. In File Explorer, right-click the file, and then select **Open with...** to display a list of apps that can open the file.

> ✓ **TIP** The available file types depend on the apps installed on your computer.

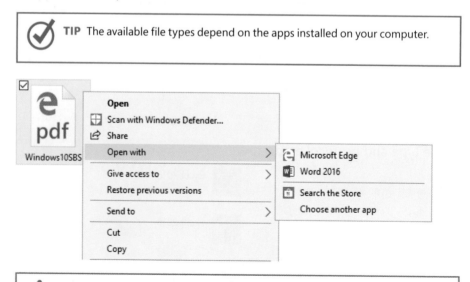

> ⚠ **IMPORTANT** Some file types display the shortcut menu in the blue and white format shown after the next step. We show you both formats in this procedure so you're not surprised to see one or the other.

2. Select **Choose another app** to display additional options. If the app you want to use isn't in the list, select **More apps** to expand the list.

How do you want to open this file?

Keep using this app

e Microsoft Edge
Open PDFs right in your web browser.

Other options

w Word 2016

Look for an app in the Store

More apps ↓

☐ Always use this app to open .pdf files

OK

How do you want to open this file?

Notepad

Office XML Handler

Paint

Snagit Editor

Windows Media Player

WordPad

Look for another app on this PC

☐ Always use this app to open .pdf files

OK

3. Select the app you want to use to open the selected type of file.

4. Select the **Always use this app to open ... files** check box (the label includes the file extension of the file you're opening), and then select **OK** to open the file and set the default app for the file type.

Or

1. Open the **Settings** window, select **Apps**, and then select **Default apps**.

2. At the bottom of the **Choose default apps** section, select **Choose default apps by file type** to display a long list of file type extensions.

3. Locate the extension for the type of file that you want to change the default app for.

> **TIP** Multiple file extensions are associated with each category of file. For example, if you want to set a default app for *all* types of images you must set the default for .bmp, .gif, .jpeg, .jpg, .png, .tif, and all other image file types. You can assign a different default app to each file type, if you have apps that can handle them differently.

14

4. Select the icon to the right of the extension, and then do either of the following:

- Select the installed app that you want to use.

- Select **Look for an app in the Store** to open the Store and display a list of apps that can open a file of that type. Install an app from the Store, and then return to the **Choose default apps by file type** pane and select that app as the default for the file type.

To specify the default app for a category

1. Display the **Default apps** pane.

2. In the **Choose default apps** section, select each task, and then do either of the following:

- Select the installed app that you want to use.

- Select **Look for an app in the Store** to open the Store and display a list of apps that can open a typical file of that type. Install an app from the Store, and then return to the **Default apps** pane and select that app as the default for the category.

To choose default apps by protocol

1. Display the **Default apps** pane. At the bottom of the **Choose default apps** section, select **Choose default apps by protocol** to display the protocol list.

2. Locate the protocol that you want to change the default app for.

3. Select the current default app, and then do either of the following:

- Select the installed app that you want to use.

- Select **Look for an app in the Store** to open the Store and display a list of apps that can handle that protocol. Install an app from the Store, and then return to the **Choose default apps by protocol** pane and select that app as the default for the protocol.

To set the file types and protocols for a specific app

1. Display the **Default apps** pane. At the bottom of the **Choose default apps** section, select **Set defaults by app** to display the Set Defaults By App pane.

2. In the **Set your default programs** list, select the app for which you want to specify file types and protocols, and then select the **Manage** button that appears.

3. In the app-specific pane, locate the file extension for which you want to change the app. To the right of the file extension, select the currently specified app or if no app has been specified, select **Choose a default**, and then in the **Choose an app** pane that opens, do either of the following:

   - Select the installed app that you want to use.

   - Select **Look for an app in the Store** to open the Store and display a list of apps that can handle that protocol. Install an app from the Store, and then return to the **Set defaults by app** pane and select that app as the default for the protocol.

Organize apps on multiple desktops

Virtual desktops, which were first introduced in Windows 10, are one of those features that you can't quite imagine how you're going to use until you take the plunge. A virtual desktop is a bit like a second monitor, or a second computer: it's a location in which you can put some of the apps or files you're working on to keep your workspace organized. A basic example would be having a work-centric desktop on which you're running Outlook and Word, and a personal desktop on which you're monitoring Facebook and Twitter. If you frequently work with a dozen app windows open at one time, organizing them on virtual desktops can be a great way of decluttering and helping you to focus on only one set of apps and tasks at a time.

You can create and manage virtual desktops from Task View or by using keyboard shortcuts. The original desktop is number 1. When you add more desktops, they are numbered consecutively.

After you create a desktop, you can drag open apps to it, or open new apps directly on that desktop. You can display or work on only one virtual desktop at a time, but it's easy to switch between them from Task View, or more quickly by using a keyboard shortcut.

14

Each desktop has a taskbar. Each taskbar displays the same pinned apps, but only those apps that are active on the current desktop have active buttons on that desktop taskbar.

> **TIP** If you have multiple instances of an app open on different desktops, the app button is active on each desktop, but pointing to it displays only the instances on that desktop.

You open a file or start an app on a virtual desktop by using the same methods you use on the standard desktop. You can't have the same instance of an app (for example, the same file) open on more than one desktop, but you can move an app instance to another desktop.

You can run multiple instances of some apps (such as the Internet Explorer, Google Chrome, and Microsoft Word desktop apps) on the same desktop or on multiple desktops. From the taskbar on each desktop, you can display thumbnails of the app instances running on that desktop.

The Store apps we tried support only one instance, whether on one desktop or on multiple desktops. If you try to open one of these apps on a different virtual desktop, Windows switches to the desktop where the app is already running.

When you finish working on a desktop, you can close it to free up system resources. If you close a desktop that contains open applications, those applications are moved to the desktop immediately to its left (for example, from Desktop 3 to Desktop 2).

To display desktops in Task View

- On the taskbar, to the right of the search box, select the **Task View** button.

- Press Win+Tab.

- On a touchscreen device, swipe in from the left edge of the screen.

  The desktops are shown at the bottom of the screen.

To create a virtual desktop

- Display the Task View of your desktop and then, in the lower-right corner of the screen, select **New desktop**.

- Press Win+Ctrl+D.

Windows creates a new virtual desktop to the right of the existing desktops, numbered with the next sequential number. The new desktop becomes the active desktop.

To move between desktops

- Display the Task View of your desktop and then, at the bottom of the screen, select the desktop you want to move to.

- Press Win+Ctrl+Right Arrow or Win+Ctrl+Left Arrow to move to the next desktop in the direction of the arrow.

To open a new instance of a running app

- Press Win+Shift+select the taskbar button.

To move an app to a different desktop

1. Display the Task View of your desktop. The available desktops are at the bottom of the screen.

2. Point to the desktop that contains the app you want to move, to display each app that is open on that desktop in the app thumbnail area of Task View.

14

3. Do either of the following:

- Right-click the thumbnail of the app you want to move. Select **Move to**, and then select the desktop you want to move the app to.

> ✓ **TIP** One of the Move To options is New Desktop. You can create a new desktop and move an app to it at the same time by selecting that option.

- Drag the thumbnail (not the title above it) to the destination desktop.

To close the current desktop

- Press Win+Ctrl+F4.

To close selected desktops

1. Display the Task View of your desktop.

2. Point to the desktop that you want to close. When a Close button (X) appears in the upper-right corner of the desktop tile, select it.

> ✓ **TIP** To quickly move all open windows and running apps to one desktop, display Task View and then close all open virtual desktops other than Desktop 1.

Monitor apps and system tasks

Windows 10 and the apps and services that run on it constantly perform an amazingly complex dance that is set to the rather boring rhythm of your computer's clock.

Every computer has a central processing unit (CPU) and every CPU has a clock speed, which is generally in the 1 GHz (gigahertz) to 4 GHz range. In very basic terms, a 2 GHz CPU can carry out two billion instructions per second. That seems like a lot of instructions, until you realize that an extremely simple task, such as typing one letter into a Word document, might require thousands of instructions. CPU speed isn't the only factor in assessing the power and efficiency of your computer, but it is one of them, and one of those that you can monitor in Task Manager.

One way to monitor the real-time flow of activities on your computer is by using Task Manager. Task Manager has two views: Fewer Details and More Details. Fewer Details view displays a simple list of the apps that are currently running on your computer. If an app is having trouble, you can quickly identify that here.

> **TIP** Task Manager opens in the same view (Fewer Details or More Details) that you last used.

More Details view offers seven tabs of information: Processes, Performance, App History, Startup, Users, Details, and Services. A lot of information is available here, and you might find it interesting to look through it all. The two tabs with information that is helpful to average computer users are the Processes and Startup tabs.

The Processes tab displays a list of all the apps and services that are running on your computer and the computer resources each process is using. Computer resource statistics include CPU, memory, disk, and network usage. The order of the processes on the tab updates constantly to sort by resource usage. You can sort in ascending or descending order of usage by any column.

14

Task Manager						— □ ✕

File   Options   View

| Processes | Performance | App history | Startup | Users | Details | Services |

Name	6% CPU	53% ⌄ Memory	0% Disk	0% Network
⌄ e Microsoft Edge (8)	0%	391.5 MB	0 MB/s	0 Mbps
e Win10SBS - Ch06 - All Documents	0%	250.8 MB	0 MB/s	0 Mbps
e Microsoft Edge Manager	0%	44.3 MB	0 MB/s	0 Mbps
e Background Tab Pool	0%	40.8 MB	0 MB/s	0 Mbps
e Cortana Devices	0%	38.5 MB	0 MB/s	0 Mbps
e User Interface Service	0%	5.9 MB	0 MB/s	0 Mbps
▣ Browser_Broker	0%	4.2 MB	0 MB/s	0 Mbps
▣ Runtime Broker	0%	3.8 MB	0 MB/s	0 Mbps
e Chakra JIT Compiler	0%	3.3 MB	0 MB/s	0 Mbps
> 📑 Microsoft Teams (5)	0.6%	243.3 MB	0.1 MB/s	0 Mbps
S Snagit Editor	0.3%	138.4 MB	0 MB/s	0 Mbps
> ⚙ Service Host: Superfetch	0.2%	93.5 MB	0 MB/s	0 Mbps
▣ Desktop Window Manager	0.6%	73.3 MB	0 MB/s	0 Mbps

⌃ Fewer details   End task

> **TIP** Some processes have multiple associated files, pages, or services running. These are indicated by a > to the left of the process name. Selecting the > expands the full process list.

The Startup tab displays a list of the apps and services that start automatically when you sign in to Windows, and their impact on the time it takes your computer to be ready. Many apps and services sneak onto this list when they're installed.

> **SEE ALSO** For information about apps that start automatically, and working on the Startup tab of Task Manager, see "Manage app startup" later in this chapter.

To start Task Manager

- Right-click an empty area of the taskbar, and then select **Task Manager**.

- Press Ctrl+Shift+Esc.

- Press Ctrl+Alt+Del and then, in the list, select **Task Manager**.

To switch between Fewer Details view and More Details view

- In the lower-left corner of the **Task Manager** window, select **More details** or **Fewer details**.

To display currently running apps

- Open **Task Manager** in Fewer Details view.

To display currently running apps and services

- Open **Task Manager** in More Details view to display the Processes tab.

To identify a nonresponsive app or service

- Open **Task Manager** in Fewer Details view, or display the **Processes** tab in More Details view. Nonresponsive apps and services are labeled *Not responding*.

To identify resource-intensive processes

1. Open **Task Manager** in More Details view to display the **Processes** tab. The current CPU, memory, storage drive, and network loads are shown at the top of the window.

2. Identify the system element with the highest load. Select that heading once to sort the running apps and services in ascending order by their effect on that load, and again to sort in descending order with the highest usage at the top. The highest usage is indicated by an orange highlight.

To quit an app or service from Task Manager

1. Open **Task Manager** in Fewer Details view, or display the **Processes** tab in More Details view.

2. Select the app or service you want to quit, and then in the lower-right corner of the window, select **End task**.

14

Manage app startup

Not all the background processes that apps run are necessary to perform every time you start your computer. It's worth your time to periodically review and refine the items that start automatically. You can identify and manage the startup of many of these apps in Task Manager.

Task Manager			— □ ✕
File Options View			
Processes Performance App history **Startup** Users Details Services			
			Last BIOS time: 6.6 seconds
Name ^	Publisher	Status	Startup impact
☁ Microsoft OneDrive	Microsoft Corporation	Enabled	High
▣ Send to OneNote Tool	Microsoft Corporation	Enabled	Low
> Ⓢ Skype for Business (2)	Microsoft Corporation	Enabled	High
> Ⓢ Snagit (4)	TechSmith Corporation	Enabled	High
> ⊞ Update (3)	Microsoft Corporation	Enabled	High
⊞ Windows Defender notificati...	Microsoft Corporation	Enabled	Low
⌃ Fewer details			Disable

You can sort items on the Startup tab by any column. The Startup Impact column indicates the level of delay caused by each item.

> 🔍 **SEE ALSO** For more information about Task Manager, see "Monitor apps and system tasks" earlier in this chapter.

There are two groups of apps that Task Manager doesn't manage startup for—Store apps and apps that start automatically because they're identified in the Startup folder that is specific to your user account. If you always use a specific app and want it to start automatically with Windows, you can put a shortcut to it in this folder.

To identify apps and services that start automatically

- Open **Task Manager** in More Details view, and then select the **Startup** tab.

To prevent an app or service from starting automatically

- On the **Startup** tab of Task Manager, select the app or service, and then select **Disable**.

To automatically start an app when Windows starts

1. In File Explorer, navigate to **C:\Users\[your account name]\AppData\Roaming \Microsoft\Windows\Start Menu\Programs\Startup**. Windows 10 automatically starts apps by using the shortcuts in this folder.

   > **IMPORTANT** The AppData folder and its contents are visible only when File Explorer is configured to show hidden items. You can always display the contents of a hidden folder by entering its path in the File Explorer Address bar. For information about configuring File Explorer, see Chapter 5, "Explore files and folders."

   > **TIP** A quicker way to open the Startup folder in File Explorer is to press Win+R to open the Run box, enter *shell:startup*, and then press Enter.

2. Drag the app from the app list on the **Start** menu to the **Startup** folder. Release the app after the word *Link* appears next to the app icon.

The next time you restart Windows, your app will start automatically.

14

Key points

- The Quick Action buttons at the bottom of the Action Center pane give you direct access to frequently used settings. You can display only the actions you intend to use, and arrange them in whatever order you want.

- You can use the Windows search feature to locate information anywhere on your computer, on storage devices connected to your computer over a network or in the cloud, and anywhere on the internet. You can search for specific categories of results and filter the results after searching.

- You can easily change the default app that opens a specific type of file—for example, if you want to open PDF files in Adobe Acrobat instead of Microsoft Edge.

- You can remain focused on a specific task workload by organizing the files and apps you use for each set of tasks on its own virtual desktop.

- From Task Manager, you can monitor the apps and services that are running on your computer to identify and exit those that are tying up CPU, memory, disk, or network resources or those that have stopped responding. You can also identify apps that start automatically when Windows starts, and stop them from doing so if they are unnecessarily typing up resources.

- You can exit an app or stop a service from within Task Manager.

Practice tasks

No practice files are necessary to complete the practice tasks in this chapter.

Configure Quick Action buttons

Perform the following tasks:

1. Display the **Action Center** pane, and identify the Quick Action buttons.

2. Expand the action button area to display all the available action buttons. Review the action buttons that are available on your computer and consider which you might use. Notice whether any buttons are a different color, and identify what that means.

3. Select the **All settings** action button to open the Settings window. Select **System**, and then select **Notifications & actions**.

4. In the **Notifications & actions** pane, select the four action buttons that you will most frequently use, and assign these to the four Quick Action button positions.

5. Open the **Action Center** pane, collapse the action button area, and ensure that the Quick Action buttons you selected are visible.

Search your computer and the web

Perform the following tasks:

1. From the taskbar search box, search for a word, simple phrase, or your first name (anything that will generate a lot of search results).

2. Scroll the search results pane, and notice the types of results the search returned. Select any category heading to display only the results in that category.

3. Filter the results to display only one type of file. Then display the remaining search results in order by date.

4. Display the **SafeSearch** settings. Notice the other settings that you can configure from the page.

5. Start File Explorer, and open the **Indexing Options** dialog box. Notice the number of indexed items and the locations that are included. If you store files in a location that isn't being indexed, modify the options to include that location. Then close the dialog box.

Specify default apps

Start File Explorer, and then perform the following tasks:

1. Locate a file of a type that you frequently work with.

2. Display the list of apps that you can use to open the file.

3. Display apps from the Store that you could install and use to open the file.

4. If you want to, change the default app for the file.

5. Display the **Default apps** pane, and review the options for setting default apps by category, by file type, and by protocol. If you want to, change the default apps to suit your preferences.

Organize apps on multiple desktops

Perform the following tasks:

1. Display Task View, and then create a virtual desktop.

2. On Desktop 2, start two apps that aren't already running.

3. Switch between the two desktops, and notice any signs of items on the other desktop.

4. Move one of the apps from Desktop 2 to Desktop 1, and confirm that the app is open on Desktop 1.

5. Close Desktop 2, and confirm that the remaining app from that desktop moved to Desktop 1.

6. Close any apps that you aren't using.

Monitor apps and system tasks

Perform the following tasks:

1. Open Task Manager. Notice the information that is available in Fewer Details view.

2. Switch to More Details view, and do the following:

   - Display each tab, and review the information that is available on the tab.

   - Notice how the information changes as your computer performs background processes.

   - Consider how and when the information will be useful to you.

Manage app startup

Perform the following tasks:

1. Display the **Startup** tab of Task Manager.

2. Sort the apps and services by their impact on the computer startup time.

3. For each item that has a **High** startup impact, look at the available information to determine what the item does.

4. Sort the apps and services by publisher.

5. Identify any app publishers in the list who you aren't familiar with. Examine the startup impact of the items associated with each unfamiliar publisher.

6. Sort the list by status. Look for any items that are already disabled from starting automatically.

7. Select one app that starts automatically, and take note of its name. Disable the app and wait for it to change status. Then enable it for automatic startup again.

8. Open the **Startup** folder associated with your user account. Add a shortcut to the Maps app to the folder so that Maps starts automatically the next time you start your computer.

Protect your computer and data

For many people, computers and other "smart" devices have become an integral part of their lives. Even if you aren't totally dependent on them, the failure of one or more of them would be at least inconvenient.

The power of modern laptops and tablets means that you can carry your information with you and easily access it for work or play. But mobile devices are more susceptible to being lost or stolen than the clunky desktop computer you abandoned, and if that happens, you could lose valuable information, and it might be misused by others.

Modern computers are reasonably robust, but the only absolute guarantee you can expect from any hardware device is that if you continue to use it long enough, it will eventually fail. A serious hardware failure might leave you stranded at a critical point in a work project, or unable to access information you need from the internet. Fortunately, it's relatively easy to get back up and running quickly these days if you make use of the Windows 10 tools that are available to protect your computer and the data on it, to recover that data if the hardware fails, and to prevent others from accessing your data if your computer is stolen.

This chapter guides you through procedures related to updating system files, configuring update options, configuring privacy settings, restoring computer functionality, backing up data manually or automatically, and restoring your system.

In this chapter

- Manage Windows updates
- Configure privacy settings
- Restore computer functionality
- Back up data
- Back up and restore your system

Manage Windows updates

The code behind operating systems is usually in a constant state of change. This might be to resolve internal or external issues—for example, threats from new viruses or the need to improve drivers for the devices you can connect to your computer. Microsoft has stated that Windows 10 will be the last version of Windows (a great reason to buy this book!), but the actual meaning of that statement is that the company plans to maintain and update this version of Windows for the foreseeable future rather than to immediately begin the development of a new version. This is in part a reflection of the agile software development methodology that Microsoft has embraced. The methodology involves multiple function-specific teams completing rapid, collaborative development cycles and continually refining processes, rather than one long-term development process driven by management.

Update Windows system files

Windows Update is part of the Update & Security category of settings. Windows Update automatically checks for, downloads, and installs updates to the operating system (including the built-in Windows Defender security software), and related files, such as device drivers, on a regular basis. If your computer is turned off or is offline when the time comes to check, you might not get an update when it first becomes available to you, but you can manually check for updates whenever you want; this is an especially good idea if your computer has been turned off for a while (for example, if you don't use it often or go on a long vacation).

If Windows Update locates available updates, it starts the process of downloading and installing them. Sometimes Windows Update delays certain update processes until a time that you're not using your computer. You can choose to run those processes immediately if you want to.

If you install an update and later wish you hadn't, you can uninstall it.

To display the Windows Update settings pane

- Open the **Settings** window, select **Update & Security**, and then select **Windows Update**.

To check for and install Windows updates

1. Display the **Windows Update** settings pane.

2. In the **Update status** area, do one of the following:

   - If no updates are currently shown, select **Check for updates**.

   - If updates are available, select **Install Now**.

   - If Windows needs to restart the computer to complete the installation of updates, first ensure that you don't need to use the computer for the next 15–60 minutes. Then save any files you're working in, close any running apps, return to this pane, and select **Restart Now**.

To display your update history

- In the **Windows Update** settings pane, at the bottom of the **Update status** area, select **View installed update history**.

15

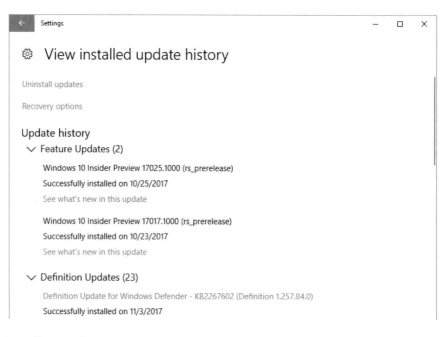

To uninstall an update

1. Display the **View installed update history** settings pane.

2. At the top of the pane, select **Uninstall updates**.

3. In the **Installed Updates** window, select the update that you want to remove, and then on the menu bar, select **Uninstall**.

> **TIP** The View Installed Update History pane displays updates installed since the last major release of Windows. If you've recently installed the Fall 2017 Creators Update or another major update, the update history might be empty.

Configure update options

Unlike previous versions of Windows, Windows 10 automatically checks for and installs updates to ensure that the security measures on your computer are current. Depending on the advanced option settings, if updates are available for Windows, the computer will either quietly install them while you aren't using it, or ask you to initiate the installation.

You also have some options for the types of updates you get and the way they're delivered to your computer. For example, Windows Update can also check for updates to other Microsoft products (such as Word, Outlook, and Skype) that are installed on your computer, and can optimize the delivery of updates by downloading them to your computer through other computers connected to yours through a local network or internet connection.

You can configure the following advanced options for Windows Update:

- **When the computer restarts** Updates are automatically downloaded and installed, but you can specify the times that you use the computer so that Windows Update will not restart your computer during your workday, if a restart is necessary. Windows Update displays a reminder when a restart is necessary, but you can opt to display additional notifications.

- **What products you get updates for** In addition to updating operating system files and drivers, you can update other Microsoft products and featured apps through Windows Update. It's a good idea to select this option because many apps and tools don't automatically update.

- **How soon you get upgrades** With some Windows 10 editions, including Professional, Enterprise, and Education (but not Home), you can defer upgrades to your computer. When you defer upgrades, new Windows features won't be downloaded or installed for several months after they're available. Deferring upgrades doesn't defer security updates, but it does prevent you from getting the latest Windows features as soon as they're available.

15

■ **How updates are delivered** This is a new and interesting feature for Windows 10. If you have several Windows 10 computers on your network and you enable this option, one computer does the download, caches the files on the network, and then sends the files to the other computers. This can substantially reduce the bandwidth you consume each month.

There is also an option, called Delivery Optimization, that allows your local computers to pass updates to and from known computers on your local network and unknown computers through the internet. This is the default update distribution model for Windows 10 Home and Windows 10 Professional. (The Enterprise and Education editions of Windows 10 are configured to pass updates to and from local network computers only.) This process helps to distribute security updates faster, but can increase your bandwidth usage. If you want more information about this, you can select the Learn More link.

■ **Get Insider Builds** You can sign up with the Windows Insider program to receive preview builds of upcoming Windows 10 versions. These builds have been tested by the product team, but they have not been released to the general public yet. You'll have earlier access to new features, but you might also have to deal with issues in those features. Microsoft suggests that you do not install a preview build on a computer that is critical to your happiness or business. If something is drastically wrong with the preview build, you might end up having to reformat and reinstall Windows from scratch.

 IMPORTANT If you decide to get Insider builds, be sure to read the topics "Restore computer functionality" and "Back up data" later in this chapter.

Windows chooses a time to install updates and restart your computer based on your activity on the computer and the working hours you stipulate, so there's less chance of interrupting your work. You can configure a time span of up to 18 hours per day during which Windows won't restart your computer without first notifying you.

⚙ Restart options

Schedule a time

We'll restart to finish installing updates when you tell us to. Just turn this on and pick a time.

◉⃝ Off

Pick a time:

| 11 | 04 | PM |

Pick a day:

Today ⌄

Show more notifications

We'll show a reminder when we're going to restart. If you want to see more notifications about restarting, turn this on.

◉⃝ Off

To configure update installation options

1. In the **Windows Update** settings pane, in the **Update settings** section, select **Advanced options**.

2. In the **Advanced options** pane, do any of the following:

   - Select or clear the **Give me updates for other Microsoft products when I update Windows** check box.

   - If available, select or clear the **Defer upgrades** check box.

   - Select **Delivery Optimization**, and turn on or off **Allow downloads from other PCs**. If you turn it on, select whether you want to accept only downloads from computers on your network (the safest option) or also from computers on other networks (the potentially faster option).

15

To specify times that Windows should not restart your computer

1. Display the **Windows Update** settings pane.

2. In the **Update settings** area, select **Change active hours**.

Active hours

Set active hours to let us know when you typically use this device. We won't automatically restart it during active hours, and we won't restart without checking if you're using it.

Start time

8	00	AM

End time (max 18 hours)

8	00	PM

Save	Cancel

3. Set the **Start time** and **End time** to indicate the time during which you don't want Windows to automatically restart. Then select **Save**.

To set a specific restart time

1. In the **Windows Update** settings pane, in the **Update settings** section, select **Restart options**.

2. Turn on **Schedule a time**, and then set the time and day you want Windows to restart your computer.

To configure restart notifications

1. In the **Windows Update** settings pane, in the **Update settings** section, select **Restart options**.

2. Turn on **Show more notifications**.

Configure privacy settings

Privacy, or at least some illusion of privacy, is important to most people. When you use a computer regularly, much of your life takes place inside that box. The operating system, the apps you use, and the sites you visit all have access to bits of information about you. Windows 10 privacy settings can limit how much of that information the apps and devices that are connected to your computer can see, and, to some extent, what the apps and devices can use that information for.

Much of the emphasis of the privacy settings is on how Microsoft and other companies can use any information they gather to present you with advertising that is theoretically more pertinent to your lifestyle than random advertising might be. From that point of view, because you are going to be presented with ads anyway, it seems like a benefit to have those ads more accurately related to your interests.

In the end, it is up to you to consider the benefits, or lack thereof, in sharing your information.

> **TIP** The placement of ads on websites provides a way to defray the expense of offering you free information. If the site is useful to you and the ads aren't too distracting, then this might be acceptable. But a lot of sites show up in web searches that exist only to barrage people with ads. Your browser can block pop-up ads, but it can't automatically block inline ads. If you are tired of waiting for these ads to load before you can start scrolling through the page, search the internet for "remove ads from your browser" and peruse the results. Some of the options are pretty amazing.

In Windows 10, you can configure general privacy settings and additional settings for the following 18 categories of information:

Account info	Camera	Microphone
App diagnostics	Contacts	Notifications
Automatic file downloads	Email	Other devices
Background apps	Feedback & diagnostics	Radios
Calendar	Location	Speech, inking, & typing
Call history	Messaging	Tasks

15

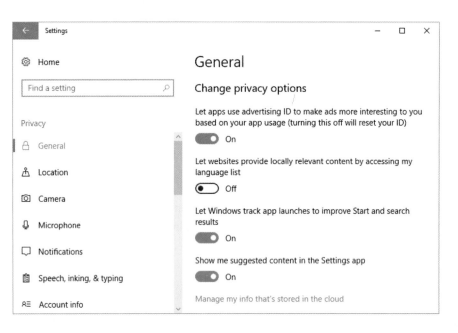

Instead of going into a lot of detail about all of these privacy settings, this chapter takes you on a quick tour and leaves it up to you to explore those areas that interest you. Sharing some of this information can be beneficial to you, and most is not harmful. Here is a bit of information that might be helpful:

- Your *advertising ID* is a unique ID that is connected to the email address you use to sign in to Windows 10. If you use a Microsoft account to sign in to OneDrive, Office 365, email, and other computers, Microsoft will accumulate information from all sources of these under this one ID.

- Many settings refer to apps that might use your information.

  Windows 10 preinstalls a lot of apps that you might never use. You can turn off the ability for the app to access your data in the settings, but if you don't want to use the app at all, it is better to uninstall it.

  > **TIP** This works only for apps that came from the App Store. If the app is part of Windows, such as Mail or Maps, then you can't uninstall it.

- You can control settings specific to each category, and within many categories you can turn on or off access for specific apps. For example, in the Microphone category, you can either prevent all apps from using your device's microphone or allow the use of the microphone and then turn access on or off for specific apps.

After you select a privacy category, there is generally a pause as Windows scans your installed apps to identify those that might need access to this category. Windows then lists these below the heading Choose Apps That Can... use or access the feature. If no apps are listed, then no currently installed apps need the feature in this category. Only Store apps appear in this list; desktop apps don't. So you could, for example, turn off camera access for the OneNote or Skype Store app, but not for the corresponding desktop app.

- Some location features, such as geofencing, are applicable only if you have installed apps that use them.

- The Speech, inking, & typing options include features that allow Windows and Cortana to "get to know you better." If you plan to use Cortana, don't turn off Getting To Know You.

Additional settings that are related to privacy and advertising in Microsoft products are available at *account.microsoft.com/privacy/ad-settings*. That page also includes links to more information about how Microsoft might use your information.

15

If you use your computer to manage your life, especially if that computer is portable, leaving many of the privacy settings enabled makes sense. It is useful to you if your computer (and Cortana) know where you are and which meetings you have scheduled and who you are exchanging email with. And sharing information about typing, voice recognition, and other activities with Microsoft can certainly help them improve Windows and their apps in the future. Give some thought to what is useful to you to share, and what isn't.

To manage privacy settings

1. In the **Settings** window, select **Privacy**.

2. Review the options in each pane. Consider how each might impact you.

3. Turn on each option you want to use, and turn off those you don't.

Restore computer functionality

Computer software tends to be updated frequently, in an effort to improve its operation, introduce new features, or increase security. But every update is also an opportunity for a little bug to creep in and cause problems. And a few years of updates, even when perfectly harmless on their own, can have the effect of scrambling the computer's brain to the point that it performs at less than ideal speeds.

Windows 10 offers several options for recovering from system problems. In order of impact, these include:

- Reverting to a system restore point, which rolls back app and driver changes that have occurred since the restore point was created but retains documents and other files created by those apps. This is often a simple fix when a problem is introduced with an app or driver update.

- Resetting the PC, which offers three levels of change:

  - Removing all apps and reverting to default settings, but retaining files.

  - Removing all apps and files, and reverting to default settings.

  - Removing all apps and files, reverting to default settings, and cleaning the hard drive. If you're planning to physically part ways with your computer, this option provides the highest level of security for your personal information.

■ Reverting to a clean installation of Windows by using the Fresh Start feature, which reinstalls and updates Windows 10 and retains your files and settings, but removes any apps that aren't installed with Windows. This is almost like having a brand-new computer.

> **TIP** Depending on your computer system and whether you participate in the Windows Insider program, it might also be possible to revert to a previous version of Windows 10. On systems that support this option, it is available in the Recovery pane of the Update & Security settings page.

Regardless of the option you select, take the time to consider the steps you need to take to protect any software licenses that have been activated on your computer. If you use Office 365 apps, you can easily reinstall them from the cloud. However, if you select a restore process that uninstalls an Adobe app, for example, the license that is assigned to your computer will be void, and it's a relatively difficult process to regain access. Before initiating a process that uninstalls an Adobe app, be sure to start the app and use the command on the Help menu to deactivate it on your computer, thus making the license available for reuse.

Create and revert to restore points

The internet is a wonderful resource, but it also exposes your computer to viruses, hackers, and other potentially harmful things.

If your computer starts performing poorly, especially if that happens just after performing updates or perhaps downloading something that installed obnoxious adware that you can't seem to get rid of, you can restore Windows to an earlier point in time, called a *restore point*. Doing this doesn't change your personal files, but it might remove recently installed apps and drivers (which could be a good thing if they are the cause of the problem).

System restore points are automatically added before significant changes are made, but if you are about to do something that makes you a bit nervous, it doesn't hurt to set one manually.

15

You create restore points from the System Protection tab of the System Properties dialog box.

> **TIP** You can create a restore point for any drive but generally need to do so for only your system drive.

When you want to restore your computer to an earlier restore point, you open the System Properties dialog box and display the System Protection tab. From there, you select the System Restore button to start the System Restore wizard.

Only the last few restore points are displayed. You can select the Show More Restore Points check box to display any others that exist.

To create a system restore point

1. Open File Explorer. In the **Navigation** pane, right-click **This PC**, select **Properties**, and then select **System protection** to display the System Protection tab of the System Properties dialog box.

2. In the **Protection Settings** section, select the drive you want to create a restore point for, and then select **Create....**

3. In the **Create a restore point** dialog box, enter a description, and then select **Create**. Windows creates the restore point, and informs you after it is done.

15

To revert to a saved system restore point

1. Open the **System Properties** dialog box and display the **System Protection** tab.

2. Select **System Restore...** to start the **System Restore** wizard. Read the introduction message, and then select **Next** to display the Restore Your Computer To The State It Was In Before The Selected Event page.

3. Select a restore point from the list, or if the restore point you want to use isn't listed, select the **Show more restore points** check box to add automatic restore points to the list, and then select a restore point.

4. Select **Scan for affected programs** to have the wizard search and display a list of programs and drivers that will be deleted or restored. Make a note of any programs or drivers you might need to reinstall after you restore your computer, and then select **Close** to return to the wizard.

5. Repeat steps 3 and 4 until you locate the checkpoint that you want to restore to. Then select **Next** to restore your computer to the selected restore point.

Refresh or reset your computer

The ability to reset your computer was first introduced with Windows 8, and has proven to be a good recovery path that requires less effort than wiping your computer, reinstalling Windows and all your apps, and recovering all your data. Refreshing retains your personal files, and resetting removes them. These two options have been rolled into the Reset This PC wizard.

Resetting your computer is a more serious action than restoring to a saved restore point; it is a bit like upgrading to a fresh version of Windows 10. Here's what happens when you reset your computer:

- You have the option of keeping your personal files (files stored in your My Documents folder).

- Your computer settings are reset to the defaults.

- Your Store apps remain installed, and your desktop apps are uninstalled. Desktop apps that were installed by the computer manufacturer might be reinstalled. A list of the removed apps is saved as a file on your desktop.

Resetting your computer reinstalls Windows and deletes all apps that weren't included in the original installation. This is a drastic action. If you plan to continue using this computer, you will want to back up all files to another location and make sure you have setup files for any desktop apps you will want to reinstall. Your computer should restart and then take a while (10 minutes to several hours, depending on various things) to complete the reset. After the reset is done, you will need to re-create your account and reinstall any missing apps.

If you're experiencing problems with your computer, first try restoring it to a saved restore point. If that doesn't solve the problem, you can escalate to resetting the computer but keeping your files, and then to resetting it completely (removing everything).

To reset your computer and keep your files

1. In the **Settings** window, select **Update & Security**, and then select **Recovery**.

2. In the **Reset this PC** section, select **Get started** to display your reset options.

15

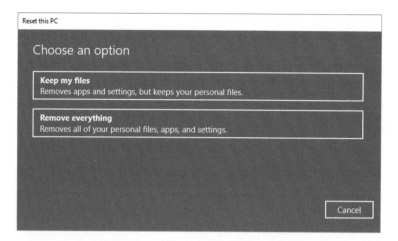

3. Select **Keep my files**. Windows scans your computer in preparation for the reset, and displays a list of apps that will be removed.

4. Review the list of apps that will be removed. If any of the apps are from Adobe or another manufacturer that requires you to release the license before you can reuse it, deactivate the apps before continuing the Reset process. When you're ready to continue, select **Next**.

    If you upgraded to Windows 10 within the past 30 days, the wizard warns you that resetting your computer will prevent you from being able to roll back to the previous version of Windows.

> ⚠ **IMPORTANT** If you want to retain the ability to roll back to your previous version of Windows using your current license, select Cancel at this point.

5. When you're ready to commit to the process, select **Next**, and then select **Reset**.

Your computer should restart and then take a while (10 to 60 minutes, depending on variables such as your internet connection speed) to complete the reset.

To reset your computer without keeping your files

1. In the **Settings** window, select **Update & Security**, and then select **Recovery**.

> ⚠ **IMPORTANT** If you have any installed apps from Adobe or another manufacturer that requires you to release the license before you can reuse it, deactivate the apps before continuing the Reset process.

2. In the **Reset this PC** section, select **Get started** to display your reset options.

3. Select **Remove everything**.

Reset this PC

Do you want to clean the drives, too?

Just remove my files
This is quicker, but less secure. Use this if you're keeping the PC.

Remove files and clean the drive
This might take a few hours, but will make it harder for someone to recover your removed files. Use this if you're recycling the PC.

Back   Cancel

4. If you want to ensure that all personal data is removed from the computer, select **Remove files and clean the drive**. Otherwise, select **Just remove my files**.

   If you upgraded to Windows 10 within the past 30 days, the wizard warns you that resetting your computer will prevent you from being able to roll back to the previous version of Windows.

> ⚠ **IMPORTANT** If you want to retain the ability to roll back to your previous version of Windows using your current license, select Cancel at this point.

5. When you're ready to commit to the process, select **Next**, and then select **Reset**.

15

To revert to a clean installation of Windows 10

1. In the **Settings** window, select **Update & Security**, and then select **Recovery**.

2. In the **More recovery options** section, select **Learn how to start fresh with a clean installation of Windows**. Then if prompted to do so, provide permission to switch to Windows Defender.

3. In the **Windows Defender Security Center**, on the **Fresh start** page, select **Get started**. In the User Account Control dialog box that prompts you to allow Windows Defender to make system changes, select **Yes**.

4. In the **Fresh start** window that opens, read the description, and then select **Next**. Windows scans your computer in preparation for the refresh, and displays a list of apps that will be removed.

5. Review the list of apps that will be removed. If any of the apps are from Adobe or another manufacturer that requires you to release the license before you can reuse it, deactivate the apps before continuing the Reset process. When you're ready to continue, select **Next**.

If you upgraded to Windows 10 within the past 30 days, the wizard warns you that resetting your computer will prevent you from being able to roll back to the previous version of Windows.

> ⚠️ **IMPORTANT** If you want to retain the ability to roll back to your previous version of Windows using your current license, select Cancel at this point.

6. When you're ready to commit to the process, select **Next**, and then select **Start**.

Back up data

Although it would be nice to believe that every "new and improved" computer will be the last one we need, the reality is that your computer will eventually wear out, be unable to support the latest technologies, fall off the kitchen counter, or get left at an international airport (and you'll never get that one back).

If you maintain a fresh backup of your data and have a system recovery drive, you will recover from a device disaster a lot faster and with less data loss than someone who isn't prepared.

Your computer, operating system, and apps are important, but they can be replaced. The personal files that are on your computer—the documents you have written, pictures you have taken, and other data—are much harder to replace. They might be worth many times the cost of a new computer. It is ironic that backing up data is so easy, and that so few people do it consistently.

These days, it's reasonably simple to store all your data in the cloud. If your organization uses Office 365, you can store work files in SharePoint and OneDrive for Business, and personal files in OneDrive. Even if you're committed to the online lifestyle, though, you probably have a few files that remain on your hard drive. It's good to have a process in place for backing up these files either manually or automatically. This topic discusses the tools you can use to do that.

15

Back up data to OneDrive

OneDrive is free online storage that comes with your Microsoft account. If you have a Microsoft account, and use it to sign in to your computer, a link to your OneDrive cloud storage is automatically created in C:\Users\[your account]\OneDrive.

> **TIP** At the time of the Windows 10 Fall 2017 Creators Update release, Microsoft is providing 5 GB of free OneDrive storage with your Microsoft account, or 1 terabyte (TB) for Office 365 subscribers. But Microsoft offers various ways to accumulate more storage. Go to *onedrive.live.com/about* and select See Plans to see the available plans for your location.

If your organization uses Office 365, you might have both a personal OneDrive account and a OneDrive for Business account. This topic is specific to personal OneDrive accounts, but much of the information also applies to OneDrive for Business accounts.

OneDrive is more than just a storage location; it is a storage location you can use to synchronize access to your files from every computer you sign in to with your Microsoft account, and from which you can share files with other people.

Every computer you sign in to with your Microsoft account credentials should automatically display your OneDrive folder in File Explorer and keep the files synchronized with those on your other devices. If you have OneDrive and OneDrive for Business accounts, these are differentiated by name in File Explorer, and by icon color in the taskbar notification area.

OneDrive for Business   Personal OneDrive   OneDrive for Business   Personal OneDrive

The Files On Demand feature of OneDrive makes it possible to see all your online files from your computer without filling your storage space with local copies. In File Explorer, the Status icon indicates whether you have an offline copy on your computer that syncs with the online version.

Icon	Status	Description
☁	Online only	Available to edit if your device is connected to the internet; available locally thereafter
⊘	Locally available	Offline copy that can be removed to free up storage space
✓	Always keep on this device	Offline copy that you want to retain offline

The online/offline status of a file is specific to the device you're working on. If you don't want files to take up space on your device, change them to Online Only to retain the version on OneDrive and any other devices you've downloaded it to. Don't delete the file, because doing so deletes the online version and any other offline versions! If you do accidentally delete a file, you can recover it from OneDrive online.

You can also sign in to your OneDrive online account and from there connect to the hard drive of any other Windows 10 computer that you sign in to with the same account, and that has OneDrive set up properly. You sign in to OneDrive online by using your Microsoft account credentials. From here you can view and share the files that are backed up to OneDrive from the computers you sign in to by using your Microsoft account.

You can access your files on OneDrive from pretty much any device, including Windows, Android, Mac OSX, iOS, Windows Phone, and Xbox systems. All you have to do is install the OneDrive app (or OneDrive for Business if you have an account of that type) from the appropriate app store.

If you work on multiple computers, you can store all your files on OneDrive so that you have access to the most up-to-date versions from any computer. If you store files locally on computers, OneDrive can help you to access those files, if you need to, by using the Fetch feature. Fetching files is a method of remotely accessing a Windows 10 computer from another computer by using your OneDrive account. You must enable the fetching of files on the computer that you intend to access remotely, and the computer must be turned on and connected to the internet.

15

To display your synchronized files on a connected computer

- Open File Explorer. In the **Navigation** pane, select **OneDrive** or **OneDrive – Personal** if you have the personal and business versions.

- In the taskbar notification area, select the **OneDrive** icon. Then on the title bar of the **OneDrive** pane, select the **Open folder** icon.

> **TIP** If the OneDrive icon isn't on the taskbar, select the Show Hidden Icons icon and then select the OneDrive icon from the hidden icons panel.

- In the taskbar notification area, right-click the **OneDrive** icon, and then select **Open your OneDrive folder**.

To open OneDrive online

- Open your browser and go to *onedrive.live.com*.

- In the taskbar notification area, right-click the **OneDrive** icon, and then select **View online**.

- In the taskbar notification area, select the **OneDrive** icon. On the title bar of the **OneDrive** pane, select the menu button (:), and then select **View online**.

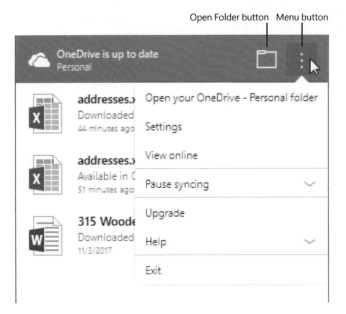

To quickly access OneDrive files you've recently worked with

1. In the taskbar notification area, select the **OneDrive** icon.

2. In the **OneDrive** pane, point to the file you want to open, select the menu button that appears to the right of the file name, and then select **Open**.

 TIP From the file-specific menu, you can open or share files or open the online storage location.

To store files on OneDrive

- Drag, or copy and paste, files from other locations to your OneDrive folder in File Explorer.

  You can place your original working files, such as Word documents, on OneDrive, and access and edit them there. Or you might want to work on your files else-where on your hard drive and drop a copy in OneDrive occasionally.

To recover a file deleted from OneDrive

1. Open OneDrive online.

2. In the left pane, select **Recycle bin**.

3. In the recycle bin, do either of the following:

   - To restore all the deleted files to their original locations, on the menu bar, select **Restore all items**.

   - To restore one or some of the files, select the check box to the left of each file you want to restore. Then on the menu bar, select **Restore**.

15

To manage OneDrive settings

1. In the taskbar notification area, right-click the **OneDrive** icon.

2. On the OneDrive shortcut menu, select **Settings** to open the Microsoft OneDrive dialog box.

To specify the folders you want to synchronize to a computer

1. Open the **Microsoft OneDrive** dialog box.

2. On the **Account** tab, select **Choose folders** to display a list of the folders on your OneDrive site, the amount of data that is stored in each folder, and the amount of storage space that is available on your computer.

3. In the folder list, select the check boxes for the folders you want to synchronize with the computer, and clear the check boxes for the folders you don't want to synchronize. As you change your selections, OneDrive keeps track of the storage space requirements.

4. Select **OK** in each of the open dialog boxes to implement your changes.

> **TIP** You configure folder synchronization independently on each computer that you connect to OneDrive, and you can make different selections on different computers. For example, you might want to synchronize your Pictures folder on your personal laptop and not on your work computer.

15

To enable the fetching of files from a computer

1. Open the **Microsoft OneDrive** dialog box.

2. On the **Settings** tab, select the **Let me use OneDrive to fetch any of my files on this PC** check box.

3. Select **OK** to close the dialog box.

4. Exit and then restart the OneDrive app by following these steps:

   a. In the taskbar notification area, right-click the **OneDrive** icon, and then select **Exit**.

   b. On the **Start** menu, in the app list, scroll or jump to the **OneDrive** entry, and select it.

 IMPORTANT You must enable file-fetching on each computer that you want to be able to fetch files from.

To fetch files remotely

1. Open OneDrive online.

2. In the left pane, select **PCs** to display a list of the computers associated with your Microsoft account that the OneDrive app is installed on.

3. In the **PCs** list, select the name of the computer you want to fetch files from to display a list of the files available on that computer.

4. Navigate to the file you want to fetch, right-click it, and select **Download**.

It is a good idea to go through this process a few times before you really need to use it, to become familiar with the process when you aren't under pressure.

Automatically back up data by using File History

If you use your Microsoft account to sign in to Windows 10, you can take advantage of OneDrive to back up files to the cloud and share them among your computers. But it is also nice to have an offline backup that maintains versions and allows you to restore earlier versions. The File History feature in File Manager helps you with this task.

15

File History can automatically back up each version of files that are in your libraries, contacts, favorites, and on your desktop. If you have files or folders elsewhere that you want backed up, you can move them into one of your existing libraries or create a new library. If you have a OneDrive account that is associated with your account, it is technically included under your Users account, so it is also included in the File History backup.

To activate File History

1. In the **Settings** window, select **Update & Security**, and then select **Backup** to display the File History controls.

> ✓ **TIP** Before you configure a File History storage location, the Backup pane displays an Add A Drive button. After you select a drive, the button changes to an Automatically Back Up My Files toggle button that is set to On.

2. To begin using File History, select **Add a drive**. Windows searches your computer and displays a list of the connected drives that you can back up files to by using File History.

Back up using File History
Back up your files to another drive and restore them if the originals are lost, damaged, or deleted.

+ Add a drive

More optio

Looking
If you creat
Restore toc
Go to Back

Back up
To have Wi
where you
network. W
a safe locat

Get more info about backup

Select a drive

FLASH (D:)
6.84 GB free of 7.22 GB

\\HIBISCUS\Pearson
1.51 TB free of 1.80 TB

\\HIBISCUS\TFS
1.51 TB free of 1.80 TB

3. Do either of the following:

- To configure File History to use a connected external drive, select the drive from the list.

- To configure File History to use a shared network folder, select **Show all network locations**, and then select the network folder.

4. In the **Backup** pane, select **More options** to display the backup frequency and scope settings.

5. In the **Backup options** pane, review the **Back up these folders** list. If you want to exclude any of these folders from the backup, select the folder, and then select **Remove**.

Back up my files

| Every hour (default) ⌄ |

Keep my backups

| Forever (default) ⌄ |

Back up these folders

+   Add a folder

Links
C:\Users\mail

Downloads
C:\Users\mail

Favorites
C:\Users\mail

> ✓ **TIP** If the Back Up These Folders list includes your local OneDrive or OneDrive for Business folders or subfolders, or other folders that contain files that are backed up elsewhere, it's probably a good idea to remove them.

6. To add a folder to the **Back up these folders** list, select **Add a folder**. In the **Select Folder** dialog box, browse to and select the folder you want to include, and then select **Choose this folder**.

15

7. If you want to specifically exclude a subfolder of a folder that you're backing up, scroll to the **Exclude these folders** section near the bottom of the **Backup options** pane, and select **Add a folder**. In the **Select Folder** dialog box, browse to and select the folder you want to exclude, and then select **Choose this folder**.

8. When you finish adding and removing folders, scroll to the top of the **Backup options** pane, and do the following:

   • Ensure that the Total Space available in the selected backup location exceeds the Size Of Backup. If it doesn't, change the backup location or remove folders from the backup.

   • Expand the **Back up my files** list, and then select a frequency between **Every 10 minutes** and **Daily**.

   • Expand the **Keep my backups** list, and then select a retention period from **1 month** to **Forever**, or select **Until space is needed** to have File History manage the retention period based on available storage space.

9. To start using File History, select **Back up now**.

> ✓ **TIP** You can also set up and manage File History from Control Panel. A few advanced settings there are not yet available in Settings.

To view versions of a file that has been backed up

1. In File Explorer, browse to and select a file that has been backed up.

2. On the **Home** tab, in the **Open** group, select **History**.

   A file viewer displays the most recently backed up version of the file. The day, date, and time of the file backup, and the number of available backups, are displayed at the top of the window.

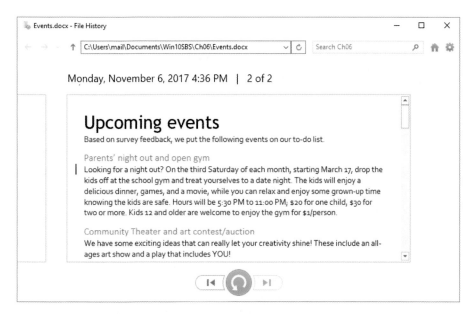

3. You can do any of the following:

   - Select the **Restore** button (the circular arrow in the green circle) to restore that version of the file to its original location.

   - Select the **Previous version** or **Next version** button (to the left and right of the Restore button) to display a different version of the file.

To manage file versions

1. In File Explorer, select a file you have previously backed up. Right-click the file, and then select **Restore previous versions** to display the Previous Versions tab of the file's Properties dialog box.

15

2. Select a file version to enable the Open and Restore buttons, and then do any of the following:

    - Select **Open** to open a read-only version of the file in its default app.

    - Select the **Open** arrow, and then select **Open in File History** to display the versions in the File History viewer.

    - Select **Restore** to restore the selected version to the file's original location.

    - Select the **Restore** arrow, and then select **Restore To** to select a different location.

Back up and restore your system

You can back up an entire drive (or drives) to a system image that contains all oper-ating system and user files, configuration information, and apps. The system image includes everything required to restore the drive to the state you capture in the image. This is a complete restoration to the imaging point, unlike the restorations provided by File History, restore points, or Reset Your PC, which bring back specific portions of the information that is stored on your hard drive. If you create a system image before your hard drive crashes, you can install a new hard drive, restore that image, and be ready to work with all your apps and data that you saved with that image.

> ⚠ **IMPORTANT** Because a system image is generally needed only if the hard drive crashes and you can't boot up, its usefulness depends on having the image files available on some form of external media. If the old hard drive is still functional, you can restore the system image to that hard drive to return it to the state it was in at the imaging point. If the hard drive no longer functions, it might not be practical to install a new hard drive and restore the image to it. You should consult an expert.

You might choose to create periodic system images to ensure that you have a recent one available. When you do, the first image you create is a complete image of the drive, and each subsequent image stores only the changes from the previous image. Because of this layered storage model, it is possible to restore the most recent image or an earlier one. In this way, restoring to a system image is similar to reverting to a specific restore point.

Backup images safeguard your data in the event of system failure, but you need to be able to start up (boot) your computer after you wipe the hard drive clean. You can start up your computer from a bootable DVD that contains installation files. You might have received a DVD from your computer manufacturer when you bought the computer. If you didn't, you will need to create some kind of boot media. Windows 10 allows you to create a bootable USB recovery drive.

15

You can quickly and easily create a recovery drive that you can use to boot up and troubleshoot problems with your computer. The recovery information is stored on a USB drive. The USB drive must have a capacity of at least 8 GB, although it might require as much as 16 GB or 32 GB. Windows will scan your computer at the beginning of the imaging process and tell you how large a drive you need. The drive doesn't have to be blank, but the process of creating the boot image reformats the drive and deletes its contents, so be sure to back up anything you want that is on the drive.

> ⚠ **IMPORTANT** A bootable recovery drive must be created in the same operating system type (32-bit or 64-bit) that you will boot into later. Ideally, you will create it on the same operating system you have backed up.

If you ever need to restore from a system image, the process will depend on whether your computer can still boot into Windows.

- If the computer can boot into Windows, follow the process described in "To restore a system image from within Windows 10," later in this topic.

- If the computer can't boot from the hard drive and you created a USB recovery drive as described in the procedure "To create a bootable USB recovery drive," you should be able to boot from that; however, the process takes a bit of effort and varies based on the specific computer.

- If the computer can't boot into Windows at all, follow the process described in "To boot from a recovery drive or disc," later in this topic.

> ✅ **TIP** If you are using a wireless or USB keyboard, your ability to get in to the BIOS will depend on the order in which the drivers for it are loaded. After you do get in, touch controls and the mouse most likely will not work.

To create a system image backup

1. Open Control Panel, and then do one of the following:

   - In **Category** view, in the **System and Security** area, select **Backup and Restore (Windows 7)**.

   - In **Large Icons** or **Small Icons** view, select **Backup and Restore (Windows 7)**.

2. In the left pane, select **Create a system image** to start the Create A System Image wizard. The wizard scans your system for storage devices that meet the requirements.

Create a system image

Where do you want to save the backup?

A system image is a copy of the drives required for Windows to run. It can also include additional drives. A system image can be used to restore your computer if your hard drive or computer ever stops working; however, you can't choose individual items to restore.

● On a hard disk

My Passport (D:) 891.69 GB free

○ On one or more DVDs

DVD RW Drive (F:)

○ On a network location

Select...

Next   Cancel

---

3. Select the location for the image. If you have created previous images, it is best to use the same location, if there is room, so all your images are in one place. Then select **Next** to display the backup settings.

15

4. Review and confirm the backup settings, and then select **Start backup** to start the backup. Windows displays a progress bar during the backup process. You can stop the process from the progress bar if you need to.

    After the backup is complete, the wizard asks whether you want to create a system repair disc.

    > ✅ **TIP** Creating a system repair disc is a good idea. You can boot your computer from it, and it contains Windows system recovery tools that you can use to restore your computer from a system image.

5. Select **Yes**, insert a blank disc in your CD/DVD drive, and then select **Create disc**.

6. After the disc is complete, select **Close** and then select **OK** to finish the process.

TIP Your first backup will take quite a while. Subsequent ones to the same location take less time.

To restore a system image from within Windows 10

1. Shut down all running apps.

2. Do one of the following to restart your computer in troubleshooting mode:

   - On the **Start** menu, select **Power**. Then hold down the **Shift** key and select **Restart**.

   - In the **Settings** windows, select **Update & Security**, select **Recovery**, and then in the **Advanced startup** section, select the **Restart now** button.

3. On the **Choose an option** screen, select **Troubleshoot**.

4. On the **Troubleshoot** screen, select **Advanced options**.

5. On the **Advanced options** screen, select **System Image Recovery**. Your screen will briefly go blank, and then display the message that Windows is preparing System Image Recovery.

6. If the computer is configured with user accounts for more than one Microsoft account, follow the System Image Recovery instructions to select your account and enter the password.

7. The system locates and displays drives that contain image files. Select the image you want to use, select **Next**, and then continue to the end of the wizard.

To create a bootable USB recovery drive

1. Do either of the following:

   - On the **Start** menu, in the app list, select the **Windows Administrative Tools** folder, and then select **Recovery Drive**.

   - Open Control Panel in **Large Icons** or **Small Icons** view, and then select **Recovery**.

2. A User Account Control message box opens. Agree to the request to allow the Recovery Media Creator to make changes to your computer. The Recovery Drive wizard starts.

15

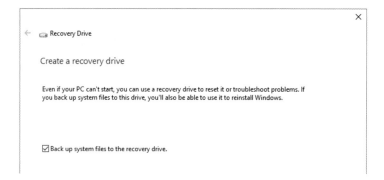

3. If you want to boot from a USB flash drive, clear the **Back up system files to the recovery drive** check box.

4. If you haven't already done so, insert the flash drive into a USB port and wait until it is recognized. Then select **Next**.

5. If multiple drives are available, select the one you want to use, and then select **Next**.

> ⚠ **IMPORTANT** Everything on the drive you select will be deleted. If you routinely back up files to an external USB hard drive, it might be among the USB drives listed. If you select the wrong device, all your backups will be gone.

6. Read and heed the warning that everything on the drive will be deleted. Make sure this is what you intend to do. Then select **Create** to start the process. A progress bar displays the progress.

7. After the process completes, select **Finish** to close the window.

> **TIP** You can follow the first few steps in the recovery process to confirm that you can boot from this drive.

To boot from a recovery drive or disc

1. Power your computer all the way down and then turn it back on.

2. If the boot process goes far enough to display the key to press to enter Setup, press it. This may be F8 or Del or some other key.

> ⚠ **IMPORTANT** Read the instructions on the screen, read your computer documentation, and search the web for more information before you make any changes in Setup. Making changes that you don't fully understand can cause problems.

3. In the BIOS Setup Utility, press your keyboard arrow keys to select an option such as Boot Options, Boot Order, or something else that includes the word *Boot*.

> ⚠ **IMPORTANT** The BIOS Setup Utility varies by computer make and model, so instructions are necessarily a bit vague. Basic instructions are usually included on the BIOS setup screen. If you have problems, search the web for information specific to your computer.

4. In the **Boot Priority Order** section (or something similar), select **1st Boot Device** and press Enter to display a list of devices.

5. Select **Removable Device** or **CD&DVD**, depending on what you want to boot from, and then press Enter.

> ⚠ **IMPORTANT** Depending on your hardware and BIOS, there might be other changes. It is best to read your computer manual or search for information about that model.

6. After making the changes, press F10 to save and exit.

7. Your computer should now boot from the USB drive and display the Options screen that appears in step 1 of the procedure "To restore a system image from within Windows 10." Follow those directions from this point forward.

15

Two-factor authentication

For the past several years, Microsoft has offered two-step identity verification as a method of protecting access to sensitive information that is associated with your Microsoft account.

If you try to sign in to your account from an unknown computer, or access sensitive information, such as advanced security settings, you are asked to verify your identity. You could initially do this by entering a key that was sent to you by email, phone, or text. More recently Microsoft has added the ability to verify your identity by using a smartphone authentication app.

If you are using the app, when you try to access a webpage that requires verification, your smartphone beeps, and when you sign in to the app, it displays, the security key and an Accept button. Tap the button and you are done.

If you are in a location where cellular access is not available, you can use the app to generate a key that you can then enter in the webpage that is requesting verification.

Starting with Windows 10, Microsoft is offering the same verification process for use when signing in to your computer and other devices. If you choose to enable this on a device, each time you sign in you will need to use one of the verification methods to complete the action.

This might seem like an unnecessary complication for a desktop computer in a secure location (though in reality there are very few such locations), but it seems like a really good idea for laptops and tablets that sometimes seem to wander off on their own.

Along with the verification methods that have been available for a while, Microsoft is planning to accept biometric information, such as facial recognition or a scanned fingerprint or eye, to access your Windows device. This option is managed by the biometric login feature, Windows Hello.

Unfortunately, this technology is dependent on hardware that few people have at the time of this writing. You can check the status of this service and find lists of compatible hardware by searching for Windows 10 Hello.

Key points

- Windows 10 self-manages the update process. You can configure update options to control how and when your computer gets updates.

- You can specify which apps have access to your calendar, camera, contacts, and other information to protect your privacy.

- If a software change causes a problem, you can revert to a system restore point to undo the change. If your computer becomes truly sluggish, you can reset it or revert to a clean installation of Windows.

- You can use the free OneDrive storage that comes with your Microsoft account to store files or file backups that you want to keep safe or have available from multiple computers.

- If you turn on file fetching, you can access files stored on any Windows 10 computer through OneDrive.

- The File History feature will automatically back up selected folders on a regular basis; you can restore older versions of files that are saved by File History.

- You can create a system image backup that allows you to do a complete restoration of your computer system in the event of a hardware failure.

15

Practice tasks

No practice files are necessary to complete the practice tasks in this chapter.

Manage Windows updates

Perform the following tasks:

1. Display the **Windows Update** pane.

2. Check for updates, or, if there are updates waiting, install them.

3. Display the update installation options, and configure the settings the way you want them.

Configure privacy settings

Perform the following tasks:

1. Display the **Privacy** page of the **Settings** window.

2. Review the settings in each pane. Consider the implications of sharing that information, and configure the settings the way you want them.

Restore computer functionality

Perform the following tasks:

1. Create a restore point.

2. In the **Settings** windows, select **Update & Security**, select **Recovery**, and then in the **Advanced startup** section, select the **Restart now** button to display the Troubleshooting screen. Investigate the options that are available from this screen so you're familiar with them if you need them in the future.

3. Display the **Recovery** pane of the **Update & Security** settings page. Explore the options to reset your computer, but do not complete the process.

Back up data

Perform the following tasks:

1. In the notification area of the taskbar, locate the **OneDrive** icon.

2. From the **OneDrive** shortcut menu, open the **Microsoft OneDrive** dialog box. Display each tab in turn, and consider the available options.

3. Review the folders that are synchronized to this computer, and configure OneDrive to synchronize only the folders you want.

4. If you work on multiple computers and want to be able to fetch files from this computer, enable that feature. (Don't forget to exit and restart the OneDrive app.)

5. Open OneDrive online and review the site options, which change from time to time and might be different from those shown in this book.

6. Display the **File History** pane.

7. If File History has not yet been configured, scan your computer system for a storage drive. If File History locates a suitable drive, do the following:

   a. Add the storage drive to File History.

   b. Display the File History options. Review the list of folders that File History backs up. Modify the list as necessary to include the folders that you want to back up, and exclude folders that you don't want to back up.

   c. Set the backup frequency, and specify how long you want to keep each version.

   d. Start the File History backup process.

8. If File History has been configured, do the following:

   a. Display the File History options. Review the list of folders that File History backs up, and modify the list as necessary.

   b. Review the backup frequency and the length of time File History retains each version. Modify these as necessary.

   c. Open one of the folders that File History backs up, and display a previous version of a file.

Back up and restore your system

There are no practice tasks for this topic.

Appendix

Keyboard shortcuts and touchscreen tips

The standard method of working with content on a Windows computer is to click the relevant commands. You can perform some tasks faster by pressing specific key combinations or, on a touchscreen device, by using specific gestures.

Keyboard shortcuts

Keyboard shortcuts provide a quick way to perform actions on the computer without taking your hands off the keyboard. Many keyboard shortcuts have become commonplace over the years, to the extent that they perform the same function in apps from almost any publisher. For example, Ctrl+C, Ctrl+X, and Ctrl+V will copy, cut, and paste in File Explorer and in many apps.

To differentiate keyboard shortcuts that control Windows from keyboard shortcuts that are specific to apps, many Windows keyboard shortcuts include the Windows logo key, which is located near the lower-left corner of the keyboard and labeled with the Windows icon. (Some keyboards have two Windows logo keys, one on each side of the spacebar.) The appearance of the icon varies based on the version of Windows that was active when the keyboard was manufactured.

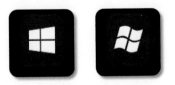

The simplest Windows 10 keyboard shortcut is to simply press and release the Windows logo key to display or hide the Start menu.

> **TIP** Because we refer to the Windows logo key a lot in this appendix, we've abbreviated the key name in multi-key keyboard shortcuts to *Win*.

Most keyboard shortcuts require that you hold down one key and then press another key. These keyboard shortcuts are presented in the form *Win+C*. Some keyboard shortcuts combine three keys; these are presented in the form *Win+Shift+M*. When invoking a three-key shortcut, press and hold the first and second keys, press the third key, and then release all three.

New in Windows 10

Most of the Windows 10 shortcuts are the same as those in previous versions of Windows, but there are a few new keyboard shortcuts that simplify interactions with features that are new or different in Windows 10. If you're familiar with the older shortcuts and just want the new ones, they are:

- **Win+A** Open the Action Center

- **Win+S** Open search

- **Win+C** Open Cortana in listening mode

> **IMPORTANT** This shortcut is turned off by default. To turn it on, open the Settings window, select Cortana, and then in the Keyboard Shortcut section, turn on Let Cortana Listen For My Commands When I Press The Windows Logo Key + C.

- **Win+Tab** Open Task View

- **Win+Ctrl+D** Add a virtual desktop

- **Win+Ctrl+Right arrow** Switch between virtual desktops you've created on the right

- **Win+Ctrl+Left arrow** Switch between virtual desktops you've created on the left

- **Win+Ctrl+F4** Close the virtual desktop you're using

Windows keyboard shortcuts

The following table lists Windows 10 keyboard shortcuts, including some that are new since the initial release of WIndows 10. Some of these keyboard shortcuts are valid only when the Windows user interface is active (not in individual apps).

To do this	Press
Display or hide the Start menu	Windows logo key
Open the Action Center	Win+A
Move the focus to the notification area	Win+B
Open or close the Cortana Listening mode window	Win+C
Display or hide the desktop	Win+D
Display the date and time pane	Win+Alt+D
Create a new virtual desktop	Win+Ctrl+D
Open the Quick Access folder in File Explorer	Win+E
Open the Feedback Hub and take a screenshot	Win+F
Open the Find Computers dialog box (in which you search for domain-joined computers)	Win+Ctrl+F
Open the Game bar (from which you capture screen shots and record video clips in games)	Win+G
Start dictation	Win+H
Open the Settings window	Win+I
Set focus to a Windows tip when one is available	Win+J
Open the Connect pane (in which you connect to wireless display and audio devices)	Win+K
Lock the computer	Win+L
Minimize all app windows (but not system windows)	Win+M
Restore minimized windows	Win+Shift+M
On a mobile device, lock the device orientation	Win+O
Open the Project pane and then cycle through presentation display modes	Win+P

To do this	Press
Activate the taskbar search box/open Cortana	Win+Q
Open the Run dialog box	Win+R
Activate the taskbar search box	Win+S
Cycle through taskbar buttons from left to right	Win+T
Cycle through taskbar buttons from right to left	Win+Shift+T
Open the Ease of Access page in Settings	Win+U
Cycle through notifications	Win+V
Cycle through notifications in reverse order	Win+Shift+V
Display the Quick Link menu	Win+X
Switch input between Windows Mixed Reality and the desktop	Win+Y
Show available commands in an app when in full-screen mode	Win+Z
Open the emoji panel	Win+Period (.) or Win+Semicolon (;)
Peek at the desktop	Win+Comma (,)
Switch to or start the app that is in the taskbar position indicated by the number	Win+number (1–0)
Start a new instance of the app that is in the taskbar position indicated by the number, if that app supports multiple instances	Win+Shift+number (1–0)
Start a new instance of the app that is in the taskbar position indicated by the number, if that app supports multiple instances, as an administrator	Win+Ctrl+Shift+number (1–0)
Switch to the last active window of the app that is in the taskbar position indicated by the number	Win+Ctrl+number (1–0)
Open the jump list of the app that is in the taskbar position indicated by the number	Win+Alt+number (1–0)
Capture an image of the current screen and save the image in the Pictures\Screenshots folder	Win+Print Screen

To do this	Press
Display the System window of Control Panel	Win+Pause/Break
Display the Task View of all open windows	Win+Tab
Switch to the next input language and keyboard (on devices configured for multiple languages or keyboards)	Win+Spacebar
Change to a previously selected input	Win+Ctrl+Spacebar
Switch to the previous input language and keyboard (on devices configured for multiple languages or keyboards)	Win+Shift+Spacebar
Start or stop Narrator	Win+Ctrl+Enter
Magnify the screen by using Magnifier	Win+Plus sign
Decrease the screen magnification when Magnifier is running	Win+Minus sign
Exit Magnifier	Win+Esc
Maximize a non-snapped window, or Snap a half-screen window to the upper corner	Win+Up arrow
Restore a non-snapped window, or Snap a half-screen window to the lower corner	Win+Down arrow
Maximize the height of the active window	Win+Shift+Up arrow
Restore or minimize the active window without changing its width	Win+Shift+Down arrow
Move a window through the left, center, and right of each screen, or move a quarter-screen window to another corner	Win+Left arrow Win+Right arrow
Move an open window to a different display	Win+Shift+Right arrow Win+Shift+Left arrow
Minimize or restore all windows other than the active window	Win+Home
Search for Windows 10 help online	Win+F1
Close the current virtual desktop	Win+Ctrl+F4
Switch to the next virtual desktop	Win+Ctrl+Left arrow Win+Ctrl+Right arrow

Taskbar keyboard shortcuts

The following shortcuts interact with taskbar buttons of pinned or running apps or groups of apps.

To do this	Press
Start a new instance of a pinned or running app	Shift+click
Start a new instance of a pinned or running app as an administrator	Ctrl+Shift+click
Open the window menu for the app	Shift+right-click
Open the window menu for the group	Shift+right-click (grouped taskbar button)
Cycle through the windows of the group	Ctrl+click (grouped taskbar button)

General keyboard shortcuts

The following shortcuts are applicable in multiple interfaces that might include system windows, app windows, File Explorer, dialog boxes, and panes.

To do this	Press
Cycle through thumbnails of open apps	Alt+Tab
Close the current app	Alt+F4
Select all content	Ctrl+A
Copy	Ctrl+C or Ctrl+Insert
Switch to the search box or Address bar	Ctrl+E
Open a new browser window	Ctrl+N
Create a new folder in File Explorer	Ctrl+Shift+N
Refresh a browser window	Ctrl+R
Paste	Ctrl+V or Shift+Insert
Close the current app window	Ctrl+W
Cut	Ctrl+X
Redo	Ctrl+Y

To do this	Press
Undo	Ctrl+Z
Close the current file or active browser tab	Ctrl+F4
Select multiple noncontiguous items	Ctrl+click
Select contiguous items	Shift+click
Open Task Manager	Ctrl+Shift+Esc
Capture an image of the current screen and save the image in short-term memory	Print Screen

Touchscreen tips

Many computers, tablets, and phones have touchscreen interfaces that you can interact with using your finger or a tablet pen, and some computer keyboards have touchpads that allow many of the same types of interactions as touchscreens.

The following table describes some specific terms that we use when describing interactions with a touchscreen.

Term	Action	Mouse equivalent
Tap	Touch your finger to the screen one time and then lift it	Click
Double-tap	Quickly tap the screen twice in the same location	Double-click
Flick	Touch your finger to the screen and quickly move it in a specific direction as you lift it	None
Press and hold	Touch the screen and wait for about one second	Right-click
Pinch	Touch the screen with two fingers and then move the fingers toward each other	None
Stretch	Touch the screen with two fingers and then move the fingers away from each other	None
Slide	Drag your finger on the screen	None
Swipe	Briefly drag your finger across an item	None

On a touch device, you can set the permitted time and distance between taps for the double-tap action, and the minimum and maximum length of hold that performs a right-click equivalent. You configure these settings in the Pen And Touch dialog box.

You can use the gestures described in the following table to manage Windows 10 user interface elements on a screen that supports 10-point touch. Other touchscreen gestures might be available on your device, depending on the hardware and drivers.

Action	Touchscreen gesture
Display the Task View of all open windows	Swipe from the left of the screen
Display the Action Center	Swipe from the right edge of the screen
Display the taskbar when it is hidden	Tap or swipe the inside edge of the screen where the taskbar is docked

You can use the gestures described in the following table to move around on the screen.

Action	Touchscreen gesture
Scroll	Swipe up, down, left, or right
Scroll quickly	Flick up, down, left, or right, and then tap to stop scrolling
Zoom in	Stretch two fingers apart
Zoom out	Pinch two fingers together

You can use the gestures described in the following table to work with text content.

Action	Touchscreen gesture
Select a word	Double-tap the word
Select a paragraph	Triple-tap the paragraph
Expand or contract a selection	Drag the selection handles

Glossary

absolute path A path that defines the exact position of a file or folder on a computer or network. See also *path*; *relative path*.

Action Center A pane that maintains a running list of notifications that you can review and take action on, if necessary. It also includes Quick Action buttons that provide access to common Windows 10 features.

activation The process of validating software with the manufacturer. Activation confirms the genuine status of a product and that the product key has not been compromised. It establishes a relationship between the software's product key and a specific installation of that software on a device.

active window The window in which a user is currently working or directing input.

Address bar In File Explorer, a text box at the top of the window, under the title bar, containing the navigation path to the current folder. Selecting the arrow after each folder name displays a list of its subfolders. In Microsoft Edge and Internet Explorer, a text box containing the web address of the currently displayed webpage.

Administrator account A type of Windows user account with access to all system files and settings, and with permission to perform all operations. Every computer must have at least one Administrator account. This account type is not recommended for daily use. See also *Standard User account*; *user account*.

All-in-One PC A desktop computer that has the internal components incorporated into the same case as the monitor.

app See *desktop app*; *Universal Windows app*.

app icon See *icon*.

aspect ratio The ratio of the width of an image, screen, or other visual element to its height.

background In a graphical user interface such as Windows, a pattern or picture that can be applied to various screen elements, such as the desktop or lock screen. Other elements, such as text, icons, and apps, are displayed on top of this background.

bandwidth The rate of data transfer, in bits per second.

bitmap (.bmp) A patent-free digital image file format that does not support transparency. A bitmap image consists of pixels in a grid. Each pixel is a specific color; the colors within the color palette are governed by the specific bitmap format. Common formats include Monochrome Bitmap, 16 Color Bitmap, 256 Color Bitmap, and 24-bit Bitmap.

blog Short for *web log*. An online journal or news/opinion column. Contributors post entries consisting of text, graphics, or video clips. When permitted by the blog owner, readers can post comments responding to the entries or to other people's comments. Blogs are often used to publish personal or company information in an informal way.

.bmp See *bitmap*.

broadband connection A high-speed internet connection such as those provided by DSL or cable modem services. Broadband connections typically transfer data at 10 megabits per second (Mbps) or faster.

browse To search for a folder or file by navigating through the hierarchical storage structure of a computer. Alternatively, to search for information on the web by following links between webpages.

browser See *web browser.*

byte A unit of measurement for data; a byte typically holds a single character, such as a letter, digit, or punctuation mark. Some single characters can take up more than 1 byte.

central processing unit (CPU) The main circuit chip in a computer. It performs most of the calculations necessary to run the computer. Also called a *processor.*

click To point to an interface element and then press the primary mouse button one time.

command An instruction you give to a computer or app.

compress To reduce the size of a set of data, such as a file or group of files, inside a compressed folder that can be stored in less space or transmitted with less bandwidth.

compressed folder A folder containing files whose contents have been compressed. Also called a *zip file.*

Content pane In File Explorer, the pane that displays files and folders stored in the currently selected folder or storage device. See also *Details pane; Navigation pane; Preview pane.*

contextual tabs See *tool tabs.*

Control Panel A Windows app that contains items through which you can control system-level features of the computer and perform related tasks, including hardware and software setup and configuration.

CPU See *central processing unit.*

credentials Information that provides proof of identification that is used to gain access to local and network resources. Examples of credentials are user names and passwords, smart cards, and certificates.

cursor The on-screen image that moves around the screen when you move your mouse. Also called a *pointer* or *mouse pointer.*

desktop The work area on a computer screen, on which you can arrange windows, icons, and shortcuts to apps, folders, and data files. The contents of the Desktop folder of your user profile appear on the desktop. You can control the appearance of the desktop by changing the theme or the desktop background, and you can add and remove files, folders, and shortcuts on the desktop.

desktop app An application that is designed to run in the Windows desktop environment.

desktop computer A computer that must be plugged in to an external power source. A typical desktop computer system includes the computer case containing the actual computer components, a monitor, a keyboard, a mouse, and speakers. See also *device.*

desktop shortcut See *shortcut.*

Details pane In File Explorer, the pane that displays details about the folder or selected items. See also *Content pane; Navigation pane; Preview pane.*

device A piece of equipment, such as a laptop, tablet, or smartphone, that runs an operating system. See also *desktop computer.*

device driver See *driver.*

dialog box A window that appears when you give a command that requires additional information. Also used to provide information or feedback about progress.

Disk Cleanup A Windows app that reduces the number of unnecessary files on your drives, which can help your computer run faster. It can delete temporary files and system files, empty the Recycle Bin, and remove a variety of other items that you might no longer need.

Disk Defragmenter See *Optimize Drives*.

domain In Windows, a logical (rather than physical) group of resources—computers, servers, and other hardware devices—on a network, that is centrally administered through Windows Server. On the internet, a name used as the base of website addresses and email addresses that identifies the entity owning the address.

double-click To point to an interface element and press the primary mouse button two times in rapid succession.

drag To move an item on the screen by pointing to it, holding down the primary mouse button, and then moving the mouse.

driver An app that enables Windows to communicate with a software app or hardware device (such as a printer, mouse, or keyboard) that is attached to your computer. Every device needs a driver in order for it to work. Many drivers are built into Windows, and most others are available through Windows Update.

dynamic Changing in response to external factors.

Edge See *Microsoft Edge*.

Ethernet A system for exchanging data between computers on a local area network by using coaxial, fiber optic, or twisted-pair cables.

executable file A computer file that starts an app, such as a word processor, game, or Windows tool. Executable files can often be identified by the file name extension *.exe*.

expansion card A printed circuit board that, when inserted into an expansion slot of a computer, provides additional functionality. There are many types of expansion cards, including audio cards, modems, network cards, security device cards, TV tuner cards, video cards, and video processing expansion cards.

expansion slot A socket on a computer's motherboard, designed to establish the electrical contact between the electronics on an expansion card and on the motherboard. Many form factors (physical dimensions) and standards for expansion slots are available. An expansion slot accepts only expansion cards of the same form factor.

Extensible Markup Language (XML) A text markup language, similar to HTML, used to define the structure of data independently of its formatting so that the data can be used for multiple purposes and by multiple apps.

extension See *file name extension*.

Favorites bar In Microsoft Edge or Internet Explorer, a toolbar located below the Address bar that provides buttons for storing web locations for easy future access, obtaining add-ons, and accessing sites that match your browsing history.

File Explorer The Windows 10 app through which users locate, open, and manage files and folders.

File History A Windows feature that allows you to recover files by maintaining a record of file versions as you make changes and backing up files to a secondary storage location.

file name extension Characters appended to the name of a file by the app that created it and separated from the file name by a period. Some file name extensions identify the app that can open the file, such as .xlsx for Microsoft Excel workbooks; and some represent formats that more than one app can work with, such as .jpg graphic files.

file recovery Reconstructing or restoring lost or unreadable files on your hard drive.

filter To display only items that match specified criteria.

flash drive See *USB flash drive*.

flick A quick, straight stroke of a finger or pen on a screen. A flick is recognized as a gesture, and interpreted as a navigation or an editing command.

Flip A feature you can use to quickly preview all open windows without selecting the taskbar. Press Alt+Tab to invoke Flip, and then to move between previews. To display the previewed window, release both keys.

folder A named storage area on a computer or device containing files and other folders. Folders are used to organize information electronically, the same way actual folders in a filing cabinet do.

frame The outer border of a window.

gadget A type of app designed to display information on the desktop. Gadgets were popular in Windows Vista and Windows 7, but have been discontinued in Windows 10 because they were vulnerable to malicious attacks.

GB See *gigabyte*.

Gbps Gigabits per second; a unit of data transfer equal to 1,000 Mbps (megabits per second).

gesture A quick movement of a finger or pen on a screen that the computer interprets as a command, rather than as a mouse movement, writing, or drawing.

.gif See *Graphics Interchange Format*.

gigabyte (GB) 1,024 megabytes of data storage; often interpreted as approximately 1 billion bytes.

glyph A graphical representation of either a character, a part of a character, or a sequence of characters.

graphical user interface (GUI) A user interface that incorporates visual elements such as a desktop, icons, and menus, so that you can perform operations by interacting with the visual interface rather than by typing commands.

Graphics Interchange Format (.gif) A digital image file format developed by CompuServe that is used for transmitting raster images on the internet. An image in this format may contain up to 256 colors, including a transparent color. The size of the file depends on the number of colors actually used.

Guest account A built-in Windows user account that allows limited use of the computer. When logged on to a computer with the Guest account, a user can't install software or hardware, change settings, or create a password. The Guest account is turned off (unavailable) by default; you can turn it on from the User Accounts window of Control Panel.

GUI See *graphical user interface*.

hardware Physical items such as computers and monitors. See also *software*.

Hibernate mode A shut-down option similar to Sleep mode, except that it saves any open files and the state of any running apps on your hard drive instead of in memory and then completely turns off the computer. When you turn on your computer to resume working, Windows retrieves information from the hard drive and restores your previous computing session.

home page In a web browser, the page or pages that open automatically when you start the browser, and that open when you select the Home button. For websites, the first page displayed when you connect to a site.

homegroup A password-protected connection among a group of computers through which you can share files and printers. A homegroup can exist only on a private network. A private network doesn't require a homegroup, and it is not necessary to join a homegroup to use the private network.

homegroup member A computer that is joined to a homegroup.

hotspot A public place (such as a coffee shop, airport, or hotel) with a wireless network that you can use to connect to the internet.

HTML See *Hypertext Markup Language*.

hub A device used to connect multiple devices of one type. See also *network hub* and *USB hub*.

hyperlink A link from a text, graphic, audio, or video element to a target location in the same document, another document, or a webpage.

Hypertext Markup Language (HTML) A text markup language used to create documents for the web. HTML defines the structure and layout of a web document by using a variety of tags and attributes.

icon A visual representation of an app, folder, file, or other object or function.

IM See *instant messaging*.

Information bar A bar that appears to notify you that there is a security issue or that a pop-up window has been blocked. You can select the bar to display a menu of actions appropriate to the situation.

information technology (IT) The development, installation, and implementation of computer systems and apps.

InPrivate Browsing A browsing mode available in Microsoft Edge and Internet Explorer that opens a separate browser window in which the places you visit are not tracked. The pages and sites do not appear on the History tab, and temporary files and cookies are not saved on your computer.

input device A peripheral device whose purpose is to allow the user to provide input to a computer system. Examples of input devices are keyboards, mice, joysticks, and tablet pens.

insertion point The point where you can insert text or graphics. It usually appears as a blinking vertical line.

instant messaging (IM) A real-time electronic communication system that you can use to "chat" and interact in other ways with other people by typing in a window on your computer screen.

interface See *user interface*.

internet service provider (ISP) A company that provides internet access to individuals or companies. An ISP provides the connection information necessary for users to access the internet through the ISP's computers. An ISP typically charges a monthly or hourly connection fee.

IP address An address that identifies a computer that is connected to the internet or a network. There are two types of IP addresses: IP version 4 (IPv4) and IP version 6 (IPv6). An IPv4 address usually consists of four groups of numbers separated by periods; an IPv6 address has eight groups of hexadecimal characters (the numbers 0–9 and the letters A–H) separated by colons.

ISP See *internet service provider*.

IT See *information technology*.

Joint Photographic Experts Group (.jpeg) A digital image file format designed for compressing either full-color or grayscale still images. It works well on photographs, naturalistic artwork, and similar material. Images saved in this format have .jpg or .jpeg file extensions.

.jpeg See *Joint Photographic Experts Group*.

.jpg See *Joint Photographic Experts Group*.

jump list A feature of Windows that provides right-click access from Start menu app links to the documents, pictures, songs, or websites a user frequently accesses.

KB See *kilobyte*.

Kbps Kilobits per second; a unit of data transfer equal to 1,000 bits per second or 125 bytes per second.

keyword A word or phrase assigned to a file or webpage so that it can be located in searches for that word or phrase. See also *tag*.

kilobyte (KB) 1,024 bytes of data storage. In reference to data transfer rates, 1,000 bytes.

laptop A term for a portable computer, referring to the fact that portable computers are small enough to set on your lap. Also called a *notebook* or *portable computer*.

library A virtual folder that isn't physically present on the hard drive but that displays the contents of multiple folders as though the files were stored together in one location.

local Located on or attached to your computer.

local account An account you can use to sign in to a computer. A local account is not connected to a Microsoft account and isn't tracked beyond the scope of the computer it exists on.

local printer A printer that is directly connected to one of the ports on a computer. See also *network printer; remote printer; shared printer*.

lock To make your Windows desktop inaccessible to other people. Most effective when your user account is protected by a password.

Lock screen The screen that appears when a user locks the computer.

Magnifier A display tool that makes the computer screen more readable by magnifying a portion of the screen in a separate window.

mail server A computer that stores email messages.

malware Software designed to deliberately harm your computer. For example, viruses, worms, and Trojan horses are malware. Also called *malicious software*.

map a drive To assign an available drive letter to a specific computer or shared folder; usually a folder located on another computer on the network. This is commonly done to create a constant connection to a network share but can also be used to maintain a connection to an internet location.

maximize To increase the size of a window so that it completely fills the screen. A maximized window cannot be moved or resized by dragging its frame.

MB See *megabyte*.

Mbps Megabits per second; a unit of data transfer equal to 1,000 Kbps (kilobits per second).

media Materials on which data is recorded or stored, such as CDs, DVDs, or USB flash drives.

megabyte (MB) 1,024 kilobytes or 1,048,576 bytes of data storage; often interpreted as approximately 1 million bytes. In reference to data transfer rates, 1,000 kilobytes.

menu A list from which you can give an instruction by selecting a command.

menu bar A toolbar from which you can access menus of commands.

metadata Descriptive information, including keywords and properties, about a file or webpage. Title, subject, author, and size are examples of a file's metadata.

Microsoft Edge A Microsoft web browser released with Windows 10 that includes built-in features such as Inking, Reading view, Sharing, and Cortana integration.

minimize To reduce a window to a button on the taskbar.

Miracast A wireless technology built in to Windows 10 that projects your screen display to TVs, projectors, and streaming media players that also support Miracast. You can use this to share what you're doing on your computer, present a slide show, or even play your favorite game on a larger screen. Previously known as *Wireless Display (WiDi)*.

modem A device that allows computer information to be transmitted and received over a telephone line or through a broadband service such as cable or DSL.

motherboard The main printed circuit board of a computer. Electronic components such as the central processing unit (CPU), memory, and peripheral expansion slots are connected to and communicate through the motherboard. Also known as a *mainboard*, *system board*, or *logic board*.

multi-touch gesture An extension of the conventional touch input feature to support gestures involving multiple fingers touching the computer or device screen at the same time.

Narrator A feature that audibly reads the text on the screen aloud and describes some events to users.

navigate To move around in a document.

Navigation pane In File Explorer, the left pane of a folder window. It displays favorite links, libraries, and an expandable list of drives and folders. See also *Content pane*; *Details pane*; *Preview pane*.

network In Windows, a group of computers connected to each other through a wired or wireless connection. A network may be as small as two computers connected directly to each other or as large as the internet.

network adapter An expansion card or other device used to provide network access to a computer or other device, such as a printer. Mediates between the computer and physical media, such as cabling, over which transmissions travel.

Network and Sharing Center A Control Panel window from which users can get real-time status information about their network, and also make changes to settings.

network discovery A network setting that affects whether your computer can find other computers and devices on the network and whether other computers on the network can find your computer.

network domain A network whose security and settings are centrally administered through Windows Server computer and user accounts.

network drive A shared folder or drive on your network that you assign a drive letter to so that it appears in the This PC window of File Explorer as a named drive.

network hub A device used to connect computers on a network. The computers are connected to the hub with cables. The hub sends information received from one computer to all other computers on the network.

network printer A printer that is connected directly to a network through a wired (Ethernet) or wireless network connection, or through a print server or printer hub. See also *local printer*; *remote printer*; *shared printer*.

network profile Information about a specific network connection, such as the network name, type, and settings.

network router A hardware device connecting computers on a network and connecting a network to the internet.

network share A shared folder on a computer on your network (not your local computer).

notification area The area at the right end of the Windows taskbar that displays system icons (such as those for the clock, volume, network connection, power, and Action Center) and system and app notification icons. On Windows 10 computers, the user can control the display of both system icons and app notifications in the notification area.

OEM See *original equipment manufacturer*.

offline Not connected to a network or to the internet. Also used to describe time that you will be away from your computer.

OneDrive The Microsoft cloud storage service that lets users access and share documents, photos, and other files from anywhere.

online Connected to a network or to the internet. Also used to describe time that you will be working on your computer.

on-screen keyboard A keyboard representation on the screen that allows users to type using touch, a tablet pen, or other input device.

operating system The underlying programs that tell your computer what to do and how to do it. The operating system coordinates interactions among the computer system components, acts as the interface between you and your computer, enables your computer to communicate with other computers and peripheral devices, and interacts with apps installed on your computer.

Optimize Drives A Windows tool that arranges fragmented data so your drives can work more efficiently. Optimize analyzes and organizes drives on a schedule, but can also be started manually. Optimize is available on the Drive Tools tab when you select your hard drive in File Explorer.

option One of a group of mutually exclusive values for a setting, usually in a dialog box.

option button A standard Windows control that you use to select one of a set of options.

original equipment manufacturer (OEM) A company that assembles a computer from components, brands the computer, and then sells the computer to the public. The OEM might also preinstall an operating system and other software on the computer.

parallel port The input/output connector for a parallel interface device. Some types of printers connect to the computer through a parallel port.

partition A section of space on a physical hard drive that functions as if it were a separate drive.

password A security measure used to restrict access to user accounts, computer systems, and resources. A password is a unique string of characters that you must provide before access is authorized.

password hint An entry you record when you create or change your password, to remind you what the password is. Windows displays the password hint if you enter an incorrect password.

password reset disk A file you create on a flash drive or other removable media to enable you to reset your Windows password if you forget it.

path A sequence of drive and folder names, separated by backslashes (\), that leads to a specific file or folder. See also *absolute path*; *relative path*.

peer-to-peer A network, such as a workgroup, where computers and resources are connected directly and are not centrally managed by a server.

peripheral device A device, such as an external DVD drive, printer, modem, or joystick, that is connected to a computer and is controlled by the computer's microprocessor, but is not necessary to the computer's operation.

personal folder In Windows, a storage folder created by Windows for each user account and containing subfolders and information that is specific to the user profile, such as Documents and Pictures. The personal folder is labeled with the name used to log on to the computer.

phishing A technique used to trick computer users into revealing personal or financial information. A common online phishing scam starts with an email message that appears to come from a trusted source but actually directs recipients to provide information to a fraudulent website.

picture password A picture-based sign-in method that authenticates a user by checking gestures made on a picture of the user's own choosing.

PID See *product key*.

pin To fix an item, such as a tile, library, movie, game, or app, in a given area of the Windows screen, so it is always accessible in that area (for example, to pin an app to Start or to the taskbar).

PIN A numeric identification code similar to a password that a user can enter to validate his or her credentials.

pinned taskbar button A button representing an app, which appears permanently next to the search box on the taskbar. A button that is not pinned appears only when its app is running. See also *taskbar button*.

pixel The smallest element used to form an image on a computer monitor. Computer monitors display images by drawing thousands of pixels arranged in columns and rows. Each pixel displays one color. See also *screen resolution*.

plug and play A technology that enables the computer to automatically discover and configure settings for a device connected to the computer through a USB or IEEE 1394 connection.

.png See *Portable Network Graphic*.

point To position the mouse pointer over an element. Also called *hover or mouse-over*.

pointer The on-screen image that moves around the screen when you move your mouse. Also called a *cursor*.

pointing device A device such as a mouse that controls a pointer with which you can select objects displayed on the screen.

pop-up window A small web browser window that opens on top of (or sometimes below) the web browser window when you display a website or select an advertising link.

port An interface through which data is transferred via cable between a computer and other devices, a network, or a direct connection to another computer.

Portable Network Graphic (.png) A digital image file format that uses lossless compression (compression that doesn't lose data) and was created as a patent-free alternative to the .gif file format.

Power button The button near the bottom of the Windows 10 Start menu that provides access to the commands for putting the computer into Sleep mode and shutting down or restarting the computer.

Preview pane In File Explorer, a pane used to show a preview of a file selected in the Content pane. See also *Content pane*; *Details pane*; *Navigation pane*.

primary display In a multiple-monitor system, the monitor that displays the Welcome screen and taskbar. Most app windows appear on the primary display when they first open. See also *secondary display*.

printer driver See *driver*.

private network A network that requires specific credentials for access and is not available to the general public.

product key A unique registration code issued by the manufacturer of an app. The key must be supplied during the setup process to verify that you have a valid license to install and use the app. Also called a *product ID*, *PID*, *registration key*, or *CD key*.

program icon See *icon*.

progress bar or ring An animated visual indicator of the percentage of completion of a process.

property Identifying information about a file, folder, drive, device, or other computer system element. Some properties are supplied automatically and others are supplied by you. For example, the properties of a file include information such as its file name, size, modification date, title, tags, and comments.

Public folder In Windows, a storage folder system created by Windows and accessible to all user accounts on the computer. Public folders are shared by all user accounts on the computer and can be shared with other network users.

public network A network that permits anyone to connect and does not require specific credentials.

Quick Link menu The menu that appears when you right-click the Start button.

random access memory (RAM) A data storage area a computer uses to run apps and temporarily store information. Information stored in RAM is erased when the computer is switched off.

ReadyBoost See *Windows ReadyBoost*.

Recycle Bin The folder on your hard drive where Windows temporarily stores files you delete. By default, the Recycle Bin is represented by an icon on the desktop. You can recover deleted files from the Recycle Bin until you empty it.

refresh your PC To reset an operating system by using a method that restores computer settings to the defaults but retains user files and settings.

registration key See *product key*.

registry A repository for information about the computer's configuration. The registry stores settings related to the hardware and software installed on the computer. Registry settings are typically updated through the proper install and uninstall procedures and apps. You can manually update the registry, but only experienced users should undertake this task because mistakes can be disastrous.

relative path A path that defines the position of a file or folder in relation to the current location. Relative paths are frequently used in website navigational code. See also *absolute path*; *path*.

Remote Desktop Connection The client software that enables users to connect to a remote computer that has the Remote Desktop feature enabled or to a remote desktop server.

remote printer A printer that is not connected directly to your computer. See also *local printer*; *network printer*; *shared printer*.

removable media Anything used for information storage that is designed to be easily inserted into and removed from a computer or portable device. Common removable media include CD and DVD discs, in addition to removable memory cards.

reset your PC To reset an operating system by using a method that restores computer settings to the defaults and removes user files and settings.

resolution See *screen resolution*.

restore down To return a window from a maximized state to its previous size.

restore point A snapshot of your computer system settings taken by Windows at regular intervals and before any major change, such as installing an app or updating system files. If you experience problems with your system, you can restore it to any saved restore point without undoing changes to your personal files.

ribbon An area in a window in which commands and other controls are displayed in functionally related groups. A ribbon can be divided into multiple views, known as tabs, and every tab can contain multiple groups of controls. Typically, a ribbon appears at the top of a window.

right-click To point to an interface element and press the secondary mouse button one time.

right-drag To move an item on the screen by pointing to its title bar or handle, holding down the secondary mouse button, and then moving the mouse. A shortcut menu displaying possible actions appears when you release the mouse button.

root Short for root folder or root directory. The highest or uppermost level in a hierarchically organized set of information. The root is the folder from which all other folders branch.

router See *network router.*

screen resolution The fineness or coarseness of detail attained by a monitor in producing an image, measured in pixels, expressed as the number of pixels wide by the number of pixels high. See also *pixel.*

screen saver A blank screen, picture, or moving images that Windows displays after a specified period of inactivity. A screen saver can be used to save power or to hide information while you are away from your desk.

ScreenTip Information that appears when you point to an item.

scroll bar A vertical or horizontal bar that you move to change the position of content within a window.

search The process of seeking a particular file or specific data. A search is carried out by an app through comparison or calculation to determine whether a match to some pattern exists or whether some other criteria have been met.

search provider A company that provides a search engine that you can use to find information on the internet.

search term The term you type in the search box of the taskbar, Settings window, or any File Explorer window. Windows then filters the contents of the available storage locations or of the folder window's Content pane to include only the items that contain the search term.

secondary display In a multiple-monitor system, the monitor onto which you can expand apps so that you can increase your work area. See also *primary display.*

share To make local files or resources available to other users of the same computer or other computers on a network.

shared component A component, such as a DLL file, that is used by multiple apps. When uninstalling an app that uses a shared component, Windows requests confirmation before removing the component.

shared drive A drive that has been made available for other people on a network to access.

shared folder A folder that has been made available for other people on a network to access.

shared printer A printer connected to a computer that has been shared with other computers on a network. See also *local printer; network printer; remote printer.*

shortcut A link, usually represented by an icon, that opens an app, data file, or device. For example, selecting a shortcut to Microsoft Word starts Word.

shortcut menu A menu displayed when you right-click an object, showing a list of commands relevant to that object.

shut down To initiate the process that closes all your open apps and files, ends your computing session, closes network connections, stops system processes, stops the hard drive, and turns off the computer.

sign in To start a computing session by entering your credentials.

sign out To stop your computing session without affecting other users' sessions.

single sign-on (SSO) account An account type that permits a user to log on to a system once with a single set of credentials to access multiple apps or services.

Sleep mode A Windows feature that saves any open files and the state of any running apps to memory and then puts your computer into a power-saving state.

SmartScreen An intelligent spam-filtering solution integrated across all Microsoft email platforms.

Snap A Windows feature that enables users to easily display two documents side by side, maximize a single document, and expand a window vertically by simply dragging window borders to the edge of the screen.

Snipping Tool A Windows tool used to capture a screen shot, or snip, of any object on the screen, and then annotate, save, or share the image.

software Apps that you use to do things with hardware. See also *hardware*.

software piracy The illegal reproduction and distribution of software.

sound card Hardware that enables audio information and music to be recorded, played back, and heard on a computer.

Sound Recorder The app that facilitates recording voice from a microphone, in addition to saving, editing, playing and sharing recorded audio clips.

spam An unsolicited and typically unwelcome message, often commercial or political in nature, transmitted via the internet as a mass mailing (sometimes as if from a fictitious user or domain) to a large number of recipients.

speech recognition The ability to interpret vocal commands or convert spoken words into computer-readable text. Speech recognition apps enable you to control an application or enter text by speaking into a microphone, rather than by using a keyboard.

spyware Software that can display advertisements (such as pop-up ads), collect information about you, or change settings on your computer, generally without appropriately obtaining your consent.

Standard User account A type of Windows user account that allows the user to install software and change system settings that do not affect other users or the security of the computer. This account type is recommended for daily use. See also *Administrator account*; *user account*.

Start menu A list of options displayed when you select the Start button. The Start menu is your central link to all the apps installed on your computer, in addition to all the tasks you can carry out with Windows 10.

Start screen An alternative full-screen version of the Start menu that displays either pinned tiles or the app list.

Store See *Windows Store*.

subfolder A folder nested within another folder.

surf the web To browse information on the internet.

sync To reconcile the differences between files, email, appointments, and other items stored on one computer, device, or in the cloud with versions of the same files on another computer, device, or in the cloud. After the differences are determined, both sets of items are updated.

system cache An area in the computer memory where Windows stores information it might need to access quickly, for the duration of the current computing session.

system drive The hard drive on which the operating system is installed.

system folder A folder created on the system drive that contains files required by Windows 10.

System Restore A tool used to restore your computer to a previous state, if a problem occurs, without losing your personal data files (such as Microsoft Word documents, browsing history, drawings, favorites, or email).

tab In a dialog box, a separate page of settings within the dialog box window; the tab title indicates the nature of the group. You can display the settings by selecting the tab.

tabbed browsing An internet browser feature that enables you to open and view multiple webpages or files in one window by displaying them on different tabs. You can display a page by selecting its tab, or display a shortcut menu of options for working with a page by right-clicking its tab.

tag In File Explorer, a keyword assigned to a file. See also *keyword*.

tap (touch) A gesture represented by placing a finger or tablet pen on the screen and then lifting it up.

Task Manager A tool that provides information about apps and processes running on the computer. Using Task Manager, you can end or run apps, end processes, and display a dynamic overview of your computer's performance.

task pane A fixed pane that appears on one side of an app window, containing options related to the completion of a specific task.

taskbar A bar on the desktop that displays buttons you can select to run apps, tools, and commands, in addition to buttons representing the windows of open apps and files.

taskbar button A button on the taskbar representing an open window, file, or app. See also *pinned taskbar button*.

taskbar search A search box from which you can locate apps, Control Panel items, settings, files, email messages, and web results containing the search string, grouped by category.

terabyte (TB) 1 trillion bytes, often incorrectly used to denote 1,099,511,627,776 (10244) bytes of data storage. (The correct term is tebibyte.) In reference to data transfer rates, 1,000 GB.

theme A set of visual elements and sounds that applies a unified look to the computer user interface. A theme can include a desktop background, screen saver, window colors, and sounds. Some themes might also include icons and mouse pointers.

tile A moveable object on the Start screen that opens apps or other customized content, such as pinned websites.

tile folder An expandable group of Start screen tiles represented on the Start screen by a single tile that displays the icons of the tiles within.

title bar The horizontal area at the top of a window that displays the title of the app or file displayed in the window, in addition to buttons for controlling the display of the window.

tool tabs In an app that uses the ribbon command structure, a ribbon tab that hosts tools for working with a specific type of file or folder and appears when a file or folder of that type is selected.

toolbar A horizontal or vertical bar that displays buttons representing commands that can be used with the content of the current window. When more commands are available than can fit on the toolbar, chevrons (>>) appear at the right end of the toolbar; selecting the chevrons displays the additional commands.

UAC See *User Account Control*.

UNC See *Universal Naming Convention*.

Uniform Resource Locator (URL) An address that uniquely identifies the location of a website or page. URLs are used by web browsers to locate internet resources.

Universal Naming Convention (UNC) A system for identifying the location on a network of shared resources such as computers, drives, and folders. A UNC address is in the form \\ComputerName\SharedFolder.

Universal Serial Bus (USB) A connection that provides data transfer capabilities and power to a peripheral device. See also *USB hub*; *USB port*.

Universal Windows app An app that is built by using the Universal Windows Platform (UWP), which was first introduced in Windows 8 as the Windows Runtime. Universal Windows apps should run on any Windows 10 device, from a phone to a desktop computer.

upgrade To replace older hardware with newer hardware or an earlier version of an app with the current version.

URL See *Uniform Resource Locator*.

USB See *Universal Serial Bus*.

USB flash drive A portable flash memory card that plugs into a computer's USB port. You can store data on a USB flash drive or use all or part of the available drive space to increase the operating system speed. See also *Windows ReadyBoost*.

USB hub A device used to connect multiple USB devices to a single USB port, or to connect one or more USB devices to USB ports on multiple computers. The latter type of USB hub, called a sharing hub, operates as a switch box to give control of the hub-connected devices to one computer at a time. See also *Universal Serial Bus*; *USB port*.

USB port A connection that provides both power and data transfer capabilities to a hardware device. See also *Universal Serial Bus*; *USB hub*.

user account On a Windows computer, a uniquely named account that allows an individual to gain access to the system and to specific resources and settings. Each user account includes a collection of information that describes the way the computer environment looks and operates for that particular user, in addition to a private folder not accessible by other people using the computer, in which personal documents, pictures, media, and other files can be stored. See also *Administrator account*; *Standard User account*.

user account button The button on the Start menu that provides access to the commands for changing user account settings, locking the computer, or logging off from Windows.

User Account Control (UAC) A Windows security feature that allows or restricts actions by the user and the system to prevent malicious apps from damaging the computer.

user account name A unique name identifying a user account to Windows.

user account picture An image representing a user account. User account pictures are available only for computer-specific user accounts and not on computers that are members of a network domain.

user credentials See *credentials*.

user interface (UI) The portion of an app with which a user interacts. Types of user interfaces include command-line interfaces, menu-driven interfaces, and graphical user interfaces.

video projector A device that projects a video signal from a computer onto a projection screen by using a lens system.

virtual Representative of an object that doesn't exist. Examples are virtual folders (called *libraries*) and virtual printers.

virtual desktop A work area on a computer screen that contains different groups of apps or content open and available for different tasks or aspects of your life.

virtual printer An app that "prints" content to a file rather than on paper. When viewed in the file, the content looks as it would if it were printed.

virus Malware that replicates, commonly by infecting other files in the system, thus allowing the execution of the malware code and its propagation when those files are activated.

web An abbreviation of *World Wide Web*. A worldwide network consisting of millions of smaller networks that exchange data.

web browser A software app used to display webpages and to navigate the internet, for example, Microsoft Edge or Internet Explorer.

web log See *blog*.

webcam A camera for use with a computer to transmit a video picture.

website A group of related webpages that is hosted by an HTTP server on the World Wide Web or an intranet. The pages in a website typically cover one or more topics and are interconnected through hyperlinks.

Welcome screen The screen that appears when you start your computer, containing a link to each active user account.

WEP See *Wired Equivalent Privacy*.

WiDi See *Miracast*.

Wi-Fi Protected Access (WPA) A security method used by wireless networks. WPA and WPA2 encrypt the information that is sent between computers on a wireless network and authenticate users to help ensure that only authorized people can access the network. WPA2 is more secure than WPA.

wildcard character In a search operation, a keyboard character, such as an asterisk (*), a question mark (?), or a pound sign (#), that represents one or more characters in a search term.

window A frame within which your computer runs an app or displays a folder or file. Several windows can be open simultaneously. Windows can be sized, moved, minimized to a taskbar button, maximized to take up the entire screen, or closed.

Windows Defender Initially provided in earlier versions of Windows as anti-spyware, an app that now serves as anti-virus software in Windows 10.

Windows Firewall A security feature that is used to set restrictions on what traffic is allowed to enter your network from the internet.

Windows ReadyBoost A feature introduced in Windows 7 that makes it possible to increase the available system memory by using a USB flash drive as a memory-expansion device. See also *USB flash drive*.

Windows Store The online store where users can learn about and download apps, games, music, and more for Windows devices.

Windows To Go A feature of Windows 10 Enterprise and Windows 10 Education that provides a predefined image of a computer from a USB flash drive instead of installing the image on the computer.

Windows Update A feature through which Windows catalogs your computer's hardware and software components, communicates with the Microsoft Update online database, and identifies any updates that are available for your operating system, software, or hardware drivers.

Wired Equivalent Privacy (WEP) An algorithm-based security protocol designed for use with wireless networks. WEP was the original wireless network security protocol and, although not as secure as the more recent Wi-Fi Protected Access (WPA) protocol, is still an option in most wireless router configurations.

Wireless Display (WiDi) See *Miracast*.

wizard A tool that walks you through the steps necessary to accomplish a particular task.

workgroup A peer-to-peer computer network through which computers can share resources, such as files, printers, and internet connections.

WPA See *Wi-Fi Protected Access.*

XML See *Extensible Markup Language.*

XML Paper Specification (XPS) A digital file format for saving documents. XPS is based on XML, preserves document formatting, and enables file sharing. XPS was developed by Microsoft but is platform-independent and royalty-free.

XPS See *XML Paper Specification.*

zipped folder See *compressed folder.*

Index

About the author

Joan Lambert has worked closely with Microsoft technologies since 1986, and in the training and certification industry since 1997. As President and CEO of Online Training Solutions, Inc. (OTSI), Joan guides the translation of technical information and requirements into useful, relevant, and measurable resources for people who are seeking certification of their computer skills or who simply want to get things done efficiently.

Joan is the author or coauthor of more than four dozen books about Windows and Office apps (for Windows, Mac, and iPad), five generations of Microsoft Office Specialist certification study guides, video-based training courses for SharePoint and OneNote, QuickStudy guides for Windows and Office apps, and the GO! series book for Outlook 2016.

Blissfully based in America's Finest City, Joan is a Microsoft Certified Professional, Microsoft Office Specialist Master (for all versions of Office since Office 2003), Microsoft Certified Technology Specialist (for Windows and Windows Server), Microsoft Certified Technology Associate (for Windows), Microsoft Dynamics Specialist, and Microsoft Certified Trainer.

Windows 10 Step by Step, Second Edition, is based on the original book coauthored by Joan and her father, Steve Lambert. Joan's first publishing collaboration with Steve was the inclusion of her depiction of *Robots in Love* in one of his earliest books, *Presentation Graphics on the Apple Macintosh* (Microsoft Press, 1984).

Steve Lambert started playing with computers in the mid-1970s. As computers evolved from wire-wrap and solder to consumer products, he evolved from hardware geek to programmer and writer.

Steve has written or coauthored more than 20 books on developing technologies, including *Presentation Graphics on the Apple Macintosh, Creative Programming in Microsoft Basic*, the CD-ROM *The New Papyrus*, and *Internet Basics: Your Online Access to the Global Electronic Superhighway.* Steve is also the author of *Built by Anhalt*, a biographical exploration into the life and architecture of the famed Seattle architect Fred Anhalt.

Steve has specialized for many years in the conversion of content from one format to another, including projects such as the Microsoft Programmer's Library in 1988 and the conversion of the 25-volume Funk & Wagnalls Encyclopedia for the initial Microsoft Encarta CD-ROM. He has created several content authoring and delivery systems, including those used by the Microsoft Mastering Series, the Quick Course Series, and numerous pubStudio titles that are published by Microsoft and several US government agencies. He is a strong advocate of good template design and of using Microsoft Visual Basic for Applications (VBA) automation to smooth out the conversion, assembly, formatting, and validation of content for delivery via print, e-book, or web.

Acknowledgments

I am extremely thankful for the unflagging support and contributions of Jaime Odell, Kathy Krause, and Susie Carr at OTSI—this book (and so many others) wouldn't exist without America's Finest Publishing Team! Thank you also to Jeanne Craver and Laura Acklen for catching visual and technical glitches, and to Laura Norman at Pearson Education and Kim Spilker and the team—past and present—at Microsoft Press for the opportunity to continue doing what I love to do.

Finally, I am so very grateful for the support of my daughter, Trinity, and my stepmom, Grace, for taking care of me, us, the dogs, and the House of Awesomeness, while I took care of business.

OTSI specializes in the design and creation of Microsoft Office, SharePoint, and Windows training solutions and the production of online and printed training resources. For more information about OTSI, visit *www.otsi.com*.

We hope you enjoy this book and find it useful! Updates to this edition were guided by feedback submitted by readers of previously published *Windows Step by Step* books. If you find errors in this book, have a request for the next edition, or would like to pass along other feedback, you can use the process outlined in the introduction.

Now that you've read the book...

Tell us what you think!

Was it useful?
Did it teach you what you wanted to learn?
Was there room for improvement?

Let us know at http://aka.ms/tellpress

Your feedback goes directly to the staff at Microsoft Press,
and we read every one of your responses. Thanks in advance!